ASSER International Sports Law Series

For further volumes:
http://www.springer.com/series/8858

Jack Anderson
Editor

Leading Cases in Sports Law

ASSER PRESS

Springer

Editor
Jack Anderson
School of Law
Queen's University Belfast
Belfast, Antrim
UK

ISSN 1874-6926
ISBN 978-90-6704-908-5 ISBN 978-90-6704-909-2 (eBook)
DOI 10.1007/978-90-6704-909-2

Library of Congress Control Number: 2013932333

Published by T.M.C. ASSER PRESS, The Hague, The Netherlands www.asserpress.nl
Produced and distributed for T.M.C. ASSER PRESS by Springer-Verlag Berlin Heidelberg

Printed on acid-free paper

Springer is part of Springer Science+Business Media (www.springer.com)

Series Information

Books in the *ASSER International Sports Law Series* chart and comment upon the legal and policy developments in European and international sports law. The books contain materials on interstate organisations and the international sports governing bodies, and will serve as comprehensive and relevant reference tools for all those involved in the area on a professional basis.

The Series is developed, edited and published by the ASSER International Sports Law Centre in The Hague. The Centre's mission is to provide a centre of excellence in particular by providing high-quality research, services and products to the sporting world at large (sports ministries, international—intergovernmental—organisations, sports associations and federations, the professional sports industry, etc.) on both a national and an international basis. The Centre is the co-founder and coordinator of the Hague International Sports Law Academy (HISLA), the purpose of which is the organisation of academic conferences and workshops of international excellence which are held in various parts of the world. Apart from the Series, the Centre edits and publishes *The International Sports Law Journal.*

Series Editors
Dr. David McArdle
e-mail: d.a.mcardle@stir.ac.uk

Dr. Ben Van Rompuy
e-mail: b.van.rompuy@asser.nl

Marco A. van der Harst, LL.M.
e-mail: m.van.der.harst@asser.nl

Editorial Office
ASSER International Sports Law Centre
T.M.C. Asser Institute
P.O. Box 30461
2500 GL, The Hague
The Netherlands
www.sportslaw.nl

Editor's Introductory Remarks and Acknowledgements

In edited collections of this nature it is often the case that the editor will use the introductory remarks to pronounce, rather grandly, on the volume's underlying and unifying theme or themes. That will not happen here. The substance and form of the collective term "sports law" covers an eclectic amalgam of various applications of traditional branches of the law and, at best, it is hoped that eclecticism is encapsulated in the various contributions to this collection. If a single theme is to be found threading its way through this collection, it is one that demonstrates the breadth and depth of sports law scholarship worldwide. Put simply, this book is not just about leading sports law cases; it is about leading sports law cases as analysed by leading sports law scholars. Authors or contributions based on case law from at least nine jurisdictions spanning the common and civil law traditions are represented—Australia; Belgium; Canada; England and Wales; Scotland; South Africa; Sweden; New Zealand; and the United States. Moreover, the case law ranges from the superior courts of the United States, the United Kingdom and the European Union (EU) to what can now be called sport's very own international court of justice—the Court of Arbitration for Sport.

Two points need to be made before briefly introducing the contents of this collection.

The first is directed towards the contributors and it is simply to express my thanks to them for their professionalism and patience in filing their contributions. The quality of this book is due to them alone, and has nothing to do with my editing skills. In fact, to paraphrase Denning MR's celebrated maxim in *Enderby Town FC v Football Association* (1971), "better a good writer than a bad editor"; and this book is full of good writers. Editing this collection was primarily a matter of arranging the case law into six parts reflecting what I thought were topics historically fundamental to the emergence of sports law (Parts I–III) and those which continue to prompt legal analysis of sporting practices (Parts IV–VI). Further, the book's chapters have also been edited into such a way that they are can be read in a self-contained manner for ease of dedicated study. Each chapter contains a reference list of its own and cross-referencing within and between chapters has been kept to a minimum.

The second point is directed at you, the reader. No doubt many of you will be perplexed as to why certain cases have made it into this collection, and others have not. There are some prosaic reasons as to why this book is limited to twenty or so cases—such as deadlines, word count, author availability and the wish to avoid an overlap with other texts from the ASSER International Sports Law Series and notably *CAS and Football: Landmark Cases*, edited by Alexander Wild and published in 2012 by TMC Asser Press and Springer. Those explanations aside, the rationale for the selected cases in this volume is otherwise straightforward: *I* wanted them to be included because I think they best portray the domestic, regional, inter- and supra-national dimensions to sports law. If you think that there is a case or arbitral award that should have been included, or, better still, one that should be included in (I hope) a second volume—and in particular, but not limited to, a jurisdiction such as Germany, France, Spain, Italy, Russia, China or Brazil—then please contact me and engage with the debate on my blog at http://blogs.qub.ac.uk/sportslaw. In any event, all comments are welcome at jack.anderson@qub.ac.uk, including any ideas on the contents of a second volume and especially from the younger generation of sports law academics, scholars and practitioners!

I write these remarks as the London 2012 Olympic Games come to a close. In his remarks at the opening ceremony to the Games, the President of the International Olympic Committee, Jacque Rogge said, "In a sense, the Olympic Games are coming home tonight. This great, sports-loving country is widely recognised as the birthplace of modern sport." Many sports can indeed trace their origins as codified pursuits to the Victorian era. How and why this happened and, more particularly, what the law contributed to the development of modern sport is central to this book's first chapter on *Abbot v Weekly* (1665).

So as Association Football and other sports emerged in codified and league form in the 1860s; so on the other side of the Atlantic (on St. Patrick's Day in 1871), the National Association of Professional Baseball Players was founded and professional league baseball was born. The "ensuing colorful days" of early baseball were breathlessly recounted in 1972 by Mr. Justice Blackmun in the US Supreme Court decision of *Flood v Kuhn*. In that decision, the long-standing exemption of professional baseball from US antitrust laws, established in *Federal Baseball Club v National League* in 1922, was recognised plainly as an "aberration", in the light of the Supreme Court's subsequent findings that other interstate professional sports were not similarly exempt, but, nevertheless, it was held an established aberration with which the US Congress acquiesced, and which the US Supreme Court reiterated was entitled to the benefit of stare decisis. The second chapter contains a brilliant analysis of the root cause of this aberration by one of the US's leading sports law scholars, Professor Roger Abrams.

The leading EU sports law scholar, Professor Richard Parrish, follows with a case synthesis on *Walrave and Koch* when for the first time the Court of Justice of the European Union ("CJEU") donned a sports jersey and did so in the most unlikely of settings—on a pace making bike for cycling races. Parrish demonstrates that the principles established by the CJEU in *Walrave and Koch* were indeed pathfinders in the development of EU sports law. The final chapter in the first part of this book is by Professor Ian Blackshaw who gives an analysis of proceedings that were fundamental to the contemporary authority of the Court of Arbitration for Sport ("CAS").

Professor Blackshaw's analysis is important in revealing that although CAS can now be seen in terms of a world supreme court for sport, it must not be forgotten that a limited means of appeal from CAS to the Swiss Supreme Court remains and that in this supervisory role, the Supreme Court of that country can have an important say in the operation and administration of key aspects of contemporary sport.

Returning to the opening ceremony of the London Olympics of 2012, the Olympic flame was brought to the host stadium by David Beckham on a speed boat along the Thames. "Becks" encapsulates the commercial spirit of modern football, both on and off the field of play. What Part II of this book illustrates is how much footballers such as Beckham owe to Mr. George Eastham and Mr. Jean-Marc Bosman and their stories are well told respectively Simon Boyes and Professor Stefaan Van den Bogaert. In many ways, the chapter on *Bosman* is this book's fulcrum. The chapter illustrates that, thanks to the CJEU's ruling in *Bosman*, the contractual servitude of football's past has been replaced by the contractual mobility of its present. Moreover, Van den Bogaert illustrates that *Bosman* was a serious but necessary breach of the administrative autonomy of sport, and not just football, and one that has led subsequently to various legislative and policy making initiatives domestically, at an EU level, and even internationally.

Part III of this book contains three very different approaches to when the private business of sport becomes the public business of law. The first by Chris Davies on *Finnigan v NZRFU* reviews the role that sporting boycotts played in the international campaign against the apartheid regime in South Africa and especially in the 1980s. Michael Beloff QC's piece reflects on the rather odd refusal by the Court of Appeal in England and Wales to the permit the judicial review of the decisions of sports bodies, including those in receipt of large amounts of public money. Professor Stephen Weatherill's contribution on *Meca Medina* grasps with EU law's reach "beyond the touchline". Characteristic of all three pieces is the sports body's initial reluctance, even refusal, to acknowledge that the ordinary courts were an appropriate palladium to discuss or provide a remedy for disputes of a specifically sporting nature. Further, all three cases demonstrate that the private self-regulatory bubble in which sport operated for much of the twentieth century has well and truly burst. As Professor Weatherill has said on numerous occasions; so far as the law is concerned, sport is special but not *that* special.

Continuing on the theme of the London Olympics, the Games finally saw the demise of one of the most shameful world records in athletics when in their gold medal winning performance at London, the US women's 4 × 100 m relay team broke one of the oldest records in world athletics set by the East German women's team in Canberra in 1985. In the mid-1980s, the old GDR state-sponsored doping programme of athletes was at its height, and when followed by the Ben Johnson affair in 1988 at the Seoul Olympics and a decade thereafter of doping-related scandal at the Tour de France, the sporting world finally acted and founded the World Anti-doping Agency. Part IV of this book opens with Hazel Hartley's reflections on the Diane Modhal affair and thus provides an insightful commentary on the challenges faced by individual athletes, sports governing bodies and the courts in a high profile anti-doping dispute in the pre-WADA era. Post-*Modahl*, we see the emergence of CAS as the ultimate arbitrator of doping-related disputes. CAS and the procedures surrounding doping control were both tested to their limits in CAS 98/211 *B v FINA* where an Irish swimmer presented a robust legal defence to accusations the there was, well, too much whiskey in the jar. Neville Cox gives an expert review of this award, which was CAS's first public hearing, as does John O'Leary on the Tim Montgomery award where we see the emergence of the "comfortable satisfaction" standard of proof in anti-doping decisions. Finally, David McArdle uses the *Pechstein v ISU* proceedings to comment authoritatively on blood profiling as a means of identifying dope cheating in sport.

Part V of this book contains the good, the bad and the commercial. Professor Steve Cornelius recounts through interviews and case analysis one the most inspirational athletes and stories in sport—that of double amputee, Paralympian and, now, Olympian, Oscar Pistorious. Pistorious' will to compete and to get the best out of himself at every turn contrasts starkly with the behaviour of the defendants in *R v Amir and Butt* on which Simon Gardiner, at Chap. 18, highlights the elemental threat to the integrity of sport presented by "spot-fixing" gambles. Chapters 16 and 17 by, respectively, Lefevere and Veermesch's and Lindholm and Kaburakis, consider two decisions of the EU courts on the exploitation of sports broadcasting rights. Lefevere and Veermesch's chapter captures the lucrative nature and fundamental importance of TV revenues to the financial stability of modern sport and especially football; while Lindholm and Kaburakis, in their review of the Karen Murphy proceedings at the CJEU, contend that the competition law aspects of *Murphy* have been understated in subsequent commentary. TV money has long been central to the operation of major league sport in the United States but so also has the manner in which the various franchises within US major league sport have sought to organise themselves as a collective in order to maximise the commoditisation of their "product". The latter is reviewed comprehensively in substance and in context by Professor Matt Mitten in his observations on the recent US Supreme Court decision in *America Needle*.

Violence (amongst spectators, between players and towards animals) is central to Part VI. Geoff Pearson illustrates that there is more, much more, to the policing and prosecution of football spectator-related violence than a dry technical review of the hybrid standard of proof for certain statutory offences enunciated by the English Court of Appeal in *Gough and Smith.* Similarly, Mark James subjects the Court of Appeal's approach to player on player violence in *Barnes* to detailed scrutiny in a manner which places the debate in its full context and outside its narrow application of the relevant parts of the Offences against the Person Act 1861. Laura Donnellan then reviews the various challenges to the Hunting Act 2004's ban on the hunting with dogs of certain wild mammals, including foxes and hares in England and Wales. In this, Donnellan analyses Lord Bingham's assertion in the House of Lords that "whatever one's view of the 2004 Act, it must be seen as the latest link in a long chain of statutes devoted to what was seen as social reform. It may be doubted if any country has done more than this to try and prevent the causing of unnecessary suffering to animals."

The final chapter has echoes in the aforementioned speech by IOC President Rogge at the opening ceremony of the London Games. In that speech, Rogge noted proudly that all 204 participating countries included female competitors for the first time and that this was a "major boost for gender equality." Rogge could make this claim because a few minutes earlier two extraordinary women had just filed past alongside the flag of Saudi Arabia, which until then had been one of the few countries not to select female athletes—its Ministry for Education still bans physical education for girls. Nevertheless, on reading Hilary Findlay's review of the *Sagen* proceedings prior to the Vancouver Winter Olympics of 2010 and the history of the IOC with regard to the inclusion of women in sport more generally, Rogge's self-congratulatory tone grates. Findlay also concludes, in a manner which neatly closes the collection as a whole, that the IOC, although ostensibly a private actor, has rapidly developed a powerful global administrative capacity and one which has on occasion placed itself outside the norms and jurisdiction of domestic law and courts. The manner in which sports law regulates the activities of the IOC, WADA and large sports organisations such as FIFA, possibly as part of the debate on global administrative law more generally, will be central to the immediate evolution of sports law both practically and theoretically.

In conclusion, I would like to use this introduction to acknowledge my colleagues at the School of Law, Queen's University Belfast for their personal and professional support and in particular Professor Gordon Anthony, a supporter of the Manchester Red Devils franchise now playing out of the New York Stock Exchange, and Professor Sally Wheeler, a supporter of Aston Villa, of which little more need be said. I am also extremely grateful to all at the T.M.C. Asser Instituut and Asser Press. Rob Siekmann who was involved in the initial commissioning stages of this book and later the ever efficient and ever pleasant Karen Jones and also Marjolijn Bastiaans, responsible for production and, of course, the Director and Publisher at TMC Asser Press, Philip van Tongeren.

Finally and as stated earlier, these introductory remarks were written as the London 2012 Olympic Games drew to a close. On one of the last nights of the men's diving competition I watched with my son (aged 4 and three quarters) and daughter (aged 2 going on 16). After one of Tom Daley's slightly less than perfect dives my daughter piped up, "good but a bit splashy". As analysis goes, I thought it concise but incisive. On reading this volume, I hope you will feel the same about its analysis of leading cases in sports law.

Thanks to Teresa, Daniel and Katherine, Mum and Dad.

Belfast, August 2012 Jack Anderson

Contents

Part I
The Emergence of Sports Law

Chapter 1
Abbot v Weekly (1665) 83 ER 357; 1 Lev 176

Jack Anderson

Abstract Trespass for breaking his close; the defendant prescribes, that all the inhabitants of the village, time out of memory…had used to dance there at all times of the year at their free will, for their recreation, and so justifies to dance there: issue was on the prescription, and a verdict for the defendant, and to save his costs the plaintiff moved in arrest of judgment, that this prescription to dance in the freehold of another, and spoil his grass, was void, especially as it is laid…at all times of the year, and not at seasonable times; and that 'twas also ill laid in the inhabitants, who although they may prescribe in easements…yet they ought to be easements of necessity, as ways to a church…and not for pleasure only, as this case is. Second, if it be good, it ought to have been laid by way of custom in the town, and not by prescription in the persons…..but by the Court, this is a good custom, and it is necessary for inhabitants to have their recreation.

Contents

J. Anderson (✉)
School of Law, Queen's University, Belfast BT7 1NN, UK
e-mail: jack.anderson@qub.ac.uk

J. Anderson (ed.), *Leading Cases in Sports Law*,
ASSER International Sports Law Series, DOI: 10.1007/978-90-6704-909-2_1,

1.1 Introduction

The above abstract needs some translation, both textual and contextual.

It is an extract from the English Reports' account of legal proceedings from the mid-seventeenth century in which the claimant instigated an action against the inhabitant of an unnamed village in Oxfordshire for trespass of his freehold, private property. The "trespass" arose from village dances, which the claimant complained were not just a summer phenomena ("at seasonable times") in this particular village but could occur at any time in the year and which always spoiled his grass. The defendant argued that, although the green space or "close" in question was enclosed (most likely by a hedge), the inhabitants of the village had, since "time immemorial", danced on this particular village green and thus had over time acquired the right to use it for recreational purposes.

The disputed right would now, in the technical language of property law, more properly be described as an "easement".[1] The acquisition process was by way of "prescription".[2] The claimant (who was obviously a man of status: owning the freehold to a property large enough to have an accompanying enclosure; and having the means to sustain protracted litigation) countered that, although the villagers may benefit from an easement of necessity over another's private property in order, for example, to permit them to go to church; they should not benefit from a widely drawn easement for pleasure only. No court, the claimant argued, should recognise villagers' right to dance on another's ground at all times of the year. The Court of King's Bench held for the villagers holding that the right in question was customary in nature and a "good custom" at that because "it is necessary for inhabitants to have their recreation."

It is this recognition of a "right to recreation" that is the starting point for this article and, more broadly, how, over the following two centuries, the courts in England, through interpretation and application of common law principles, and later statute, had an influential and hitherto understated role in the birth of modern sport in Britain.[3] In this vein, this article traces the subsequent precedential pattern of *Abbot v Weekly* with regard to the development of recreational rights surrounding village greens and, later, urban public spaces in England. Moreover, and centrally, the article highlights that at a critical juncture in the development of modern sport in Britain—the mid-nineteenth century—the law helped embed not just a *space* for sport in the emerging industrialised and increasingly urbanised

---

[1] In plain language, an easement is right to cross (a right of way) or otherwise use someone else's land for a specified purpose.

[2] In this instance, prescription meant the acquisition of an easement by uninterrupted and unhidden use over a long period. Technically, the period entailed continuous and open use of the easement from "time immemorial", which was fixed in the legal memory of English common law at 1189 i.e., before the reign of Richard I.

[3] For a sports historian's view of the law's influence on the regulation of sport at the material time see Vamplew 2007b, 2009. The author would also like to thank Professor Vamplew for his insightful comments on an earlier draft of this chapter.

environment but also the *place* of sport in the Victorian era's evolving socio-economic landscape.[4]

The *Abbot v Weekly* precedential trail ends at the turn of this century when the then House of Lords addressed the issue of the registration of village greens wherein proof of the playing of lawful sports, games and informal recreations was often integral to attempts by claimants to establish (or deny) user rights to the land in question.[5] Accordingly, this short article, which has begun with an account of the first reported case considering customary recreation rights—and, arguably, the first recorded "sports law" case in the UK—will end with reference to the small handful of genuinely sports law-related proceedings ever to make the jurisdiction's senior superior court.

Before that story is told, however, it is necessary to begin *in media res* by giving a brief overview of the social, economic and political factors which together ensured that the origins of many modern, codified sports can be traced to the values, morals and laws of mid-nineteenth century Britain.

1.2 The Civilising Process, Law and the Birth of Modern Sport

There is, no doubt, a correlation between the sophistication, frequency and range of organised sports events and the technological, economic and military power of the "host" society. Sporting events were, for instance, an integral and popular part of the societal calendars of Ancient Greece and Imperial Rome.[6] In contemporary terms, the four major leagues sports in North America continue to dominate sporting "rich lists" in terms of annual revenue streams and player salaries.[7] In the mid-nineteenth century, Britain and its Empire, as the world's leading industrial power, would leave an inedible mark on the development of contemporary sport. Dedicated leisure time and increased disposable income, allied to developments in communication and transport meant that not only could most sections of Victorian society read about sports events more or less as they happened but some could also easily travel to and cheaply attend these events. This rise in the popularity and accessibility of sport meant that some sports could sustain a professional code, augmenting basic revenue

---

[4] This chapter is informed by a similar, but much more erudite, account of the law's role contribution to the birth of modern sport by McArdle 2000, Chap. 1.

[5] See, for example, *R (Beresford) v Sunderland City Council* [2003] UKHL 60; [2004] 1 AC 889.

[6] For a recent account of "ancient" sport, from Homer to Byzantium, see generally Potter 2011.

[7] See Sawer 2010 in an article that draws from sports finance data available at www.sportingintelligence.com.

from gate receipts by attracting commercial sponsorships and thus in turn leading to the beginning of the mass "consumption" of sport.[8]

A number of other less tangible factors also helped nurture and sustain sport's first meaningful wave of "start-up" regulatory bodies, including the establishment of the Football Association in 1863; the Rugby Football Union (1871); the Yacht Racing Association (1875); the Amateur Athletics Association (1880); the Amateur Rowing Association (1882); the Amateur Swimming Association (1886); the Hockey Association (1886); the Lawn Tennis Association (1888); the Badminton Association (1893); and the Northern Rugby (League) Football Union (1895).[9] Three of these factors are noteworthy.

The first is that sport was seen by the governing and moneyed elite of the material time as providing a vital cathartic outlet for the industrialised and urbanised masses of the era. Sport could be used with powerful symbolism to demonstrate a commonality between all in society and, simultaneously, deference to one's betters. The elite's education in the classics would have alerted them to the regular distraction of the Roman mob by the *panem et circenses* of imperially sponsored events at the Coliseum. Moreover, the folk history, among the landed elite, and in particular of the French Revolution, remained fresh, as epitomised by George Trevelyan's exaggerated lament, "if the French noblesse had been capable of playing cricket with their peasants, their chateaux would never have been burnt."[10] The self-serving and self-interested extent of the elite's interest in "sport for all"—to which the maintenance of the social and political status quo was in fact central—will be expanded upon later. For now, the socio-political catharsis provided by sport helps, to some extent, explain why from the mid- to late nineteenth century the proletarianism and professionalisation of sport, epitomised by working class football, and otherwise completely at odds with the Corinthian ideal of the "gentleman amateur", was partly indulged.[11] Most symbolically of all, on 25 April 1914, that "indulgence" received the royal seal of approval when George V became the first reigning monarch to attend the FA Cup final. The year and timing of the gesture, as Europe and the world drew towards war, is, of course, hugely relevant. Those Burnley and Liverpool supporters in the 72,000 attendance at Crystal Palace would, a summer later, be asked to swap the terrace for the trench.

The second factor in the promotion of sport at the material time is captured in the cultural conditioning notion of "manly character". That concept encapsulated not only the historical connotations of practice at sport as a means of preparing men for war but also Victorian ideals on masculinity, social Darwinism, muscular

---

[8] The research on the history and development of sport in Britain at the material time is voluminous. Nonetheless, three monographs that continue to reward on re-reading include Birley 1993; Holt 1990 and Vamplew 1988.

[9] For a witty review of how the British "invented" these sports see generally Norridge 2008.

[10] Cited by Holt 1990, 268.

[11] See generally Hargreaves 1986. In the sport of rugby this, essentially, class-based distinction led in the 1890s to the schism between rugby union and rugby league. See generally Collins 2006.

Christianity and even imperial superiority.[12] The manner in which sport was seen as a means of building character, learning about manhood and inculcating the habit of victory at home and abroad was seen to greatest effect in English public schools who understood that "through sport boys acquire virtues which no books can give them; not merely daring and endurance but better still temper, self-restraint, fairness, honour, unenvious appropriation of another's success and all that 'give and take' of life which stands a man in good stead when he goes forth in the world and without which, indeed, his success is always maimed and partial."[13]

The third factor in the promotion of sport can be set against the backdrop of the social, economic and political developments that marked the gradual decline in Europe of feudal, agrarian, kin-based societies and the beginnings of industrialisation and urbanisation, allied to centralised government. In short, as western societies became more advanced in terms of political and economic structure, Elias,[14] (as later interpreted by Dunning and others) outlined how such societies had engaged in a parallel "civilising process" influencing personal, social *and* sporting relationships.[15] Put simply, Elias and Dunning contend that a lowering of the "threshold of repugnancy" towards acts of inter-personal violence had a significant influence on the development of modern sport.[16] During the nineteenth century, this civilising process, it is claimed, was an underlying feature in the development of a bourgeois model of sport whereby in order to fit in with the emerging "respectable" values of the (predominately) metropolitan middle class, popular sports of the pre-industrial era either had to submit to codification and rid themselves of their association with alcohol, gambling, violence, animal cruelty and the inobservance of the Sabbath; or face proscription.[17]

Central to this article is the contention that a fourth factor assisted in the development of modern sport i.e., the general law and the judiciary. Arguably, during the half-century 1830–1880, the general law and the courts played an understated instrumental role in this civilising process through which "rational" recreations[18] and sport appropriate to the newly industrialised and orderly urbanised landscape of mid-nineteenth century Britain were promoted and formalised into what we today recognise as their modern form. Three examples of this process are noteworthy. First, the 1830s saw an increase in what might be called "pugilistic prosecutions" whereby the criminal law in various actions—assault, affray, riot or illegal assembly—was used both as an attempt to eradicate

[12] See further Mangan 2011.

[13] Quoted by Haley 1978, 119.

[14] Elias 1978 and Elias and Dunning 1986.

[15] On this "reform of popular culture" see further Burke 2009.

[16] It must be noted that the Elias and Dunning's approach has been criticised for placing too much emphasis on a "violence reduction" rationale in the formalisation of sport at this time. Compare, for instance, Vamplew 2007, 161–171.

[17] See, for example, Agozino 1996, 163–188; Malcolm 2002, 37–57 and Sheard 1997, 31–57.

[18] See generally Bailey 1978.

the practice of bare fisted fighting and coerce the prize fighting fraternity into adopting rules as regularised and sanitised (in relative terms) as the Queensberry Rules (1865).[19] Second, the 1830s also saw the proscription of numerous blood sports involving the baiting or fighting of animals contrary to the Cruelty to Animals Act 1835 and similar legislative provisions in 1849, 1876 and 1911.[20] Third, enforcement of section 72 of the Highways Way Act 1835,[21] in conjunction with section 54(17) of the Metropolitan Police Act 1839,[22] helped ensure that the "riotous rampage" that was pre-industrial football, often held on religious holidays or pattern days such as Shrove Tuesday, evolved into the "more domesticated, commercialised and spatially contained form"[23] that we recognise today.

In overall terms, the combined influence that the civilising process, the law and the courts had on sport at the material time assisted in suppressing traditional and dangerously unconstrained and improvised sports event, and transforming them into events that became as easily regulated and supervised as the blast of the factory whistle. Symbolic manifestations of this link can be found in the various Factory Acts of the era, which eventually led in most industries to the stoppage of work at 2 pm on Saturdays and thus, in turn, to the tradition of holding football matches one hour later,[24] and also in the Bank Holiday Act of 1871 which, according to Walvin, was "a landmark in the emergence of modern leisure patterns for it transformed old religious holidays into secular days of recreation sanctioned by the state."[25] It must also be noted that these reforms were a unique experience in nineteenth century Europe—the five and a half day working week was referred to as *la semaine anglaise*—and they go to understanding Britain's marked influence on the then development and, later, the spread of new forms of sport and recreation.[26]

The influence that the civilising process, the law and the courts had on sport was not confined to the mid-nineteenth century. As Hunt shows, it can be traced to and from the medieval era.[27] A statute in 1388 from the reign of Richard II, for instance, prohibited labourers from "playing at Tennis or Football and other Games called Coits, Dice, Casting of the Stone and other importune Games" on

---

[19] Anderson 2006, 265–287.

[20] See Radford 2001, 33–98.

[21] The provision made it a criminal offence for any person to obstruct the highway by playing at "Football or any other Game on any Part of said Highways, to the Annoyance of Any Passenger or Passengers."

[22] The provision made it an offence to "play at any game to the annoyance of the inhabitants or passengers" and it authorised a constable to take any person committing such an offence into custody without warrant.

[23] See further Vorspan 2000, 905–908.

[24] Walvin 1975, 50–56.

[25] Walvin 1975, 55.

[26] Huggins 2004, 15–16.

[27] Hunt 1995, 5–29.

Sundays and holy feast/saint days[28] and similar statutes followed in 1477,[29] 1495,[30] 1503,[31] 1511,[32] 1514[33] and 1541.[34] Variously, these "Unlawful Games" statutes—often supported by royal proclamation[35]—sought to prohibit "vain, dishonest, unthrifty and idle"[36] sports associated with alcohol, gambling and vagrancy to the detriment of the practice of a sport such as archery, which in the absence of a standing army was seen as central to the realm's military preparedness for war.[37]

Finally, this essentially moral regulation of sport throughout the above ages (at no stage, even in the Victorian era, can it be said that a centralised, deliberative governmental "policy" on sport existed) prompted by the civilising process and facilitated by the law can be used to explain *what* type of sports were played or emerged at a particular time; *how* they were played and evolved in terms of rules and codification; *when* they were played such as on Saturday afternoons; and even *who*—labouring, middle or upper class—played a particular sport. The core of this short piece is—and using *Abbot v Weekly* as an example—to argue that the combination of the civilising process, the law and judgments of the courts of mid-nineteenth century Britain also had an influential role in *where* sport was played.

1.3 A Place and Space for Sport and Recreation

At first it must be clarified that the sport or recreations at issue are not the established or newly professional sports of the mid-nineteenth century but what would now be called "grassroots" or recreational sport. The key question is where, in the absence of any central or local government support for sport and recreation, could such sport be played? What local facilities did the "Sunday league" footballers of the mid-nineteenth century or the local cycling or cricket or athletic club access and use?

In terms of infrastructure and facilities, sports such as horse racing, cricket and golf benefitted from their connections with the landed and moneyed elite of the era.

[28] 12 Ric 2 c6, Unlawful Games (1388).

[29] 17 Edw 4 c3, Unlawful Games (1477).

[30] 11 Hen 7 c17, Unlawful Games (1495).

[31] 19 Hen 7 c12, Unlawful Games (1503).

[32] 3 Hen 8 c3, Unlawful Games (1511).

[33] 6 Hen 8 c2, Unlawful Games (1514).

[34] 33 Hen 8 c9, Unlawful Games (1541).

[35] Hunt 1995, 19–21.

[36] 39 Edw 3 c23, Unlawful Games (1365).

[37] For the specific example of the attempts to proscribe football during the period see Bushaway 1982, 250–252 and Dunning and Sheard 1979, Chap. 1.

For instance, the site of Ascot racecourse (located just six miles from Windsor Castle in Berkshire and with an equine history stretching back to the reign of Queen Anne in the early eighteenth century) formally was secured through the Windsor Forest Enclosure Act of 1813, which entrusted heath land in the area into the ownership of the Crown with the proviso that it would be retained as a racecourse for public use: "which piece of Ground shall be kept and continued as a Racecourse for the Public Use at all times, as it has usually been."

Similarly, the history of Edgbaston cricket ground in Birmingham owes its origins to the fact that from the 1820s onwards the Calthorpe estate, the landowners of the eponymous suburb, imposed restrictive clauses in covenants for leasing land prohibiting the building of "low class" housing as well as "any workshops or other kinds of shops, nor any place or places for carrying on any trade or manufacture nor any brewshop, alehouse or tea garden."[38] Consequently, when in the mid 1880s Warwickshire Cricket Club asked to lease a 12 acre site in the area, then used as meadows, their request was granted because, according to Hignall, it created "a positive externality" that further enhanced the genteel nature of the suburb.[39]

Later still in the 1890s, Lowerson notes that as a golf club membership boomed among the middle classes, clubs sought to expand their use of commons land adjacent to urban areas as courses and driving areas—and particularly the sandy heath lands in the London area.[40] Objections, sometimes taking the form of legal proceedings, by locals, who enjoyed customary rights to ramble, play football or even graze animals on the commons, were regularly faced down by golf clubs who "had the advantage of their own commercial or professional experience, with solicitors members as key figures. They also had a sense of sporting aggression and the collective power of clubs to reinforce their encroachments."[41] In short, while golf clubs could collectively subsume the costs of defending a legal action; individual, local residents most likely did not wish to take the risks of having to pay the costs of instigating and sustaining legal proceedings. By the mid-1890s, the Commons Preservation Society, a national conservation body for commons areas, was reporting bluntly that "golf clubs practically monopolise the commons."[42]

By this decade recreations favoured by the moneyed industrial elite as their gentleman-amateur sport of choice benefitted both from the demise of the legal device that was the strict settlement, whereby the landed classes sought to tie their estates dynastically, and the *noveaux riches* financial capacity to lease or buy undeveloped green areas near urban centres.[43] Moreover, and as Baker observes,

---

[38] Hignall 2002, 63.

[39] Hignall, 64.

[40] Lowerson 1995, 143–153.

[41] Lowerson 1995, 148.

[42] Commons Preservation Society 1893–1896, 47.

[43] Under a strict settlement the immediate "owner" of the estate had very limited means of generating revenue from the land by way of, for example, leasing or mortgaging it or part thereof.

the great agricultural depression of the 1880s gave rise to "strong desires among landowners to be able to convert land into more profitable investments."[44] Leasing land in or near urban areas to emerging sports clubs was one such means of investment and indeed the desire to make the investment pay all year round for the benefit of members saw many cricket clubs adopt a "winter" sport i.e., football.[45] An illustration of this pattern can be seen in the incorporation in 1894 of the Bath and County Recreation Ground Company, which leased 15 acres near the city from the Forster family, holders of the Bathwick Estate. According to the company's prospectus, its object was to develop grounds, on what is still colloquially known as "the Rec", in such a way "as to render it suitable for County Cricket Matches, Law Tennis Tournaments, Football Matches and other sports."[46]

Arguably, the most pertinent example of the relationship at the material time between those who owned land and were willing to sell it and those who had the money to rent or buy it in order to support their leisure interests, occurred as far back as 1854 when a local land agent and chairman of Sheffield Cricket Club, Michael Ellison, arranged the leasing of an 8.5 acre site later called Bramall Lane. This link between the estate of the premier ducal title in England and the stadium that is apparently the oldest major stadium in the world still hosting professional football matches, epitomises this period in sports history. Moreover, the impact that the civilising/rational recreation process had on nineteenth century British sporting life is summarised neatly in the objectives of the new company—the Sheffield United Cricket and Football Club Ltd—incorporated to buy Bramall Lane from the Duke of Norfolk for £10,000 on Ellison's death in 1899. The objects of the new company were stated to be:

> To promote and practice the play of cricket, football, lacrosse, law tennis, bowls, bicycling and tricycling, running, jumping, physical training and the development of the human frame, and other athletic sports, games and exercises of every description, and any other game, pastime, sport, recreation, amusement or entertainment, but not pigeon shooting, rabbit coursing, or racing for money.[47]

Outside of these bourgeois models of sporting membership—the "incorporated club" and all the social and economic advancement that term entailed for this nascent middle class—the question remained as to where those not of that class

---

(Footnote 43 continued)
This meant that not only did strict settlements concentrate landholding within an ever declining landed elite but it also meant that many estates became financially unviable for lack of investment. The overall economic undesirability of this system resulted in legislative changes such as the Settled Estate Acts of 1856 and 1877, as supplemented by the Settled Land Acts 1882, 1890 and 1925.

44 Baker 2002, 295.

45 See Walvin 1975, 61–62 on the "cricketing" history of founding members of the football league (Derby County FC and Preston North End FC) and both Sheffield clubs.

46 *Bath and North East Somerset Council v HM Attorney General and Anor* [2002] EWHC 1623 (Ch), para 9.

47 Clareborough and Kirkham 1999, 12–13.

might *play* sport. There were accessible and relatively inexpensive places to *watch* sport. For instance, leading football grounds of the era, many designed by the Scottish architect Archibald Leitch, were often reflective of, and integral to, the emerging functional urban landscape.[48] And yet, mass spectator sport was one thing; but if the personal, economic, health and moral benefits of this emerging notion of recreationalism were to gain any enduring societal traction, then mass participative sport would also have to be promoted and assisted in its development. In this, one of the great hindrances to "participative recreationalism", and one that would test the strength of Victorian social engineering to it limits, was something that for centuries before hand had been at the heart of British sport—the local pub.

1.4 Out of the Village Pub and Onto the Village Green

As Collins and Vamplew note, it is "difficult to underestimate the importance of the drinking place to pre-industrial societies."[49] In England, the pub was long the fulcrum of village life: it served as a meeting place for socialising, doing business, finding work, travel and the organisation of everything from fairs to political activity. Collins and Vamplew estimate that by the sixteenth century the alehouse was the main area for staging sports events in England with the grounds of such "disorderly houses or "places of publick entertainment", as a 1751 Act called them,[50] providing the space "in which sports as diverse as skittle, quoits, bowls, boxing, wrestling, tennis, foot-racing, cricket and any number of activities featuring animals could be staged."[51] The publican, the authors note, was often the organiser, promoter, bookmaker and, of course, caterer (drink and food) for the event.

The activities and mores of the "sporting pub" were at odds with the temperate, rule-bound values demanded in mid-nineteenth century Britain and during the period the "coercive weight of the law fell heavily on the public houses".[52] Two avenues of attack were opened: the regulation of the gambling and licensing laws. Many of the sports traditionally held in or adjacent to pubs were little more than adjuncts for gambling. Consequently, by targeting gambling in pubs—on pain of, at least, a fine or possibly the revocation of the publican's licence—traditional alehouse sports were discouraged. This process begun with offence contained in section 21 of the Alehouse Act 1828 for those licensed publicans who "knowingly suffered any unlawful games or any gaming whatsoever". It continued with the catch-all offence provided in section 1 of Betting Houses Acts 1853 and also

[48] See generally Inglis 2005. Leitch designed stands for Arsenal, Manchester United, Chelsea, Everton, Liverpool, Tottenham, Aston Villa, Hearts and Glasgow Rangers.

[49] Collins and Vamplew 2002.

[50] 25 Geo 2 c36, Disorderly Houses (1751).

[51] Collins and Vamplew 2002, 5.

[52] Vorspan 2000, 935.

included section 17 of the 1872 Licensing Act, which, on its face, contained a strict liability offence of "suffering any gaming" on the licensed premises.[53]

The overall effectiveness, and indeed the actual enforcement of the above legislation, have been questioned.[54] In any event, the pub and publican were well placed to adapt in providing meeting places, playing fields and sponsorship for emerging football clubs.[55] Moreover, while it was all very well to attempt to restrict gambling in pubs in order that it might have an adverse affect on the sports events that took place on such premises ("the stick"); if patrons were to be attracted to the benefits of participating in sport, as opposed to the manifold attractions of having a social drink while watching and betting on the outcome of an event, then alternative, easily accessible venues would have to be provided ("the carrot").

In the mid- to late nineteenth century in Britain such alternatives came from a number of sources. One source has been mentioned already—cricket clubs looking for a winter sport in order to maintain income and membership. Others included sports facilities and outlets provided by the leading "gateways" into working class communities, such as churches and schools; by private entities such as those driven by charitable or philanthropic patronage; by voluntary organisations emanating from within working class communities themselves, such as factory teams and at workingmen's clubs; as a result of state (legislative) intervention; or the consequence of the (re)interpretation of existing common law principles on access to public spaces and the right to recreation.

What follows is a brief and separate outline of each "alternative source"—community gateways; private entities and the legally protected right to recreation—though in reality at the material time local sports facilities and clubs emerged from a combination of these interrelated social institutions.

An illustration of this can be seen in an overview of the historical origins of Southampton FC.[56] In the early 1880s the church curate at St Mary's in the city, a Reverend Arthur Baron Sole, established the St Mary's church football team. They played their matches on the adjacent Deanery field which also hosted cricket matches involving the Deanery Cricket Club and its winter offshoot, founded by local school teachers, called Deanery FC. Over the next decade or so the church-based team evolved incorporating members of the young men's association at St Mary's Church (thus becoming St Mary's Young Men's Association FC) and possibly also members of Southampton Rangers, a team made up of shipbuilders working for Oswald and Mordaunt Ltd (thus becoming Southampton St Mary's FC from November 1885).

Initially, St Mary's (as they were know locally and hence the still-used nickname the Saints) played their matches on Southampton Common, where they had

53 For an account of the related case law see Vorspan 2000, 935–948.

54 Miers 2004, 239–241 and at Chap. 9.

55 Collins and Vamplew 2002, 10ff.

56 See generally Chalk and Holley 1987.

to compete for space with ramblers, pedestrian foot racers and even those locals entitled to collect berries on the common. Southampton Common, which has a history stretching back to the thirteenth century, was, in the immediate pre-industrial era, used mainly as an area for the grazing of cattle. In the 1830s it had seen its long-term common rights threatened by the enclosure of the nearby Shirely Common. The Southampton Marsh Improvement Act 1844 protected its use for public recreation, including sport.

As for St Mary's FC, as it became more successful in local competitions and on entering the FA Cup in 1891, it began more frequently to hold matches at bigger grounds—such as the nearby County Ground but also the Antelope Ground, which was owned in freehold by the church and which had been leased for cricket matches from the 1830s mainly to the predecessors of what is now Hampshire Cricket Club. On winning the Southern League in 1897, the club incorporated as a limited company and became Southampton FC. Shortly afterwards it moved grounds to the Dell. One hundred and one years and one FA Cup later, ground was broken at a new stadium, which given its close physical proximity to the club's ecclesiastical roots, has been called St Mary's Stadium.

To reiterate, although, of course, not all local football clubs developed into one which could compete at the elite professional level; nevertheless aspects of the above potted history of Southampton FC, and the manner in which the club and its facilities evolved, are reflective of the influences that ensured that local sport and clubs became embedded in communities nationwide.

1.4.1 Gateways

In line with the belief in the benefits underpinning muscular Christianity—that a healthy body complimented a healthy, moral and religious mind—Walvin notes that in the mid- to late nineteenth century, "churches provided the main entry into working-class communities" and that younger clergy in particular "seized on football as an ideal way of combating urban degeneracy" in such communities.[57] Consequently, churches, he claims, spawned hundreds of local football teams nationwide with many of the sport's most famous clubs beginning life as church teams and including five of the twelve founding members of the football league in 1888 (Aston Villa, Bolton, Burnley, Everton and Wolves). Moreover, as seen above in Southampton's case, fields attaching to churches often served as the initial home for sports clubs.

This adjacent land was often part of a church's "glebe" i.e., land serving as part of a clergyman's benefice and providing income. Although the freehold in such land rested with the clergyman, statutes dating from the Reformation restricted the alienation of such land. As demand for building and amenity development sites

[57] Walvin 1975, 56.

near urban areas increased in the nineteenth century, the law was relaxed. For example, under the Ecclesiastical Leasing Acts of 1842 and 1858, glebe lands could be let for a period of up to 99 years. In addition, the Glebe Land Act 1888 permitted the clergy to sell, exchange or gift such land under strict conditions and often to the benefit of the local "labouring classes" for allotments or a site for local amenities ranging from village halls to local water or sewage facilities or, sometimes, as recreational pitches for the emerging sports clubs of the 1880s.[58]

As again seems to be the case in Southampton, some of these churches were also connected locally through voluntary schools and with the impetus gained from the Education Act 1870, whereby the state extended elementary schooling opportunity nationwide, Walvin notes that this new state education system provided "public school and University men" with an opportunity to put their belief that "through sport boys acquire virtues which no books can give them" into practice through increased physical education instruction, the establishment of inter-school competitions and the founding of old boys football clubs or Edwardian-style boys clubs.[59] These school teacher-led initiatives, not all of whom, as Mangan and Hickey recently noted,[60] were of a privileged public school background "became of crucial importance in generating and maintaining youthful commitment to football, particularly among working-class boys whose recreational opportunities were limited."[61]

The broad influence of the manly character/muscular Christianity movement on English education was subsequently reflected in recommendations by the Royal Commission on Education 1886–1888, which called for the extension of systematised physical exercises especially for schools in towns[62] and later implemented through the Education Code of 1891, which for the first time imposed a duty of care upon the state for the physical welfare of children thus encouraging sporting instruction, the building of adjacent playgrounds and outdoor activity.[63] Nevertheless, according to Rose, the percentage of time devoted to physical education remained extremely low in the immediate pre-War period—often not

[58] In terms of primary research on this point, it is well to note that from its establishment in 1889, the Board of Agriculture undertook annual reports of transactions, proceedings and other statistical data relevant to the Glebe Lands Act 1888 and on other related provisions, which also, indirectly, would have made land available for sporting and recreational purposes. See, for instance, the first of these reports in Board of Agriculture 1890, (5947) xxv 315.

[59] Walvin 1975, 59. See also Rose 1991, 140–141.

[60] See Mangan and Hickey 2009 on the "missing men" and their role as school teachers in the spread in popularity of association football at the material time.

[61] Walvin 1975, 59.

[62] See the Elementary Education Acts 1888, (5485) xxxv 1, 216, recommendation 110.

[63] Plans for newly built or fitted elementary schools were obliged, for instance, to provide for a playground. See Education Department's Code of Regulations, 1891 (6272) lxi 141, schedule IV, building rule 15.

more than 15 min a week and mainly consisting of desk bound imitations of War Office drills and marches.[64]

Moreover, the shallowness of the success of the manly character/muscular Christianity movement was revealed in the performance of the British armed forces during the Boer War of 1899–1902, which seemed to suggest a grave deterioration in the physical fitness of the average soldier. In a period of geopolitical uncertainty, the British Empire could no longer afford to be distracted nor led by the gentleman-amateurishness of what Kipling excoriated as "the flannelled fools at the wicket and the muddied oafs at goal" and some serious consideration had to be given to practical means of improving the physical well-being and hardiness of, in particular, the young urban poor in key population centres. Accordingly, and in moves that echoed Henry VIII's legislation in the 1500s promoting only those sports suitable to prepare men for war, Government reports in the immediate aftermath of the Boer War reinforced the need for schools to provide and maintain play areas; to integrate physical education meaningfully into the curriculum away from War Office instructions on drills and exercise and towards Swedish-style gymnastic drills; training more and better qualified PE teachers and encouraging the much greater use of school and public playgrounds for organised games.[65] The Board of Education published the first Syllabus on Physical Exercise in 1904 and the syllabus—revised in 1905, 1909, 1919 and 1933 and with increasing emphasis on games and athletic competition—laid the foundation for the contemporary regulation of school sports in Britain.

1.4.2 Private Entities

Walvin notes that trade unions and factory groups provided "an ideal base for working men to organise recreation in their spare time" and industrial football teams in particular mushroomed rapidly in the mid-nineteenth century in England, and especially in the north and midlands.[66] Shipbuilders were, as noted, part of the story of the foundation of Southampton FC, as were, for example, railway workers in the foundation of the oldest club in the current English Premier League, Stoke, (founded by workmen on the North Staffordshire Railway in 1863) and in the establishment of the Premier League's most successful club, Manchester United, whose origins can be traced back to 1878 and a team formed by workmen in the carriage and wagon department of the Lancashire and Yorkshire Railway Company at Newton Heath. In addition, these factory, trade union and industrial teams were also supported in a structural way by the emerging working men's club

[64] Rose 1991, 142–143.

[65] See the three volume *Report of the Inter-Departmental Committee on Physical Deterioration.* 1904 (2175) xxxii 1; (2210) xxxii 145; and (2186) xxxii 655.

[66] Walvin 1975, 60.

movement, which provided permanent playing and meeting facilities for local sports clubs.[67]

Moreover, and in line with the social philosophy underpinning rational recreationalism, a number of industrialists saw the social, economic and political benefits of sporting-related patronage. This ranged from increased goodwill and loyalty towards the company; to increased productivity as a result of spending more time at play than with alcohol; and included an effort to distract workers from deeper political debate and wider trade union or party political organisation. Consequently, industrial benefactors were willing to underwrite the provision of recreational facilities for workers and the general public. For example, as early as 1851, Titus Salt, a wealthy Bradford industrialist, was ensuring that his model industrial village of Saltaire included sporting and recreational facilities for his mill workers and other workers in the village who might on occasion need a "good day out".[68] Furthermore, by the end of the century large industrial estate type projects, such as the development of Trafford Park by the Manchester Ship Canal Company in the late 1890s, also involved the setting aside of recreational zones.[69]

In sum, and as seen above, the proselytisation of the social, economic, moral and political benefits of "rational recreation" by the industrialist and bourgeoisie classes of the mid to late nineteenth century was underpinned by a wide variety of motivations ranging from, on the one hand, a benignly paternalistic and genuinely altruistic interest in the benefits of recreation for all (i.e., a broad "societal" interest in promoting sport) to, on the other hand, a patronisingly manipulative and cynically self-interested promotion of rational recreation (i.e., a narrow "sectoral" interest). Among sports historians of the era, the sectoral motivation tends to be favoured as an explanation for the motivations underpinning the rational recreation movement. According to this approach, the rational recreation movement can therefore be understood from the perspective that, if the working class of the era kept drinking and pursuing violent sport then, in the absence of alternative leisure facilities, these activities might, as they had done on occasion in the past, collectively prove a seditious threat to the social and political status quo in the form of associated criminality such as rioting, affray, gambling, vagrancy, illegal assembly and civil disobedience.

Lowerson uses the example of the establishment of golf clubs—what he calls those bastions of "middle-class ambitions and anxieties"[70]—in the later nineteenth century to underpin this point on the manipulative and cynical interest of the few in the recreation of the many. In illustration, he cites the advice given by a leading

[67] For a review of the working men's club movement within the context of rational or participative recreationalism see Bailey 1978, Chap. 5.

[68] Wigglesworth 1996, 65.

[69] See generally Nicholls 1996, 20–65.

[70] Lowerson 1995, 125.

figure in the sport during the era, Colt,[71] to golf clubs in trying, ostensibly, to reach agreements with local residents on increasing golf exclusive times and spaces on commons areas:

> …two difficulties exist—the commoners and the commonable beasts. The commoners need at times a lot of tact—the commonable beasts an even temper and considerable patience. Both are apt to resent interference in their rights; the former retaliate at times by digging up the best putting green with their spades, and the latter by destroying it with their hoofs. The best plan to get over both difficulties is to encourage the commoners to play golf themselves, and, if a club be started for them, and the ways and means provided for them to enjoy the game, the manners of the commonable beasts are apt also to improve. In time an annual match can be held between the parent club and the commoners' club, and during the subsequent convivial evening leave may be obtained for making a few more necessary bunkers, even at the expense of the commonable beast. These hazards must, however, be made with discretion…pedestrians have a nasty way of objecting to being hit be a golf ball.[72]

Overall, whether this investment in, and the promotion of, sport by the emerging industrialised elite was, to paraphrase Tranter, for "health, prestige or profit", it has, no doubt, had an enduring and academically well documented influence on sport in modern Britain.[73] And yet there is one other underlying factor which contributed to the success of the rational recreation movement of the Victorian era and concomitantly the rise of modern sport. That motivation is one of "guilt" and, specifically, guilt on the part of the newly emerging industrialist and middle classes. How that guilt arose and how the law was used instrumentally to assuage that guilt is the focus of the remainder of this chapter.

1.5 The Right to Recreation: Enclosure

As Cunningham observes:

> For much of the eighteenth century in both town and country most people had access to some kind of public space: space which they might use individually—to walk on, to pursue game in, to graze animals on—or collectively—as the forum for political activity or communal entertainment. Such space was public in the sense that it was owned communally and belonged to everyone; hence everyone had equal rights to it.[74]

---

[71] Henry Shapland Colt (1869–1951), who read law at Cambridge in the later 1880s, was a leading golf architect in the first quarter of the twentieth century. The Oxford Dictionary of National Biography notes that as a designer Colt was aware of the social tensions arising in England from the great expansion of golf as a middle-class game at the time. Although Colt promoted the development of working class clubs, the Oxford DNB notes that "this arrangement did nothing to challenge the social distinctions that were already entrenched in the game". See http://www.oxforddnb.com/view/article/41096.

[72] Colt 1912, 15–16.

[73] See Tranter 1998, Chap. 5.

[74] Cunningham 1980, 76.

This notion of a public communal space is fundamental to, for instance, an understanding of *Abbot v Weekly* and both to the sense of grievance felt by the villagers at the attempt to restrict their use of the close and also to the empathy of the court towards the "good and necessary" custom of using the close for recreational purposes.

Nevertheless, and within a century of *Abbot v Weekly*, Cunningham notes that the extant landed elite had benefitted from a mass appropriation of public spaces for their own exclusive, private use and "as a corollary to it, they frowned on and become suspicious of public gatherings of the lower orders for whatever purpose."[75] In this, Cunningham is referring impliedly to the success of the enclosure movement, which had a profound impact on the evolution of the agricultural, economic and social landscape of England and Wales during the period in question—from the early eighteenth century to the mid-nineteenth century.[76] The enclosure process—facilitated by way of parliamentary enclosures i.e., local, private or public Acts of Parliament called Inclosure Acts—involved the removal of "communal" rights, control and ownerships over the stated land and its conversion into a state where the owner had sole access and control of that land—often called "severalty" or unity of possession.[77] Generally, it is estimated that during the material period just over one-fifth of England (seven million acres) was enclosed by way of these (5,000 or so) parliamentary enclosures, two-thirds of which was arable land and one-third common or waste land.[78]

In abridged form, the purpose of the enclosure movement was twofold. In the first place, it was designed to address a perceived weakness in the then agricultural practice of farming scattered strips of arable land in large open fields. Accordingly, the enclosure movement was said to promote more compact, more productively farmed units of land. Second and similarly, so-called "waste" land (heath, scrub-, moor-land etc.) was earmarked for more productive use and, as the industrial revolution gathered momentum, commons located near expanding urban centres was seen as both a squander of valuable development land (housing, industrial or residential) and a "major source of social evils" given that such commons sometimes acted as a hiding and meeting place for criminals (petty thieves to highway robbers); illegal sporting events (bare fisted prize fights) and events linked with excess alcohol and gambling.[79]

The pressures that the enclosure movement gradually brought to bear on recreational uses of land of the kind protected in *Abbot v Weekly* can be seen in *Fitch*

[75] Cunningham 1980, 76.

[76] What follows has benefitted from Chap. 1 in Kain et al. 2004.

[77] Private Enclosure Acts driven by the concerns of local, landed elites became a feature of the legal landscape from the 1750s and become so frequent that, for the sake of parliamentary efficacy, public general Enclosure Acts were thought necessary. The first of these appeared in 1801, another in 1836 with a consolidating provision, later amended, in 1845.

[78] For further sources and maps see www.nationalarchives.gov.uk/records/research-guides/enclosure.htm.

[79] Kain 2004, 4.

v Rawling, a case from the late eighteenth century.[80] In that case, the Court of Common Pleas noted that, although an *Abbott v Weekly*-type custom for "all the inhabitants of a parish to play at all kinds of lawful games, sports and pastimes in the close of another at all seasonable times of the year at their own free will and pleasure" could be upheld; a similar, if more widely drawn custom, "for all persons for the time being, being is said parish" lacked the "certainty" necessary for the validation of such a right. The underlying view of the court was that only the immediate parishioners or inhabitants of a specified locality should benefit from the customary right of recreation otherwise—and this view was very much one that informed the courts more generally for the first half of the nineteenth century—the owners of such open, unenclosed property would, in effect, be divested of this land.[81]

By the mid-nineteenth century, this perspective can be seen in, and encapsulated by, decisions such as *Dyce v Hay*[82] where it was held, bluntly, that widely drawn, customary rights or easements of a recreational nature on behalf of the public generally would be "entirely inconsistent with the right of property".[83] Further, during the stated period from *Fitch v Rawling* in 1795 to *Dyce v Hay* in the 1850s, the courts used the legal technicalities surrounding the recognition of customary rights—in order to be validly recognised the custom had to be proved certain; reasonable in itself; commencing from time immemorial; and continued without interruption[84]—to restrict the recreational use not just of village greens but even to limit access to, and the use of, beaches for swimming.[85] Moreover, and as noted previously in the context of the development of golf clubs in the period, individual local residents were unlikely to take the risk of meeting hefty legal costs in order to establish user rights to commons and thus such rights were "widely lost".[86] Reflecting on this process in 1865, a House of Commons Select Committee Report on Open Spaces decried the courts' restrictive interpretation and application of customary, recreational rights in the first half of the nineteenth century and went so far as to argue that legislation was needed to reverse the process and particularly so as to provide and protect accessible recreational areas in an increasingly urbanised society.[87]

---

[80] *Fitch v Rawling and others* (1795) 126 ER 614; 2 Hy BL 393.

[81] For references to similar case law and principle see Vorspan 2000, 928–929.

[82] *Dyce v Hay* (1852) 1 Macq 305.

[83] *Dyce v Hay* (1852) 1 Macq 305, 309.

[84] See, for example, *Tyson v Smith* (1838) 112 ER 1265; 9 Al & Ed 406, 421.

[85] *Blundell v Catterall* (1821) 106 ER 286; 5 B & Ad 553. In that case, the Court of King's Bench held that, in the absence of custom or usage or prescriptive right and taking account that the shore in question was vested in an individual, the public had no common law right to bathe in the sea and to pass over the seashore, between the ordinary high and low water marks, for that purpose on foot or with horses or vehicles even where it could be done without creating any nuisance.

[86] Lowerson 1995, 148.

[87] *First Report from the Select Committee on Open Spaces (Metropolis)*. 1865 (178) viii, 259.

In a broader sociological analysis of the same period, Cunningham surmises that in the immediate pre- and early Victorian era leisure had become "increasingly class bound" whereby what he calls the "leisure class" retreated to their fenced-off private enclosures to enjoy their pursuit of choice.[88] Nevertheless, he argues, by the end of the first quarter of the nineteenth century some members of the middle class had become alarmed at a process that entailed the "privatisation" of certain socially acceptable leisure activities for the privileged few and the prohibition of many traditional pursuits enjoyed by many. Consequently, their accompanying guilt or, in a spirit of what might, appropriately, be called their sense of "fair play", some reformers sought to create a "new kind of public leisure" that would be communal in nature and in benefit. As stated earlier, these recreational activities, unlike those of the past—which had involved the baiting of animals or bare fisted prize fighting or those which were little more that an excuse for riot and tumult (football) or excess gambling and alcohol—would be visible, controlled and rational is such as way as to be in tune with the emerging mores and values of Victorian Britain. If, however, this rational or participative recreationalism were to mean anything in substance—and if, for example, the moral, health and social objectives of increased sporting participation were to be realised—then *space* had to be provided for such pursuits and particularly in the rapidly emerging urban landscape of the period. In sum, the demand of land supply for factories and housing and the enclosure of commons and judicial restrictions on customary rights meant that green spaces within urban environments were being threatened and eliminated. A *place* for sport and recreation would have to be found, and quickly.

As early as 1833, contributions to the House of Commons Select Committee on Public Walks were highlighting the dangers associated with lack of space and amenities in urban areas throughout the country.[89] A Mr John Stock, a magistrate for the county of Middlesex, gave evidence to the Committee on the marked decline of open spaces for the "humbler" class of Londoner and in an evocative recollection remembered "the fields at the back of the British Museum being covered every night in the summer by at least from 100 to 200 people at cricket, and at other sports" but that now the increase of "building and enclosures" had seen the demise of such pursuits.[90] Mr Stock agreed forcefully upon questioning that formal places of exercise would "wean" the humbler classes from "public houses and drinking shops, into which they are now driven".[91] Similarly, a public health expert, a Mr JP Kay, complained that the "operative [working class] population of Manchester enjoys little or no leisure during the week" and on Sunday sank into "abject sloth", "listless apathy" and "reckless sensuality".[92] He concluded that the health of the lower classes of Manchester in the 1830s was

---

88 Cunningham 1980, 76.

89 *Report from the Select Committee on Open Spaces*. 1833 (448) xv, 337.

90 *Report from the Select Committee on Open Spaces* 1833, 18.

91 *Report from the Select Committee on Open Spaces* 1833, 18.

92 *Report from the Select Committee on Open Spaces* 1833, 18.

"much depressed" by the combined influences of "municipal evils" and "constant toil" and that open park spaces adjacent to the city were needed for the healthful benefit of the populace as a whole.[93]

In overall terms, one of the Committee's recommendations summaries many of the points made immediately above and thus is worth citing at length:

> Your Committee feel convinced that some Open Places reserved for the amusement (under due regulations to preserve order) of the humbler classes, would assist to wean them from low and debasing pleasures. Great complaint is made of drinking-houses, dog fights, and boxing matches, yet, unless some opportunity for other recreation is afforded to workmen, they are driven to such pursuit. The spring to industry to which occasional relaxation gives, seems quite as necessary to the poor as to the rich.[94]

1.6 The Right to Recreation: Expansion

As Vorspan notes, this "conviction that open urban spaces would promote rational recreation and provide a counter-attraction to less deserving amusements persisted and indeed intensified as the [nineteenth century] advanced."[95] Again, a combination of private benefactors (e.g., the aforementioned Duke of Norfolk donated Sheffield its first public park in 1847)[96]; local and nationwide organisations (e.g., the Commons Preservation Society founded in 1865 and Britain's oldest national conservation society)[97] and later the public purse (in the form of ratepayers' money) helped purchase and develop public parks and other amenities in urban areas.[98] The law was also used to secure open spaces for urban leisure activities with Parliament enacting a series of provisions—the Metropolitan Commons Acts 1866–1878; the Public Health Acts 1875–1890; the Commons Acts 1876–1899; the Open Spaces Act 1890 and the Commons Act 1908—permitting, empowering and sometimes mandating local authorities to provide residents with dedicated areas to play games and enjoy general recreation.

In many ways, this legislative response could be deemed as a "counter-enclosure" movement with the underlying idea being to protect and manage—rather than enclose—common land in recognition of its value as an open space for recreation. Indeed, the beginnings of this regulatory movement can be marked by the enactment of the Inclosure Act 1845, which expressly tried to preserve existing greens and commons. Under the 1845 Act permanent salaried Enclosure Commissioners were appointed with the power to issue enclosure awards without

---

93 *Report from the Select Committee on Open Spaces* 1833, 66.

94 *Report from the Select Committee on Open Spaces* 1833, 8.

95 Vorspan 2000, 915.

96 Cunningham 1980, 151.

97 Now called the Open Spaces Society. See further www.oss.org.uk/history.

98 See Malcolmson 1973, 110.

submitting them to parliament for approval. Further, the Commissioners allocated plots or allotments to locals which they considered to be a fair equivalent "in full and perfect satisfaction" of pre-existing open lands and common rights and which could be used securely by residents for the "playing of games or of enjoying other species of recreation."[99]

In parallel to these provisions, Vorspan highlights a broad and active judicial support for the preservation of municipal, recreational land.[100] Returning to the aforementioned Southampton Common and that city's local Marsh Act of 1844, the case of *Attorney-General v Mayor, Aldermen and Burgesses of the Corporation of Southampton*[101] concerned an attempt by municipal officials to move a traditional cattle fair to an area located within the protected commons and specifically to site known as the "Cricket Ground." The court held that any attempt by the authorities to move the fair to the disputed site would violate the provisions of the 1844 Act, which mandated that the site be "put and kept" in proper condition for recreational purposes. In addition, and in due recognition of the recreational rights protected under the 1844 Act, Vice-Chancellor Sir John Stuart restricted the city authorities from further action upon the "Cricket Ground" by way of a perpetual injunction.

Later in the nineteenth century, Vorspan detects a similar judicial activism in support of recreational rights through a leniency in the application of the various criteria—certainty, reasonableness, immemoriality and continuity—that previously had hindered efforts by local residents to prove and protect the existence of customary recreational rights.[102] A case in illustration is that of *Warrick v Queen's College, Oxford.*[103] The litigation principally surrounded a dispute between the College, as the manorial rights holders to a common adjacent to the town of Plumstead in Kent, and the residents of the town. The commons, it was claimed, had been used for centuries by residents for various recreational and allotment purposes. From the 1850s onwards, the suburban growth of the town (and mainly consisting of workers from the Woolwich munitions factory in London who later helped establish Arsenal FC) led the College authorities to seek various ways of financially exploiting the land either by selling parts of it for building or, later, by leasing it to the War Office as an exercise grounds for the military. In the case at hand, the then Master of the Rolls found in favour of the customary rights of the town residents given the "distinct evidence that for a long time past the green had been used as a place of pastime by the inhabitants of the parish of Plumstead."[104]

[99] Inclosure Act 1845, s30.

[100] Note the extensive case law cited by Vorspan 2000, 917–921.

[101] *Attorney-General v Mayor, Aldermen and Burgesses of the Corporation of Southampton* (1858) 65 ER 957, 1 Giff 363.

[102] Note the case law collated by Vorspan 2000, 929–935.

[103] *Warrick v Queen's College, Oxford* (1870) LR 10 Eq 105.

[104] Disturbances and even riots about the use of Plumstead Common continued well into the next decade, and especially in 1876. See further Allen 1997, 61–77 and George 2011, 195–210.

In fact, by the early part of the twentieth century, reform of property law not only abolished the manorial system noted in the above litigation, it also further sought to safeguard commons land and especially those "lungs of the city" i.e., commons adjacent to major urban areas. Section 193 of the Law of Property Act 1925, for instance, introduced a statutory right of public access to certain commons, whilst, section 194 of the same Act made it a requirement that ministerial consent would have to be obtained before any works that might prevent or impede access could be carried out on any common which remained subject to customary rights at the material time.

1.7 Conclusion

Mention of Oxford in the *Warrick v Queen's College* proceedings returns us neatly back to *Abbot v Weekly*. So as it was deemed "necessary" for the inhabitants of the unnamed Oxfordshire village of the mid- to late seventeenth century "to have their recreation"; equally, it was deemed necessary, two centuries later, for the emerging town of Plumstead to have a dedicated space for sport. The comparison between *Abbot v Weekly* and *Warrick v Queen's College, Oxford* must, however, end there. The infrastructural, social, economic and political landscape of the south eastern corner of Britain, as in other parts of the UK, had, during the centuries in question, undergone a, at times, revolutionary change. Therefore, at first instance, although "the right to recreate" appears to have survived industrialisation, urbanisation and the huge technological advances of the era, there is, in fact, little substantial comparison between the recreations and sports pursued by the residents of Plumstead in the 1860s and those pursued on an irregular, spontaneous basis by the claimants in *Abbot v Weekly* in the 1660s. In short, village, suburban and inner city life in the Britain of the second half of the nineteenth century was increasingly planned, regulated and confined; and so were the sports and leisure activities its inhabitants pursued.

A pattern of litigation and legislation surrounding the right to recreate on the village green or on the local commons continued throughout the twentieth century. The Commons Registration Act 1965, for example, was a rather belated and limited attempt to deal, through a registration process, with the loss of commons land and principally as a result of the building of suburban houses, motorways and changes in agricultural practices in the post World War II era. At the turn of this century, litigation again involving Oxfordshire-based residents, and concerning the use and designation of village greens, exercised the House of Lords in *R* v *Oxfordshire County Council (Ex p Sunningwell Parish Council)*[105] and *Oxfordshire CC v Oxford*

[105] *R v Oxfordshire County Council (Ex p Sunningwell Parish Council)* [1999] UKHL 28; [2000] 1 AC 335.

City Council.[106] More recently, still the Commons Act 2006 and the Countryside and Right of Way Act 2000 included initiatives in respect of the registration of commons and village greens; the use and management of commons and a new statutory right of access for open-air recreation to mountain, moor, heath, down and registered common land ("the right to ramble").

Finally, to ramble too much more on the above path would overly distract from the principal point of this piece, which has been to highlight that at a critical juncture in the evolution of modern sport i.e., at the zenith of the Victorian era, the law played a key instrumental role in facilitating the objectives of those influential few who, for various reasons (rational recereationalism, muscular Christianity, public health etc.), took the view that participation in codified, regulated sport was, on balance, a good thing. Admittedly, there was little that was initiatory about both the sports-related judicial pronouncements and legislation of the Victorian era—the role of law was always only instrumental and consequential to other policy drivers and objectives; nevertheless, so as the actions of William Webb Ellis and other public school boys have become somewhat exaggerated, even apocryphal, in the influence they might have had as the midwives of modern sport; so the role of the law in assisting in the spread of organised sport at the material time has, in my view, been somewhat underplayed. In sum, what I have tried to do here is not just give an introduction to the legal history of what we now like to call "sport" but also to give an historical overview of what we now like to call "sports law".

References

Allen R (1997) The battle for the common: politics and populism in mid-Victorian Kentish London. Soc Hist 22:61–77

Agozino B (1996) Football and the civilizing process: penal discourse and the ethic of collective responsibility in sports law. Int J Sociol Sport 24:163–188

Anderson J (2006) The legal response to prize fighting in England and America. North Irel Leg Q 57:265–287

Bailey P (1978) Leisure and class in Victorian England: rational recreation and the contest for control. Routledge and Kegan Paul, London

Baker JH (2002) An introduction to English legal history, 4th edn. Butterworths LexisNexis, London

Birley D (1993) Sport and the making of Britain. Manchester University Press, Manchester

Board of Agriculture (1890) Report of proceedings under the inclosure acts, the metropolitan commons acts, the drainage and improvement of land acts, the copyhold acts, the universities and college estate acts, tithe rentcharge acts and glebe lands act 1888, 1889. (5947) xxv 315

Burke P (2009) Popular culture in early modern Europe, 3rd edn. Ashgate, Farnham

Bushaway B (1982) By rite: custom, ceremony and community in England, 1700–1800. Junction, London

Chalk G, Holley D (1987) Saints! a complete record of Southampton Football Club, 1885–1987. Breedon Books, Derby

[106] *Oxfordshire CC v Oxford City Council* [2006] UKHL 25; [2006] 2 AC 674.

Clareborough D, Kirkham A (1999) Sheffield United Football Club, 1889–1999: a complete record. Sheffield United FC, Sheffield
Collins T (2006) Rugby's great split: class culture and the origins of Rugby League Football. Routledge, Abingdon
Collins T, Vamplew W (2002) Mud, sweat and beers: a cultural history of sport and alcohol. Berg, Oxford
Colt H (1912) The construction of new courses. In: Sutton M (ed) The book of the links: a symposium on golf. WH Smith, London
Commons Preservation Society (1893–1896) Commons preservation society: report of the executive committee of proceedings during the years 1893–1896. Eyre and Spottiswoode, 1897
Cunningham H (1980) Leisure in the industrial revolution, c1780–c1880. Croom Helm, London
Dunning E, Sheard K (1979) Barbarians, gentlemen, and players: a sociological study of the development of Rugby football. Robertson, Oxford
Elementary Education Acts (1888) Final report of the commissioners appointed to inquire into the Elementary Education Acts in England and Wales. 1888 (5485) xxxv 1, 216
Elias N (1978) The civilising process. Blackwell, Oxford
Elias N, Dunning E (1986) Quest for excitement: sport and leisure in the civilizing process. Blackwell, Oxford
George D (2011) The Plumstead Common Riots of 1876: a study in Mid-Victorian protest. Lond J 36:195–210
Haley B (1978) The healthy body and Victorian culture. Harvard University Press, Cambridge
Hargreaves J (1986) Sport, power and culture: a social and historical analysis of popular sports in britain. Polity Press, Oxford
Hignall A (2002) Rain stops play: cricketing climates. Frank Cass, London
Holt R (1990) Sport and the British: a modern history. Clarendon Press, Oxford
Huggins M (2004) The Victorians and sport. Continuum, London
Hunt A (1995) The Role of law in the civilizing process and the reform of popular culture. Can J Law Soc 10:5–29
Kain P et al (2004) The enclosure maps of England and Wales, 1595–1918. Cambridge University Press, Cambridge
Inglis S (2005) Engineering archie. English Heritage, London
Lowerson J (1995) Sport and the English middle classes, 1870–1914. Manchester University Press, Manchester
Malcolm D (2002) Cricket and the civilizing process. Int Rev Sociol Sport 37:37–57
Malcolmson RW (1973) Popular recreations in English s 1700–1850. Cambridge University Press, Cambridge
Mangan J, Hickey C (2009) Soccer's missing men: school teachers and the spread of association football. Routledge, London
Mangan J (2011) 'Manufactured' masculinity: making imperial manliness morality and militarism. Routledge, London
McArdle D (2000) From boot money to Bosman: football society and the law. Cavendish, London
Miers D (2004) Regulating commercial gambling. Oxford University Press, Oxford
Nicholls R (1996) Trafford Park: the first hundred years. Phillamore, Andover
Norridge J (2008) Can we have our balls back, please? How the British invented sport. Allen Lane, London
Potter D (2011) The victor's crown. Quercus, London
Radford M (2001) Animal welfare law in Britain: regulation and responsibility. Oxford University Press, Oxford
Rose L (1991) The erosion of childhood: child oppression in Britain, 1860–1918. Routledge, London
Sawer P (2010) Top of the big money leagues. The Sunday Telegraph, London, 28 Mar, Sport, 15
Sheard K (1997) Aspects of boxing in the western civilizing process. Int Rev Sociolo Sport 32:31–57

Tranter N (1998) Sport, economy and society in Britain, 1750–1914. Cambridge University Press, Cambridge
Vamplew W (1988) Pay up and play the game: professional sport in Britain, 1875–1914. Cambridge University Press, Cambridge
Vamplew W (2007a) Empiricist versus sociological history: some comments on the civilizing process. Sport Hist 27:161–171
Vamplew W (2007b) Playing with the rules: influences on the development of regulation in sport. Int J Hist Sport 24:843–871
Vamplew W (2009) Sports without rules: hunting, shooting and fishing in Edwardian Britain. Eur Stud Sport Hist 2:34–51
Vorspan R (2000) Rational recreation and the law: the transformation of popular urban leisure in Victorian England. McGill Law J 45:891–973
Walvin J (1975) The people's game: a social history. Allen Lane, London
Wigglesworth N (1996) The evolution of English sport. Frank Cass, London

Chapter 2
Federal League Baseball Club of Baltimore v National League et al. 259 US 200 (1922)

Roger I. Abrams

Abstract The claimant, a baseball club, sought review of a decision of the United States Court of Appeals of the District of Columbia, which reversed a judgment awarding the club damages for a conspiracy by the defendants to monopolise the baseball industry in violation of federal antitrust/competition law, namely the Sherman Act 1890. The claimants alleged that the defendants had conspired by purchasing or inducing all other clubs in the claimant's former league to leave that league. The United States Supreme Court affirmed the decision of the US Court of Appeals and held that the conduct charged against the defendants was not an interference with interstate commerce as prohibited by, and within the meaning of, the Sherman Act. The US Supreme Court's rationale was that, although competitions between the various clubs required extensive and repeated travel across state lines by players and officials, such travel was merely incidental to baseball competitions. The business of providing and organising public baseball games for profit between professional clubs in rival league formats was not interstate commerce: baseball was purely a state affair and thus America's "national game" was not subject to federal antitrust law.

Contents

R. I. Abrams (✉)
Richardson Professor of Law, School of Law, Northeastern University, Boston, MA 02115, USA
e-mail: r.abrams@neu.edu

J. Anderson (ed.), *Leading Cases in Sports Law*,
ASSER International Sports Law Series, DOI: 10.1007/978-90-6704-909-2_2,

2.1 Introduction

The history of American baseball is filled with stories of glorious athletes competing on the field of play and not-so-glorious businessmen who sought the public's entertainment dollar and were willing to violate both moral and legal standards to achieve their goals.[1] Starting in 1876 with the creation of the National League of Professional Baseball Clubs, entrepreneurs used the collusive tools of a business cartel to control their enterprise, depress the salaries of the players who brought in the crowds of paying customers and crush any potential business competition.[2] The eight original club owners in the National League allocated geographic territories so there would be no intra-league competition for spectators. They agreed to a uniform schedule of prices for tickets and bound their players to a reserve system that prevented the athletes from moving from one club to another for higher salaries. They also gave the President of the League the power to discipline and exclude clubs that failed to follow the League's rules.[3] The business model worked brilliantly. While other professional baseball leagues came and went during the nineteenth century,[4] the National League remained predominant until the turn of the century.

In 1901, a former sportswriter from Cincinnati, Bancroft Johnson, devised a business scheme that would create a rival circuit to the National League. He renamed the minor Western League, of which he was President, the "American League" and vowed to steal away the best players from the National League by paying them better salaries. The Nationals fought back, but ultimately decided it was preferable to merge with the rival Americans. With the end of the "civil war" in the baseball business in 1903, the merged National and American Leagues operated "Organized Baseball" for over a decade as an oligopoly without major league competition. They also made sure their players returned to the strict reserve system and were paid only a modest salary.[5]

Organized Baseball remained a closed enterprise, and entrepreneurs who sought to purchase existing baseball clubs were rejected out of hand. Thwarted from joining the inner circle of the baseball business, in 1913 a collection of

---

1 Seymour and Seymour 1960 and Seymour and Seymour 1971.

2 Abrams 1998.

3 In its initial 1876 season, two clubs failed to complete their entire schedule of games. League President William Hulbert expelled the Philadelphia and New York clubs from the National League, Powers 2003.

4 The American Association lasted from 1882 until 1891; the Union Association (1884) and the Players League (1890) each played one season, see further Abrams 1998, 18–22.

5 Wilber 2007.

businessmen created their own circuit, the Federal League, as a "minor league" and then the following season declared themselves a "major league" in competition for the patronage of spectators across the country. Federal League owners followed the model employed by Ban Johnson that had proven so successful for the American League in 1901. They announced their intention to induce baseball's star players to sign with the new league for much higher salaries and bonuses. Management also offered players a five-percent annual salary increase and the right to change clubs after ten years. Organized Baseball responded by threatening to blacklist for life any players who jumped to the Federal League.[6]

Initially, the Federal League scored some significant business victories. Joe Tinker of the famous Tinker-to-Evers-to-Chance double play combination that played for the Cubs from 1902 to 1912, returned to Chicago to manage the Chicago Whales at double the salary he was paid by the Cincinnati Reds.[7] Hal Chase, Russ Ford and Mordecai "Three-Finger" Brown followed suit to play in the Federal League. In total, the Federal League attracted 81 major leaguers who were spread across its eight franchises.[8]

Some clubs in the American and National Leagues filed suits against the players who had defected, claiming they had violated their contracts' perpetual reserve clauses. They prevailed in cases where the players had actually breached their employment agreements mid-term, but the courts generally refused to enforce the reserve system's option clause once a player's contract had expired.[9] The Federal League responded with litigation of its own, suing the club owners of Organized Baseball under the antitrust laws, claiming an illegal restraint of trade.[10]

2.2 The Antitrust Laws

In 1890 the United States Congress enacted the Sherman Act, a statute designed to protect participants in the American free market system against unfair competition from business rivals who, by combining their economic strengths, caused economic harm to business competitors. Section 1 of the Sherman Act prohibited any "contract, combination or conspiracy in restraint of trade," a broad proscription against predatory economic activity that would be enforced by federal authorities. With Congress' passage of the Clayton Act in 1914, private parties could sue to recover damages caused by anti-competitive conduct. If the allegations were proven, the federal court would then treble the damages under the terms of the statute.[11]

---

[6] Wiggins 2008 and Abrams 1998, 53–58.

[7] Bogen 2003.

[8] Abrams1998, 54.

[9] Abrams 1998, 54.

[10] Santo and Mildner 2010, 11.

[11] Duquette 1999, 10–14.

Under the American federal system of government, in enacting these laws Congress exercised its power under the United States Constitution to regulate commerce "among the several states." By the terms of the statutes, the proscriptions of the Sherman and Clayton Acts applied only to commercial activity that affected "interstate commerce." This requirement would prove critical in the baseball litigation to come.[12]

The Federal League filed suit under the antitrust laws against Organized Baseball in federal court in Chicago where the case would be heard by Judge Kenesaw Mountain Landis, later to become baseball's most famous commissioner. Landis had developed a reputation as a "trustbuster," even summoning John D Rockefeller to court to answer on behalf of Standard Oil. Judge Landis imposed a $29 million fine on his company. (Like many of his judicial pronouncements, however, Landis' edict was reversed on appeal.)

Judge Landis had a particular fondness for the national pastime of baseball. He told the lawyers for the Federal League in open court that he would not look kindly upon any court action that would harm America's great game: "Any blows at the thing called baseball would be regarded by this court as a blow to a national institution."[13] Landis was true to his word, and he took the Federal League's suit against Organized Baseball under "advisement" for a year. Without the prospect of a victory in court, the Federal League lacked the economic staying power to continue its challenge to Organized Baseball. The League folded after the 1915 season.

The Federal League owners then pursued an out-of-court settlement of its dispute with Organized Baseball.[14] The parties began meeting secretly to discuss peace. On 13 December 1915 at a dinner at the Republican Club in New York City they struck a deal. Organized Baseball made generous financial offers to the Federal League, but only to those businessmen who owned clubs in cities where there were existing American or National League franchises. Two Federal League owners were also allowed to purchase existing Major League clubs. The owner of the Federal League's Chicago Whales, Charles Weeghman, bought the Chicago National League club, the Cubs.[15] Phil Ball, the owner of the Federal League's St. Louis Terriers, was allowed to buy the St. Louis Browns of the American League.[16]

Organized Baseball made penurious offers to Federal League club owners located in cities without rival American or National League franchises, including Baltimore. Ned Hanlon was the principal shareholder of the Terrapins club of Baltimore. A long-time baseball man who had played in the National League in the 1880s and 1890s and then managed various clubs for 19 years until joining the

---

[12] See Judson 1905 for a contemporary discussion of the meaning of "interstate commerce".

[13] Seymour and Seymour 1971, 212 and Ginsburg 1995, 142.

[14] Duquette 1999, 9.

[15] Within a few years, due to economic reverses, Weeghman would have to sell the Chicago franchise to his partner William Wrigley. In 1926, Wrigley changed the name of the club's north side ballpark from Cubs Park to Wrigley Field, thus providing free advertising for his chewing gum, see Wood and Hazucha 2008, 41.

[16] Golenbock 2001, 74.

Federal League venture, Hanlon had attempted without success to purchase an existing club in Organized Baseball. The major leagues offered him a modest payout of $50,000 in settlement. Hanlon had personally invested many times that amount in establishing the Baltimore club and building a suitable stadium. He was insulted not only by the meagre buyout offer but also by the public comments made by major league owners that derogated his adopted hometown of Baltimore. (One baseball magnate reportedly called Baltimore "a minor league city, and not a hell of a good one at that.")[17] In order to seek financial redress and as a matter of personal pride, Hanlon brought suit under the federal antitrust laws against Organized Baseball, its club owners and his fellow Federal League owners who had been allowed to purchase major league franchises. Hanlon's suit—a frontal attack on the hegemony of Organized Baseball—would make baseball history.[18]

2.3 Hanlon's Lawsuit

Hanlon filed his antitrust complaint in federal court in the District of Columbia. He alleged that the owners of the clubs in Organized Baseball had successfully sought to "wreck and destroy" the Federal League. They did so by monopolising the best ballplayers under baseball's "illegal" reserve system. The complaint stressed the "humiliation" suffered by the citizens of Baltimore which "tended to lessen" the city's "standing and prestige." Using hyperbole not uncommon in legal papers of the era, Hanlon accused Organized Baseball of carrying out "transactions which amount to nothing less than bribery." No other case, he said, ever showed "such an example of ruthless conduct toward a competitor, or of shameless disregard of his fundamental property rights." These businessmen (Hanlon's complaint termed them "despots") combined to restrain the free market in violation of the Sherman Act 1890 which proscribed such anti-competitive behavior.[19]

Baseball's reserve system had first been instituted by the eight club owners of the National League in 1879. During the first three years of the National League, baseball players had "revolved" around the League from one club to another, sometimes in the middle of a season. They would play for whichever club offered them the highest salary at any given moment. Needless to say, this practice was opposed by National League club owners who were forced to pay ever higher salaries to their baseball talent.

Arthur Soden, owner of the Boston club, felt the financial pain of revolving players when in 1879 his two stars, George Wright and Jim O'Rourke, jumped to

---

17 Abrams 1998, 56. Charles Ebbets, the owner of the Brooklyn Dodgers, also reportedly insulted Baltimore for having too many black residents to have an adequate fan base, see Seymour and Seymour, 1960, 244.

18 Abrams 1998, 56.

19 Abrams 1998, 56.

play for Providence. Soden was incensed: "What man in his right mind would invest money in this kind of business? Today he may have some assets. Tomorrow he may have none."[20] Soden proposed to his fellow National League club owners that they agree—perhaps the more accurate economic term is "collude"—to reserve five players each as the exclusive property of their clubs. Teams only had a dozen or so players at the time, and retaining the rights to the five best players would be sufficient to add stability to the lineup. The plan worked brilliantly. Unable to sell their services in a free market of employing clubs, player salaries dropped immediately.[21]

Under the owners' new personnel scheme, all players would sign the same standard form contract, and each contract would contain an option clause that allowed the club to retain the right to resign that player upon the contract's expiration. The player was not free to enter into a contract to play baseball for another club. This diminished every player's bargaining power. The player had the choice of playing for the club that reserved him at the salary the club offered or going home to work in a mill or on the farm. The reserve system was then combined with a league-wide "blacklist." Players who sought better terms and conditions of employment from clubs in a rival league would be placed on an "ineligible list" and banned from playing again for any club in Organized Baseball. Within a few years, the reserve system was expanded to cover all the players signed by every major league club.

The owners of the National League clubs, joined by the owners of the American League clubs after the merger of 1903, controlled their most valuable assets, their players, for life. No major league club would risk injuring their joint venture by tampering with another club's reserved players. Confronted by the unyielding collusion of the club owners, players accepted their fate.[22] In general, the fans of the game were disinterested. Most would have gladly changed places with the players and played a child's game for a living, even if their pay level was modest.[23]

Organized Baseball appreciated the threat posed by a rival league that would place teams in many cities that had previously been the exclusive reserve of major league clubs. After all, the National League had faced rival circuits in the nineteenth century and, in fact, it succumbed to the rivalry of the American League after two years of economic warfare at the start of the twentieth century. The creation of the Federal League posed a significant challenge to Organized Baseball's territorial exclusivity, but the rival could only succeed if it could poach

---

20 Caruso 1995, 317.

21 Abrams 1998, 45–48.

22 White 1996, 61. The players briefly attempted to form a rival league of their own, the Players League, in 1890, but it was a short-lived experiment in free competition. The National League crushed the players' venture by bribing and threatening their financial supporters, see Koszarek 2006.

23 White 1996, 66.

the best players from the major leagues.[24] This was where the established reserve system and lifetime blacklist would prove effective economic weapons for the major leagues. Although for some marginal performers the Federal League offered a great opportunity, for the stars of the game jumping to the new circuit would risk their entire baseball careers if the new league should fail. Only a few stars were willing to do so. Without the marquee attractions of Ty Cobb, Honus Wagner, Walter Johnson, Nap Lajoie, Eddie Collins, Grover Cleveland Alexander or Christy Mathewson, the Federal League was doomed.

As part of his federal court suit, Ned Hanlon would ultimately have to show that Organized Baseball's reserve system, combined with the lifetime blacklist, "restrained trade," keeping competitor employers (the clubs in the Federal League) from hiring baseball players who had completed their employment contracts with major league clubs. The economic impact of this system on the rival circuit would not be very difficult to demonstrate. The scheme allowed major league franchises to monopolise the players market and, as a result, kept Federal League owners from competing effectively for the public's patronage. However, even before the merits of the case could be reached, Ned Hanlon faced a formidable hurdle. He would have to show that baseball's reserve system affected the interstate market, that baseball was a form of interstate "trade" or "commerce." Ultimately, this would prove to be an insurmountable barrier to the court litigation.[25]

In the trial court, Hanlon scored an initial victory. After an unsuccessful effort was made to reach a settlement, Federal District Judge Wendell P Stafford ruled that offering exhibitions of baseball to the public constituted a business in interstate commerce covered by the Sherman Act and that, by virtue of the reserve system, Organized Baseball had restrained "trade," i.e. the ability of business rivals to employ willing employees, the baseball players. He left to the jury the determination of the extent of the damages suffered by the Baltimore Federal League club. The jury assessed damages at $80,000, which were tripled to $240,000 under the provisions of the Clayton Act.[26] Judge Stafford added $24,000 in attorney's fees to Hanlon's recovery.[27] It was a remarkable victory for Hanlon and the free market, but it would not survive on appeal.

In the United States Court of Appeals for the District of Columbia, George Wharton Pepper, the attorney for the major leagues, argued that the antitrust laws did not apply to baseball because the activity was not a "business." "Baseball," he wrote in his brief, was "a spontaneous output of human activity... and not in its nature commerce." The Court of Appeals, in a decision by Chief Justice Constantine J. Smyth, agreed with Pepper, holding that baseball was not commerce. It was simply a game, and, as such, it was not subject to the proscription of the Sherman Act. Justice Smythe wrote: "The fact that the [club owners] produce

[24] Abrams 1998, 56.

[25] White 1996, 72.

[26] White 1996, 71. In current dollars, Hanlon's damages would be valued at $2.7 million.

[27] White 1996, 71.

baseball games as a source of profit, large or small, cannot change the character of the games. They are still sport, not trade."

The opinion of the Court of Appeals focused on the distinction between personal services, such as lawyering and lecturing, and the transportation of "goods" which would be "commerce" covered by the antitrust laws. Addressing the statutorily required element of interstate commerce, the court ruled that the game of baseball was "local in its beginning and in its end." (Justice Smyth did not concern himself with the "middle," the transport of men and material across state lines.) As a result, the court ruled that the antitrust laws simply did not apply.[28] Hanlon appealed, and the United States Supreme Court issued a writ of certiorari to hear and resolve this important legal dispute involving America's favorite pastime.

2.4 To the Supreme Court, While Controversy Reigned

On 19 April 1922, the day before the baseball season opened in the District of Columbia, the Supreme Court of the United States heard oral arguments in the *Federal Baseball* appeal. Chief Justice William Howard Taft, the former president of the United States, presided. Taft was a great lover of the national game. As a teenager, he was offered a professional contract to catch for the Cincinnati club, but he broke his arm and attended Yale College instead.[29] As president, Taft initiated the custom of the nation's chief executive throwing out the first ball on Opening Day. He is also credited with originating the "seventh-inning stretch" at National Park in the Nation's Capital on Opening Day in 1910. Taft was a man of considerable girth and abundant torso. (The Washington Senators club had installed a couch in the front row for his comfort.) It is said that Taft stood up midway through the seventh inning to stretch his limbs. The crowd stood up out of respect for the president, and a new custom was initiated.

Only months before they appeared in his court the club owners of Organized Baseball had offered Chief Justice Taft the new position of Commissioner of Baseball, but Taft declined. Taft had always wanted to be Chief Justice of the United States, even more than becoming President or presiding over the business of baseball. While president, he had once said "there is nothing I would have loved more than being chief justice of the United States," President Harding nominated him in 1921. Despite his devotion to the law and to the court, Taft did not believe that the job offer from the respondents in the Federal Baseball case warranted his recusing himself from hearing the dispute that would determine the future of the business of baseball.[30]

---

[28] *National League of Professional Baseball Clubs v Federal Baseball Club of Baltimore*, 269 Fed 681, 685 (DC Circuit, 1920).

[29] Watterson 2006, 84.

[30] Abrams 1998, 57.

Baseball in the spring of 1922 was just beginning to recover from a crisis in public confidence created by the disastrous Black Sox scandal that broke in October 1920. A Chicago grand jury had indicted eight players from the American League champion Chicago White Sox who, it was alleged, had thrown the 1919 World Series against the Cincinnati Reds in exchange for payments from notorious New York City gambler Arnold Rothstein. Two of the accused players had confessed to their perfidy. The nation followed the criminal trial throughout the summer of 1921. The two players' confessions, however, had mysteriously disappeared, and the Chicago jury acquitted their heroes on 2 August 1921. Notwithstanding the jury verdict, baseball needed to cleanse itself, and the newly appointed commissioner of baseball Kenesaw Mountain Landis would step up to the plate. He banned the acquitted players from professional baseball for life. "Baseball," Landis explained, "is something more than a game to an American boy; it is his training field for life's work. Destroy his faith in its squareness and honesty and you have destroyed something more; you have planted suspicion of all things in his heart."[31]

If the Black Sox scandal jeopardised the legitimacy of the nation's premier sport, *Federal Baseball* risked its business stability. Ned Hanlon's attack on the autonomy of Organized Baseball could have undermined the entire enterprise. If baseball could not control its player resources through the reserve system, club owners might be forced to return to the personnel system of the very early days of the professional game with players "revolving" from club to club as free agents. Organized Baseball wanted no part of free competition, and it drew the lines of defense around its cartel. The business of the game would have to triumph decisively over dissenters like Hanlon.

2.5 The Arguments to the Court

In its brief to the Supreme Court, the petitioner Baltimore Federal League club made the case for the interstate character of major league baseball. Each club, it wrote, "symbolizes the great city that it represents to those assembled to witness the contest."[32] Waxing poetic, the petitioner's brief stated: "The personality, so to speak, of each club in a league is actually projected over state lines and becomes mingled with that of the clubs in all the other States."[33] This business of baseball also contained "the element of intersectional rivalry" between east and west.[34]

---

31 Abrams 1998, 155.

32 *Federal Baseball Club of Baltimore v National League* et al. 259 US 200, 202 (1920).

33 *Federal Baseball Club of Baltimore v National League* et al. 259 US 200, 203 (1920).

34 *Federal Baseball Club of Baltimore v National League* et al. 259 US 200, 202 (1920). In 1922, of course, "west" in Organized Baseball meant only as far as St. Louis, which was also its southernmost outpost. The Federal League, however, had a franchise further west in Kansas City.

Baseball is a money-making enterprise, something the District of Columbia Court of Appeals seemed to ignore in its opinion. Gate receipts are shared with the visiting clubs which travel from state to state.[35] The net profits the clubs earned were then invested in building ballparks in the various states. Interstate activity is thus the essential part of the business and endures "continuously." The business of professional baseball can operate only if baseball clubs are "ambulatory" across state lines.[36]

To address the expected argument by the respondents that there could be no "commerce" in baseball because there were no "commodities" that crossed state lines, the plaintiff cited the 1824 Supreme Court decision of *Gibbons v. Ogden*,[37] a staple of every law school constitutional law class. That case involved the state regulation of river navigation. There were no commodities directly involved, although the ships in question did carry goods. It was the interstate navigation that was the critical factor in the Court's decision. *Gibbons v. Ogden* offered a broad reading of the scope of the interstate commerce clause from constitutional adjudication a century earlier, but it may not have accurately reflected the more constrained judicial view in the early twentieth century of the reach of the interstate commerce clause.

In his argument before the Supreme Court, George Wharton Pepper for Organized Baseball again made the case for the non-applicability of the antitrust laws. He urged the Justices to recognise the importance of the case before them. The national pastime was at stake, and "the very existence of baseball depended upon its exemption from the antitrust laws."[38] The Supreme Court seemed inclined to agree with Pepper's pretentious exaggeration, although all other businesses were bound by the antitrust laws, and even baseball complied with all other state and federal statutes and regulations. Within a few weeks, the Supreme Court would issue a unanimous decision written by Justice Oliver Wendell Holmes upholding the result in the Court of Appeals and creating the antitrust exemption sought by Organized Baseball.

2.6 The *Federal Baseball* Opinion

In his opinion for the Court, Justice Holmes wrote that the antitrust laws did not apply in Ned Hanlon's case because "the business [of] giving exhibitions of baseball" did not affect interstate commerce.[39] He did not rely on the precise rationale offered by the Court of Appeals, that baseball was not a commercial

---

[35] *Federal Baseball Club of Baltimore v National League* et al. 259 US 200, 203 (1920).

[36] *Federal Baseball Club of Baltimore v National League* et al. 259 US 200, 203 (1920).

[37] *Gibbons v Ogden* 9 Wheat 189; 22 US 1 (1824).

[38] Abrams 1998, 57.

[39] *Federal Baseball Club of Baltimore v National League* et al. 259 US 200, 209 (1920).

business. An enterprise that sold tickets to spectators was obviously a commercial business. Furthermore, Holmes acknowledged that baseball clubs crossed state lines to "play against one another in public exhibitions for money." According to Holmes, however, this interstate travel was "a mere incident, not the essential thing."[40]

Reflecting the then current notions of "commerce," Holmes wrote that "personal effort, not related to production, is not a subject of commerce."[41] Business activities that presented baseball entertainment, he stated, were "purely state affairs," and, as such, beyond the reach of federal legislation based upon the Commerce Clause of the United States Constitution.[42] Holmes then used two examples taken from Justice Smyth's decision in the Court of Appeals. A firm of lawyers and the Chautauqua Lecture Bureau would not be engaging in interstate commerce simply because persons associated with those entities crossed state lines to perform their work.[43]

The Court's opinion cites only one prior Supreme Court case, *Hooper v. California*,[44] in support of its conclusion that "the transport [across state lines] is a mere incident, not the essential thing," which is the local baseball exhibition itself.[45] *Hooper v. California* had held that the sale of insurance policies did not constitute interstate commerce even if insurance companies crossed state lines to market those policies. Issuing insurance policies was not the transaction of commerce. They were not "commodities to be shipped and forwarded from one state to another and then put up for sale."[46] The "transportation" across state lines was "merely incidental" to the business of selling insurance.[47] Similarly, in professional baseball, it was the presentation of the game that was the "essential thing," the display of personal effort, not the transport of clubs from state to state. The game, an exhibition of athletic skills, was not trade or commerce. Thus, as a result of *Federal Baseball*, America's national pastime was held outside the reach of the federal antitrust laws because the business of baseball did not affect interstate commerce.

---

40 *Federal Baseball Club of Baltimore v National League* et al. 259 US 200, 209 (1920).

41 *Federal Baseball Club of Baltimore v National League* et al. 259 US 200, 209 (1920).

42 *Federal Baseball Club of Baltimore v National League* et al. 259 US 200, 208 (1920).

43 *Federal Baseball Club of Baltimore v National League* et al. 259 US 200, 208 (1920).

44 *Hooper v California* 155 US 648 (1895).

45 *Federal Baseball Club of Baltimore v National League* et al. 259 US 200, 209.

46 *Hooper v California* 155 US 648, 654 (1895).

47 The Supreme Court ultimately overruled *Hooper v California* in *US v. South-Eastern Underwriters Assn* 322 US 533 (1944). However, it would never overrule *Federal Baseball Club of Baltimore v National League* et al.

2.7 Analysis of *Federal Baseball*

The Supreme Court's decision in *Federal Baseball* has received abundant criticism from commentators.[48] Most have written from the perspective of later history after the Supreme Court dramatically expanded the reach of the Interstate Commerce Clause in response to the legislation of the New Deal. Using this gloss, *Federal Baseball* is an absurd declaration of limited federal power to regulate businesses that, by their very nature, affect more than one state. One central purpose of the American federal union of states was to provide for the uniform national regulation of economic activities that involved more than one state.

A few commentators wrote approvingly of the case, including M Lindsey Cowen, then a student editor of the *Virginia Law Review* and later dean of the law schools at the University of Georgia and Case Western Reserve University. As long as baseball was governed in a "benevolent" manner and "the public receives the quality of sports it wants," Cowan wrote, then Holmes' decision was acceptable.[49]

The case is best analysed from the notions of interstate commerce current in 1922. It would be unfair to evaluate the decision based on changes in reasoning, circumstances and jurisprudence that would not be announced for another decade and a half. As such, the Holmes opinion accurately applies notions of constraints on federal governmental power extant in the late nineteenth and early twentieth centuries. The problem with Holmes' opinion, however, is that its focus was misdirected. He ignored the interstate commercial realities of the business of baseball. His conclusion that the "essential thing" of baseball was the personal performance of the players on the field while "transportation" across state lines was "merely incidental" does not reflect the business realities of the game in the 1920s.

There could be no doubt that the men who created and enforced the reserve system and blacklist were engaged in operating a business that was only profitable because of its interstate nature. Through the territorial exclusivity which they created and maintained, they limited local business competition. No major league clubs faced in-state competition in their league with the single exception of the Brooklyn and New York National League franchises. Combined with personnel practices that were intended to restrain the free movement of players from club to club across state lines, the club owners of Organized Baseball had designed and implemented a combination that restrained the free market in player personnel that would otherwise move in interstate commerce. Even in the early 1920s, this would constitute trade or commerce affecting employers in many states.[50]

Holmes' analogies to a law firm and a lecture bureau were inapposite. A 1920s law firm did not travel across state lines to engage other law firms in an

---

48 Berger 1983, 209–226; McDonald 1998, 102–105; and Van Roo 2010, 381–401.

49 An early student case note appearing in the *Harvard Law Review* and focusing on the decision in the Court of Appeals offered approval as well, see Anon 1921, 559. See also Rogers 1977, 620 and Grow 2010, 568.

50 White 1996, 81.

entertainment endeavor. They did not follow a schedule of interstate travel mandated by a centralised organisation, such as a league office. In fact, the practice of law is essentially local in nature requiring bar admission or special permission in other states in order to "perform." The same is the case with regard to a lecture bureau. Chautauqua sent its lecturers across state lines not to engage in scheduled commercial entertainment contests. Baseball was quite different. It involved regularised, pre-scheduled commercial entertainment events across state lines where the "essential thing" was that the competition came from out of state to take on the local team. Moreover, the employees who played the game were not local; they hailed from many states across the country.

American courts follow the rule of stare decisis.[51] A court decision stands as precedent to be followed in the future in similar situations by the same court or lower courts. Thus, when the Supreme Court took certiorari in a case the following term in *Hart v BF Keith Vaudeville Exchange*,[52] involving the applicability of the antitrust laws to the vaudeville business, *Federal Baseball* would stand as the controlling precedent. Baseball and vaudeville shared much in common. Both involved the transportation of persons and equipment across state lines for the purpose of providing commercial entertainment.[53]

The *Federal Baseball* precedent should have required the Supreme Court to conclude that vaudeville did not affect interstate commerce because the interstate travel was "merely incidental" to the business, and therefore the antitrust laws did not apply. Yet, in another unanimous decision written by Justice Holmes, the Supreme Court determined that the antitrust laws could apply to the business of vaudeville. The lower court had relied upon *Federal Baseball* in dismissing the complaint in *Hart v BF Keith Vaudeville Exchange*.[54] How could the two cases possibly be reconciled?

Holmes wrote in his opinion that the vaudeville business involved "the transportation of vaudeville acts, including performers, scenery, music, costumes and whatever constitutes the act, so that it is said that there is a constant stream of this so-called commerce from State to State."[55] It could be, Holmes suggests, that "what in general is incidental, in some instances may rise to a magnitude that requires it to be considered independently."[56] Apparently, moving sets and costumes across state lines could be trade or commerce triggering antitrust applicability, but moving players, uniforms, bats and balls would not. If that was Holmes' distinction, it was genuine sophistry. The only way the two cases can be reconciled is by concluding that one involved baseball and the other vaudeville—a difference

---

[51] Wells 1878.

[52] *Hart v BF Keith Vaudeville Exchange* 262 US 271 (1923).

[53] See generally Lewis 2007 and Kibler 1999.

[54] *Hart v BF Keith Vaudeville Exchange* 262 US 271, 273 (1923).

[55] *Hart v BF Keith Vaudeville Exchange* 262 US 271, 273 (1923).

[56] *Hart v BF Keith Vaudeville Exchange* 262 US 271, 274 (1923).

that cannot constitute a distinction worthy of recognition at law or under the Constitution.

What then explains *Federal Baseball*? Could the Supreme Court have shown special solicitude for the *Federal Baseball* respondents simply because they presented baseball games? Although their attorney did make that precise argument to the Supreme Court, nowhere in Holmes opinion does he refer to any special or unique nature of the respondents' business. If he did state that baseball was entitled to a singular status because of its hold on the American psyche, his opinion would have been subject to even greater scorn than it has received. Yet, when compared with the vaudeville case from the following term, it is hard to reach any other conclusion. Placed in its very best light, *Federal Baseball* reflects the contemporary constrained view of the reach of interstate commerce, an approach the Court would follow, for the most part, until the New Deal. Seen as an aberration, *Federal Baseball* is worthy of its status as an historical oddity.

2.8 Conclusion: The Impact of *Federal Baseball*

Any benign assessment that *Federal Baseball* was simply an error in judgment announced by the Supreme Court ninety years ago is rebutted by the subsequent impact of the case. Although some lower courts raised serious questions about the efficacy of the precedent,[57] it was followed, but only with regard to baseball. All other American sports were held to be covered by the antitrust laws.

The Supreme Court revisited the *Federal Baseball* precedent in two subsequent cases. In both cases, the Court reaffirmed its adherence to the *Federal Baseball* holding. In *Toolson v New York Yankees*, the Court majority let stand the *Federal Baseball* precedent in a per curiam opinion, leaving the repair of the antitrust laws to Congress, if any was to occur.[58] In *Flood v. Kuhn*, in a 5-4 decision, the Court admitted its original error in *Federal Baseball*, but it still declined to repudiate its transgression.[59]

Under a regime of antitrust immunity, major league club owners fought against threats to their hegemony from the Mexican League in the 1940s using the same collusive personnel tools that had crippled the Federal League.[60] Organized Baseball was able to perpetuate its personnel system through the 1960s until the time when the players had organised an effective union as a countervailing force.[61]

---

[57] In *Salerno v American League of Professional Baseball Clubs* 429 F 2d 1003, 1005 (2d Cir, 1970), Judge Henry Friendly wrote in a concurrence: "We freely acknowledge our belief that *Federal Baseball* was not one of Mr. Justice Holmes' happiest days.".

[58] *Toolson v New York Yankees* 346 US 200 (1953).

[59] *Flood v Kuhn* 407 US 258 (1972). See generally Abrams 2007, 181–207.

[60] McKelvey 2006.

[61] Miller 2004.

Although the reserve system has now been substantially modified through collective bargaining with the Player Association and under federal law,[62] baseball remains the only sports business without antitrust constraints.

Ned Hanlon, the protagonist in *Federal Baseball*, was finally elected to the Baseball Hall of Fame in 1996 based on his exemplary performance as a manager in the National League. In the 1890s while manager of the Baltimore Orioles, Hanlon designed an innovative offensive strategy using the "hit-and-run," bunting and the "squeeze play." He later won two pennants while guiding the Brooklyn club. His Hall of Fame plaque in Cooperstown does not mention his antitrust suit against Organized Baseball.

References

Abrams R (1998) Legal bases: baseball and the law. Temple University Press, Philadelphia

Abrams R (1999) Before the flood: the history of baseball's antitrust exemption. Marquette Sports Law J 9:307–313

Abrams R (2007) Blackmun's list. Va Sports Entertain Law J 6:181–207

Anon (1921) Case note: interstate commerce—what constitutes interstate commerce—professional baseball. Harv Law Rev 34:559

Berger R (1983) After the strike: a re-examination of professional baseball's exemption from the antitrust laws. Univ Pittsburgh Law Rev 45:209–226

Bogen G (2003) Tinker, evers, and chance: a triple biography. McFarland & Co, Jefferson

Caruso G (1995) The braves encyclopaedia. Temple University Press, Philadelphia

Duquette J (1999) Regulating the national pastime: baseball and antitrust. Praeger, Westport

Ginsburg D (1995) The fix is in: a history of baseball gambling and game fixing scandals. McFarland & Co, Jefferson, NC

Golenbock P (2001) The spirit of St Louis: a history of St Louis Cardinal and Browns. HarperCollins, New York

Grow N (2010) Defining the business of baseball: a proposed framework for determining the scope of professional baseball's antitrust exemption. Univ Calif Davies Law Rev 44:557–623

Judson F (1905) The law of interstate commerce and its federal regulation. TH Flood & Co, Chicago

Kibler M (1999) Rank ladies: gender and cultural hierarchy in American vaudeville. University of North Carolina Press, Chapel Hill

Koszarek E (2006) The players league: history, clubs, ballplayers and statistics. McFarland & Co, Jefferson

Lewis R (2007) From traveling show to vaudeville: theatrical spectacle in America, 1830–1910. John Hopkins University Press, Baltimore

McDonald K (1998) Antitrust and baseball: stealing homes. J Supreme Court Hist 23:88–128

McKelvey G (2006) Mexican raiders in the major leagues: the Pasquel brothers vs. organised baseball (1946). McFarland & Co, Jefferson

Miller M (2004) Whole different ball game: the inside story of the baseball revolution. Ivan R Dee, Lanham

Powers A (2003) The business of baseball. McFarland & Co, Jefferson

[62] In 1998, Congress enacted the Curt Flood Act that stated that major league players were covered by the antitrust laws. The statute did not cover minor league players or business relationships between major and minor league club owners, see further Abrams 1999, 307–313.

Rogers C (1977) Judicial reinterpretation of statutes: the example of baseball and the antitrust laws. Houston Law Rev 14:611–634
Santo C, Mildner G (2010) Sport and public policy: social, political, and economic perspectives. Human Kinetics, Champaign
Seymour H, Seymour D (1960) Baseball: the early years. Oxford University Press, New York
Seymour H, Seymour D (1971) Baseball: the golden years. Oxford University Press, New York
Van Roo B (2010) One trilogy that should go away without a sequel: why the baseball antitrust exemption should be repealed. Marquette Sports Law Rev 21:381–401
Watterson J (2006) The games presidents play: sports and the presidency. The John Hopkins University Press, Baltimore
Wells J (1878) A treatise on the doctrines of res adjudicata and stare decisis. Mills & Co, Des Moines
White G (1996) Creating the national pastime: baseball transforms itself. Princeton University Press, Princeton
Wiggins R (2008) The federal league of base ball clubs: the history of an outlaw major league, 1914–1915. McFarland & Co, Jefferson
Wilber W (2007) The arrival of the American league: Ban Johnson and the 1901 challenge to National League Monopoly. McFarland & Co, Jefferson
Wood G, Hazucha A (eds) (2008) Northsiders: essays on the history and culture of Chicago Clubs. McFarland & Co, Jefferson

Chapter 3
Case C-36/74 *Walrave and Koch* [1974] ECR 1405

Richard Parrish

Abstract The claimants, Dutch nationals, offered their services for remuneration to act as pacemakers on motorcycles in medium distance races for participants (called "stayers") who cycled in the lee of the motorcycle. The claimants provide their services under agreements with the stayers or the national associations or with sponsors. The first defendants, as the rule making body for the sport, and including its world championships, endorsed a regulation that provided "as from 1973 the pacemaker must be of the same nationality as the stayer". The claimants considered this provision to be incompatible with EU law in so far as it prevented a pacemaker of one Member State from offering his services to a stayer of another Member State. The claimants brought an action against the defendant in a court in Utrecht for a declaration that the rule was void and an order that the defendants allow them to compete at the world championships. The Utrecht court took the view that questions of the interpretation of EU law arose and referred a number of questions to the European Court of Justice for preliminary ruling.

Contents

Richard Parrish, Professor of Sports Law.

R. Parrish (✉)
Department of Law and Criminology, Centre for Sports Law Research,
Edge Hill University, Ormskirk, Lancashire L39 4QP, UK
e-mail: Parrishr@edgehill.co.uk

J. Anderson (ed.), *Leading Cases in Sports Law*,
ASSER International Sports Law Series, DOI: 10.1007/978-90-6704-909-2_3,

3.1 Introduction

Walrave and Koch was the first occasion that the Court of Justice of the European Union ("CJEU") considered the relationship between sport and European law. At issue were four considerations. First, did the absence of an EU sports competence preclude the application of EU law to sporting activity? Second, if so, how could EU law draw a distinction between those sporting rules and practices that should remain outside the reach of the Treaty and those that should be subject to judicial scrutiny? Third, were the acts of privately established sports bodies subject to the Treaty provisions on the free movement of workers and the freedom to provide services, or did those provisions only bind public bodies? Finally, can certain prohibitions contained in the European Treaty invalidate a provision contained in the rules of an international association covering countries that are not subject to the jurisdictional reach of European law?

The CJEU's treatment of these issues structured sport's relationship with EU law for many years. However, recently the application of the judgment to contemporary sports cases has been questioned. First, modern policy and constitutional developments linked to the concept of EU citizenship rights has undermined the divide drawn by the CJEU concerning the separation of sporting rules and economic activity. Second, the CJEU's attempt to construct a category of purely sporting rules, which nonetheless carry economic effects, but which are outside the reach of the Treaty has been criticised and undermined by recent jurisprudence. Third, now that purely sporting rules are to be assessed within the Treaty framework, questions of how to approach the connection between sport and EU law, particularly on sensitive issues such as nationality discrimination in sport, have been re-ignited.

3.2 Facts of the Case

The dispute arose in motor-paced cycling, a sport in which a cyclist (the stayer) follows in the slipstream of a motor-powered pacemaker. This allows the stayer to achieve speeds well in excess of an unaided cyclist. At the time, it was standard for the pacemaker to enter into a contract with the stayer, a cycling association or a sponsor. The sport is regulated by the Union Cycliste International ("UCI"), a body also responsible for supervising the national association's running of world championships. In November 1970, the UCI reviewed its rules on the conduct of motor-paced races for the forthcoming medium distance world cycling championships. From 1973, the pacemaker and the stayer were required to be of the same nationality. This was justified by the UCI on the grounds that world championships were intended to be competitions between national teams.

The rule change had consequences for two Dutch professional pacemakers, Bruno Walrave and Noppie Koch, both believed to be amongst the best pacemakers around. Walrave and Koch entered into contracts with non-Dutch stayers, including Belgians and Germans but in order to participate at the world championships, the pacemakers would have needed to team up with Dutch stayers. Both believed there to be a paucity of good Dutch stayers and consequently Walrave and Koch had fears for their livelihood.

Having failed to persuade the UCI to reverse its decision, the two pacemakers initiated proceedings against the UCI, the Dutch cycling association and, because the championships were to be held in Spain, the Spanish cycling association. At the time Spain was not a member of the European Union and the Spanish association was later dismissed from the litigation. The case was brought before the Arrondissementsrechtbank (District Court) in Utrecht in 1973 with the pacemakers seeking the repeal of the rule and an injunction requiring the UCI to allow the pacemakers to take part in forthcoming events. Somewhat unusually for such a low level court, the District Court referred to the CJEU a number of questions on the compatibility of the UCI nationality rule with certain provisions of European law, particularly those concerning nationality discrimination within the context of legislation securing the free movement of workers and services.[1]

3.3 Sport as Economic Activity

The CJEU initially had to establish whether EU law was applicable to sport. Paragraph 4 of the ruling established that, "having regard to the objectives of the Community, the practice of sport is subject to Community law only in so far as it constitutes an economic activity within the meaning of Article 2 of the Treaty".[2] This was a statement of orthodox European law—in other words at the time the Treaty only regulated economic activity. Paragraph 4 gave rise to claims advanced by sports bodies that sport was in fact a non-economic activity and therefore not subject to European law.

[1] The preliminary reference procedure at the time was regulated by Article 177 of the EC Treaty, now Article 267 of the Treaty on the Functioning of the European Union (TFEU).

[2] Case 36/74 *Walrave and Koch* [1974] ECR 1405, para 4.

Debates concerning whether sport was, or indeed is, an economic activity are now largely settled.[3] In 1989, for instance, Weatherill argued that Article 2 of the Treaty was of such breadth that "there can be no doubt that professional football, which represents a minor but genuine aspect of the market economy, is subject to the Treaty rules designed to achieve a single market".[4] Of course, more recent developments in professional football suggest that the extent of economic activity is no longer minor. Not all sports are as economically significant as football yet the breadth of Article 2 of the Treaty still serves to draw these sports within the scope of the Treaty (now the categories and areas of Union competence can be found in Articles 2–6 of the Treaty on the Functioning of the European Union "TFEU"). Indeed, in *Walrave and Koch* the CJEU regarded economic activity as having the character of gainful employment or remunerated service[5] and later in *Donà v Mantero* the CJEU made clear that this applied to professional and semi-professional players.[6] Nearly twenty years later in *Bosman* the CJEU rejected submissions that "sport is not an economic activity"[7] and that "only the major European leagues may be regarded as undertakings" and that clubs in other leagues carry out only "negligible" economic activity.[8] Indeed, in *Deliège* the CJEU found that an amateur judoka *was* carrying out economic activity. As the CJEU acknowledged, "leading sports personalities could receive, in addition to grants and other assistance, higher levels of income because of their celebrity status, with the result that they provided services of an economic nature".[9]

3.4 Rules of Purely Sporting Interest

Having established that the economic dimension of sport is subject to European law, the CJEU had to wrestle with a second issue. Should an exception from the general prohibition of nationality discrimination be made for certain sporting rules, such as those concerning the composition of national teams? If the answer was in the affirmative, how could European law accommodate such an exception? Advocate General Warner considered such an exception to be necessary and that it was a matter of "common sense" that national teams should consist only of nationals of that country.[10] For Warner, the legal basis supporting the exception

[3] For an extended discussion on sport as economic activity see Van den Bogaert 2005, 40–75.

[4] Weatherill 2007a, 18.

[5] Case 36/74 *Walrave and Koch* [1974] ECR 1405, para 5.

[6] Case 13/76 *Donà v Mantero* [1976] ECR 1333, para 12.

[7] Case C-415/93 *Bosman* [1995] ECR I-4921, para 72.

[8] Case C-415/93 *Bosman* [1995] ECR I-4921, para 70.

[9] Case C-51/96 and C-191/97 *Deliège* [2000] ECR I-2549, para 13.

[10] Opinion of Advocate General Warner in Case 36/74 *Walrave and Koch* [1974] ECR 1405, 1426.

lay in the application of the so-called "officious bystander" test. This test, familiar to those with knowledge of the English contract law, is applied by courts seeking to imply a term into an agreement.

In his view, the original drafters of the Treaty did not have in their contemplation the opening up of national teams to non-nationals and therefore they had no reason to expressly provide such an exception. Warner argued that had the officious bystander asked those signing the Treaty of Rome in 1957 whether the rules on non-discrimination were intended to allow foreigners to play for national teams, he or she would have received short shrift.[11] However, the fact that sport played no part in the Rome, or indeed the later Accession negotiations, cannot necessarily be taken to prove that point. That assessment may underestimate the strength of federalist arguments advanced at the time of the Rome negotiations that European integration should seek to eliminate, and not protect, national rivalries. The fact that federal ambitions were merely implied into the original Rome agreement whereas economic objectives were made express was not a reflection that federalism was defeated in 1957. Rather political expediency demanded that federal union be achieved through economic means.[12] This point is not made in support of the goal of applying the principle of non-discrimination to national sports teams, but rather as evidence of the weakness of the officious bystander test.

The Commission's approach to the matter, submitted by way of "Observations to the Court" in *Walrave*, was to propose locating the exception within the reasoning of CJEU in *Sotgiu*.[13] In that case, an Italian national working in Germany received less favourable treatment than equivalent German workers. The CJEU found that the discrimination in question did not amount to such if account was taken of objective differences between the situations of different workers. This reasoning did not find favour with Mr Warner. Indeed, transposing the logic of *Sotgiu* to *Walrave* is problematic given that the difference in treatment in the composition of national sports teams is not explicable on objective grounds unconnected to nationality, but rather as a direct consequence of an athlete's nationality. In other words, the reason for the discrimination is to maintain the purity of the national make up of that team.

The CJEU's solution was to assert in para 8 that the prohibition on nationality discrimination "does not affect the composition of sport teams, in particular national teams, the formation of which is a matter of purely sporting interest and as such has nothing to do with economic activity".[14] The CJEU then went on to

---

[11] Opinion of Advocate General Warner in Case 36/74 *Walrave and Koch* [1974] ECR 1405, 1426.

[12] The relevant European integration literature is too voluminous for summary here but for a useful introduction see O'Neill 1996.

[13] Case 152/73 *Sotgiu* [1974] ECR 153.

[14] Case 36/74 *Walrave and Koch* [1974] ECR 1405, para 8.

explain that "this restriction on the scope of the provisions in question must however remain limited to its proper objective".[15]

Paragraph 4 is clear—sport has nothing to fear from European law whenever it is practiced as a non-economic activity. This is not a question of justifying restrictions that fall within the scope of the Treaty, but a statement that non-economic activity falls outside it. Paragraph 8 is less clear. Are rules of "purely sporting interest" also non-economic rules or does para 8 establish a wider exception which allows certain sporting practices carried out as economic activity to be removed from the scope of the Treaty because their primary motivation is sporting and has "nothing to do with economic activity"?

Two issues suggest that non-economic activity and purely sporting rules can be different. First, if non-economic activity falls outside the scope of the Treaty as per para 4, then there was no need to elaborate further in para 8 on the limitation on the prohibition on discrimination unless that paragraph is referring to sport as economic activity. Second, the CJEU provides an example of circumstances in which the prohibition on nationality discrimination does not apply. Reference to "the composition of sport teams, in particular national teams", clearly locates the national teams within this exception, but it also raises the prospect of discriminatory selection criteria being permissible in the composition of other sports teams. Here the CJEU departed from the Opinion of Advocate General Warner who clearly saw the exception as only applying to national teams. According to Warner, nationality discrimination in sport is incompatible with European law unless the rule in question is "aimed at the constitution of national teams".[16] The reason for this, according to Warner, is that national teams should consist only of nationals of the country it represented.

The CJEU's reference to "the composition of sport teams, in particular national teams" appears to have persuaded Advocate General Trabucchi, in the slightly later case of *Donà v Mantero*, that club football could also benefit from the *Walrave* para 8 exception. *Donà v Mantero* concerned nationality restrictions in Italian club football and a challenge to these rules brought by a football agent who had attempted to recruit players from abroad. The referring Italian court, the Giudice Conciliatore di Rovigo, sought guidance from the CJEU on a number of points including whether the nationality requirement for playing in professional football matches in Italy was compatible with European law. In his Opinion delivered on 6 July 1976, Trabucchi argued that considerations of purely sporting interest could justify the imposition of restrictions on the signing of or at least on the participation in official championship matches of foreign players so as to ensure that the winning team would be representative of the state of which it is the champion team. Trabucchi considered this reasonable given that the team which

---

[15] Case 36/74 *Walrave and Koch* [1974] ECR 1405, para 9.

[16] Opinion of Advocate General Warner in Case 36/74 *Walrave and Koch* [1974] ECR 1405, 1427.

wins the national championship is often chosen to represent its own state in international competitions.[17]

Trabucchi's reasoning has been attacked by those who do not see a club side as being a representative eleven analogous to a national team. As Weatherill argues, players are not selected for their club sides for the purpose of representing the country should that club qualify for European club competitions by dint of their performance in the national league.[18] This can be contrasted with the motivation underlying selection choices for national teams. In *Donà v Mantero* the CJEU, adopting slightly different language to that found in para 8 of *Walrave and Koch* argued that rules adopted by a sporting organisation which limit the right to take part in football matches as professional or semi-professional players solely to the nationals of the State in question, are incompatible with European law unless such rules exclude foreign players from participation in certain matches for reasons which are not of an economic nature, which relate to the particular nature and context of such matches and are thus of sporting interest only.[19] Whereas in *Walrave and Koch* national teams were removed from the reach of the Treaty prohibitions on nationality discrimination on purely sporting grounds, the *Donà v Mantero* judgment appeared to accept that the composition of a team might be driven by non-sporting considerations. *Donà v Mantero* has therefore been interpreted as narrowing the scope of the para 8 exception established in *Walrave and Koch*.[20]

The question of whether the composition of sports teams, particularly national teams, can be characterised as being a question of purely sporting interest can be approached from two angles. First, one could seek to undermine the connection. It is clear that in the early 1970s, just as today, national teams carry out economic activity. Matches between national teams generate income by way of ticket sales, broadcasting agreements and sponsorship. Players can also be remunerated to represent national teams and a player's earning potential and market value are increased through representative honours. Clearly, matches between national teams do have something to do with economic activity.

The second approach, and the one favoured by the CJEU in *Walrave and Koch*, was to consider the motives behind nationality discrimination. In the case of selecting a national team, even though the practice of sport involving national teams may have an economic dimension, as long as the motives behind the discriminatory selection criteria are deemed to be of purely sporting interest, the Treaty prohibitions do not apply. As Advocate-General Trabucchi explained in *Donà v Mantero* "even sporting activities run on a business basis may nevertheless fall outside the application of the fundamental rules of the Treaty against

[17] Opinion of Advocate General Trabucchi in Case 13/76 *Donà v Mantero* [1976] ECR 1333, 1344.

[18] Weatherill 2007a, 21.

[19] Case 13/76 *Donà v Mantero* [1976] ECR 1333, para 19.

[20] This is the opinion of the Advocate General Lenz in Case C-415/93 *Bosman* [1995] ECR I-4921 para 138. See also Parrish and Miettinen 2008, 84; Van den Bogaert 2005, 342 and McCutcheon, (2000) 132–133.

discrimination in cases where the restrictions on the ground of the player's nationality are based on purely sporting considerations".[21] These purely sporting considerations are, according to Weatherill, connected to "national pride and identity outside the economic sphere".[22] The CJEU's position in *Walrave and Koch* was therefore that non-economic activity fell outside the scope of the Treaty, as did rules which entailed economic activity but which were motivated by a purely sporting interest as long as the rule remained limited to its proper objectives.

In *Walrave and Koch*, the question of what constituted a "national team" was left unanswered by the CJEU as was the more specific question of whether the pacer and the stayer amounted to a national team. Although Advocate-General Warner conceded that this "makes all the difference",[23] he nevertheless advised against providing guidance on this, despite being invited to do so by the Commission in its Observations.[24] Warner did not want to transgress the border between interpreting European law and applying it, the latter being the function of the referring court. Ultimately, on the question of application, the national court did not act upon the guidance provided by the CJEU as Walrave and Koch declined to press for a judgment because the UCI had allegedly threatened to withdraw paced cycle racing from the World Championships.[25] This denied the sporting world of guidance as to the scope and meaning of the para 8 exception. Van den Bogaert speculates that the question of whether the pacer and stayer formed a national team was finely balanced.[26]

3.5 The Collective Regulators Question

In sport private parties such as sports governing bodies adopt rules regulating the employment opportunities of other private individuals, such as athletes. So in *Walrave and Koch* the rules of the UCI had an impact on the employment prospects of the cyclists. Later in *Bosman*, at issue were UEFA rules regulating player transfers that restricted the movement of professional footballers. In *Piau*, FIFA player agent rules placed qualitative restrictions on who could practice as a football agent.[27] Normally it is for a public authority to regulate a private profession. Where this

---

[21] Opinion of Advocate General Trabucchi in Case 13/76 *Donà v Mantero* [1976] ECR 1333, 1344.

[22] Weatherill 2007a, 20.

[23] Opinion of Advocate General Warner in Case 36/74 *Walrave and Koch* [1974] ECR 1405, 1427.

[24] Opinion of Advocate General Warner in Case 36/74 *Walrave and Koch* [1974] ECR 1405, 1426.

[25] Weatherill 2007a, 24.

[26] Van den Bogaert 2005, 360.

[27] Case T-193/02 *Piau* [2005] ECR II-209, para 102.

public regulation restricts a worker's freedom of movement, the private individual is able to invoke rights protected under the Treaty. So Article 45TFEU, regulating freedom of movement for workers, is vertically directly effective as the individual possess rights that they can enforce against the state. The issue in *Walrave and Koch* was whether this Treaty article carried horizontal direct effect. In other words can it be invoked by one private party, such as an athlete, against another, such as a governing body?

In *Walrave and Koch*, Advocate-General Warner suggested that Article 48 of the Treaty (now Article 45TFEU) "binds everyone" and Article 59 of the Treaty (now Article 56TFEU) relating to freedom to provide services is "apt to relate to restrictions imposed by anyone".[28] Therefore from the Advocate-General's perspective, these provisions bind public authorities in the Member States and also private persons within the EU. The CJEU took a slightly different approach by establishing, for the first time, that the prohibition on discrimination contained in the free movement passages of the Treaty applied not only to the actions of public authorities but also to rules of any other nature aimed at collectively regulating gainful employment and services.[29] Reference to collective regulators in this passage is significant as it appears to rule out the binding effect on individual employers, such as an individual sports club. However, the term collective regulator clearly covers those sports governing bodies whose rules have the effect of controlling the activities of the individual employers.

Reference to the binding effect on collective regulators has been maintained by the CJEU in its sports jurisprudence.[30] However, in other non-sporting contexts, case law since *Walrave and Koch* suggests individual employers as well as collective regulators are bound by horizontally directly effective Treaty articles. So in the equal pay case of *Defrenne* the CJEU held that "the prohibition on discrimination between men and women applies not only to the action of public authorities, but also extends to all agreements which are intended to regulate paid labour collectively, as well as to contracts between individuals".[31] Similarly, in *Angonese* the CJEU concluded that "the prohibition of discrimination on grounds of nationality laid down in Article 48 of the Treaty [now Article 45TFEU] must be regarded as applying to private persons as well".[32]

The CJEU's reasoning in *Walrave and Koch* was threefold. First, free movement within the EU would be compromised if the abolition of barriers of national

[28] Opinion of Advocate General Warner in Case 36/74 *Walrave and Koch* [1974] ECR 1405, 1424.

[29] Case 36/74 *Walrave and Koch* [1974] ECR 1405, para 17.

[30] See, for instance, Case C-415/93 *Bosman* [1995] ECR I-4921, para 82 and Case 325/08 *Bernard* [2010] ECR I-2177, para 30.

[31] See Case 43/75 *Defrenne* [1976] ECR 455, para 39.

[32] Case 281/98 *Roman Angonese* [2000] ECR I-4139, para 36.

origin could be neutralised by obstacles resulting from the exercise of their legal autonomy by associations or organizations which do not come under public law.[33] Second, since working conditions in the various Member States are governed by provisions laid down by law or regulation and/or by agreements and other acts concluded or adopted by private persons, to limit the prohibitions in question to acts of a public authority would risk creating inequality in their application.[34] Third, the CJEU spelt out the general nature of the applicable Treaty provisions which draw no distinction between the source of the restrictions to be abolished. Consequently, this general scope of the provisions extends to agreements and rules which do not emanate from public authorities.[35]

3.6 The Jurisdictional Question

Sport is an international phenomenon. Whilst regulatory control of sport is vested at national level, national associations are affiliated to regional (often continental) and global regulatory bodies. For instance, in the case of cycling, the national associations are affiliated to the global regulator, the UCI. In football, national associations must defer to the regulatory authority of the European governing body, UEFA, who in turn respect the authority of the game's global governing body, FIFA.

In *Walrave and Koch*, the UCI raised the jurisdictional question—in other words can certain prohibitions contained in the European Treaty invalidate a provision contained in the rules of an international association covering countries not subject to the jurisdictional reach of European law? If the answer to that question was in the affirmative, the UCI contended that the rules of the (at the time) nine European Economic Community ("EEC") member states would invalidate a rule applicable to over 100 countries. The Advocate General in *Walrave and Koch* dismissed this argument. Advocate-General Warner pointed out that sovereign states are entitled to enact that a particular type of provision in the rules of an international association of private persons shall be deemed unlawful in its territory and shall not be applied there. By analogy, the same, he argued, was true for the EEC.[36] Warner was, of course, correct. To follow the logic of the UCI would be to sanction practices that could easily result in the circumvention of the rights contained within the Treaty.

The jurisdictional question had another dimension. Given that the 1973 cycling world championships were held in Spain, a country not at that time a member of the EEC, the reach of European law would, on first glance, appear limited. However, the

[33] Case 36/74 *Walrave and Koch* [1974] ECR 1405, para 18.

[34] Case 36/74 *Walrave and Koch* [1974] ECR 1405, para 19.

[35] Case 36/74 *Walrave and Koch* [1974] ECR 1405, paras 20 and 21.

[36] Opinion of Advocate General Warner in Case 36/74 *Walrave and Koch* [1974] ECR 1405, 1425.

effect of the UCI's nationality requirement was felt within the territory of the EEC because the world championships determined the choice of a pacemaker in competitions staged at national level. Consequently, European law was engaged in circumstances where a Member State national was placed at a disadvantage, albeit by a rule regulating the conduct of a tournament held outside the EU.

The CJEU agreed with this view by finding that in relation to the applicability of European law to events of world-wide significance, such as the cycling championships in question, the rule on non-discrimination applied to all legal relationships in so far as those relationships, by reason either of the place where they were entered into or the place where they took effect, could be located within the territory of the EU.[37] *Walrave and Koch* therefore laid to rest any notion that collective regulators, such as sports governing bodies, could escape the reach of European law by locating their headquarters outside the EU. It is of course well known that a number of sports governing bodies such as FIFA, UEFA and the International Olympic Committee ("IOC") are located in non-EU Switzerland.

3.7 *Walrave and Koch* Under Pressure

One of the fundamental criticisms of *Walrave and Koch* is the manner in which the CJEU sought to draw a distinction between rules of a purely sporting nature and those which carry economic effects. The solution devised by the CJEU and expressed in paras 4 and 8 of the judgment rests on an assumption that sporting activity can be separated from economic activity. In recent years this approach has come under serious strain in three important respects. First, the para 4 assertion that sport is subject to EU law in so far as it constitutes an economic activity has been overtaken by policy and constitutional developments linked to the concept of EU citizenship rights. Second, the distinction between purely sporting rules and those of an economic nature, is, as Beloff et al. argue, a "difficult one to draw".[38] Third, given that recent jurisprudence means that purely sporting rules are now to be assessed within the Treaty framework, how should future sports cases, particularly those concerning sensitive issues such as nationality discrimination, be treated?

These three issues are dealt with in turn.

3.7.1 *Citizenship Rights*

Aficionados of European sports law and policy are aware that the reference in para 4 of the judgment to the non-economic aspects of sport falling outside the reach of

[37] Case 36/74 *Walrave and Koch* [1974] ECR 1405, para 28.

[38] Beloff et al. 1999, 69.

the Treaty has been frequently cited in the sports jurisprudence of the CJEU since *Walrave and Koch*. However, modern *constitutional* and *policy* developments in the EU mean that the EU Treaty does now have an interest in non-economic activity. From a constitutional perspective, the EU's citizenship provisions, first introduced by the Treaty on European Union ("TEU"), remove the economic activity requirement thus bringing within the scope of the Treaty non-economic sporting activities previously excluded from its scope. The legal basis for the EU's citizenship provisions resides in Article 9TEU and in Articles 20 and 21TFEU. Article 21TFEU grants each EU citizen "the right to move and reside freely within the territory of the Member States, subject to the limitations and conditions laid down in the Treaties and by the measures adopted to give them effect." The "Citizenship Directive" has further strengthened the EU's citizenship provisions[39] as has the CJEU's desire to link citizenship rights with the principle of equal treatment and non-discrimination on the grounds of nationality found in Article 18TFEU. In this respect, the CJEU's approach has been described as amounting to the construction of a "fifth freedom".[40]

From a policy perspective, the EU has long stressed the social, as well as the economic, importance of sport.[41] The 1997 Amsterdam Declaration on Sport emphasised "the social significance of sport, in particular its role in forging identity and bringing people together… In this connection, special consideration should be given to the particular characteristics of amateur sport".[42] The 2000 Nice Declaration stressed the "specific characteristics of sport and its social function in Europe, of which account should be taken in implementing common policies".[43] In both the 2007 White Paper on Sport and the 2011 Communication on Sport, the Commission dedicated chapters to the "societal role of sport" in which it once again stressed the value of sport for social inclusion, integration and equal opportunities.[44] These policy statements are significant insofar as they are used by the European Commission to connect amateur sport with citizenship principles. In 2004, for instance, the Commission expressed concern that a worker's right to be joined by their family in the host country, and the integration of that family into their new surroundings, may be undermined by rules such as those adopted by the Spanish Football Federation prohibiting the issuing of amateur licences to non-Spanish nationals.[45]

The "social advantage" principle expressed in this statement is not new, but the significance lies in its connection with the non-economic aspects of a worker's life,

[39] Directive 2004/38/EC, *The Citizenship Directive* [2004] OJ L 158/77.

[40] TMC Asser Institute et al. 2010.

[41] As indeed has the CJEU in, for example, Case C-415/93 *Bosman* [1995] ECR I-4921, para 106.

[42] Declaration 29 to the Treaty of Amsterdam.

[43] Nice European Council: Presidency Conclusions 2000.

[44] European Commission 2007, Chap. 2 and European Commission 2011, Chap. 2.

[45] Commission Press Release IP/04/1222 of 13 October 2004.

such as their or their family's desire to participate in amateur sport. The CJEU has tended to adopt a wide interpretation of what constitutes a social advantage by consistently arguing that social advantages should be interpreted as meaning all advantages which, whether or not linked to a contract of employment, are generally granted to national workers because of their objective status as workers or by virtue of the mere fact of their residence on the national territory, and whose extension to workers who are nationals of other Member States therefore seems likely to facilitate the mobility of such workers within the EU.[46] From this perspective it seems reasonable to assume that access to amateur sport is a corollary to freedom of movement. This line of reasoning has indeed already been established in relation to access to leisure activities.[47]

The Commission's assertiveness on issues relating to discrimination in the non-economic aspects of sport has been enhanced by way of Article 165TFEU. Article 165TFEU provides that "The Union shall contribute to the promotion of European sporting issues, while taking account of the specific nature of sport, its structures based on voluntary activity and its social and educational function". Article 165(2)TFEU states that "Union action shall be aimed at: developing the European dimension in sport, by promoting fairness and openness in sporting competitions and cooperation between bodies responsible for sports, and by protecting the physical and moral integrity of sportsmen and sportswomen, especially the youngest sportsmen and sportswomen". Reference in Article 165TFEU to the "social" function of sport and "openness in sporting competitions" can be interpreted as extending beyond the confines of the economic aspects of sport.

The Commission's position on nationality discrimination in amateur sport following the entry into force of Article 165TFEU was revealed in a response to a question asked of them by a private party.[48] In its response the Commission argued that "following a combined reading of Articles 18, 21 and 165TFEU, the general EU principle of prohibition of any discrimination on grounds of nationality applies for all EU citizens who have used their right to free movement. This principle concerns amateur sport as well as professional sport".[49] The Commission then went on to repeat the oft cited line that "Union citizenship is destined to be the fundamental status of nationals of the Member States".[50]

The implications for sport are that the rules of amateur sports governing bodies which exclude non-nationals from participation in their competitions may need amending to reflect the fact that as citizenship rights do not depend on the performance of economic activity, amateur players can rely on equal treatment rights. It may not therefore be permissible to exclude such individuals on non-economic

---

[46] Case C-249/83 *Hoeckx* [1985] ECR 973, para 20.

[47] Case C-334/94 *Commission v France* [1996] ECR I-1307, paras 21–23.

[48] Details of the letter have been published in Engelbrecht 2010, 105–106.

[49] Engelbrecht 2010, 105.

[50] Engelbrecht 2010, 105. The phrase derives from Case C-184/99 *Grzelczyk* [2001] ECR I-6193, para 31.

grounds as per *Walrave and Koch*. Furthermore, a worker's right to be joined by their family in the host country, and the integration of that family into their new surroundings, should not be undermined by discriminatory nationality rules employed by sports governing bodies. According to the Commission, this position has been strengthened by the entry into force of Article 165TFEU which confers on the EU a supporting competence in the field of sport. This assessment is of course "subject to the limitations and conditions laid down in the Treaties and by the measures adopted to give them effect"[51] such as the express Treaty derogations and applicable secondary legislation.

3.7.2 Inflated Expectations and the Demise of Rules of Purely Sporting Interest

Despite the very limited nature of the sporting exception developed in *Walrave and Koch*, much has since been asked of para 8 of that judgment. An independent review of European football carried out by former Portuguese sports minister José Luis Arnaut in 2006 recommended sweeping many rules and practices of sports governing bodies outside of the reach of European law. The reasoning was that even though such rules and practices carried economic consequences for those affected by them, their promulgation was motivated by purely sporting considerations. From the perspective of the sport's governing bodies, one can understand the allure of only considering the *intention* of a rule and not its *effect* but that approach is not standard EU legal orthodoxy.[52] Arnaut's reasoning received critical contemporary comment[53] and is difficult to reconcile with the CJEU's attitude in *Bosman* on 'the difficulty of severing the economic aspects from the sporting aspects of football'.[54]

The demands placed by sports bodies on *Walrave and Koch* have been unrealistic. After all, *Walrave and Koch* did not exempt sport from the scope of the Treaty, it actually connected the economic aspects of sport to the Treaty and imposed binding obligations on sports bodies who acted in the capacity as collective regulators. From this perspective, it is misguided to assume that the judgment can be interpreted as placing significant activities of an economic sector such as sport outside the reach of EU law, particularly given that the CJEU insisted that any restriction on the scope of the Treaty must remain limited to its proper objective.

This assumption, whether misguided or not, has now been laid to rest by the CJEU's decision in *Meca-Medina*, a ruling curiously given little treatment by

[51] Article 21(1)TFEU.

[52] For a sports specific discussion on this issue see Beloff et al. 1999, 71–72.

[53] See Miettinen 2006, 57–62 and Wathelet 2007, 3–12.

[54] Case C-415/93 *Bosman* [1995] ECR I-4921, para 76.

Arnaut.[55] Whereas in previous rulings the CJEU attempted to maintain *Walrave and Koch's* "awkward formulation"[56] embodied in para 8; in contrast in *Meca-Medina* the CJEU returned to legal orthodoxy by considering both the intention *and* effect of a contested measure. *Meca-Medina* concerned a challenge brought by two swimmers against a doping sanction imposed on them following a failed test. Hearing an appeal against a Commission Decision to reject the swimmers complaint,[57] the Court of First Instance (now the General Court) treated the anti-doping rules as being of purely sporting interest. It found that anti-doping rules concerned an exclusively "non-economic aspect of that sporting action, which constitutes its very essence".[58]

On further appeal, the CJEU dismissed this reasoning by finding that "it is apparent that the mere fact that a rule is purely sporting in nature does not have the effect of removing from the scope of the Treaty the person engaging in the activity governed by that rule or the body which has laid it down".[59] In determining whether the contested rule fell within the scope of Article 101TFEU, the CJEU found that "account must first of all be taken of the overall context in which the decision of the association of undertakings was taken or produces its effects and, more specifically, of its objectives. It has then to be considered whether the consequential effects restrictive of competition are inherent in the pursuit of those objectives… and are proportionate to them."[60]

The CJEU's approach in *Meca-Medina* has effectively "eliminated" the *Walrave and Koch* "purely sporting interest" rule[61] although one can conceive of a small number of genuinely sporting rules devoid of economic effects, such as the off-side rule in football.[62] The definition of a rule as being of purely sporting interest unrelated to economic activity is now not sufficient in itself to remove the rule in question from the scope of the Treaty, in this context the competition law provisions. Therefore, if a rule carries economic effects, even those of an ancillary nature, its compatibility with the specific requirements of EU law must be examined irrespective of the nature of the rule. Ultimately, the CJEU found that the objective of the anti-doping rules was to ensure fair sporting competitions with equal chances for all athletes as well as the protection of athletes' health, the integrity and objectivity of competitive sport and ethical values in sport. The restrictions (the effect) caused by the anti-doping rules were considered by the CJEU to be inherent in the organisation and proper conduct of competitive sport and the means of achieving it were deemed to be proportionate. Therefore, whilst

---

[55] Case C-519/04 P *Meca-Medina* [2006] ECR I-6991.

[56] Weatherill 2007b, 50.

[57] Comp 38.158 *Meca-Medina*, Decision of 1 August 2002.

[58] Case T-313/02 *Meca-Medina* [2004] ECR II-3291, para 45.

[59] Case C-519/04 P *Meca-Medina* [2006] ECR I-6991, para 27.

[60] Case C-519/04 P *Meca-Medina* [2006] ECR I-6991, para 45.

[61] Weatherill 2007a, 345.

[62] Weatherill 2007b, 60.

Meca-Medina departs from *Walrave and Koch* with respect to the force of rules of purely sporting interest, it confirms the importance of proportionality control expressed in *Walrave*.

3.7.3 Justifying Direct Discrimination?

It is to be recalled that following *Walrave and Koch* and *Donà v Mantero*, nationality discrimination related to the composition of a national team is permissible under European law, not because it is a justified restriction, but because such rules fall outside the scope of the Treaty for reasons of "purely sporting interest". The demise of the purely sporting interest exception prompted by *Meca-Medina* has cast some doubt on whether the purely sporting exception for national team sport can be maintained. If purely sporting rules are now to be assessed within the Treaty framework, how should future cases concerning nationality discrimination be treated? The orthodox approach to directly discriminatory measures would be to cite the express Treaty derogations of public policy, public security or public health.[63] Indirectly, discriminatory measures, and indeed non-discriminatory measures, would only escape condemnation if they satisfy the standards governing objective justification, namely the rule or practice must proportionately pursue a legitimate aim.

Once Advocate-General Trabucchi's support for nationality restrictions in club football was rejected by the Court in *Donà v Mantero* it appeared that only rules concerning the composition of national teams fell outside the scope of Treaty. This would seem to have been confirmed in *Bosman* in which the CJEU condemned the use of nationality quotas in the composition of club teams entering European club competitions organised by UEFA. However, the CJEU's approach to nationality discrimination in *Bosman* raised two important issues. First, at para 128 the CJEU made reference to "teams representing their country". Clearly this includes national teams, but it could also, conceivably, apply to club teams. As Van den Bogaert points out, if the CJEU had wanted to limit the exception to national teams only, here was an opportunity to say just that.[64] Reference to "teams representing their country" has not re-appeared in the sports related jurisprudence of the CJEU since.

The second important issue arising out of *Bosman* is that in relation to the contested nationality quotas the CJEU chose to consider the full spectrum of nationality discrimination (direct, indirect and non-discriminatory) as "restrictions" under EU free movement law. It then chose to consider whether these acts could be justified. In doing so the CJEU appeared to entertain submissions seeking to justify direct nationality discrimination that were not linked to the Treaty derogations. So, for instance, the CJEU accepted the legitimacy of promoting

[63] Article 45(3)TFEU.

[64] Van den Bogaert 2005, 346.

competitive balance in sport but went onto to find that the nationality quotas in place were ill equipped at securing this objective.[65] Similarly the CJEU rejected arguments based on a clubs links with the Member State in which it is established[66] and the need to protect the national team.[67] In relation to the question of justifying directly discriminatory acts, Van den Bogaert sees some merit in this approach even though it is somewhat unorthodox.[68]

The CJEU's treatment of the disputed international transfer system in *Bosman* also added some uncertainty to *Walrave and Koch's* construction of the sporting exception. The CJEU made reference to rules or practices, albeit in the context of non-discriminatory transfer rules, which are "justified on non-economic grounds related to the particular nature and context of certain matches".[69] This raised the prospect that the *Walrave and Koch* sporting exception was in fact a form of justification and not an exception from the Treaty at all. Weatherill disagrees by arguing that whilst the choice of words ("justified") was "peculiar", the CJEU had in fact confirmed its earlier approach in *Walrave and Koch* and *Donà v Mantero*.[70]

In theory, at least, the demise of the purely sporting interest rule therefore exposes directly discriminatory measures to condemnation unless such measures can be justified with reference to the express Treaty derogations. As there appears to be no connection between sporting rules and these derogations, Article 45(3)TFEU should be "discarded" as a means of justifying national eligibility rules.[71] Notable authorities have also dismissed the relevance of the public service exemption found in Article 45(4)TFEU.[72] For this exemption to be relevant an argument must be made that participation in national team sports derives from powers conferred by public law. The argument has some very limited merit in countries with interventionist national sports laws such as France in which the state delegates organisational responsibility to sports governing bodies and imposes obligations on players to accept international call-ups. However, it still remains a considerable leap to suggest that this amounts to employment in the public service as required by Article 45(4)TFEU.

What then should be the legal formula supporting the proposition that European law permits only players who possess the nationality of a state to play in that country's national team? According to Advocate-General Lenz in *Bosman*, this proposition is "obvious and convincing" although as he further acknowledged, it is "not easy to state the reason for it".[73]As the *Bosman* case did not concern the

---

65 Case C-415/93 *Bosman* [1995] ECR I-4921, para 135.

66 Case C-415/93 *Bosman* [1995] ECR I-4921, para 131.

67 Case C-415/93 *Bosman* [1995] ECR I-4921, paras 133–134.

68 Van den Bogaert 2005.

69 Case C-415/93 *Bosman* [1995] ECR I-4921, para 76.

70 Weatherill 2007a, 99.

71 Van den Bogaert 2005, 338.

72 Weatherill 2007a, 25 and Van den Bogaert 2005, 339.

73 Case C-415/93 *Bosman* [1995] ECR I-4921, Opinion of Advocate General Lenz, para 139.

question of national eligibility, Lenz added no further comment although he did reject the argument that the right of freedom of association enjoyed by sports bodies should not be undermined by an individual athlete's right of free movement. Advocate-General argued that only an interest of the association which is of paramount importance could justify a restriction on freedom of movement.[74] In *Deliège*, Advocate-General Cosmas returned to this issue by arguing that "the pursuit of a national team's interests constitutes an overriding need in the public interest which, by its very nature, is capable of justifying restrictions on the freedom to provide services".[75]

Of course, in future cases the CJEU may decide to simply repeat para 8 of *Walrave and Koch* so that national team sports continue to receive protection from the prohibition on nationality discrimination. However, this may be considered unsatisfactory by those who observed the CJEU's firm stance limiting the use of purely sporting rules expressed in para 27 of *Meca-Medina*, and indeed as a consequence of the economic reality of modern national team sport. The solution, proposed in a 2010 European Commission-sponsored *Study on the Equal Treatment of Non-Nationals in Individual Sports Competitions* ("Non-nationals Study"), in which the author participated, is two-fold.[76]

First, national eligibility rules, whilst falling under the EU's free movement rules, could be considered as being incapable of definition as a restriction pursuant to those rules because they derive from a need inherent in the organisation of international sporting competitions. This approach follows the logic of *Deliège* and *Meca-Medina* in which this "inherent rules" doctrine was introduced and refined. Applying this doctrine to national eligibility rules would still require additional judicial development given that *Deliège* and *Meca-Medina* concerned non-discriminatory restrictions. The benefit of the inherent rules doctrine lies in the recognition that national team sport is an economic activity and that when the restrictive effects of nationality clauses go beyond what is necessary and inherent to organise matches between national teams, the rule would constitute a restriction of free movement. As the Non-nationals study argued, this conclusion is entirely consistent with the CJEU's assertion in *Donà v Mantero* that the restriction on the scope of the provisions in question must remain limited to its proper objective and cannot be relied upon to exclude the whole of a sporting activity from the scope of the Treaty.[77]

Second, the Non-nationals Study suggested that national eligibility rules may be apt for justification under the Treaty framework. The difficulty of relying on the express Treaty derogations is outlined above, as is the apparent unavailability of open ended objective justification, an orthodox view being that this is only

[74] Case C-415/93 *Bosman* [1995] ECR I-4921, Opinion of Advocate General Lenz, para 216.

[75] Case C-51/96 and C-191/97 *Deliège* [2000] ECR I-2549, Opinion of Advocate General Comas, para 84.

[76] TMC Asser Institute et al. 2010.

[77] TMC Asser Institute et al. 2010, 225.

available to acts not amounting to direct discrimination. The Non-nationals Study suggests that the CJEU may wish to allow such objective justification to be available to defend directly discriminatory measures, subject to proportionality control. As is explained above, this approach was implied in *Bosman* and further mooted by Advocate-General Cosmas in *Deliège*.[78] The Non-nationals Study also speculates that the prospects for the recognition of such a sports specific mandatory requirement have been enhanced following the entry into force of Article 165TFEU. Article 165 requests that the Union contributes "to the promotion of European sporting issues, while taking account of the specific nature of sport, its structures based on voluntary activity and its social and educational function."[79] The constitutional strength of Article 165TFEU has however been disputed by those who question whether it extends an obligation to the EU institutions to respect the specific nature of sport in the application of other Treaty competences, such as those concerning the non-discrimination and the fundamental freedoms.[80] This situation is different to that found in other Treaty competencies, such as the provisions on environmental protection and public health, which do contain horizontal clauses.

3.8 Conclusion

The *Walrave and Koch* judgment is notable for four reasons. First, it confirmed that only the economic aspects of sport are subject to European law. Second, that even where there is an economic dimension, the Treaty will not touch certain sporting practices, particularly those relating to the composition of national teams, the formation of which is a matter of purely sporting interest and as such has nothing to do with economic activity. Third, *Walrave and Koch* was ground breaking in that it established that the prohibition on discrimination contained in the free movement passages of the Treaty applied not only to the actions of public authorities but also to rules of any other nature aimed at collectively regulating gainful employment and service such as those developed by sports governing bodies. Finally, the judgment clearly established that sporting practices can be subject to review by EU law even though the rule emanates from outside the EU.

Despite featuring as an enduring landmark in the sports jurisprudence of the CJEU the decision making practice of the European Commission and even the occasional case heard by the Court of Arbitration for Sport,[81] the *Walrave and Koch* judgment has come under serious strain. The uncomfortable attempt in para

[78] Case C-51/96 and C-191/97 *Deliège* [2000] ECR I-2549, Opinion of Advocate General Comas, para 84.

[79] Article 165(1)TFEU.

[80] Edge Hill University et al. 2010.

[81] See, for instance, CAS 98/200 *AEK Athens and Slavia Prague v UEFA*, paras 79, 80 and 90.

4 to separate sport from economic activity can no longer be sustained, particularly given commercial developments in modern sport and the EU's interest in citizenship rights. Similarly, reference to rules of purely sporting interest contained in para 8 of the judgment must now be interpreted very narrowly in light of the CJEU's judgment in *Meca-Medina*. Nevertheless, the horizontal effect and the jurisdictional question still has the effect of drawing sporting rules and practices into the reach of the Treaty and even when those rules and practices are promulgated outside the territory of the EU.

References

Beloff M et al (1999) Sports law. Hart, Oxford

Edge Hill University et al (2010) The Lisbon Treaty and EU sports policy. Tender No EAC/19/2009, Study for the Education and Culture Committee, European Parliament, Brussels

Engelbrecht G (2010) Discrimination against EU Nationals in amateur sports. Int Sports Law J 1–2:105–106

European Commission (2007) White paper on sport, COM(2007) 391 final

European Commission (2011) Developing the European dimension in sport, COM(2011) 12 final

McCutcheon P (2000) National eligibility rules after *Bosman*. In: Caiger A, Gardiner S (eds) Professional sport in the EU: regulation and re-regulation. TMC Asser Press, The Hague, pp 127–139

Miettinen S (2006) The independent European sports review: a critical overview. Int Sports Law J 3–4:57–62

Nice European Council: Presidency Conclusions (2000) Declaration on the specific characteristics of sport and its social function of which account should be taken in implementing common policies. www.european-council.europa.eu/council-meetings/conclusions. Accessed 25 Jan 2012

O'Neill M (1996) The politics of European integration. Routledge, Abingdon

Parrish R, Miettinen S (2008) The sporting exception in European Union law. TMC Asser Press, The Hague

TMC Asser Institute et al (2010) Study on the equal treatment of non-nationals in individual sports competitions. Tender No EAC/19/2009, Commissioned by the Directorate-General for Education and Culture, European Commission, Brussels

Van den Bogaert S (2005) Practical regulation of the mobility of sportsmen in the EU post *Bosman*. Kluwer International Law, The Hague

Wathelet M (2007) Sport governance and EU legal order: present and future. Int Sports Law J 3–4:3–12

Weatherill S (2007a) On overlapping legal orders: what is a 'purely sporting' rule. In: Bogusz B et al (eds) The regulation of sport in the European union. Edward Elgar, Cheltenham, pp 48–73

Weatherill S (2007b) European sports law: collected papers. TMC Asser Press, The Hague

Chapter 4
CAS 92/A/63 *GUNDEL v FEI*

Ian S. Blackshaw

Abstract A German equestrian competitor appealed a decision of the International Equestrian Federation's ("FEI's") Judicial Commission to the Court of Arbitration for Sport ("CAS"). The decision was disciplinary in nature and involved the imposition of a suspension and fine on the competitor as a result of his horse testing positive for a prohibited substance. Although it reduced the fine (marginally) and the suspension (from three months to one), CAS dismissed the substance of the appeal. Gundel then sought to challenge the CAS award at the First Civil Division of the Swiss Federal Supreme Tribunal ("SFST" or "Swiss Supreme Court") on the grounds that CAS did not offer sufficient guarantees of independence and impartiality to rule in his appeal such that CAS awards could not be deemed recognisable and enforceable as international arbitral awards. The SFST, whose competency to hear a public law appeal against CAS rested in an application of the Swiss Federal Statute on Private International Law, dismissed Gundel's application and held that on balance CAS satisfied the essentials of a "true" arbitral tribunal.

Ian S. Blackshaw is an International Sports Lawyer and Visiting Professor and Fellow at the TMC Asser Institute's International Sports Law Centre, The Hague; a Member of the Court of Arbitration for Sport and has recently been awarded an Honorary Doctor of Laws of Anglia Ruskin University, Chelmsford and Cambridge, United Kingdom, where he is a Founder Member of The International Law Unit of the University.

I. S. Blackshaw (✉)
TMC Asser Institute's International Sports Law Centre, Court of Arbitration for Sport and Anglia Ruskin University, Cambridge, UK
e-mail: ian.blackshaw@orange.fr

J. Anderson (ed.), *Leading Cases in Sports Law*,
ASSER International Sports Law Series, DOI: 10.1007/978-90-6704-909-2_4,

Contents

4.1 Introduction

CAS 92/A/63 *Gundel v FEI*, and including the subsequent proceedings at the First Civil Division of the SFST,[1] is certainly a landmark case in sports law as it led to a ground-breaking change in the organisation and governance of the CAS, which had been established ten years before in 1983. *Gundel v FEI* is inextricably bound up with the history and subsequent development of the CAS and the effects of *Gundel v FEI* on the CAS are still being felt today and will probably continue to be so in the foreseeable future. Before discussing the decision, some historical background on the CAS and its organisation and role in relation to the settlement of sports-related disputes would not be out of place and would help to put *Gundel v FEI* into its proper context.

4.2 The Court of Arbitration for Sport

At the beginning of the 1980s, an increasing number of international sports disputes and the lack of any independent body to deal with them in a flexible, quick, inexpensive and binding manner prompted a number of international sports federations to look at this situation and see what could be done. Soon after assuming the Presidency of the International Olympic Committee ("IOC") in 1981, the late Juan Antonio Samaranch had the idea of creating a sports court that would become "the supreme court of world sport". The following year at an IOC Meeting in Rome, the late Judge Keba Mbaye, from Senegal, an IOC member and at the time a member of the International Court of Justice, was asked to chair a

[1] Decision 4P.217/1992 of 15 March 1993; ATF 119 II 271 and translated at 1 Digest of CAS Awards 1993, 561–575 and (1993) 8 *Mealey's International Arbitration Reports* 12–18. See also Blackshaw 2009, 109–117.

working party with the aim of preparing the statutes of a sports dispute resolution body that, in time, would become known as the CAS.

In 1983, the IOC officially ratified the Statutes of the CAS, which came into force on 30 June 1984. On the same date, the CAS became operational under the late Judge Mbaye as its first President, a position he occupied with distinction until his death in 2007.

4.2.1 The First Ten Years

The 1984 CAS Statutes were supplemented by a set of procedural regulations. Both were slightly modified in 1990. Under these regulations, the CAS was composed of 60 members appointed by the IOC, the International Federations ("IFs"), the National Olympic Committees ("NOCs") and the IOC President—15 members each. The IOC President had to choose members outside the other three groups. All the operating costs of the CAS were borne by the IOC. In general, the proceedings were free of charge, except for financial disputes, in which the parties could be required to pay a share of the costs. The CAS Statutes could be modified only by the IOC meeting in General Session, on the proposal of the IOC Executive Board.

The CAS Statutes and Regulations provided for only one kind of contentious procedure, irrespective of the nature of the dispute. In addition, there was also a "consultation procedure" open to sports bodies or individuals. Through this procedure, which no longer exists, the CAS could give a legal opinion on any sports-related issue.

In 1991, the CAS published a "Guide to Arbitration", which included several model arbitration clauses, including one for incorporation in the statutes or regulations of international sports federations. This clause foresaw the creation of special rules to settle disputes arising out of a decision taken by a sports federation (the "Appeals Procedure"). The first such body to adopt this clause was the FEI.

4.2.2 The Gundel Case

The next significant development was in February 1992 when a horse rider, named Elmar Gundel, lodged an appeal for arbitration by the CAS based on an arbitration clause in the FEI statutes, in which he challenged a decision rendered by the FEI. This decision, which followed a horse doping case, disqualified the rider, suspending and also fining him. CAS 92/A/63 *Gundel v FEI* found partly in favour of the rider (the suspension was reduced from three months to one month). Dissatisfied with the CAS ruling, Gundel filed an appeal with the SFST. He disputed the validity of the award, on the grounds that it was rendered by a tribunal that did not meet the conditions of impartiality and independence needed to be considered as a proper arbitration court under Swiss Law. In its judgment of 15 March 1993, the SFST recognised the CAS as a true court of arbitration and noted, *inter alia*, that the CAS was not an organ of the FEI; that it did not receive instructions from that federation; and that it retained sufficient autonomy with regard to it, in that it placed at the disposal of the CAS only three arbitrators out of the maximum of 60 members of which the CAS was composed.

However, in its judgement, the SFST drew attention to numerous links between the CAS and the IOC: the fact that the CAS was financed almost exclusively by the IOC; the fact that the IOC was competent to modify the CAS Statutes; and the considerable power given to the IOC and its President to appoint CAS members. In the SFST's view, such links would be sufficiently serious to call into question the independence of the CAS if the IOC were a party to proceedings before it. As Matthieu Reeb, Secretary General of the CAS, subsequently remarked: "The Federal Tribunal's message was thus perfectly clear: the CAS had to be made more independent of the IOC both organizationally and financially."[2]

In short, *Gundel v FEI* led to some major reforms of the CAS in 1994. The main findings and rationale of the SFST will be discussed and reviewed anon; for now a potted history of the CAS and the Gundel-inspired reforms to its organisation and governance are discussed.

4.2.3 The 1994 Gundel Reforms at CAS

As a result of *Gundel v FEI* at the SFST, the CAS Statutes and accompanying regulations were completely revised to make it more efficient and to modify its institutional structure so as to make it more independent of the IOC, which had sponsored it since its creation. The most important change was the creation of an International Council of Arbitration for Sport ("ICAS") to deal with the running and financing of the CAS, thereby taking the place of the IOC. Another major change was the creation of two Arbitration Divisions of the CAS (the "Ordinary Division" and the "Appeals Division") in order to make a clear distinction between disputes of sole instance and those arising from a decision rendered by a sports body. The CAS reforms were enshrined in a new Code of Sports-related Arbitration ("CAS Code"), which came into force on 22 November 1994. All these reforms were approved on 22 June 1994 with the signing of the so-called "Paris Agreement".[3] Although the 1994 reforms were instrumental in minimising the IOC's overt control over the funding and governance of the CAS, the issue of institutional independence, as a measure of good governance, continues to be an

---

[2] Blackshaw et al. 2006, 34. *See further* Reeb 1998, 2002, 2004.

[3] The Paris Agreement is reproduced under its formal title "Agreement related to the Constitution of the International Council of Arbitration for Sport" at 2 Digest of CAS Awards 2002, 883.

ongoing challenge for the CAS and, according to Downie, it remains debatable whether such reforms provided sufficient independence from other influential international sporting organisations.[4]

4.3 The Legal Status of and Challenges to CAS Awards

Awards made by the CAS, like other international arbitral awards, are legally enforceable generally in accordance with the rules of international private law, and also specifically under the provisions of the New York Convention on the Recognition and Enforcement of Foreign Arbitral Awards of 10 June 1958. The CAS is also recognised under the European Convention on the Recognition of the Legal Personality of International Non-Governmental Organizations of 24 April 1986. So, the CAS decisions are legally effective and can be enforced internationally. This is particularly important in the case of disputes involving intellectual property rights, especially trademarks, which are generally of a territorial nature. The CAS awards can be legally challenged in the SFST by a dissatisfied party, but only in very limited circumstances, under the provisions of article 190(2) of the Swiss Federal Code on Private International Law of 18 December 1987.[5] This article reads (in translation) as follows:

> [The Award] can be attacked only if (a) a sole arbitrator was designated irregularly or the arbitral tribunal was constituted irregularly; (b) if the arbitral tribunal erroneously held that it had or did not have jurisdiction; (c) if the arbitral tribunal ruled on matters beyond the claims submitted to it or failed to rule on one of the claims; (d) if the equality of the parties or their right to be heard in an adversarial proceeding was not respected; or (e) if the award is incompatible with Swiss public policy.

In practice, perhaps ground (d) is the most important one, and permits the SFST to act in a supervisory manner to remedy "breaches of fundamental principles and essential procedural guarantees which may be committed by the arbitrators called upon to decide in his case."[6] Although there have been a number of legal challenges to CAS awards,[7] this chapter will principally discuss *Gundel v FEI* and also the *Lazutina and Danilova* proceedings from 2002 and 2003, both of which centrally involved the questioning of the independence of the CAS from the IOC, in view of its association with and partial funding by the IOC.[8]

---

[4] Downie 2011.

[5] See generally the thorough review by Rigozzi 2010, 217–265.

[6] *Canas v ATP* Decision 4P.172/2006 of 27 March 2007; ATF 133 III 235 and translated at (2007) 1 *Swiss International Arbitration Law Reports* 65, 86. See originally CAS 2005/A/951 *Canas v ATP*.

[7] See Mitten 2009, 54.

[8] See originally CAS 2002/A/370 *L v IOC*, CAS 2002/A/397 *L v FIS*; and CAS 2002/A/371 *D v IOC*, CAS 2002/A/397 *D v FIS* and, on appeal to the SFST, *A & B v IOC and FIS* 4P.267/2002;

4.4 The Gundel Case

The SFST's decision in *Gundel v FEI*, as already noted, constituted a major turning point in the development of the CAS. The fundamental question raised by the appellant concerning the independence of the CAS was essentially whether, as its founders claimed it to be, the CAS was a true arbitral tribunal independent of the parties, which freely exercised complete juridical control over the decisions of the associations brought before it, and in this case the FEI. The SFST noting both the manner in which CAS's arbitrators were then nominated (i.e., offering the parties the possibility of designating as an arbitrator or umpire one of at least fifteen persons belonging neither to the FEI nor to other sports associations) and other aspects of the then CAS Statutes guaranteeing the independence in operation of the arbitrators (e.g., the solemn declaration of independence signed by each CAS member before s/he takes office), the SFST was generally satisfied that the CAS offered the guarantees of arbitral independence upon which Swiss law made conditional the valid exclusion of ordinary judicial recourse. Nevertheless, the SFST did have certain reservations with regard to the independence of the CAS with respect to the "organic and economic ties" existing between it and the IOC. And in this the SFST observed that the IOC was competent to modify the CAS Statute; it underwrote the operating costs of CAS; and the IOC played a considerable role in the appointment of the CAS's membership.

The IOC was not a party to the *Gundel v FEI* proceedings and thus its observations on the CAS/IOC relationship remained moot for almost a decade until the *Lazutina and Danilova* proceedings.

4.5 Lazutina and Danilova

In the stated proceedings, two Russian cross-country skiers, Larissa Lazutina and Olga Danilova unsuccessfully questioned the independence of CAS at the SFST in 2003. The skiers were disqualified by the IOC after the 2002 Winter Olympic Games in Salt Lake City for doping offences. The International Ski Federation ("FIS") suspended both of them for two years. Their appeal to CAS, calling for the IOC and FIS decisions to be overruled, was dismissed. Their subsequent legal challenge to the SFST—on the grounds that CAS, because it was a "vassal" of and received some funding from the IOC, was not a truly independent body—was also dismissed. The SFST held that CAS offered all the guarantees of independence and impartiality to be regarded as a real court of arbitration, even where the IOC—as in the Russian skiers' case—was a party to its proceedings.

(Footnote 8 continued)
4P.268/2002; 4P.269/2002; and 4P.270/2002 of 27 May 2003 and translated at 3 Digest of CAS Awards 2004, 674–695.

The appellants had sought to distinguish their case from *Gundel v FEI* on the ground that their situation was exacerbated by the fact that the IOC was a party to the stated proceedings. In an extremely thorough judgment the SFST held that, on the whole the 1994 reforms were such that CAS had the necessary independence to pass judgment in a case involving the IOC without any fear of partiality or prejudice towards the claimants. The SFST did however note that some improvements could be made in terms of transparency in the appointment of arbitrators, in the sense that it thought it preferable if the published list of CAS arbitrators indicated clearly by whom they were nominated so that the parties "would then be able to appoint their arbitrator with full knowledge of the facts. For example, it would prevent a party in dispute with the IOC, in the belief that he was choosing an arbitrator completely unconnected to the latter, from actually appointing a person who was proposed by that organisation."[9]

The SFT's response to the claimants' argument on the close financial links between the IOC and CAS is useful in that it has application to many other quasi-independent, arbitral bodies in sport and thus is worth citing at length:

> …it should be added that there is not necessarily any relationship of cause and effect between the way a judicial body is financed and its level of independence. This is illustrated, for example, by the fact that State courts in countries governed by the rule of law are often required to rule on disputes involving the State itself, without their judges' independence being questioned on the ground that they are financially linked to the State. Similarly, the CAS arbitrators should be presumed capable of treating the IOC on an equal footing with any other party, regardless of the fact that it partly finances the Court of which they are members and which pays their fees.[10]

In the present case, the claimants also challenged the independence of the appointed arbitrators (danger of bias) and their conduct (breach of natural justice) during the hearings. The allegations concerning misconduct, which related to the calling of witnesses, were dismissed by the SFST, which held that, minor procedural errors apart, fundamentally the equality of the parties and their right to a fair hearing was respected throughout the proceedings. The claim as to lack of impartiality was also rejected but, again, in its dismissal, the SFST laid down some important guidelines for arbitration in sport more generally. The essence of the claimants' argument was that at least one of the arbitrators in the stated proceedings had worked with the IOC's principal lawyer in previous CAS hearings and that more generally the relatively small number of CAS arbitrators (and international sports lawyers) meant that "they forge such close personal and professional relationships with one another that their independence is affected when, at a later time and in different roles, they are involved in cases submitted to the CAS."[11]

---

[9] *A & B v IOC and FIS* 4P.267/2002; 4P.268/2002; 4P.269/2002; and 4P.270/2002 of 27 May 2003 and translated at 3 Digest of CAS Awards 2004, 686.

[10] *A & B v IOC and FIS* 4P.267/2002; 4P.268/2002; 4P.269/2002; and 4P.270/2002 of 27 May 2003 and translated at 3 Digest of CAS Awards 2004, 688.

[11] *A & B v IOC and FIS* 4P.267/2002; 4P.268/2002; 4P.269/2002; and 4P.270/2002 of 27 May 2003 and translated at 3 Digest of CAS Awards 2004, 689.

On this point, the SFST took a pragmatic approach noting that in the small world of international sports arbitration, and is frequent in private arbitration, relations between arbitrators and lawyers are, because of professional necessities, much more frequent than judicial proceedings but that that of itself should not be considered a ground for challenge. Proof of prejudice should, according to the SFST, go beyond "purely subjective reactions" and be evaluated on a case-by-case basis with reference to the existence of any "objective facts which are likely, for the rational observer, to arouse suspicion concerning the arbitrator's independence."[12] Otherwise, the SFST held, one should assume that experienced arbitrators "are capable of rising above the eventualities linked to their appointment when they are required to render concrete decisions in discharge of their duties."[13]

The approach of the SFST is a useful one. Sports communities tend to be relatively small and provided that certain precautions are taken, subjectively based suspicions as to bias, prejudice and conflicts of interest, should not be permitted to overly hinder the work of sports arbitral tribunals. In this, it is of interest to note that following the stated case the CAS Code was revised somewhat in 2004 in order to address this issue. The revised 2004 CAS Code reiterated that CAS members must, upon their appointment, exercise their functions personally with total objectivity and independence and in conformity with the operating CAS Code. Moreover, members of ICAS could neither appear on the list of CAS arbitrators nor could they act as counsel to one of the parties in proceedings before the CAS.[14] The President of either of CAS's divisions also had to spontaneously disqualify himself if, in arbitration proceedings assigned to his Division, one of the parties was a sports-related body to which he belonged, or if a member of the law firm to which he belonged was acting as arbitrator or counsel.

On 29 September 2009, ICAS announced, at its annual meeting, that it was to amend the CAS Code in order to prohibit CAS arbitrators and mediators from acting as counsel before CAS. The accompanying media release stated that the "prohibition of the double-hat arbitrator/counsel role was decided in order to limit the risk of conflicts of interest and to reduce the number of petitions for challenge during arbitrations." CAS Code S18 now includes the following: "CAS arbitrators and mediators may not act as counsel for a party before CAS." Finally, the CAS Code expressly states that, on pain of a "legitimate doubt" as to their independence, "every arbitrator shall be and remain independent of the parties and shall immediately disclose any circumstances likely to affect his independence with respect to any of the parties."[15]

---

[12] *A & B v IOC and FIS* 4P.267/2002; 4P.268/2002; 4P.269/2002; and 4P.270/2002 of 27 May 2003 and translated at 3 Digest of CAS Awards 2004, 691. See also Blackshaw 2011, 10–11.

[13] *A & B v IOC and FIS* 4P.267/2002; 4P.268/2002; 4P.269/2002; and 4P.270/2002 of 27 May 2003 and translated at 3 Digest of CAS Awards 2004, 692.

[14] CAS Code, S5.

[15] CAS Code, R33. The challenge must be brought to ICAS (R34) and can result in the removal (R35) and/or replacement (R36) of the arbitrator. See also CAS Code, S19. ICAS may remove, temporarily or permanently, an arbitrator from the list of CAS members if they breach their duty

In sum, in the stated proceedings, the Swiss Supreme Court was satisfied that the CAS was no longer "the vassal of the IOC."[16] The SFST highlighted evidence supplied by the Secretary General of CAS that of the twelve cases submitted between 1996 and 2003 in which the IOC was the respondent, the IOC had won eight but lost four.[17] Although as the SFST observed, this statistic had "indicative value" only, it did provide concentre evidence of CAS's independence and authority. Put simply, by the turn of the 21st century interested parties appeared to have more confidence in CAS, a confidence that was reflected in the statistics on CAS applications and in a number of developments that expanded CAS's "reach" into the world of sports disputes.[18]

Finally and on the development of the CAS generally, the SFST made the following pertinent remarks, which may be regarded as a ringing and enduring endorsement by the SFST of the legal status and position of the CAS in the world of sport:

> ...the CAS is growing rapidly and continuing to develop. An important new step in its development was recently taken at the World Conference on Doping in Sport, held in Copenhagen at the beginning of March 2003. This Conference adopted the World Anti-Doping Code as the basis for the worldwide fight against doping in sport. Many States, including China Russia and the United States of America, have adopted the Copenhagen Declaration on Anti-Doping in Sport. Under the terms of Art. 13.2.1 of the new Code, the CAS is the appeals body for all doping-related disputes related to international sports events or international-level athletes. This is a tangible sign that States and all parties concerned by the fight against doping have confidence in the CAS. It is hard to imagine that they would have felt able to endorse the judicial powers of the CAS so resoundingly if they had thought it was controlled by the IOC.
>
> This new mark of recognition from the international community shows that the CAS is meeting a real need. There appears to be no viable alternative to this institution, which can resolve international sports-related disputes quickly and inexpensively...Having gradually built up the trust of the sporting world, this institution which is now widely recognised...remains one of the principal mainstays of organised sport.[19]

(Footnote 15 continued)
of confidentially regarding the disclosure to any third party of any facts or other information relating to proceedings conducted before CAS.

[16] *A & B v IOC and FIS* 4P.267/2002; 4P.268/2002; 4P.269/2002; and 4P.270/2002 of 27 May 2003 and translated at 3 Digest of CAS Awards 2004, 688.

[17] *A & B v IOC and FIS* 4P.267/2002; 4P.268/2002; 4P.269/2002; and 4P.270/2002 of 27 May 2003 and translated at 3 Digest of CAS Awards 2004, 688. In addition, the three arbitrators in the stated proceedings had all been part of CAS Panels that had ruled against the IOC.

[18] Anderson 2010, 87.

[19] *A & B v IOC and FIS* 4P.267/2002; 4P.268/2002; 4P.269/2002; and 4P.270/2002 of 27 May 2003 and translated at 3 Digest of CAS Awards 2004, 688–689.

4.6 Conclusion

The decision of the SFST in *Gundel v FEI* in its day had a considerable impact upon the future organisation and governance of the CAS and the repercussions of the decision, which concerns the legal status of the CAS as an independent arbitral tribunal under Swiss Law, are still being felt today—and may well continue be felt in the foreseeable future. In *Gundel v FEI*, the SFST noted that the impartiality of an arbitral tribunal is undermined when the primary financial benefactor is a party to the arbitration. In view of the continuing part reliance of the CAS on funds from the IOC and its affiliates, it is arguable that even the present reformed governance structure and arrangements may still have the potential to undermine the institutional independence of the CAS. To reduce this financial dependence, it has been suggested that the CAS should charge more for its services and become self-funding.[20] That debate is for another day. For now, and as the CAS continues to evolve further, *Gundel v FEI*, it is submitted, will continue to be a beacon that will ensure that, as its founders intended, the CAS not only becomes the "supreme court of world sport", but also a body whose organisation, governance, procedures and decisions the international sporting community can rely on—not only for impartiality, but also for legal certainty and effectiveness in delivering sporting justice in a timely and inexpensive manner.

References

Anderson J (2010) Modern sports law. Hart, Oxford

Blackshaw IS (2009) Sport, mediation and arbitration. TMC Asser Press, The Hague

Blackshaw IS (2011) Challenging the independence of CAS arbitrators. World Sports Law Rep 9(9):10–11

Blackshaw IS et al (2006) The Court of Arbitration for Sport: 1984–2004. TMC Asser Press, The Hague

Downie R (2011) Improving the performance of sport's ultimate umpire: reforming the governance of the Court of Arbitration for Sport. Melb J Int Law 12:315–356

Mitten M (2009) Judicial review of olympic and international sports arbitration awards: trends and observations. Pepperdine Disput Resolut J 9:51–67

Reeb M (ed) (1998) Digest of CAS awards I. Staempfli Publishers, Berne

Reeb M (ed) (2002) Digest of CAS awards II. Kluwer Law International, The Hague

Reeb M (ed) (2004) Digest of CAS Awards III. Kluwer Law International, The Hague

Rigozzi A (2010) Challenging awards of the Court of Arbitration for Sport. J Int Dispute Settl 1:217–265

[20] Downie 2011, 315–356.

Part II
Player Mobility Versus Contractual Stability

Chapter 5
Eastham v Newcastle United FC Ltd [1964] Ch 413

Simon Boyes

Abstract At the material time, professional football players in England were typically employed with their club through written contracts of 12 month's duration. A player also had to register with the Football League (the league of 92 professional clubs in England) and the Football Association (the governing body of the sport in England) and while so registered could only play for that club. At the end of the season, the employing club had the choice either to retain the player at a reasonable wage or put the player up for transfer to another club for a fee. If retained, the player was debarred from playing for another club and until he resigned with the retaining club, no contract of employment existed. If the club wanted to transfer the player, they would set a transfer fee and although a player could not be transferred without their consent; nevertheless, if he was on the transfer list he could not seek re-employment except with a club willing to pay the fee. A dissatisfied player had a limited means of appeal to the league management committee. In the stated case, the claimant, a professional footballer registered with a league club, asked to be transferred. The club had, however, given him notice of retention and thus refused to release him. The player refused to resign with the retaining club and sought to challenge football's "retain and transfer system" principally by arguing that it was an unreasonable restraint of trade.

Contents

S. Boyes (✉)
Nottingham Law School, Nottingham Trent University, Nottingham NG1 4BU, UK
e-mail: simon.boyes@ntu.ac.uk

J. Anderson (ed.), *Leading Cases in Sports Law*,
ASSER International Sports Law Series, DOI: 10.1007/978-90-6704-909-2_5,

5.1 Introduction

The case of *Eastham v Newcastle United* is of significance for a number and variety of reasons, which combine to mean that it remains of contemporary as well as historical interest. The case has much to offer to a modern analysis of sports law in a range of respects. In its historical perspective, the case was both a contributor to, and evidence of, a shift in the balance of power between professional footballers and their employer clubs. *Eastham v Newcastle United* played a key role in rebalancing the employment relationship between club and player and came at a time when players had made minimal progress from being treated as "chattels", as counsel for Eastham put it to the High Court,[1] to acquiring at least a limited degree of freedom in the exercise of their professional activities.

From the standpoint of the development of sports law, the *Eastham* case represents a significant advance in the approach to permitting challenges to the rules and regulations of sports governing bodies through the English courts. Further, the case can also be recognised as an accurate indicator of the approach that would come to be adopted in subsequent litigation, most notably in the case of *Bosman*.[2] Most particularly the case established the pattern of sporting values acquiring recognition as meriting legal protection.

5.2 Historical Context

Eastham v Newcastle United formed part of wider events that effected a fundamental shift in the status of professional football players, their relationships with their employer clubs and regulatory bodies in England. Players had only formally been permitted to enjoy "professional" status since 1885, though illicit "boot-money" payments had been commonplace up to that point in time.[3] Accompanying the introduction of professionalism, and following the inception of the Football League in 1888, the authorities also introduced a system of annual player registration, with the aim of preventing players "hopping" between clubs.

[1] *Eastham v Newcastle United Football Club* [1964] 1 Ch 413, 427.

[2] Case C-415/93 *Bosman* [1995] ECR I-4192.

[3] See, for example, Taylor 2001, 101–118.

Quite unintentionally it seems, this system of registration became the basis of a transfer system between clubs, as they would trade a player's registration in return for a fee.[4]

The issue of contractual stability was litigated almost immediately in *Radford v Campbell,*[5] in which case Nottingham Forest—not then a member of the Football League—sought an injunction to prevent a player breaking a contract with the club in order to sign with Blackburn Rovers. The claim, which was unsuccessful, is of less importance than the attitude of the Master of the Rolls in the Court of Appeal, as summarised by McArdle: "Lord Esher's contempt for the sport, and particularly for professionalism and the clubs' obsession with 'winning their games', drips from the judgment; the Court ought not to involve itself with something so trivial as football".[6] There was, it seems, no kindly judicial disposition towards professional sport at this time.

A further inhibition on professional players was introduced in 1900, with the introduction of a maximum wage. The initial balance in the relationship was hugely in favour of the clubs and such restrictions were a continual source of dispute between the players and the clubs and regulatory bodies between the 1890s and 1950s, with little real change being effected. The enmity between the players and regulators reached a peak in 1909, following the establishment of a players' union—the Association Football Player's Union (which eventually evolved to become the Professional Footballers' Association)—in 1907, which the authorities sought to eradicate.[7]

The rolling disputes of this period once again found a home in the courts in the case of *Kingaby v Aston Villa,*[8] where the retain and transfer system first fell to be considered. However, due principally to a calamitous misjudgement by counsel for Kingaby, the claim failed having been premised upon an allegation of malicious behaviour on the part of Aston Villa, and not challenging directly the validity of the retain and transfer system as being in restraint of trade. Had it not been for this error, it could well have been that matters would have been settled half a century before *Eastham.* As it was, it was not until 1961, against the background of threatened strike action, that the maximum wage was finally abolished and the players reached a settlement with the football authorities on payments to out of contract players retained by clubs. It was against this turbulent background that the *Eastham v Newcastle United* litigation arose.

---

4 Magee 2006.

5 *Radford v Campbell* (1890) 6 TLR 488.

6 McArdle 2002, 266. See also McArdle 2000 and Grayson 1996.

7 See Dabshceck 1991, 221–238.

8 *Kingaby v Aston Villa* (1912) *The Times* 28 March.

5.3 Factual Background

Eastham v Newcastle United concerned a challenge to the rules of the English Football Association ("the FA") and Football League ("the League") relating to the system of "retain and transfer", governing the movement of players between clubs. The claimant in the action, George Eastham, was a professional footballer of some note,[9] whose playing contract with Newcastle United had expired. However, the combination of the rules of the FA, the sport's regulator, and the League, the organiser of the premier English league competition, meant that Newcastle United could still retain his registration, even though his contractual relationship had ended. The result of this was that, despite the absence of a contract between him and Newcastle United, the claimant was prevented from moving to another club unless Newcastle agreed to release his registration.

Eastham was unable to mount a successful challenge to the "retain and transfer" scheme within football's regulatory structures, though Newcastle, seeking to avoid the matter being litigated, eventually succumbed to his demands for a transfer to Arsenal for a fee of £47,500. By the time matters had been resolved in his favour, Eastham had spent three months in professional limbo and so continued to pursue his claim in the High Court. He claimed declarations against Newcastle United, the FA and the League that his contract with the club, the rules of the FA and the regulations of the League constituting the "retain and transfer" system were inapplicable to him as being in unreasonable restraint of trade and, or in the alternative, *ultra vires* and hence unlawful as being in breach of contract. In sum, Eastham argued that the retention system had the effect of impeding his ability to pursue further employment and make use of his abilities as a professional footballer after the termination of his contract.

The FA was, and remains, the governing body of association football in England; its rules are binding upon all players and member clubs. As now, any player wishing to represent a member club was obliged to lodge his registration for that club with the FA. The player may then only represent the club which holds his registration and may not appear for any other. Players representing a club playing in the League were also required to register their club affiliation with the League. Under the regulatory scheme in place at the time players were employed on a twelve-month contract; at the conclusion of that agreement the club could, subject to continuing to offer the player a reasonable wage, choose to retain a player's registration and thus the exclusive right to his services. The FA had the capacity to refuse a club the right to retain a player if it considered the wage offered to be insufficient. Retained players were barred from representing any other League club, with no limits on the length of time for which a player could be retained

---

[9] George Eastham made 525 Football League appearances for Newcastle United, Arsenal and Stoke City, scoring 74 goals. Eastham won 19 caps for England, scoring two goals and was a squad member for both the 1962 and 1966 World Cup Finals, though he did not make an appearance in either tournament.

despite not being contractually bound to the club. A transfer to another club was possible upon a payment of a fee to the retaining club from the player's new club. Thus a player would be limited to seeking employment with clubs willing and able to meet the asking price. A player dissatisfied with either the terms offered or transfer fee required by the retaining club, could make an appeal to the League's Management Committee in the hope of obtaining a "free-transfer", in which case the player could not be retained, nor a fee demanded. A transfer to a club outside of the League was, in any case, available to a retained player on condition that FA rules were complied with. However, this was of marginal importance as prospects for full-time professional players outside of the League were extremely limited.

5.4 Contribution to the Development of Sports Law

Eastham v Newcastle United made a significant contribution to the development of sports law in a number of key respects and notably access to the courts in challenges to sports governing bodies and the mode of application of the law in such cases.

5.4.1 Challenging Sports Governing Bodies: Access to English Courts

A key reason for the continued significance of *Eastham v Newcastle United* is its importance in establishing the accountability, through the English courts, of sports governing bodies. The case represents a landmark in the development of the law in this area, and taken in its contemporary context would have been just as an astonishing intervention as was that in *Bosman* some thirty years later. Barely a decade earlier, the Court of Appeal had decided that another sports governing body, the Jockey Club, was possessed of an absolute and unfettered discretion to withdraw a race horse trainer's license and thus his livelihood, without even the benefit of a hearing in accordance with the rules of natural justice.[10] It had only been recently established in *Baker v Jones*[11] that the decisions of sports governing bodies could be scrutinised in contract on the basis of *ultra vires*, and in *Davis v Carew-Pole*[12] that the rules of natural justice applied to sports disciplinary matters. To move from this to a position where the application of an established rule could

[10] *Russell v Duke of Norfolk* [1949] 1 All ER 109. Note though the dissenting judgment of Denning LJ, at 119–120, which more accurately represents the position that would come to be adopted by English courts.

[11] *Baker v Jones* [1954] 2 All ER 553.

[12] *Davis v Carew-Pole* [1956] 1 WLR 833.

itself be scrutinised and overturned was a significant development of the law. This much is emphasised by the *dicta* of Megarry V-C in the later case of *McInnes v Onslow-Fane*, concerning a challenge to the British Boxing Board of Control, in the context of the more limited demands of natural justice:

> I think that the courts must be slow to allow any implied obligation to be fair to be used as a means of bringing before the courts for review honest decisions of bodies exercising jurisdiction over sporting and other activities *which those bodies are far better fitted to judge than the courts*. This is so even where those bodies are concerned with the means of livelihood of those who take part in those activities. The concepts of natural justice and the duty to be fair must not be allowed to discredit themselves by making unreasonable requirements and imposing undue burdens. Bodies such as the board which promote a public interest by seeking to maintain high standards in a field of activity which might otherwise become degraded and corrupt *ought not to be hampered in their work without good cause.*[13]

In this context, the judgment in *Eastham v Newcastle United* can be seen as a bold intercession by the High Court. The decision even to consider the legality of the regulatory framework demonstrates a hitherto unseen level of scrutiny. The defendants to the claim had argued strongly that their expertise in, and special appreciation of, matters pertaining to the regulation of football meant that it would be inappropriate for the court even to permit itself jurisdiction to appraise the rules—particularly as similar systems were in place across the globe. Wilberforce J, however, took an important step in determining that the dispute was justiciable:

> It was said that this system, the combined system of registration, retention and transfer fees, or something like it, is operated in all professional leagues and has been so operated for a long time. This is claimed as evidence that those who know best consider it to be in the general interest of the game. I do not accept this line of argument. The system is an employers' system, set up in an industry where the employers have succeeded in establishing a united monolithic front all over the world, and where it is clear that for the purpose of negotiation the employers are vastly more strongly organised than the employees. No doubt the employers all over the world consider the system a good system, but this does not prevent the court from considering whether it goes further than is reasonably necessary to protect their legitimate interests.[14]

Further emphasising this point, Wilberforce J determined that the court's scrutiny was not just limited to the contractual question of *ultra vires* in ensuring compliance with the relevant rules and regulations, but also extended to testing these against the requirements of public policy.[15] Thus, for the first time, a situation arose in which a court was willing to give genuine consideration to the validity of the rules of a sport's governing body. This is of no small significance to

---

[13] *McInnes v Onslow-Fane* [1978] 1 WLR 1520, 1535, author's emphasis. This passage was cited as applicable in restraint of trade cases pertaining to sport by Scott J in *Gasser v Stinson*, Unreported, Queen's Bench Division, 15 June 1988, Scott J, at page 16 of the official transcript.

[14] *Eastham v Newcastle United Football Club* [1964] Ch 413, 438.

[15] *Eastham v Newcastle United Football Club* [1964] Ch 413, 440.

those regulated by such organisations which have "a monopoly in an important field of human activity".[16]

This newfound capacity for scrutiny was accentuated by the court's attitude to the standing of the claimant. The defendant parties to the claim all made arguments to the effect that Eastham was a stranger to the rules of the FA and League and thus had no entitlement to challenge. Further, it was contended that, even were it the case that the rules were unlawful as being in restraint of trade, this had the simple effect of making them unenforceable and that it remained open to the clubs to continue on a voluntary basis. Wilberforce J adopted a realistic view of the rules as being aimed at the employee players and saw their right to seek and secure employment as an important public interest and thus that a declaration could be granted, irrespective of the existence of a cause of action for the claimant.[17]

In taking this position Wilberforce J demonstrated that, in deciding restraint of trade cases, the courts would not necessarily be swayed by the specialist abilities and knowledge of a sport's governing body, nor by the seeming disconnect between the rules and regulations of a sport and those subject to them, even where the restrained party was not a direct party to the agreement giving rise to a restriction.

This perspective set the standard for an expansive approach in following cases, with the restraint of trade doctrine being held to be applicable in a variety of situations: to a suspended *amateur* athlete deriving *indirect* financial reward from her participation in athletics[18]; to a group of Test cricketers banned after agreeing to participate in an "unofficial" competition[19]; and to a football club denied entry to the Football League having failed to satisfy ground-grading criteria.[20] Thus restrictions of an economic nature imposed by a sports governing body, whatever particular form they take, are likely to fall for consideration under the doctrine of restraint of trade following *Eastham v Newcastle United*.[21] But, more than this, the case established the broader modern trend for sports governing bodies to be open to challenge in the English courts as a matter of public policy, particularly where matters of livelihood or reputation are at stake and occasionally irrespective of the existence of an established cause of action.[22]

---

[16] *Russell v Duke of Norfolk* [1949] 1 All ER 109, 119, Denning LJ.

[17] *Eastham v Newcastle United Football Club* [1964] Ch 413, 441–443.

[18] *Gasser v Stinson*, Unreported, Queen's Bench Division, 15 June 1988, Scott J.

[19] *Greig v Insole* [1978] 1 WLR 302.

[20] *Stevenage Borough Football Club v Football League* (1996) *The Times* 1 August 1996; (1997) Admin LR 109 (CA).

[21] Compare however with the position adopted by McKay J in *Chambers v British Olympic Association* [2008] EWHC 2028 (QB) to the effect that a restriction on a small part of an athlete's activities—in this case selection for, and participation in, the Olympic Games—was insufficiently broad to engage the restraint of trade doctrine.

[22] See *Nagle v Feilden* [1966] 1 All ER 689, and in particular the judgment of Denning LJ at 119–120, for an extension of jurisdiction beyond the realms of restraint of trade. See also *Bradley v Jockey Club* [2004] EWHC 2164; [2005] EWCA Civ 1056, as it relates to the extension of a

The *Eastham v Newcastle United* case is also indicative of the vociferous approach to scrutiny of the economic restrictions imposed by sports governing bodies adopted by English courts. Economic consequences for the aggrieved party can be identified as a consistent trigger for the stretching or extension of jurisdiction, if not remediation, before the English courts; much of this approach can be seen to be rooted in the sea change manifested in *Eastham v Newcastle United* and locates this type of litigation firmly in the domain of private law, which is evidenced by the much more conservative approach to standing adopted in claims for judicial review against sports governing bodies in English law.[23] This aspect of sports law is also indicative of the importance of early case law in establishing the approach of the courts—the judgment of the Court of Appeal in *Law v National Greyhound Racing Club*[24] had a profound impact on subsequent judgements; effectively "locking out" sports governing bodies from the judicial review process, and thus *Eastham v Newcastle United* is of great significance in establishing a more liberal early approach in the private law context.

5.4.2 Establishing the Balance in Sports Restraint of Trade Cases

Though the issue of access to the court was decided resoundingly in favour of the claimant, the substantive part of his claim was dealt with in more circumspect manner by the High Court.

In considering whether there was an unreasonable restraint and, if so, whether it was justified, Wilberforce J chose to consider the retention and transfer elements of the rules separately. In terms of the retention system, Wilberforce J stated that to restrain players' liberty to utilise their skills in some other employment, after their employment with a particular club had ceased, would be considered as being contrary to public policy, were it not possible to demonstrate that the restraint was in the interests of both parties and in the public interest.[25] The practical effects of the retention provisions were considered by the judge who noted that they were used by clubs as a tool to obtain a transfer fee for a player who, in reality, they did not wish to retain.[26] Thus, as in this particular case, a situation could arise where a

(Footnote 22 continued)
private law "supervisory jurisdiction" over the decisions of sports governing bodies, irrespective of the existence of a contract or other legal relationship.

[23] See *Law v National Greyhound Racing Club Ltd* [1983] 1 WLR 1302; *R v Jockey Club ex p Aga Khan* [1993] 1 WLR 909; *R (o/a Mullins) v Jockey Club Appeal Board* [2005] EWHC 2197 (Admin). For commentary see Anderson 2006, Beloff 2009, Pannick 1997 and Beloff and Kerr 1996.

[24] *Law v National Greyhound Racing Club Ltd* [1983] 1 WLR 1302.

[25] *Eastham v Newcastle United Football Club* [1964] Ch 413, 428.

[26] *Eastham v Newcastle United Football Club* [1964] Ch 413, 430.

player who was adamant that they would not resign with their existing club could be denied the opportunity to utilise their skills. Wilberforce J considered that placing such players on the retained list would "substantially interfere with their right to seek other employment – and I emphasise this – does so at a time when they are not the employees of the retaining club. That seems to me to operate substantially in restraint of trade".[27]

Wilberforce J then went on to evaluate the transfer system in isolation from the retention provisions. He considered that the transfer system alone imposed a less serious restraint upon the player than the retention system. Even though an out of contract player was still not free to seek employment as long as he remained on the transfer list—except where a club was willing to meet the fee set by his old club—the player had other courses of action open to him. A transfer listed player could apply to the Football League Management Committee for a free transfer if he felt the fee to be excessive. He could also transfer to a club outside of the Football League without payment of a fee. Thus the imposition of the restraint was mitigated in two ways.

Wilberforce J concluded that the combination of retain and transfer operated in unjustifiable restraint of trade, but refused to decide whether the transfer system in itself would also be regarded in this manner.

This is consistent with the later jurisprudence developed in *Bosman*. In that litigation, the Court of Justice of the European Union condemned a Belgian system similar to that of retain and transfer. However, as in *Eastham v Newcastle United*, the court chose not to outlaw the transfer element of the scheme, despite Advocate General Lenz's opinion that the transfer system itself was unlawful as being in breach of European Union competition law. This is not only consistent with the approach adopted in "transfer" cases, but also establishes the pattern evident in a variety of later cases that, while rejecting an absolute exclusion of scrutiny, there has, nevertheless been a good deal of judicial reserve evident in the application of the law to the substance of each case. The attitude assumed has been to delve into the regulatory sphere of sports governing bodies but only to effect change at the margins, leaving the core elements of the regulatory system relatively untouched. This remains true today—even with the much greater interest and involvement of the European Commission in the "transfer" element of professional football, the core principle that players may be tied to their clubs, subject to minor limitations, remains true.[28]

The impact of the judgment is not limited to the domain of legal approaches to "transfer" systems—though the *Eastham v Newcastle United* judgment has had an undoubted influence in this sphere beyond its own jurisdiction[29]—but the case is also an allegory for the "supervisory" approach of the English courts in matters

---

27 *Eastham v Newcastle United Football Club* [1964] Ch 413, 431.

28 See further the debate initiated by the award in CAS 2007/A/1298-1300 *Webster, Hearts & Wigan Athletic FC.*

29 See, for instance: *Blackler v New Zealand Rugby Football League* [1968] NZLR 547; *Elford v Buckley* [1969] 2 NSWR 170; and *Buckley v Tutty* (1971) 125 CLR 353.

pertaining to sports regulation, which was implicit in many such judgments before being made manifest in the judgment of Richards J in *Bradley v Jockey Club*.[30] On this basis, the courts will move to intervene in obvious cases of injustice, but refrain from revision of matters which might be regarded as reasonable in its broadest sense.

From this perspective, *Eastham v Newcastle United* is of particular significance as it establishes the capacity of the courts to consider the legality of the substance of sports governing bodies' rules and regulations, not just the policing of *ultra vires* behaviour within the rules as is largely the case in the contract and public policy cases. These cases are characterised by challenges to measures adopted under a governing body's rules and not to the reasonableness or lawfulness of the rules themselves. Substantive claims on this basis beyond *ultra vires* are largely contingent upon adducing overarching statutory or common law rights, such as those protected under the principles of natural justice, which are consistently read in by courts considering sports regulatory structures. *Eastham* demonstrated and established the capacity of the restraint of trade doctrine to be utilised in direct challenge to those rules and regulations, not just in relation to measures adopted under their auspices.

5.4.3 Sporting Values as Legitimate Objectives for Protection

When considering the question of the reasonableness of the restraints imposed by the system Wilberforce J did not deem the mainstream, established justifications of protection of trade secrets and prevention of canvassing of customers as legitimate interests and also ruled out any suggestion that the employer could prevent the player from using skills acquired through employment with the club.[31]

However, the judge did consider that interests specific to the organisation of football could be regarded as legitimate objects for protection in the context of an action for restraint of trade. Wilberforce J felt that he was able to look beyond the traditional justifications for imposing post-termination restraints, suggesting that others might be considered to be reasonable in the particular circumstances, stating:

> I think it would be wrong to pass straight on to the conclusion that no … interest—and, therefore, no possible justification for the restraint exists. Regard must be had to the special character of the area in which the restraints operate—different from that of industrial employment—and to the special interests of those concerned with the organisation of professional football.[32]

[30] *Bradley v Jockey Club* [2004] EWHC Civ 2164 (QB); [2005] EWCA Civ 1056.

[31] *Eastham v Newcastle United Football Club* [1964] Ch 413, 431.

[32] *Eastham v Newcastle United Football Club* [1964] Ch 413, 432.

During the litigation the defendants had put forward a number of justifications for the retain and transfer system, premised on the special interests and character of professional football. Newcastle United had argued that a contract in restraint of trade was not illegal on the basis that, without that system in place, the wealthier clubs would sign up all the best players and thus a competitive imbalance would arise between the clubs participating in the league competition, with a resultant reduction of uncertainty of outcome of results and parallel decline in interest amongst spectators.

Wilberforce J rejected the defendants' argument that without the retention system in place the richer clubs would, when players became freely available at the end of each season, be in a position to accumulate the best players to the detriment of the public and the majority of the FA and League's member clubs. He suggested that richer clubs already tended to accumulate the better players and did not believe that this would be substantially affected by the abolition of the retention system. This was particularly so because it was open for clubs to award players longer term contracts. Assertions that a player might be worse off under a long-term contract than under the retention system were dismissed by the judge, because of the unlimited time over which a player could be retained, and thus effectively restrained from employment. Wilberforce J also felt that factors such as family ties, loyalty to a club and a desire for first-team football would also stem the agglomeration of players by the wealthier teams.

However, what is noteworthy is the recognition in the judgment of competitive balance as a football-specific, legitimate objective meriting protection, albeit in this case the protection went further than necessary to effect such safeguarding. In addition to noting practical limitations to the concentration of the best players within a few, rich clubs, Wilberforce J also put forward less restrictive alternatives which could legitimately support this objective, such as offering players longer term contracts tying them to the club, making the employment relationship a more balanced and consensual one and eradicating the need for the more severe retention element of the system. In addition, on the subsidiary issue of the maintenance of team stability, Wilberforce J also acknowledged the desirability of clubs being able to build and maintain a team over a period of time—but retained the view that longer, carefully managed player contracts could also legitimately address this concern, as well as repressing the "evil" of the poaching of players.[33]

This contractual approach could, it was said, also address the need to protect clubs' investment in the development and training of young players. Wilberforce J was not wholly convinced of the legitimate nature of this interest. This was principally because there was limited evidence of significant investment by the clubs, but maintained his view that a club's special interest could be protected

33 *Eastham v Newcastle United Football Club* [1964] Ch 413, 436.

adequately through longer term contracts or through a special measure aimed at just those younger players rather than through the imposition of a general restriction applicable to all players.[34]

In considering the transfer system in isolation from the retention element Wilberforce J, whilst acknowledging that it did have a restrictive effect upon players, considered this to be less so and thus requiring of less justification: "[I]t does not appear to me to be so very objectionable".[35]

In this context, the transfer system was regarded as being justified by its redistributive impact between clubs and its capacity to facilitate the movement of players between employers:

> [It] provides a means by which the poorer clubs can, on occasions, obtain money, enabling them to stay in existence and improve their facilities; and, rather more generally, that it provides a means by which clubs can part with a good player in a manner which will allow them to secure a replacement ... Given the need to circulate players, money is necessarily a more efficient medium of exchange than barter, and the system helps both money and players to circulate. Looked at in this way the system might be said to be in the interests of the players themselves.[36]

These elements of the judgment have particular significance as being the first instance, in English law at least, of the acknowledgement of sports specific values as legitimate balancing considerations for a court considering the validity of a sports governing body's measures and rules. More pertinently these have application not only in the context of restraint of trade actions, but also in those cases brought on the basis of breach of contract or public policy and domestic competition law.

5.5 The Practical Effects

The immediate impact of the decision was to force the football authorities, albeit reluctantly,[37] into negotiations with the Professional Footballers Association. The resultant changes were relatively conservative, but a number of modifications were made that were of considerable benefit to professional players.

At the end of each season each League club would be required to specify those of its players it sought to "retain" and those to be placed on the "transfer list". Those players whose services the club sought to retain had to be offered terms and had a period of 28-days in which to agree or decline. If, by 30 June, the player had not resigned with a club then a dispute was presumed to exist, in which case the

[34] This measure now exists worldwide following the amendments to football's transfer system post-*Bosman* i.e., Article 20 of the FIFA Regulations for the Status and Transfer of Players.

[35] *Eastham v Newcastle United Football Club* [1964] Ch 413, 437.

[36] *Eastham v Newcastle United Football Club* [1964] Ch 413, 437–438.

[37] Furmston 1964, 214.

Management Committee of the League could adjudge the situation at the behest of either the player or the club. If the dispute continued beyond 30 July, then a newly created independent tribunal could make a determination in relation to the new contract offered, the question of retention and any transfer fee demanded for transfer listed players. This was to be concluded by the end of September. Of greatest significance, clubs were required to continue to pay players—even though not under contract—at their previously contracted rate.[38]

This approach remained substantially in favour of the clubs and was some distance from any true conception of "free-agency" of the sort that emanated from the aftermath of *Bosman*. In 1978 the system was further reformed, the principle being introduced that players were free to move at the conclusion of their contracted period, irrespective of the wishes of the employer club—though a fee for the player's registration could still be payable by the new club with disputed fees being arbitrated by a "Transfer Tribunal" as required. The amended position was still short of a position of genuine freedom of contract but nonetheless represented a significant shift in the power relations between club and player. It can also be said with a high degree of confidence that, had this system been in place more widely and particularly in Belgium, the *Bosman* litigation and its aftermath would not have arisen in the form that it did.

The shift in the employment relationship cannot, in its entirety, be seen as a consequence of the *Eastham v Newcastle United* decision—some reforms were already underway in parallel with the litigation—but the judgment was undoubtedly a significant component in effecting the change, in the same way that the *Bosman* litigation was a catalyst for fundamental reform of the status of professional players on a global scale.

5.6 Conclusion

In light of the above analysis there is a persuasive body of evidence in support of the conclusion that *Eastham v Newcastle United* is deserving of being accorded "landmark" status. Not only does it represent a watershed in the relations between employee professional players and employer football clubs, but it can be seen as being instrumental in changing that relationship in English law and other Commonwealth jurisdictions.

Moreover, the case has made an indelible imprint on the legal approaches to sports governing bodies in England, with Wilberforce J's pragmatic and insightful approach—both to the justiciability of sporting rules and regulations and the acknowledgement of the validity of sporting interests as legitimate objects for protections—continuing to find favour in England and beyond in the half-century since the judgment.

---

[38] Greenfield and Osborn 1998, 39.

References

Anderson J (2006) An accident of history: why the decisions of sports governing bodies are not amenable to judicial review. Common Law World Rev 35:173–196

Beloff M (2009) Watching out for the googly: judicial review in the world of sport. Judic Rev 14:136–141

Beloff M, Kerr T (1996) Why Aga Khan was wrong. Judic Rev 1:30–33

Dabshceck B (1991) 'A man or a puppet? The football association's 1909 attempt to destroy the association football players' union. Int J Hist Sport 8:221–238

Furmston M (1964) Retain and transfer system offside. Mod Law Rev 27:210–216

Grayson E (1996) The Ralph banks road to *Bosman* via *Eastham*, *Greig v Insole* and beyond. Sport Law J 4:19–23

Greenfield S, Osborn G (1998) Contract and control in the entertainment industry. Ashgate, Aldershot

Taylor M (2001) Beyond the maximum wage: the earnings of football professional in England, 1900–39. Soccer Soc 2:101–118

Magee J (2006) When is a contract more than a contract? Professional football contracts and the pendulum of power. Entertain Sports Law J 4(2) Online. www2.warwick.ac.uk/fac/soc/law/elj/eslj/issues/volume4/number2/magee. Accessed 2 Feb 2012

McArdle D (2000) One hundred years of servitude: contractual conflict in English professional football before *Bosman*. Web J Curr Leg Issues 2 Online. http://webjcli.ncl.ac.uk/2000/issue2/mcardle2.html. Accessed 2 Feb 2012

McArdle D (2002) Ignoring the inevitable: reflections on the intervention of the English courts in football's contract disputes. Eur Sports Manag Q 2:264–275

Pannick D (1997) Judicial review of sports bodies. Judic Rev 2:150–153

Chapter 6
From Bosman to Bernard C-415/93; [1995] ECR I-4921 to C-325/08; [2010] ECR I-2177

Stefaan Van den Bogaert

Abstract The Bosman (Full citation: Case C-415/93 *Union royale belge des sociétés de football association ASBL v Jean-Marc Bosman, Royal club liégeois SA v Jean-Marc Bosman and others and Union des associations européennes de football (UEFA) v Jean-Marc Bosman* [1995] ECR I-4921) proceedings involved a reference from the Court of Appeal, Liège in Belgium seeking a preliminary ruling on two questions raised by a Belgian-born professional footballer, Jean-Marc Bosman, and relating to the compatibility with EU law of certain player transfer rules then applying in European professional football. The questions referred to the Court of Justice of the European Union (CJEU) by the Court of Appeal, Liège for a preliminary ruling were as follows: Articles 48, 85 and 86 of the Treaty of Rome of 25 March 1957 to be interpreted as (i) prohibiting a football club from requiring and receiving payment of a sum of money upon the engagement of one of its players who has come to the end of his contract by a new employing club; (ii) prohibiting the national and international sporting associations or federations from including in their respective regulations provisions restricting access of foreign players from the European Community to the competitions which they organise? In answer, the CJEU held that Article 48 of the EEC Treaty (free movement of workers) precluded the application of rules laid down by sporting associations, under which a professional footballer who is a national of one Member State may not, on the expiry of his contract with a club, be employed by a club of another Member State unless the latter club has paid to the former club a transfer, training or development fee. It also held that Article 48 of the EEC Treaty precluded the application of rules laid down by sporting associations under which, in matches in competitions which they organise, football clubs may field only a limited number of professional players who are nationals of other Member States. The impact that

Stefaan Van den Bogaert, Professor of European Law and Director of the Europa Institute.

S. Van den Bogaert (✉)
Leiden Law School, Leiden University, Steenschuur 25, 2311 ES Leiden, The Netherlands
e-mail: s.van.den.bogaert@law.leidenuniv.nl

J. Anderson (ed.), *Leading Cases in Sports Law*,
ASSER International Sports Law Series, DOI: 10.1007/978-90-6704-909-2_6,

the Bosman judgment has had on the legal, administrative and financial landscape of professional football in Europe has been profound and is accounted for in this chapter with reference inter alia to recent case law, such as the Bernard proceedings, (Full citation: Case C-325/08 *Olympique Lyonnais SASP v Olivier Bernard and Newcastle UFC* [2010] ECR I-2177) and also the continuing debate on efforts to promote "homegrown" players in professional football.

Contents

6.1 Introduction

On 15 December 1995, the undivided attention of the sporting world was focused for once on Luxembourg. That day, the CJEU delivered its judgment in the *Bosman* case,[1] outlawing certain aspects of the traditional transfer system and also the so-called "3+2" nationality clauses in professional football in Europe for infringing the rules on free movement for workers laid down in the European Treaties. In almost no time, this ruling acquired a place in the Court's "Hall of Fame" of legendary judgments.[2] In the first place, this is due to the fact that it called for drastic changes to be put in place in the football industry. As an immediate consequence, clubs could no longer ask for a transfer sum when one of their EU/EEA football players at the end of his contract intended to move to a club in another EU/EEA country. Sporting associations were also no longer authorised to impose limitations on the number of EU/EEA sportsmen to be fielded during official matches. But the actual impact of the decision goes far beyond the mere

[1] Case C-415/93 *Bosman* [1995] ECR I-4921.

[2] From the wealth of analysis, see, for instance, Dubey 2000; O'Keeffe and Osborne 1996; Thill 1996; Van den Bogaert 2005; Weatherill 1999, 346–350 and the four contributions (of respectively Ilesic; Weatherill; Van den Bogaert and Infantino and Mavroidis) in Poiares Maduro and Azoulay 2010, 475–506.

circumstances of the case, or the sphere of football. It yields consequences for sports in general. It can safely be stated that *Bosman* constitutes the genesis of European sports law. It also perfectly illustrates how European law, albeit indirectly via the free movement and/or competition law provisions, also applies to economic aspects in other sectors of society for which the EU may not have been given any—or only complementary—express competence to act. Furthermore, several of the statements of principle established or reaffirmed by the CJEU in *Bosman* have become of great relevance for the development of European law. And, also important, because of all the media attention it received, the *Bosman* case allowed for ordinary European citizens to get acquainted with the existence, role and functioning of Europe's supreme court. It is fair to state that *Bosman* constitutes to date the most well-known judgment in the history of the CJEU. More than fifteen years have now passed since it was rendered. In these years, the judgement has been extensively discussed, debated, applauded and criticised. Here follows yet another account of the case, the judgment and its impact on sports.

6.2 In the Beginning...

In preliminary, it must be observed that the legal setting of the case was not unequivocally clear. Sport had not been included in the original Treaty of Rome. It was the then European Court of Justice that established in 1974 in *Walrave*[3] and reiterated two years later in *Donà*[4] that sport nonetheless forms part of European law insofar as it constitutes an economic activity within the meaning of the European Treaties. Subsequently, the Court proceeded in these cases to address the conformity with EU free movement law of the contested rules of, respectively, the International Cycling Union and the Italian Football Federation.

Contrary to common expectations, these judgments did not lead to a stream of challenges against the compatibility with EU law of certain sports rules and practices before national courts and tribunals. Sporting associations are often formidably powerful and influential private organisations. The ranks were closed in sporting circles. Rather than accepting the applicability of European law, the federations tried to ignore the Court's dicta or comply with them only reluctantly and to the minimum extent possible. The protagonists in *Walrave* were strongly dissuaded from pressing for a judgment before the national court after the then Court of Justice had rendered its preliminary ruling, as the International Cycling Union threatened to remove the discipline in which they were active from the programme of the next World Championships.[5] Moreover, the Italian football

[3] Case 36/74 *Walrave and Koch* [1974] ECR 1405, para 4. Discussed generally at Chap. 3 of this volume.

[4] Case 13/76 *Donà v Mantero* [1976] ECR 1333, para 12.

[5] Van Staveren 1989, 67.

federation even tried to ignore the consequences of the *Donà* decision, although ultimately it was forced to comply with its terms when a similar request for a preliminary ruling was referred to the then Court of Justice.[6] From a practical point of view both decisions appeared thus to have caused nothing but a "storm in a teacup". Afterwards, it was business as usual. Most sporting associations continued to regulate and settle their affairs autonomously, operating on the assumption that they were practically immune from legal intervention from outside. It would effectively take almost 20 years before another dispute concerning sports regulations would reach the stadium of the Court in Luxembourg.

When, in 1990, Jean-Marc Bosman commenced legal proceedings to challenge the rules that prevented him from freely contracting with the club of his choice, even though he was no longer contractually bound to his previous club, he exposed himself to heavy pressure from the football establishment to drop the case or at least come to a settlement out of court. He had to resist various kinds of cunning legal manoeuvres to slow down the process of the case before the various courts. Had it not been for his perseverance, stubbornness and dogged determination to defy the football system, there would simply not have been a *Bosman* case at all. Who knows how long the transfer rules and nationality clauses would have continued to exist without Bosman? Ultimately, one player thus managed to defeat the whole football establishment, a story reminiscent of David's mythical victory over Goliath. The Court's ruling in Bosman's favour clearly conveys the message that citizen's rights are to be taken seriously under EU law. But then again, there is also a darker side: to vindicate his rights, Bosman basically had to sacrifice his career. One career for all players' freedom at the expiry of contracts was a high price to pay.

6.3 *Bosman*: The Facts

It is well worth briefly recalling the facts of the dispute, if only to illustrate the magnitude of the impact of the case. First, it is now a well-established rule that footballers are free to move to another club once they arrive at the end of their contract. The credit for this must entirely go to Jean-Marc Bosman. For this had not always been common practice in professional football. At the material time, and this is not even 25 years ago, Belgian first division football club RC Liège was still entitled to receive a transfer sum for the transfer of one of its players, Jean-Marc Bosman, to French second division club US Dunkerque even if he had served the terms of his contract with RC Liège and was thus no longer contractually bound to the club. The transfer ultimately fell through, because RC Liège refrained from requesting the Belgian Football Association ("KBVB") to send the

[6] Request for a preliminary ruling, presented by an ordonnance of the 'Procura della Repubblica italiana de Salerno', Case 46/79 *Criminal proceedings v Gennaro Brunetti*, 28 April 1979, OJ C 107/14.

international transfer certificate to the French Football Federation ("FFF") and, as a result, Bosman was prevented from playing for another team for the entire 1990–1991 season.[7] He then instituted the legal proceedings which would ultimately bring him to Luxembourg five years later.

Secondly, it is often lost out of sight that this aspect of the football transfer system was not the only rule that was at stake in this case. Bosman also challenged the lawfulness of the then applicable UEFA "3+2" nationality clauses, claiming that these rules could impede his career. According to this "3+2" rule, national associations were permitted to limit to three the number of foreign players whom a club could field in any first division match in their national championships, plus two players who had played in the country of the relevant national association for an uninterrupted period of five years, including three years as a junior. The same "3+2" limitation also applied to matches in UEFA's European Cup competitions for club teams.[8] Again thanks to Mr Bosman this rule appears now as a relic from an already long forgotten past. For instance, in the 2010 UEFA Champions League final, Italian champions Internazionale defeated Germany's Bayern Munich with a team of 4 Argentine footballers, 3 Brazilians, 1 Dutchman, 1 Romanian, 1 player from the Republic of Macedonia and 1 player from Cameroon. Only one Italian came on the pitch, as a substitute, in the dying seconds of the game. Even the coach of the *nerazzurri* was not Italian, but rather the *Special One* from Portugal, José Mourinho. And this is by no means an exceptional example. In sum, *Bosman* liberalised even globalised the labour market for football players in Europe.

6.4 *Bosman*: The CJEU's Judgment

In *Bosman*, the CJEU first dismissed all arguments contesting the Court's jurisdiction to hear the case, firmly reaffirming that sport falls under the scope of EU law to the extent it constitutes an economic activity.

Concerning the contested transfer rules, the Court observed that those rules are "likely to restrict the freedom of movement of players who wish to pursue their activity in another Member State by preventing or deterring them from leaving the clubs to which they belong even after the expiry of their contracts of employment with those clubs, and therefore the transfer rules could be regarded as an obstacle to the freedom of movement of workers."[9]

Turning to the issue of justification, the Court accepted that the aims of maintaining a balance between clubs by preserving a certain degree of equality and

---

[7] Case C-415/93 *Bosman* [1995] ECR I-4921, para 33.

[8] Interestingly, for the purposes of those clauses, nationality was defined in relation to whether the player could be selected to play in a country's national or representative team. See Case C-415/93 *Bosman* [1995] ECR I-4921, para 25.

[9] Case C-415/93 *Bosman* [1995] ECR I-4921, paras 99 and 100.

uncertainty as to results and of encouraging the recruitment and training of young players were, in principle, legitimate objectives, "in view of the considerable social importance of sporting activities, and in particular football, in the Community."[10] This statement remains of crucial importance, for it means that, in the CJEU's view, not every transfer rule is automatically infringing the free movement provisions. It clearly signals the readiness of the Court to regard a particular transfer system in conformity with the Treaty provisions, provided it actually pursues these legitimate aims in a proportionate way. However, this condition ultimately appeared not to be fulfilled by the transfer rules at stake in *Bosman*.

Firstly, the Court rejected the argument that the application of the contested transfer rules was an adequate means of maintaining financial and competitive balance in the world of football. It considered that those rules neither precluded the richest clubs from securing the services of the best players, nor prevented the availability of financial resources from being a decisive factor in competitive sport, thus considerably altering the balance between clubs.[11] Secondly, while acknowledging that the prospect of receiving transfer, development or training fees might indeed likely encourage football clubs to seek new talent and train young players,[12] the Court held that in actuality the prospect of receiving such fees could not be either a decisive factor in encouraging recruitment and training of young players or an adequate means of financing such activities, particularly in the case of smaller clubs.[13] It reached this conclusion on the grounds that: (i) it is impossible to predict the sporting future of young players with any certainty; (ii) only a limited number of such players go on to play professionally; and (iii) the transfer fees are by nature contingent and uncertain and are in any event unrelated to the actual cost borne by clubs of training both future professional players and those who will never play professionally.

In the end, the Court subtly hinted that these aims, even though illegitimate *in se*, "could be achieved at least as efficiently by other means which do not impede the freedom of movement for workers"[14] almost casually referring to the opinion of Advocate General Lenz in this respect.[15] And it left it at that. This unmistakably (and still) constitutes an invitation to the football authorities to develop an alternative transfer system in conformity with the Treaty.

In addition, and concerning the contested nationality clauses, the Court established the existence of an obstacle to the freedom of movement, holding that "in so far as participation in such matches is the essential purpose of a professional player's activity, a rule which restricts that participation obviously also restricts

---

[10] Case C-415/93 *Bosman* [1995] ECR I-4921, para 106.

[11] Case C-415/93 *Bosman* [1995] ECR I-4921, para 107.

[12] Case C-415/93 *Bosman* [1995] ECR I-4921, para 108.

[13] Case C-415/93 *Bosman* [1995] ECR I-4921, para 109.

[14] Case C-415/93 *Bosman* [1995] ECR I-4921, para 110.

[15] Case C-415/93 *Bosman* [1995] ECR I-4921, Opinion of Advocate-General Lenz, paras 226 *et seq.*

the chances of employment of the player concerned."[16] The "3+2" rule also failed to pass the justification hurdle. None of the arguments put forward by the sporting associations and by the intervening governments succeeded in convincing the Court.

First, the CJEU unequivocally quashed the argument based on the role served by the nationality clauses to maintain a traditional link between a club and country. According to the Court, a football club's links with the Member State in which it is established cannot be regarded as any more inherent in its sporting activity than its links with its locality, town or region. It pointed out that there exists no such rule restricting the right of clubs to field players from other regions, towns or localities in official matches either.[17] Secondly, the Court also failed to be convinced by the supposed indispensability of the nationality clauses for the good of the national team. It observed that although the right to freedom of movement "by opening up the employment market in one Member State to nationals of the other Member States, has the effect of reducing workers' chances of finding employment within the Member State of which they are nationals, it also, by the same token, offers them new prospects of employment in other Member States."[18] In addition, the Court noted that football clubs were obliged to release their foreign players for official matches of their national team.[19] Thirdly, the Court also ruled that the nationality clauses are not an appropriate means to preserve a certain competitive equilibrium between clubs: these clauses may prevent the richest clubs from engaging the best foreign players, but there are no rules limiting the possibility for such clubs to recruit the best national players and "thus undermining that balance to the same extent."[20]

6.5 *Bosman* and the Birth of "European Sports Law"

The *Bosman* judgment yielded important and far-reaching consequences both for football specifically in the matter of transfer rules and the nationality clauses, but also for sport and sports law in general. Moreover, *Bosman* conveys the loud and unequivocal message that sportsmen have rights under EU law, and that they can also effectively enforce them before the ordinary courts. Federations have definitively and irrevocably lost their aura of immunity under EU law. They remain primarily competent to organise and regulate any given sporting discipline, but their autonomy is conditional, in the sense that the sporting associations must take into account the exigencies of EU law. By the same token, when dealing with

---

[16] Case C-415/93 *Bosman* [1995] ECR I-4921, para 120.

[17] Case C-415/93 *Bosman* [1995] ECR I-4921 para 131.

[18] Case C-415/93 *Bosman* [1995] ECR I-4921, para 134.

[19] Case C-415/93 *Bosman* [1995] ECR I-4921, para 133.

[20] Case C-415/93 *Bosman* [1995] ECR I-4921, para 135.

sports-related issues, the EU institutions will also have due regard for the specificity of sport.[21] This unquestionably constitutes the most important lesson from *Bosman*.

In the aftermath of *Bosman*, athletes started making use of the possibility of vindicating their EU rights either to or before the European Commission, the General Court and the CJEU.[22] For instance, in *Deliège,* the CJEU was asked to rule on the compatibility with the freedom to provide services of the rules laid down by the responsible judo federations as regards the requirement that professional sportsmen be authorised or selected by their national federation to be able to take part in an international competition.[23] These selection rules inevitably had the effect of limiting the number of participants in a tournament. However, such a limitation was regarded as being "inherent in the conduct of an international high-level sports event, which necessarily involves certain selection rules or criteria being adopted."[24] Therefore, such rules could not in themselves be regarded as constituting a restriction on the principle of freedom of movement.[25]

The *Lehtonen* case concerned a dispute involving a Finnish basketball player wishing to play for a Belgian team in the play-offs after the regular season but registered to play after the transfer deadline. The Court held that the material rules on the transfer deadlines constituted an obstacle to the free movement of workers. However, the Court also acknowledged that "the setting of deadlines of transfers for players may meet the objective of ensuring the regularity of sporting competitions", again displaying openness to the specificity of sport.[26] It further specified that "late transfers might be liable to change substantially the sporting strength of one or the other in the course of the championship, thus calling into question the comparability of results between the teams taking part in that championship, and consequently the proper functioning of the championship as a whole."[27] Ultimately, the CJEU left it to the national court to ascertain whether different transfer windows for players from different countries could be objectively justified.

In the early years after *Bosman*, most sport-related cases invariably concerned that of freedom of movement. Gradually, this picture has changed. Nowadays, the courts also tackle sports cases involving EU competition law issues and most notably in *Meca-Medina*, where the compatibility of the international doping rules with EU competition law was at stake.[28] The CJEU stipulated in principled terms that the compatibility of rules with the Treaty provisions cannot be assessed in the

---

[21] On the "specificity" of sport in an EU context see generally Parrish and Miettinen 2008.

[22] See generally Weatherill 2003; Van den Bogaert and Vermeersch 2006 and Bogusz et al. 2007.

[23] Case C-51/96 and C-191/97 *Deliège* [2000] ECR I-2549, para 42.

[24] Case C-51/96 and C-191/97 *Deliège* [2000] ECR I-2549, para 64.

[25] See further Van den Bogaert 2000.

[26] Case C-176/96 *Lehtonen et al. v FRSB* [2000] ECR I-2681, para 53.

[27] Case C-176/96 *Lehtonen et al. v FRSB* [2000] ECR I-2681, para 54.

[28] Case C-519/04 P *Meca-Medina* [2006] ECR I-6991.

abstract: for the purposes of application of a Treaty provision to a particular case, account must first of all be taken of the overall context in which the rule was taken or produces its effects and, more specifically, of its objectives; then, it has to be considered whether the consequential restrictive effects it produces are *inherent* in the pursuit of those objectives and are *proportionate* to them.[29] Concretely, the Court ruled, first, that the general objective of the contested anti-doping rules was to combat doping, in order for competitive sport to be conducted fairly; and that this included the need to safeguard equal chances for athletes, athletes' health, the integrity and objectivity of competitive sport and ethical values in sport.[30] Secondly, it held that the effect on athletes' freedom of action of the penalties imposed in the federation's rules to enforce the doping ban, must be considered to be, in principle, inherent in the organisation and proper conduct of competitive sport, whose very purpose is to ensure healthy rivalry between athletes.[31] Finally, the CJEU did not find a violation of the proportionality principle. It therefore concluded that the anti-doping rules did not in law constitute a restriction of competition incompatible with the common market even if they in fact had ancillary effects that did restrict competition.[32]

Meca-Medina is an important judgment, perhaps the most important sports-related one since *Bosman*. This certainly has to do with the fact that it concerns doping and that it is the first time the CJEU actually applied EU competition law rules to sport and immediately seems to have set the scene for later decisions, but also because the judgment perfectly illustrates once again how EU law is applied to sports: on a case-by-case basis, requiring compliance with the Treaty provisions but contemporaneously having regard to the specificity of sport.[33]

The *Bosman* judgment has not only led to increased litigation at both a national and EU level but it has also given a renewed impetus to sports-related regulatory activities at EU legislative and policy-making level encapsulated in 2007 by the Commission's White Paper on Sport.[34] Importantly, in the 2009 Lisbon Treaty, sport was included as an official EU policy by way of Article 165TFEU. For the first time, the EU has been given the explicit authorisation to act in the field of sport. The insertion also has a symbolic character, for it "legitimizes" initiatives and actions already taken in the domain of sport. Moreover, Article 165TFEU can be said to demarcate the level playing field of the EU in sport, outlining a division of competences between the EU, its Member States and the sporting associations. The primary competence remains in the hands of the Member States and the federations and EU competence is limited to supporting, coordinating and complementary action. Although Article 165TFEU is not expected to bring about any substantial

---

[29] Case C-519/04 P *Meca-Medina* [2006] ECR I-6991, para 42.

[30] Case C-519/04 P *Meca-Medina* [2006] ECR I-6991, para 43.

[31] Case C-519/04 P *Meca-Medina* [2006] ECR I-6991, para 45.

[32] Case C-519/04 P *Meca-Medina* [2006] ECR I-6991, para 55.

[33] *Meca-Medina is* discussed generally at Chap. 9 of this volume.

[34] White Paper on Sport, COM(2007) 391 final.

changes in the application of the Treaty free movement and competition rules to sport, its very presence illustrates the enduring influence of the *Bosman* judgment. Truly, *Bosman* can be considered as the genesis of EU sports law.

6.6 Football Transfer Rules, Post-*Bosman* and Today

The *Bosman* ruling evidently exerted its most direct and immediate impact on transfer rules and nationality clauses in sports. Concerning transfer rules, the judgment was clear: transfer sums for transfers within the EU/EEA of professional out-of-contract EU/EEA players were incompatible with EU law. It must be remembered that the Court only outlawed this specific aspect of the transfer system; it had not invalidated the entire transfer system. This did not mean that the other aspects of the transfer system, relating to, inter alia, transfers within one Member State, transfers involving third-country nationals or to non-EU/EEA countries, were necessarily compatible with EU law; the Court had simply not expressed itself on these issues and wisely left it to the football authorities to come up with alternatives to the existing system at the time. However, when the football authorities made it plain that they were not going to make any further changes to the transfer system apart from the one to which they were constrained after *Bosman*, the European Commission ultimately started infringement proceedings against some of the residual aspects of the transfer system.

With the unappealing perspective of another "loss" at the CJEU looming in the background, the football authorities, UEFA and FIFA, reluctantly started thoroughly revising football's transfer system, in close consultation with the European Commission. In 2001, a radically renewed transfer system emerged, which managed to secure the approval of the Commission, inducing it to bring an end to the infringement procedure. The main features of the revised FIFA Regulations on the Status and Transfer of Players were the protection of minors; respect for contracts; a new system to compensate clubs for the training of young players; a "solidarity" mechanism; and a new system of dispute resolution.[35] Since 2001, these rules have been slightly amended on a number of occasions. This new transfer system has been widely received as a major improvement. Whether it is now entirely "EU proof" is yet uncertain. The CJEU has not had to pronounce itself on it yet. Until proof of the contrary, the transfer system can thus continue to regulate international transfers of players. This however does not mean that since *Bosman* the transfer rules have gone entirely unchallenged. Two aspects of the new transfer system, namely the rules concerning a training compensation for young players and the rules concerning the respect for contracts, have already led to judicial disputes.

[35] For a detailed analysis see Van den Bogaert 2005, Chap. 5.

On the former issue, the *Bernard* proceedings concerned a dispute about the payment of damages for unilateral breach by the player of his obligations under the French Professional Football Charter applicable at the material time.[36] According to French labour law, football club Olympique Lyonnais was entitled to receive compensation for the training of talented youngster Olivier Bernard after he had left Lyon for Newcastle United in the English Premier League, thereby contravening the rules of the French Professional Football Charter. The French Supreme Court referred the case to Luxembourg for a preliminary ruling.

The CJEU held that rules which require a "joueur espoir", at the end of his training period, under pain of being sued for damages, to sign a professional contract with the club which trained him, are likely to discourage that player from exercising his right of free movement and must therefore be considered as a restriction on freedom of movement for workers.[37] Subsequently, the Court confirmed its admission from *Bosman* that "the objective of encouraging the recruitment and training of young players must be accepted as legitimate."[38] Ultimately, however, the CJEU concluded that the French system could not be upheld because the damages to be paid for unilateral breach of contract were calculated in a way which was unrelated to the actual costs of the training, and therefore went beyond what was necessary to encourage recruitment and training of young players and to fund those activities.[39]

In football circles, there was little concern about Bernard given that since 2001 the new FIFA rules had replaced the French rules at issue. Indirectly, there was an anxiety to hear what, if anything, the CJEU might say about extant FIFA regulations on player transfers. Indeed, the CJEU was explicitly asked to express its opinion on the lawfulness of the FIFA rules under EU law, but refrained from doing so and limited itself to adjudicating solely on the narrow issue at hand. Be that as it may, the CJEU did make a number of statements in the judgment that could be of relevance to assess the conformity of FIFA's regulations with EU law. For example, in para 45 of *Bernard*, the Court stated that a scheme providing for the payment of compensation for training must take "due account of the costs borne by the clubs in training both future professional players and those who will never play professionally." At para 50, the CJEU added that the compensation must not be "unrelated to the actual costs of the training." These appear to be the parameters set by the Court: the compensation for training may be higher than what is strictly needed to train the specific player concerned, but it may not be so high as to be unrelated to the costs of training. Arguably, if the system of training

[36] Case C-325/08 *Bernard* [2010] ECR I-2177.

[37] Case C-325/08 *Bernard* [2010] ECR I-2177, paras 35–37.

[38] Case C-325/08 *Bernard* [2010] ECR I-2177, para 39.

[39] Case C-325/08 *Bernard* [2010] ECR I-2177, paras 48–50.

compensation set out in the FIFA Regulations on the Status and Transfer of Players is considered to remain within these limits, this bodes well for this aspect of the transfer system.[40]

Secondly, the Court of Arbitration for Sport ("CAS") has confronted a number of disputes on the maintenance of contractual stability between professional footballers and clubs. Article 17 of the FIFA Regulations on the Status and Transfer of Players deals with the consequences of unilateral breach of contract without just cause. The provision provides that the party in breach shall always pay compensation. In addition, a sporting sanction shall also be imposed, consisting of a four or six month restriction on playing in official matches, if the breach takes place within the protected period.[41] In the case of *Webster*, involving a Scottish player who moved from Hearts to Wigan after he had served three years of his four-year contract and only after he had been sidelined by Hearts in the preceding months for not agreeing to extend his contract, CAS awarded Hearts a compensation of £150,000, an amount corresponding to Webster's salary for one season, and upheld the two week suspension the FIFA Dispute Resolution Chamber had imposed.[42] This modest compensation fee stands in stark contrast to the compensation CAS awarded in *Matuzalem*. In that dispute, a Brazilian football player, Matuzalem, moved to Real Zaragoza despite a still running contract with Shakthar Donetsk in Ukraine. It was undisputed that the unilateral breach occurred outside the protected period. However, in this instance, CAS imposed a compensation fee of almost €12 million to be paid to the Ukrainian club, taking into account not only the salary of the player but also his market value and the club's lost earnings, i.e., the missed transfer fee.[43] On appeal on 28 March 2012, the Swiss Federal Court ruled that CAS had committed a serious and manifest infringement of the rights of the Brazilian player. Much legal uncertainty about Article 17 FIFA Regulations remains and one must always be careful not to draw too many general conclusions or precedent about fact-specific arbitration awards. A CJEU ruling on the conformity of Article 17 with EU law might be necessary. Does another *Bosman* await?

6.7 Nationality Clauses, Post-*Bosman* and Today

Bosman also had a significant impact on the use of nationality clauses in sport. It must however not be forgotten that *Bosman* was not the first judgment of the CJEU in which it expressed itself on nationality discrimination in sports. In *Walrave*, the

[40] See further Van den Bogaert 2010.

[41] The protected period amounts to a period of two or three years after the signing of the contract, depending on whether the player was over or under 28 years old at the time of signing the contract.

[42] CAS 2007/A/1298-1300 *Webster, Hearts & Wigan Athletic FC*.

[43] CAS 2008/A/1519-1520 *Matuzalem, FC Shakhtar Donetsk (Ukraine) & Real Zaragoza SAD (Spain)*.

Court adopted a hands-off approach in relation to matches between national teams, ruling that the free movement provisions "do not prevent the adoption of rules or of a practice excluding foreign players from participation in certain matches for reasons which are not of an economic nature, which relate to the particular nature and context of such matches and are thus of sporting interest only."[44] It immediately added, though, that the "restriction on the scope of the provisions in question must remain limited to its proper objective and cannot be relied upon to exclude the whole of a sporting activity" from the scope of the Treaty.[45] Conversely, in *Donà*, the Court for the first time ruled out nationality discrimination in sport, holding that a rule allowing only nationals to take part in matches organised by the responsible national federation was contrary to Articles 18, 45 and 56 TFEU.

The Court's subsequent dismissal of the "3+2" nationality clauses in *Bosman* appears to close the door for sporting federations to treat domestic players more favourably than foreign players with the nationality of a country belonging to the EU or the European Economic Area.[46] The *Bosman* decision forced the sporting associations to fully liberalise the EU sports employment market for sportsmen from EU/EEA countries. In the wake of the *Bosman* ruling, entire hordes of EU/EEA athletes have made use of their free movement rights. In football, foreign players nowadays take up a significant portion of the total number of players in any given league in Europe. Sport can be considered as a paradigm of migration in Europe. As a result, a typical team squad in many a sporting discipline is nowadays composed of a mixture of national players, EU citizens and also third-country nationals.

Be that as it may, to be perfectly clear, the Court's ruling in *Bosman* did not signal the end of nationality clauses at club level. The judgment only concerned the Treaty rights of EU/EEA citizens. Many sporting associations decided to cling to quota with regard to third-country nationals. In 2003, the Court was invited for the first time to express its opinion on the legality of such nationality requirements. *Kolpak* involved a professional handball goalkeeper of Slovak nationality who played in the German second division and who challenged the rule of the German handball federation, stipulating that clubs were entitled to field only two non-EU/EEA nationals in official matches.[47] At the material time, Slovakia was not yet an EU Member State. The Court concluded that Kolpak, who was legally employed in Germany, could legitimately invoke Article 38(1) of the Association Agreement concluded between the European Communities and Slovakia, which conferred the right to equal treatment to Slovak nationals as regards working conditions, remuneration and dismissal in the EU in relation to the host Member State's

[44] Case 36/74 *Walrave and Koch* [1974] ECR 1405, para 8. See also Case 13/76 *Donà v Mantero* [1976] ECR 1333, para 14 and Case C-415/93 *Bosman* [1995] ECR I-4921, paras 76 and 127.

[45] Case 13/76 *Donà v Mantero* [1976] ECR 1333, paras 14–15 and Case C-415/93 *Bosman* [1995] ECR I-4921, paras 76 and 127.

[46] Case C-415/93 *Bosman* [1995] ECR I-4921, paras 115–120.

[47] Case C-438/00 *Deutscher Handballbund eV v Kolpak* [2003] ECR I-4135.

nationals.[48] Again, the CJEU showed no inclination to accept the arguments to justify the contested rule, which were grossly the same as in *Bosman*.[49]

The potential impact of this decision is far-reaching: the EU have concluded international agreements containing a similar equal treatment clause with a large number of third-countries and, arguably, a lot of them seem to fulfil the criteria for direct effect.[50] Admittedly, the dispute in *Kolpak* concerned a national from a country that was, at the time of the proceedings, on the verge of becoming an EU Member State. The impression could therefore not entirely be discarded that the final outcome, in particular the CJEU's stance on the justification issue, might have been different had the case involved a sportsman from a non-accession country. After *Kolpak*, the situation was thus not completely clarified yet. An excellent occasion to settle the issue presented itself two years later.

In *Simutenkov*, a Russian footballer playing for Tenerife complained about the fact that the Spanish football federation had issued a licence as a non-Community player, subjecting him to the quota for non-EU/EEA nationals.[51] In its judgment, the CJEU followed exactly the same line of reasoning as in *Kolpak*, enabling Simutenkov to base his claim for an EU licence directly on Article 23(1) of the Partnership Agreement concluded between the EU and Russia. The Court refrained from entering into an in-depth analysis of the justification issue, seemingly conveying the message that the hard line it had previously adopted with regard to nationality discrimination of EU/EEA nationals is to be extended to privileged third-country nationals. For these non-EU/EEA sportsmen to be able to challenge nationality clauses, it suffices that they are legally employed in a host EU Member State and can rely upon a directly effective equal treatment provision included in an international agreement establishing a partnership between the EU and their country of origin, regardless of whether accession to the EU is envisaged or not. In strict legal terms therefore, the lifeline of nationality clauses at club level in sport appears now thinner than ever, certainly bearing in mind the well-established practice in some (southern) European countries to relatively easily offer third-country nationals (especially South Americans) a national passport and thus also EU citizenship status through a quick naturalisation procedure.

Nevertheless, many sporting federations still have not abandoned the idea of nationality clauses altogether and this despite the fact that a radical reversal of the Court's approach with regard to nationality requirements also appears unlikely at this point. FIFA has for quite some time continued to debate the introduction of a "6+5" rule, according to which clubs must start official matches with 6 players eligible to play for the national team of the club's country. The rule received strong backing in football circles, but as it is clearly at odds with the *Bosman*

48 Case C-438/00 *Deutscher Handballbund eV v Kolpak* [2003] ECR I-4135, para 58.

49 Case C-438/00 *Deutscher Handballbund eV v Kolpak* [2003] ECR I-4135, paras 53–57.

50 See the contemporaneous case notes by Dubey 2005 and Van den Bogaert 2004.

51 Case C-265/03 *Simutenkov v Ministerio de Educación y Cultura and RFEFl* [2005] ECR I-2579.

judgment, FIFA has so far refrained from introducing it.[52] Within Europe, the European football association, UEFA, has adopted a home-grown rule, providing that each club must have a certain number of domestically trained players under contract. This rule applies only for matches in UEFA competitions, but UEFA encourages the national federations to apply it domestically. According to this "4+4" rule, a minimum four players out of a squad of maximum 25 must have received their training at the club itself; another four must have been trained by other clubs from the same country. At first sight, UEFA's home-grown rule appears to be favouring local players and therefore inevitably runs the risk of being qualified as indirectly discriminatory. Nonetheless, there is large—and also significant political—support for this rule, including at an EU level. Certainly, if this rule were to be challenged it would provide the CJEU with another excellent opportunity to clarify the position of the EU on nationality clauses.

Interestingly, so far, little attention had been paid to nationality discrimination in individual sports. A recent study for the European Commission on equal treatment of non-nationals in individual sports has shown that in many, if not most, individual sports regulations in the 27 EU Member States, instances of nationality discrimination, direct or indirect, still occur.[53] A lot of work thus remains to be done in this field.

6.8 Conclusion

Bosman may not have been the first sports-related judgment of the CJEU, but it was certainly the first that caught everyone's attention. *Bernard* illustrates that more than fifteen years, many judicial proceedings, legislative activities and policy documents later, *Bosman* remains the point of departure and centre of gravity—the Alpha and Omega if you like—of an entire body of law that has moved beyond merely transfer rules and nationality clauses and can now safely be termed European sports law. In sum, *Bosman* is still good law but it will be interesting to see whether that will still be the case in ten years or so ….

References

Bogusz B, Cygan A, Szyszczak E (eds) (2007) The regulation of sport in the European Union. Edward Elgar Publishing, Cheltenham

Dubey JP (2000) La libre circulation des sportifs en Europe. Bruylant, Brussels

[52] An "Expert Opinion" by the Institute for European Affairs in Dusseldorf concluded that the "6+5 Rule" could be seen to be compatible with EU Law. The report is available online at http://inea-online.com/download/regel/gutachten_eng.pdf. Accessed 31 July 2012.

[53] See further TMC Asser Institute et al. 2010.

Dubey JP (2005) Case note on *Kolpak*. Common Market Law Rev 42:499–522
O'Keeffe D, Osborne P (1996) L'affaire Bosman: un arrêt important pour le bon fonctionnement du Marché Unique Européen. Revue du Marché Unique Européen 1:17–44
Parrish R, Miettinen S (2008) The sporting exception in European Union law. TMC Asser Press, The Hague
Poiares Maduro M, Azoulay L (eds) (2010) The past and future of EU law—the classics of EU law revisited on the 50th anniversary of the Rome Treaty. Hart, Oxford
Thill M (1996) 'L'arrêt "Bosman" et ses implications pour la libre circulation des sportifs à l'intérieur de l'Union Européenne dans des contextes factuels différents de ceux de l'affaire "Bosman". Revue du Marché Unique Européen 1:89–117
TMC Asser Institute et al (2010) Study on the equal treatment of non-nationals in individual sports competitions, Tender No EAC/19/2009. Commissioned by the European Commission, Directorate-General for Education and Culture, Brussels
Van den Bogaert S (2000) The Court of Justice on the Tatami: Ippon, Wazari or Koka. Eur Law Rev 25:554–563
Van den Bogaert S (2004) And another uppercut from the Court of Justice to nationality requirements in sports regulations. Eur Law Rev 29:267–275
Van den Bogaert S (2005) Practical regulation of the mobility of sportsmen in the EU post Bosman. Kluwer Law International, The Hague
Van den Bogaert S (2010) De zaak Bernard: het Hof van Justitie van de EU laat opleidingsvergoedingen toe in het Voetbal. Nederlands Tijdschrift voor Europees Recht 8:265–272
Van den Bogaert S, Vermeersch A (2006) Sport and the EC Treaty: a tale of uneasy bedfellows? Eur Law Rev 31:821–840
Van Staveren H (1989) Proceedings of the 18th colloquyum on European law: sport and the law. Council of Europe, Strasbourg
Weatherill S (1999) "European Football Law" in Collected courses of the Academy of European Law, vol VII, Book I. Kluwer Law International, The Hague, pp 339–382
Weatherill S (2003) 'Fair Play Please': recent developments in the application of EC law to sport. Common Market Law Rev 40:51–93

Part III
When the Private Business of Sport Becomes the Public Business of Law

Chapter 7
Finnigan v NZRFU (1985)

Chris Davies

Abstract When the New Zealand Rugby Football Union ("NZRFU") accepted an invitation to tour South Africa in 1985, two plaintiffs sought an injunction to prevent the All Blacks from leaving the country. The main issue was of standing, with it being held that, despite the plaintiffs not being members of the NZRFU, there were interlocking contracts with the local clubs, of which they were members, which provided a sufficient link with the national governing body. An injunction was therefore granted on the basis that there was a prima facie case that it was in the public and national interest that the tour be prevented from taking place. Accordingly, the tour was cancelled, even though the matter did not go to a full trial. Within a decade, the All Blacks were playing against South Africa and the apartheid system, which the plaintiffs were opposed to, had been abandoned. The Finnigan proceedings encapsulate the relationship between sport and politics but also have some relevance to contemporary sport's attitude to racism and discrimination on the field of play.

Contents

C. Davies (✉)
School of Law, James Cook University, Queensland, Australia
e-mail: chris.davies@jcu.edu.au

J. Anderson (ed.), *Leading Cases in Sports Law*,
ASSER International Sports Law Series, DOI: 10.1007/978-90-6704-909-2_7,

7.1 Introduction

The 1995 Rugby World Cup ("RWC"), held in South Africa, culminated in the sight of the South African President, Nelson Mandela, and South African rugby captain, Francois Pienaar, standing together on the victory dais, both clad in green Springbok jerseys bearing the number six. It was a sight unimaginable, and unthinkable, even four years earlier when South Africa had not been allowed to participate in the previous RWC, and when Mandela had only just been released from jail after spending 27 years as a political prisoner. It was also just ten years after two New Zealand rugby supporters had taken legal action to successfully prevent the New Zealand All Blacks from commencing a tour to South Africa in 1985. This paper will examine the stated proceedings, *Finnigan v New Zealand Rugby Football Union Inc*,[1] in regard to the politics of the time and the legal issues it raised, before looking at its long-term significance in relation to sport and to sports law. First, however, a brief examination of sport's involvement in the international opposition to South Africa's apartheid system is needed.

7.2 Sport and the Apartheid System

The apartheid system involved the situation where the original inhabitants of the country were denied political rights by the ruling white minority in South Africa. It was a system that not only prevented non-whites from being able to vote and hold down government jobs, but also the opportunity to represent South Africa in sport.[2] The inequity of this situation was highlighted by the case of coloured cricketer, Basil D'Oliveira, who had captained a non-white South African team against Kenya in 1956, but in 1960 was forced to move to England in order to further his cricketing career.[3] He played for five years in the Central Lancashire League with Middleton before joining English County side, Worcestershire,

---

[1] Note that there are in fact three decisions relating to this case: *Finnigan v New Zealand Rugby Football Union Inc (No 1)* [1985] 2 NZLR 159 covers the initial application for an interlocutory injunction, *Finnigan v New Zealand Rugby Football Union Inc (No 2)* [1985] 2 NZLR 181 involves the interim interlocutory decision, while *Finnigan v New Zealand Rugby Football Union Inc (No 3)* [1985] 2 NZLR 190 involves the application to the Court of Appeal for conditional leave to appeal to the Privy Council.

[2] It is usually taken that the only coloured cricketer to have represented South Africa before the abolishment of apartheid was Charles Llewellyn who played in the early 1900s and was a member of the 1910–1911 South African team that toured Australia. However, when this claim was made in the mid-1970s by a cricket historian, Llewellyn's surviving daughter denied that he was either "coloured" or, as had also been claimed, ever racially abused by teammates. See further Merrett 2002, 26.

[3] Wilde 2011, 40.

earning his first English cap in 1966 at the age of 34, and going on to play a total of 44 Test matches.[4]

In 1968, D'Oliveira's selection for England became a major international political issue. After scoring 158 against the Australian touring team, he was initially left out of the England team that was subsequently selected to tour South Africa. However, when another player had to withdraw due to injury, D'Oliveira was called into the team. South African Prime Minister, John Forster, immediately claimed that "the MCC team is not the team of the MCC but of the anti-apartheid movement."[5] A little over a week later the MCC had cancelled the tour in what was to become the first of many tours of South Africa cancelled by countries opposed to apartheid.[6] Although the 1970 South African rugby union tour of Australia meanwhile did go ahead, it was marked by strong protests before, during and after each of the Test matches. The 1971–1972 South African cricket tour of Australia, however, was cancelled, with Australian cricket having no official contact with South Africa until the early 1990s.

Reflecting on the sport-related responses to South Africa's apartheid system, it should be noted that Australia, one of the countries which led the way in regard to sporting boycotts, did not allow Indigenous Australians to have the vote until 1962, and they were not considered to be citizens of their country until 1967. Restrictive government policies also had a great impact on their ability to be involved in sport. Cricket, for instance, quickly became an established sport in Australia soon after European settlement, and, despite the fact that the first touring team to England in 1868 was an all-Indigenous side, over the next hundred years or so very few Indigenous Australians reached the pinnacle of sport in Australia due to blatantly racist and protective policies of successive Australian governments. While Indigenous Australians considered suitable to be integrated into mainstream Australian society were removed from their families, others were required to live on missions where, under the relevant legislation, such as the Protection of Aborigines Act and the Restriction of the Sale of Opium Act 1897 (Qld), they had to seek permission from appropriate authorities if they wanted to even temporarily leave the mission.[7]

New Zealand proved to be more accommodating than Australia in regard to both making tours of South Africa and allowing South African teams to tour New

---

[4] Wilde 2011, 40. D'Oliveira scored 2,484 runs for England at an average of 40.06 and also took 47 Test wickets.

[5] Obituary, *The Australian*, 12.

[6] The MCC is the Marylebone Cricket Club. Formed in 1787, the MCC, rather than the English Cricket Board, selected English teams for overseas tours up until the 1980s.

[7] For instance, this was the situation that faced Queensland fast bowler, Eddie Gilbert, during the 1930s. Despite the fact that he had the talent to play cricket at first-class level, including impressive first-class figures of 87 wickets at 28.97, and despite the fact that he had dismissed Don Bradman for duck in a Sheffield Shield match in Brisbane in 1931, his opportunities to play were restricted by his race. For more information on Gilbert's career see Colman and Edwards 2002.

Zealand. These tours, however, did not take place without considerable public backlash and especially from the late 1960s. In *Parsons v Burk*,[8] for instance, the plaintiff sought a court order to prevent the All Blacks from leaving New Zealand for a tour of South Africa and Southern Rhodesia (now Zimbabwe). The application was made seeking a writ of *ne exeat regno*.[9] Hardie Boys J stated that this was a writ "originally issued in attempts against the safety of the State" and could be used "to prevent any subject from quitting the country."[10] In times of peace it was limited to cases involving "absconding debtors or persons evading justice", though it "might possibly still be used as a State writ to prevent persons leaving the realm in time of war."[11] His Honour then stated that even historically it was only speculation as to when a private citizen could take such a writ to the Chancellor, and even then it was likely only to be taken out "for the King so that at least it must have been for the same purposes – great political objects and purposes of State, for the safety and benefit of the realm". It was then held that as the "application lacks either qualification, it must fail accordingly."[12]

New Zealand faced further public unrest throughout the 1970s and, eventually, legal action, when the Springboks toured in 1981. Similar to the 1970 Springboks tour of Australia, it was marked by continuous protests by many New Zealand citizens with Casey J later commenting that the tour "was a disaster both for rugby football and for the community". It was a sign that New Zealand was a country widely, and sometimes violently, split over the issue of its sporting contact with South Africa, with "otherwise perfectly respectable people at odds with the law for the first time."[13] As there had been in 1970, there was also an attempt to prevent the tour taking place through legal processes. In *Ashby v Minister of Immigration*,[14] the plaintiffs claimed that the decision of the Minister of Immigration to grant temporary entry permits to the Springboks was invalid. This was based on the argument that the Minister, when exercising this discretion to grant such visas, had to take into consideration, and be consistent with, the 1965 International Convention on the Elimination of all Forms of Racial Discrimination. This had been ratified by New Zealand[15] and implemented into domestic law by the Race Relations Act 1971.[16] It was noted by Richardson J that Article 3 of the 1965 Convention expressly condemned racial segregation and apartheid,[17] and he also noted that Article 6 of the 1977 International Declaration against Apartheid in

---

8 *Parsons v Burk* [1971] NZLR 244.

9 *Parsons v Burk* [1971] NZLR 244.

10 *Parsons v Burk* [1971] NZLR 244, 246.

11 *Parsons v Burk* [1971] NZLR 244, 246.

12 *Parsons v Burk* [1971] NZLR 244, 247.

13 *Finnigan v New Zealand Rugby Football Union Inc (No 2)* [1985] 2 NZLR 181, 184.

14 *Ashby v Minister of Immigration* [1981] 1 NZLR 222.

15 *Ashby v Minister of Immigration* [1981] 1 NZLR 222, 223.

16 *Ashby v Minister of Immigration* [1981] 1 NZLR 222, 224.

17 *Ashby v Minister of Immigration* [1981] 1 NZLR 222, 227.

Sports held that "states shall deny visas and/or entry to representative of sports bodies, members of teams or individual sportsmen from any country practising apartheid."[18]

His Honour, however, pointed out that "if the terms of the domestic legislation are clear and unambiguous they must be given effect in our Courts whether or not they carry out New Zealand's international obligations."[19] It was then held that the language of the relevant section, section 14(1) of the Immigration Act 1964, was "clear and unequivocal" and "where the statutory criteria are met the Minister's discretion to grant or refuse a temporary permit is not expressly fettered in any way."[20] Richardson J therefore dismissed the appeal stating that it was "common ground that the Minister has given due consideration to the Government's perception of the national interest in exercising his discretion under s 14 in this case."[21] His decision was supported by Cooke J, and also Somers J, who made a pertinent comment at the end of his judgment when he stated:

> I would wish only to add that this appeal raised matters of great importance and some difficulty. For obvious reasons a decision on this matter is called for today. For my part I regret that there has not been available a greater time for reflection upon the issues raised.[22]

The case therefore illustrated that, despite the high aims of international law, it is always weakened by the fact that it is not, strictly speaking, law in any country, and the wording of the domestic legislation will have legal priority. Accordingly, from a legal perspective, the decision by the High Court to uphold the Minister's granting of visas was the correct one, despite the fact that the decision would appear to contradict international conventions. Whether it was morally the right decision was another matter, many New Zealanders indicating their belief that it was not by demonstrating throughout the tour. This included the dropping of flour bombs from helicopters over fields while matches were being played.

Despite New Zealand allowing the Springboks to tour in 1981, it was also clear that sporting bans were having an impact on sports loving South Africans. Its response was to tempt players with significant financial incentives to make rebel tours with unofficial cricket teams from Australia, England and the West Indies all touring South Africa at this time. In New Zealand, meanwhile, the decision in early 1985 by the NZRFU to accept an invitation for an All Blacks side to tour South Africa raised the possibility of an official side representing New Zealand in that country. It was a decision that not only re-opened public wounds, still unhealed from 1981, but also gave the New Zealand High Court another opportunity to examine the legal situation regarding New Zealand's willingness to

---

[18] *Ashby v Minister of Immigration* [1981] 1 NZLR 222, 228.

[19] *Ashby v Minister of Immigration* [1981] 1 NZLR 222, 229.

[20] *Ashby v Minister of Immigration* [1981] 1 NZLR 222, 229.

[21] *Ashby v Minister of Immigration* [1981] 1 NZLR 222, 229, 231.

[22] *Ashby v Minister of Immigration* [1981] 1 NZLR 222, 229, 234.

continue playing sport against South Africa when an injunction was sought to prevent the All Blacks from leaving the country.

7.3 Finnigan v New Zealand Rugby Football Union

7.3.1 Background Facts

On 17 April 1985, the NZRFU Council formally accepted an invitation from the South African Rugby Board ("SARB") for a New Zealand representative side to tour South Africa.[23] The plaintiffs in the subsequent proceedings were members of the Auckland University Rugby Football Club and the Teachers' Rugby Football Club. They challenged the validity of the NZRFU Council's decision, claiming it was invalid on the grounds that it had not been made in accordance with the NZRFU's rules. An injunction was therefore sought to prevent the decision from being implemented.[24]

7.3.2 The Initial Injunction Decision

The initial application for an injunction to prevent the proposed tour from proceeding was heard by Davison CJ on 6 and 10 June during which the NZRFU attempted to strike out the plaintiffs' actions. His Honour noted that the NZRFU had the power to accept the invitation from the SARB to tour South Africa,[25] and held "that the plaintiffs had no cause of action against the defendants at all."[26] This was on the grounds that they were not actual members of the NZRFU and therefore had no contractual relationship with that body.[27] The Chief Justice therefore dismissed the plaintiff's actions. The plaintiffs immediately appealed and the Court of Appeal heard the matter on 18 and 21 June.[28]

On appeal, Cooke J first noted that amendments had been made to the initial submissions and that "the hearing of the appeal covered considerably wider ground than the High Court hearing."[29] His Honour stated that "standing to a claim that an incorporated association controlling a sport has acted beyond its powers may be accorded to a person affected, even though he is not a member or in

[23] *Finnigan v New Zealand Rugby Football Union Inc (No 1)* [1985] 2 NZLR 159 at 161.
[24] *Finnigan v New Zealand Rugby Football Union Inc (No 1)* [1985] 2 NZLR 159, 161.
[25] *Finnigan v New Zealand Rugby Football Union Inc (No 1)* [1985] 2 NZLR 159, 172.
[26] *Finnigan v New Zealand Rugby Football Union Inc (No 1)* [1985] 2 NZLR 159, 174.
[27] *Finnigan v New Zealand Rugby Football Union Inc (No 1)* [1985] 2 NZLR 159, 170.
[28] *Finnigan v New Zealand Rugby Football Union Inc (No 1)* [1985] 2 NZLR 159, 175.
[29] *Finnigan v New Zealand Rugby Football Union Inc (No 1)* [1985] 2 NZLR 159, 178.

contractual relationship with the body."[30] Accordingly, although the plaintiffs were not contracted directly to the NZRFU, nevertheless, as local club members, they were "linked to it by a chain of contracts" and were therefore "part of the structure of the whole organisation."[31] It was also Cooke J's opinion that the plaintiffs could not be "dismissed as mere busybodies, cranks or other mischief makers" and "unless persons such as the plaintiffs are accorded standing, it may be well be that in reality there is no effective way of establishing whether or not the [NZRFU] is acting within its lawful powers."[32] Thus, once the plaintiffs had been granted standing, the decision as to whether an injunction should be granted could now be heard. In addition, the question now rested on whether the NZRFU had acted against its objects of promoting, fostering and developing the game of rugby in New Zealand.[33]

7.3.3 The Interim Injunction Decision

The trial for an interim injunction was heard in the High Court by Casey J on 11, 12 and 13 of July 1985, the dates in themselves being of note since they indicated both sides had underestimated the complexity of the case and as a consequence, just days before the All Blacks were due to leave for South Africa, the matter had not yet been finalised by the court. It was Casey J's opinion that the plaintiffs had a prima facie case that the present tour would not benefit New Zealand rugby, taking into account the evidence that the community remained divided, as it had been since 1981, over the issue of sporting contacts with South Africa. His Honour also noted the unanimous House of Representatives statement against the tour and "Mr Finnigan's evidence of a peaceful protest of some 26,000 people filling Queen St [Auckland]."[34] Casey J also noted the "unique importance" of the decision, both in regard to the effect it could have on New Zealand's relationship with other countries, and on its own community.[35] Casey J held:

> I am satisfied that such a situation requires that body [NZRFU] (or any other in a similar position) to exercise more than good faith in reaching its decision; it must also exercise that degree of care which it had been found appropriate to impose on statutory bodies in the exercise of their powers affecting the legal rights or legitimate expectation of the public. Broadly speaking, on this basis the [NZRFU] Council must act reasonably as well as honestly, paying regard to the relevant considerations for the benefit of New Zealand rugby...The interest of the public and of the nation in not having the tour go ahead is a most potent factor...The tour is contrary to a clear direction from the Government because

30 *Finnigan v New Zealand Rugby Football Union Inc (No 1)* [1985] 2 NZLR 159, 178.

31 *Finnigan v New Zealand Rugby Football Union Inc (No 1)* [1985] 2 NZLR 159, 178.

32 *Finnigan v New Zealand Rugby Football Union Inc (No 1)* [1985] 2 NZLR 159, 179.

33 *Finnigan v New Zealand Rugby Football Union Inc (No 1)* [1985] 2 NZLR 159, 180.

34 *Finnigan v New Zealand Rugby Football Union Inc (No 2)* [1985] 2 NZLR 181, 185.

35 *Finnigan v New Zealand Rugby Football Union Inc (No 2)* [1985] 2 NZLR 181, 186.

> of the harm it would do to our national interests; to the unanimous resolution of the Parliament for the serious harm it would do to New Zealand's interest at home and abroad; and to the spirit of the Gleneagles Agreement to which the country is fully committed. There is also the risk of violence and bloodshed – even loss of life – to black Africans so eloquently testified to by Mr Sofile.[36]

An injunction was therefore granted on 13 July (damages were, unsurprisingly, considered to be an inadequate remedy) and the plaintiffs gave an undertaking to cover any losses. Two days later, on 15 July, the Chairman of the NZRFU, Mr C Blazey, made the announcement that it would not be practical for the tour of South Africa to go ahead.[37] It follows that a feature of the case was that the plaintiffs were able to achieve their objective on the basis of establishing no more than a prima facie case since no trial was actually heard to decide the issue. The NZRFU, however, lodged an application to the Court of Appeal seeking leave to appeal to the Privy Council on the matter; despite the fact that such a ruling could not affect the decision not to tour. Indeed, that application was not heard until November and December 1985, long after the tour had been cancelled.

7.3.4 The Privy Council Appeal Application

The ground for the application was in relation "to the extent that the judgment was adverse to the union [NZRFU]."[38] In the early part of his judgment, Cooke J noted:

> In circumstances of such importance in the history of the sport in New Zealand it seemed to this Court right that persons lawfully associated with the sport should be able to obtain a ruling from the Courts as to whether the acceptance of the invitation had been in accordance with the Union's constitution.[39]

Cooke J went on to state that the courts had "remained open" to hear all of the NZRFU's evidence and contentions,[40] and it had only been by agreement of the parties that retaining the injunction was deemed unnecessary. Further, there was, he observed, no need for an actual trial to decide the matter as the tour had been abandoned for practical, time-related reasons.[41] Accordingly, given that it could not be ignored the proposed appeal was "academic" on the substantive issue, Cooke J held that leave should not be granted and the motion dismissed.[42]

---

[36] *Finnigan v New Zealand Rugby Football Union Inc (No 2)* [1985] 2 NZLR 181, 186–188. Mr Stofile was a Presbyterian Minister from South Africa who was a witness for the plaintiffs.

[37] *Finnigan v New Zealand Rugby Football Union Inc (No 2)* [1985] 2 NZLR 181, 189.

[38] *Finnigan v New Zealand Rugby Football Union Inc (No 3)* [1985] 2 NZLR 190, 192.

[39] *Finnigan v New Zealand Rugby Football Union Inc (No 3)* [1985] 2 NZLR 190, 193.

[40] *Finnigan v New Zealand Rugby Football Union Inc (No 3)* [1985] 2 NZLR 190, 196.

[41] *Finnigan v New Zealand Rugby Football Union Inc (No 3)* [1985] 2 NZLR 190, 197.

[42] *Finnigan v New Zealand Rugby Football Union Inc (No 3)* [1985] 2 NZLR 190, 199.

Richardson J expressed similar views, stating that to grant leave in this case would "be contrary to the well-settled principle that in the exercise of discretion leave must be refused where the substratum of the present litigation between the parties has gone and there is no matter remaining in actual controversy and requiring decision."[43] McMullan J opined that because "the present case was rather unique – both as to the nature of the tour and the situation of the plaintiffs",[44] it was unlikely that a decision on standing in *Finnigan* would provide a binding precedent as it was unlikely that future proceedings would involve plaintiffs "linked to the Union in the very same way as these plaintiffs were linked."[45] Further, he argued, it was also likely that "the constitution and rules of other sporting bodies may differ from those of the Union."[46] McCarthy J, meanwhile, acknowledged that there were some grounds for the Union's fears that the ruling in the case left it open for people without voting rights, and with only a distant connection to the sport, now having the capacity to influence and restrain decisions made by sporting organising bodies. Nevertheless, McCarthy J still held that the "substance of the plaintiff's case for relief" had effectively dissipated.[47] Finally, Somers J, likewise, agreed with such reasoning,[48] and thus leave was unanimously refused.

7.4 Significance of *Finnigan*

What was clearly accepted by the various judges in the above proceedings was that, in the specific words of Justice Cooke, "its bearing on the image, standing and future of rugby as a national sport the decision challenged is probably at least important as—if not more important—than any other in the history of the game in New Zealand."[49] In light of such sentiments, it is perhaps a little ironic that in effect no real decision was made in the case. Although the plaintiffs were successful in achieving their goal of preventing the 1985 All Blacks from touring South Africa, it was never determined that they had a genuine case, and the proceedings were determined ultimately on the prima facie basis of an order for injunctive relief.

While the author accepts the High Court's decision not to grant leave to the Privy Council on the grounds that it was, from a legal perspective, an academic exercise; from a sports governance perspective, a full decision would, clearly, have

[43] *Finnigan v New Zealand Rugby Football Union Inc (No 3)* [1985] 2 NZLR 190, 199.
[44] *Finnigan v New Zealand Rugby Football Union Inc (No 3)* [1985] 2 NZLR 190, 203.
[45] *Finnigan v New Zealand Rugby Football Union Inc (No 3)* [1985] 2 NZLR 190, 203.
[46] *Finnigan v New Zealand Rugby Football Union Inc (No 3)* [1985] 2 NZLR 190, 203.
[47] *Finnigan v New Zealand Rugby Football Union Inc (No 3)* [1985] 2 NZLR 190, 207.
[48] *Finnigan v New Zealand Rugby Football Union Inc (No 3)* [1985] 2 NZLR 190, 207.
[49] *Finnigan v New Zealand Rugby Football Union Inc (No 1)* [1985] 2 NZLR 159, 179.

been the preferable option since it would have clarified with more certainty whether members of individual clubs could legally challenge a governing body's decision. The analogy the author would make is the *South Sydney v News Ltd* cases involving South Sydney's legal challenge to its exclusion from the National Rugby League ("NRL"), the claim there being on an interpretation of the invalid exclusionary provisions under section 45 of the then Trade Practices Act 1974 (Cth).[50]

After losing at the original trial, South Sydney was successful on appeal to the Full Court of the Federal Court,[51] which meant that the club was allowed back into the NRL competition. News Ltd, partners in the NRL, sought special leave to the High Court, despite making it clear that even if it won its High Court case, South Sydney would still be allowed to remain in the NRL. Accordingly, prima facie, it may have appeared to be little more than an academic exercise, since the practical reason for the case, namely whether South Sydney should be allowed to compete in the NRL, was no longer an issue. However, from a sports governance perspective, the High Court challenge was still significant since the 4-1 decision reversing the Full Court of the Federal Court's decision indicated that the terms used by the NRL to originally exclude South Sydney were valid, and similar provisions could be used if it ever wanted to restructure its competition at a later date.[52]

Despite *Finnigan* not reaching a final decision, it is suggested that it still provides judicial reasoning in relation to the issue of standing in regard to an incorporated association controlling sport. It is suggested that the case indicates that an affected party does not necessarily have to be a member, or in a contractual relationship, to a governing body, since in the stated case "a potent factor" was the public and national interest in the tour not going ahead.[53] From a sports law perspective, a point of further interest was the acknowledgment that, although the plaintiffs were not directly contracted with the NZRFU, as club members they were linked to it by means of "a chain of contracts."[54] It is further suggested that sport, as a whole, has become even more reliant on contractual agreements in the 25 years since *Finnigan*, either directly or through these interlocking contracts between various levels of a sports organisation, and thus this aspect of the Finnigan judgment appears of even greater contemporary relevance.[55]

There is little doubt that, at first instance, most people would classify *Finnigan* as a "racism in sport" case, and yet, unlike *Ashby*, no mention was made in the

[50] Note that this act has been repealed and replaced by the Competition and Consumer Act 2010 (Cth). The relevant section (45) of the Trade Practices Act 1974 (Cth), has, however, been retained as section 45 of the new act.

[51] For a discussion of the original trial and appeal to the Full Court of the Federal Court see Davies 2001, 121–129.

[52] For a discussion on the High Court decision see Davies 2003a, 116–128.

[53] *Finnigan v New Zealand Rugby Football Union Inc (No 2)* [1985] 2 NZLR 181, 188.

[54] *Finnigan v New Zealand Rugby Football Union Inc (No 1)* [1985] 2 NZLR 159, 178.

[55] See, for example, Davies 2003b, 190–202.

proceedings in regard to racism, or of it being a case involving a breach of an anti-racism-related national or international provision. However, in another (UK) case originating from the apartheid era, *Wheeler v Leicester City Council*,[56] the council's defence was based on section 71 of the Race Relations Act 1976. The case arose after three members of the Leicester Rugby League were chosen for the 1984 England tour to South Africa. Leicester City Council's response was to draft four questions relating to whether the rugby club considered that the decision to tour was "an insult to the large proportion of the Leicester population" and whether the club would press the Rugby Football Union and the players to call off and pull out of the tour respectively. In this, the council clearly indicated that only affirmative answers would be acceptable.[57] In its response, the club stated that it joined "the council in condemning apartheid but recognise that there are differences of opinion over the way in which the barriers of apartheid can be broken down."[58] No solution, however, was found in the following weeks, with the council deciding to sanction the club by banning it from using the Welford Road recreation ground (the club's home ground) for 12 months.[59]

The club then sought a judicial review of the decision. Eventually, the then House of Lords stated that the council did have power under section 71 of the Race Relations Act 1976 to consider the best interests of race relations in regard to its management of the recreation ground. However, in demanding the club provide affirmative answers to the four questions in order to ensure the club accepted its views and position, the House of Lords took the view that the council had acted unreasonably.[60] It was, therefore, a situation where "the court should interfere because of the unfair manner in which the council set about obtaining its objective",[61] and since the club had done no wrong, "the council could not use their statutory powers...in order to punish the club."[62] In sum, *Wheeler* illustrates that the issue of whether there should be official tours to South Africa was, as in New Zealand, a divisive one in England at the time.[63]

---

[56] *Wheeler v Leicester City Council* [1985] 1 AC 1054.

[57] *Wheeler v Leicester City Council* [1985] 1 AC 1054, 1074.

[58] *Wheeler v Leicester City Council* [1985] 1 AC 1054, 1075.

[59] *Wheeler v Leicester City Council* [1985] 1 AC 1054, 1075.

[60] *Wheeler v Leicester City Council* [1985] 1 AC 1054, 1078.

[61] *Wheeler v Leicester City Council* [1985] AC 1054, 1079.

[62] *Wheeler v Leicester City Council* [1985] AC 1054, 1080. Around the same time in Australia, the Australian Cricket Board's attempt to ban "rebel" players from touring and playing in South Africa was held to be an unreasonable restraint of trade. See *Hughes v Western Australian Cricket Association* (1986) 69 ALR 660, 703.

[63] Demonstrations by protestors opposed to sports participants from South Africa competing in England were frequent at the time and had been since the 1960s and 1970s. Note, for example, *Brutus v Cozens* [1973] AC 854 where a protest by anti-apartheid demonstrators at the All England Lawn Tennis Club, Wimbledon, during a doubles match involving a South African player, was held not to be insulting behaviour under section 5 of the Public Order Act 1936.

Returning to the present case, notwithstanding the administrative law technicalities, the *Finnigan* proceedings should, no doubt, still be reflected upon principally through its connection to the broader issue of racism in sport. *Finnigan* was about more than the litigious efforts of two ordinary New Zealanders to challenge the decision of a sports body. *Finnigan* was more than that; much more. It encompassed international anti-apartheid boycotts, conventions and a global public consensus that, at the height of the Cold War era, was unprecedented. Most powerfully, *Finnigan* was a "bottom-up" challenge by ordinary sport-loving people so that there would never again be a repeat of the scenario whereby players of the calibre of Basil D'Oliveria were denied the opportunity to play for their country of birth simply because of the colour of their skin.

In contemporary sports regulation, the attitude towards racism is one of zero tolerance. For example, the International Olympic Committee's ("IOC's") Olympic Charter, still, perhaps, a document with constitutional status in world sport, is uncompromising in its stance: in the sixth "Fundamental Principles of Olympism" it is stated that any form of discrimination based on "race, religion, politics, gender or otherwise is incompatible to the Olympic Movement."[64] Further, under the "Mission and Role of the IOC", the Charter holds that one of the IOC's duties and functions is "to act against any form of discrimination affecting the Olympic Movement."[65]

And yet, in the same week in 2011 of the announcement regarding the passing of Basil D'Oliveira, the man who inadvertently became a symbol of why sporting boycotts of South Africa were necessary, news also broke of players in the English Premier League (EPL) being accused of making racist comments during matches. It follows that, although statutory-based provisions and policies restraining people of certain races from representing their country may be a thing of the past, the issue of racist comments by players in the sporting arena, or from the spectators in the stands, remains a problem for sport. In the stated incidents, the first involved Liverpool's Luis Suarez who was accused of racially abusing Manchester United's Patrick Evra. Suarez was subsequently suspended for eight matches, and fined £40,000, by an independent regulatory commission appointed by the Football Association.[66] Chelsea's John Terry, meanwhile, was accused of racially abusing Anton Ferdinand of Queen's Park Rangers and in the summer of 2012 will face charges based on racially aggravated public order offences.[67] The manner in which the two incidents were/are being dealt is, in many ways, indicative of modern sports law, i.e. such matters can either be handled internally, with the sport's governing body relying on contractual terms to take actions against players, or externally by state authorities relying on relevant legislation or a combination of both.

---

[64] Olympic Charter 2011, 11.

[65] Olympic Charter 2011, 14.

[66] Barrett 2011, 24.

[67] Hughes 2011, 24.

7.5 Conclusion

The *Finnigan* case was about two plaintiffs who, unlike their government or the NZRFU, wanted to prevent New Zealand's world famous rugby team, the All Blacks, from touring South Africa in 1985. It was therefore a stand by two individuals who represented the views of many New Zealanders, namely that their country should not show any support for a country for which a racist-based apartheid system was the political norm. It was a case, therefore, very much relating to a time when there was a collision between sport and politics. Yet, less than a decade later, the apartheid system had imploded and all New Zealanders were unequivocally welcoming the resumption of games between these two great rugby rivals. While it is impossible to say what, if any, direct impact the *Finnigan* case had on this happy outcome, there is little doubt that sporting and trade boycotts did hasten the demise of the apartheid system. As a case involving an important legal challenge to the last proposed All Black tour prior to the end of the apartheid era, *Finnigan* therefore deserves its place as one of the most significant cases in international sports law. While recent events have shown that the issue of racism has not been totally eradicated in today's sport, it is an issue that sport is better equipped to deal with than it was back in 1985.

References

Barrett T (2011) Liverpool fury at Suarez penalty. The Australian, 22 Dec, 24

Colman M, Edwards K (2002) Eddie Gilbert: the true story of an aboriginal cricketing legend. ABC Books, Sydney

Davies C (2001) South Sydney v News Ltd. James Cook Univ Law Rev 8:121–129

Davies C (2003a) News Ltd v South Sydney District Rugby League Football Club Ltd. James Cook Univ Law Rev 10:116–128

Davies C (2003b) Post-Bosman and the future of soccer is contract law. J Contract Law 19:190–202

Hughes M (2011) Terry to captain England despite racial abuse charge. The Australian, 23 Dec, 24

Merrett C (2002) Sport and race in colonial natal: C.B. Llewellyn, South Africa's first black test cricketer. Natalia 32:19–35

Obituary (2011) Cricketer who helped to end apartheid dies. The Australian, 21 Nov, 12

Olympic Charter in force from 8 July (2011) www.olympic.org/Documents/olympic_charter_en.pdf. Accessed 31 July 2012

Wilde S (2011) D'Oliveira's legacy: a symbol of injustice broke down racial barriers. The Australian, 21 Nov, 40

Chapter 8
R. v. Disciplinary Committee of the Jockey Club ex p. the Aga Khan [1993] 1 WLR 909

Michael Beloff

Abstract The applicant sought to apply for judicial review of a decision by the Jockey Club, in order to quash a decision that a horse owned by him should be disqualified for failing a drugs test. The Court of Appeal held that, although the Jockey Club controlled most of the racing in the UK, it was not in any sense an organ of government. It was a private organisation, bound to its members by contract, and therefore the appropriate remedies against it were private law in nature and there was neither the amenability nor the scope for judicial review of the decision of the sporting body.

Contents

Michael Beloff QC, MA (Oxon) is a member of the Court of Arbitration for Sport, Steward of the Royal Automobile Club and Ethics Commissioner, London 2012.

M. Beloff (✉)
Blackstone Chambers, Blackstone House, Temple, London EC4Y 9BW, UK
e-mail: clerks@blackstonechambers.com

J. Anderson (ed.), *Leading Cases in Sports Law*,
ASSER International Sports Law Series, DOI: 10.1007/978-90-6704-909-2_8,

8.1 Introduction

In *R v Disciplinary Committee of the Jockey Club ex p the Aga Khan* ("*Aga Khan*"),[1] the Court of Appeal decided that a decision of the Jockey Club's disciplinary committee was not amenable to judicial review. I had a transient role in the case, being originally instructed on behalf of the Aga Khan. My advice that the claim could not succeed at first instance, and was unlikely to succeed at all, was unpalatable to those instructing me, and I was "jocked off" in favour of the legendary Sydney Kentridge QC, the Lester Piggott (in terms of talent, not tax avoidance) of the Bar. But though my pride and pocket were hurt, my powers of prophecy were unimpaired. Even Sir Sydney could ride this particular claim into the winner's enclosure.

The Court of Appeal left open the question whether a decision of the club could ever be susceptible to judicial review so the ratio of the case relates strictly to the decision made, not the body making it. But the case put a substantial roadblock in the path of any litigant seeking to challenge by judicial review a decision of a sporting body. That road block has now, as a result of subsequent cases, become a seemingly impenetrable barrier. In this essay I shall seek to answer three questions. How did this come about? Was the conclusion correct? Does it matter?

8.2 Factual and Legal Background

The short facts of the case were these. On 10 June 1991 at Epsom the Aga Khan's brilliant filly Aliysa[2] won the Oaks—indisputably the most famous and prestigious race exclusively open to horses of the feminine gender. The conventional drugs test administered to winners (they dope horses don't they?) revealed the presence of a prohibited substance, metabolite of camphor. The horse was duly disqualified pursuant to the rules of racing. The Aga Khan sought to challenge the decision by way of judicial review as vitiated by fundamental unfairness. The threshold issue was whether—whatever the facts—that remedy was available.

The issue was no virgin one; it had a history. In the seminal judgment in *O'Reilly v Mackman*,[3] Lord Diplock acknowledged that English law recognised a difference between private and public law describing "progress towards a comprehensive system of administrative law" and as having "been the greatest achievement of the English Courts" in my judicial lifetime.[4] He held also that, materially to the matter under consideration, given the procedural reforms for judicial review, implemented by rules of court in 1979 and consolidated in the

[1] *R v Disciplinary Committee of the Jockey Club ex p. the Aga Khan* [1993] 1 WLR 909.

[2] Whose ancestors included Shirley Heights and Mill Reef, both Derby winners.

[3] *O'Reilly v Mackman* [1983] 2 AC 237.

[4] *O'Reilly v Mackman* [1983] 2 AC 237, 279.

Supreme (now Senior) Courts Act 1981, it would prima facie be an abuse of process for a claimant who challenged a decision on traditional public law grounds (illegality, irrationality and procedural impropriety as the same Law Lord subsequently summarised them[5]) and so by-pass the requirement of leave (now permission) to institute judicial review proceedings as well as the strict time, limits attached to that remedy.

This remarkable piece of judicial law-making was clearly not contemplated by those who had drafted the earlier legislation, primary and secondary, which had nowhere sought to prohibit an aggrieved claimant for deploying a procedure by writ or originating summons to obtain appropriate declaratory or injunctive relief. It spawned a series of cases in which the boundaries of the so-called rule in *O'Reilly v Mackman* were explored as various administrative authorities sought to shield or postpone scrutiny of the merits of their decisions by raising a preliminary issue of lack of jurisdiction where the claimant had taken the public law route, other than by use of Order 53 or 54 CPR (the rules sequentially governing judicial review).[6]

Sports law was not immune to these unprofitable wrangles, reminiscent of the ancient disputes over the proper forms of private law action which Maitland said "still rule us from their grave",[7] (Lord Atkin later, after deployment of a famous sepulchral metaphor, suggested that in respect of them "the proper course is for the judge to pass through"[8]). In *Law v NRGC*,[9] the claimant, a trainer of greyhounds, had his licence suspended on the grounds that a dog under his charge had been tested positive. He issued an originating summons seeking both declaratory and injunctive relief as well as damages on the ground that the suspension was ultra vires the NGRC and reached in violation of the principles of natural justice. The NGRC's response was to seek to strike the action out on the basis that any claim should have been made by way of judicial review. The Court of Appeal rejected this assertion. They held that the NGRC was a domestic tribunal to which the prerogative writs had never lain. The public interest in its decisions, such as purification of the sport, did not convert it into a public authority. The powers of the Tribunal affected only "those who had voluntarily submitted themselves to the stewards' jurisdiction".[10]

There followed two cases in which the Jockey Club itself featured as putative respondent. *R v Disciplinary Committee of the Jockey Club ex p Massingberd-Mundy*

---

[5] *Council of Civil Service Unions v Minister for the Civil Service* [1985] AC 374, 409.

[6] For example, *Davy v Spelthorne* [1984] AC 262; *Wandsworth v Winder* [1985] AC 461; *Roy v Kensington & Chelsea FPC* [1992] 1 AC 624; *Mercury Communications Ltd v Director General of Telecommunications* [1996] 1 WLR 48; *Steed v Home Secretary* [2000] 1 WLR 1169; and *Clark v University of Lincolnshire & Humberside* [2001] 1 WLR 1988, as discussed by Beloff 2001.

[7] Maitland 1948, 2.

[8] *United Australian Bank v Barclays Bank* [1949] AC 1, 29.

[9] *Law v NGRC* [1983] 1 WLR 1302.

[10] *Law v NGRC* [1983] 1 WLR 1302, 1307, Lawton LJ.

("Massingberd-Mundy")[11] and *R v Disciplinary Committee of the Jockey Club ex p RAM Racecourses Ltd* ("RAM").[12] In the former a Chairman of a Panel of local stewards had had his name removed from those qualified so to act—he claimed unfairly. In the latter a racecourse proprietor had sought to hold the Jockey Club to a representation said to give rise to a legitimate expectation to introduce 60 or so new fixtures. Both claims failed on their merits; but in both cases the availability *vel non* of judicial review was examined. In the former, Neill LJ and Roch J[13] felt bound by *Law v NRGC*, but would otherwise have held that at least some decisions of the Jockey Club were open to review. In the latter, Stuart-Smith LJ and Simon Brown J felt bound to follow *Massingberd-Mundy*, though with misgivings. Three of those four judges concluded their judicial careers in the Court of Appeal; and one, Simon Brown, in the House of Lords and later the Supreme Court—a clear case, one might argue of horses for courses.

A case which was influential in the approach of those who were minded to allow judicial review to lie against powerful sporting bodies who controlled de jure and de facto their sport, or particular areas of it, was *R v Takeover Panel ex p Datafin*[14] (*"Datafin")* where Lord Donaldson MR had substituted "functions" test for "sources" as a litmus test for whether a particular body was amenable to judicial review. He said "possibly the only essential elements are what can be described as a public element which can take many different forms."[15] Simon Brown J—with a former Treasury Devil's acute eye for what that nebulous phrase "a public element" might mean—would himself in *Ram* have equated the licensing function of the Jockey Club to that operated by many bodies established by statute.

8.3 The Aga Saga

In *Aga Khan*, Sir Thomas Bingham MR said:

> I have little hesitation in accepting the applicant's contention that the Jockey Club effectively regulates a significant national activity, exercising powers which affect the public and are exercised in the interest of the public. I am willing to accept that if the Jockey Club did not regulate this activity the government would probably be driven to create a public body to do so.
>
> But the Jockey Club is not in its origin, its history, its constitution or (least of all) its membership a public body. While the grant of a Royal Charter was no doubt a mark of official approval, this did not in any way alter its essential nature, functions or standing. Statute provides for its representation on the Horserace Betting Levy Board, no doubt as a

---

[11] *R v Disciplinary Committee of the Jockey Club ex p Massingberd-Mundy* [1993] 2 All ER 207.

[12] *R v Disciplinary Committee of the Jockey Club ex p RAM Racecourses Ltd* [1993] 2 All ER 225.

[13] See the comments in *Aga Khan* [1993] 1 WLR 909, 927D–928D, Sir Thomas Bingham MR.

[14] *R v Takeover Panel ex p Datafin* [1987] QB 815.

[15] *R v Takeover Panel ex p Datafin* [1987] QB 815, 833.

body with an obvious interest in racing, but it has otherwise escaped mention in the statute book. It has not been woven into any system of governmental control of horseracing, perhaps because it has itself controlled horseracing so successfully that there has been no need for any such governmental system and such does not therefore exist. This has the result that while the Jockey Club's powers may be described as in many ways, public they are in no sense governmental. The discretion conferred by section 31(6) of the Supreme Court Act 1981 to refuse a grant of leave or relief where the applicant has been guilty of delay which would be prejudicial to good administration can scarcely have been envisaged as applicable in a case such as this.

I would accept that those who agree to be bound by the Rules of Racing have no effective alternative to doing so if they want to take part in racing in this country. It also seems likely to me that if, instead of Rules of Racing administered by the Jockey Club, there were a statutory code administered by a public body, the rights and obligations conferred and imposed by the code would probably approximate to those conferred and imposed by the Rules of Racing. But this does not, as it seems to me, alter the fact, however anomalous it may be, that the powers which the Jockey Club exercises over those who (like the applicant) agree to be bound by the Rules of the Racing derive from the agreement of the parties and give rise to private rights on which effective action for a declaration, and injunction and damages can be based without resort to judicial review. It would in my opinion be contrary to sound and long-standing principle to extend the remedy of judicial review to such a case.[16]

Hoffmann LJ said (still more emphatically):

The attitude of the English legislator to racing is much more akin to his attitude to religion (see *R v Chief Rabbi of the United Hebrew Congregations of Great Britain and the Commonwealth, ex p Wachmann* [1992] 1 WLR 1036): it is something to be encouraged but not the business of government.

All this leaves is the fact that the Jockey Club has power. But the mere fact of power, even over a substantial area of economic activity, is not enough. In a mixed economy, power may be private as well as public. Private power may affect the public interest and the livelihoods of many individuals. But that does not subject it to the rules of public law. If control is needed, it must be found in the law of contract, the doctrine of restraint of trade, the Restrictive Trade Practices Act 1976, articles 85 and 86 of the E.E.C. Treaty and all the other instruments available in law for curbing the excesses of private power.

It may be that in some cases the remedies available in private law are inadequate. For example, in cases in which power is exercised unfairly against persons who have no contractual relationship with the private decision-making body, the court may not find it easy to fashion a cause of action to provide a remedy. In *Nagle v Feilden* [1966] 2 QB 633, for example, this court had to consider the Jockey Club's refusal on grounds of sex to grant a trainer's licence to a woman. She had no contract with the Jockey Club or (at the time) any other recognised cause of action, but this court said that it was arguable that she could still obtain a declaration and injunction. There is an improvisatory air about this solution and the possibility of obtaining an injunction has probably not survived *Siskina (Owners of cargo lately laden on board) v Distos Compania Naviera SA* [1979] AC 210.[17]

Farquharson LJ reached the same conclusion with a more conservative emphasis on precedent than on principle.[18]

---

[16] *Aga Khan* [1993] 1 WLR 909, 924.

[17] *Aga Khan* [1993] 1 WLR 909, 932–933.

[18] *Aga Khan* [1993] 1 WLR 909, 924–30.

I had been a proponent in earlier writings[19] of the view that the decision in *Aga Khan* was wrong because sufficient of the *indicia* of a public law right were present—both as to the functions exercised and the body which exercised them; and I was not alone in this view.[20] I argued that the court gave too much emphasis to the contractual relationship between the parties, and too little to the absence of any real choice for anyone involved in the sport of kings (and Khans) but to submit to the Jockey Club's jurisdiction.

The absence of compulsion to undertake a regulated activity does not in other spheres bar judicial review at the suit of the "regulate" against the regulator. An applicant for a statutory licence can choose not to apply for one, but if he chooses to apply, the licensing authority's decision will be amenable to judicial review. Granted that the Jockey Club at the time of *Aga Khan* exercised virtually monopolistic powers over horse racing in Great Britain, a person who races horses could not avoid submitting to its jurisdiction. Sir Thomas Bingham himself observed: "no serious racecourse management, owner trainer or jockey can survive without the recognition or licence of the Jockey Club. There is in effect no alternative market in which those not accepted by the Jockey Club can find a place or to which race goers may resort",[21] properly applied to facts such as these, a consensuality exclusion test points in favour of, not against judicial review.[22]

While there is general agreement that no one factor is dispositive as an index of a public law function,[23] a good starting point is to consider the variety of overlapping criteria designed to particularise the broad-based functional approach of Lord Donaldson MR in *Datafin*, (and obliquely developed in cases under section 6 of the Human Rights Act 1998 ("HRA"),[24] which include those enumerated in the most recent edition of de Smith.[25]

The first criterion is whether, but for the existence of a non-statutory body, government would itself almost inevitably intervene to regulate the activity in question. This consideration weighed heavily with Rose J in deciding that the Football Association was not amenable to judicial review[26]; he thought it more likely that a television company or other entertainment industry body would step in.

---

[19] See, for example, Beloff and Kerr 1996. Where I say "I" hereafter I include Tim Kerr, now QC, in respect of all propositions and associated material relating to 1996 or earlier.

[20] See further Pannick 1997 and Griffith Jones 1997, 52–57.

[21] *Aga Khan* [1993] 1 WLR 909, 915F.

[22] Wade and Forsyth 2004, 545–547.

[23] There is "no litmus test", Fordham 1994, 188.

[24] *Aston Cantlow v Wallbank* [2004] 1 AC 546.

[25] Woolf et al. 2007, 133–138.

[26] *R v Football Association Ltd. ex p Football League Ltd.* [1993] 2 All ER 833.

In *Aga Khan*, Hoffmann LJ indicated his agreement with that analysis.[27] Subsequent developments have shown that this speculation may have been unsound. The current (UK) Minister of Sport has threatened that if the FA do not put their house in order the Government may legislate.[28] As de Smith says, "Given the huge changes in the scope of government activity, and disputes about its proper scope, it is doubtful if this criterion is a proper one".[29]

But the correct question is whether government would intervene and regulate *if no one else did*. If a function is properly to be regarded as public, the adventitious availability of a private body willing to perform it ought to be irrelevant. Sir Thomas Bingham MR (if not Hoffmann LJ) in *Aga Khan* was, for his part "willing to accept that if the Jockey Club did not regulate this activity the government would probably be driven to create a public body to do so".[30]

The second criterion is whether government has acquiesced in or encouraged the activities of the body whose decision is under challenge by providing underpinning for its work or weaving it into the fabric of public regulation[31]; or whether the body was established under the authority of government.

Acquiescence rather than active encouragement, underpinning or express authority, is the key element where a public function is being satisfactorily performed by a private body with no need for any state intervention. The Jockey Club has after all dominated British racing since its foundation in 1750 and continues to enjoy royal patronage. It was incorporated by Royal Charter in 1970 following a merger with the National Hunt Committee.[32]

The third criterion is whether the body in question exercises extensive or monopolistic powers, for instance by effectively regulating entry to a trade, profession or sport. Rose J in the *Football Association* case decided against amenability of that body to judicial review "despite its virtually monopolistic powers".[33] The Panel on Takeovers and Mergers in the *Datafin* case met this criterion.[34] So, plainly, does the Jockey Club; as Sir Thomas Bingham MR himself acknowledged:

> The Jockey Club cannot … impose contractual conditions on those who … do not enter into any contract with it. ….. The club's sanction here lies not in contract but in its

[27] *Aga Khan* [1993] 1 WLR 909, 933E.

[28] See Department for Culture, Media and Sport 2011, para 75. See generally Lewis and Taylor 2008, Chap. 1 who argue that the non-interventionist tradition of Government in Britain towards sport is being slowly eroded.

[29] Woolf et al. 2007, para 3-046, the fact that in other jurisdictions governments regulated horse racing was considered immaterial in *Aga Khan* [1993] 1 WLR 909, 932.

[30] *Aga Khan* [1993] 1 WLR 909, 922G.

[31] *Aga Khan* [1993] 1 WLR 909, 921B.

[32] Note though that in 2001 the Jockey Club's Disciplinary Committee was superseded by an Appeal Board and since 2006 regulatory functions have been carried out by an independent horse-racing authority.

[33] Cited by Sir Thomas Bingham MR in *Aga Khan* [1993] 1 WLR 909, 921B.

[34] Lloyd LJ called it "a giant's strength". See *R v Takeover Panel ex p Datafin* [1987] QB 815, 845.

> domination of the market. … For practical purposes the Jockey Club's writ runs in the British racing world, to the acknowledged benefit of British racing.[35]

In the Matter of an Application for Judicial Review by Patrick Wylie,[36] a Friendly Society, a private body, which owned rights to eel fishing on Lough Neagh in Northern Ireland was held (realistically) to be carrying out a public function when it refused a boat owner's licence to someone who fished there as a boat helper for nigh on half a century. Weatherup J said: "The regulation of fishing involves an implied duty to act in the public interest; the issues that arise are matters of public concern where direct governmental regulatory control is absent and the regulatory activities are providing a public service".[37] Hoffmann LJ noted that power, even monopolistic power, may exist in the private sphere and its exercise may be controlled by the mechanisms available for curbing excesses of private power, of which he instanced, in the passage quoted above, the restraint of trade doctrine and Articles 85 and 86 of the Treaty of Rome (now Articles 101 and 102TFEU).[38]

By that logic the monopolistic character of the body's power begs but does not answer the question whether it is exercised in the public or private sphere.

The fourth criterion is whether the aggrieved person has consensually submitted to be bound by the decision maker. As I have already pointed out that agreement to undertake the regulated activity is not the same as "agreement" to submit to a monopoly jurisdiction having decided to undertake it. I drew support from de Smith's proposition that in such a case, "judicial review ought in principle to be available to an aggrieved person, though if a contract exists a contractual claim will normally be an appropriate alternative remedy which may bar judicial review".[39]

Farquharson LJ attached importance to the contractual relationship between the Jockey Club and its members. Both he and Hoffmann LJ felt unable to distinguish the Court of Appeal's decision in *Law v NGRC* and Hoffmann LJ declined to hold that the reasoning in *Law* was affected by *Datafin*. He was reassured by the proposition that the Aga Khan had an adequate private law remedy under his contract of membership. That consideration also weighed with Sir Thomas Bingham MR, who accepted that two earlier Divisional Court decisions involving the Jockey Club were distinguishable on the ground that the applicants in those cases had no contract with the club; though the absence of a contract did not help either applicant.[40]

De Smith adds that the receipt of public funding cannot itself be of more than marginal relevance in determining amenability to judicial review. With that I respectfully agree. It is neutral; but it is certainly not inconsistent with such

---

35 *Aga Khan* [1993] 1 WLR 909, 915E-F.

36 In the Matter of an Application for Judicial Review by Patrick Wylie [2005] NIQB 2.

37 *In the Matter of an Application for Judicial Review by Patrick Wylie* [2005] NIQB 2, para 19.

38 *Aga Khan* [1993] 1 WLR 909, 932H-933A.

39 Woolf et al. 2007, 171–172.

40 *Aga Khan* [1993] 1 WLR 909, 922C.

amenability.[41] I wrote anyone seeking to invoke a private law remedy must beware the procedural banana skin placed in his path by the *O'Reilly v Mackman* principle, which makes the tail of procedure wag the dog of substance.[42] In a borderline case the only safe course is to apply for leave promptly in case in the right infringed is viewed as one arising in public law. And the existence of a contract is no guarantee that the court will not do so since, "There is no reason why a private club should not also exercise public powers".[43] Indeed a public law dispute and a private law dispute may co-exist on the same facts, either between different parties[44] or between the same parties.[45] And two celebrated contributions of Lord Denning, both in cases cited in the judgments in *Aga Khan*, serve to emphasise how similar are the functions of, respectively, domestic bodies and statutory bodies.[46]

It is instructive to compare the public/private law divide with the well-established dichotomy between state bodies, against which directly effective EU law directives may be enforced, and private sector bodies not amenable to direct effect.[47] Public functions are increasingly carried out by bodies constituted under private law by reason of privatisation, contracting out and competitive tendering. Functions which are public in nature, such as managing a prison, ought not to be regarded as any less public merely because they are carried out by a private body for reward on behalf of the state. The contracting out phenomenon is not a reason for judges to adopt a narrower view of what functions are public.[48] Market dominance ought itself to be recognised as one of the indicia of a body exercising public law functions, because market dominance negates consensuality between the decision

---

[41] Woolf et al. 2007, para 3-051.

[42] To the dissatisfaction of, inter alios, Lord Lowry. See *R v Employment Secretary ex p EOC* [1995] 1 AC 1, 34C. See further Beloff 2001.

[43] Per Hoffmann LJ in *Aga Khan* [1993] 1 WLR 909, 931B-C, citing *Swain v. Law Society* [1983] 1 AC 598.

[44] *R v Secretary of State for Education ex p Prior* [1994] ICR 877 (teacher's private law dispute with employer; public law dispute with Secretary of State).

[45] *R v City of Sunderland ex p Baumber* [1996] COD 211, QBD (psychologist's private law dispute with employer over alleged unlawful instruction; public law dispute with employer as to whether instruction ultra vires).

[46] *Nagle v. Fielden* [1966] 2 QB 633, CA (a striking example from the pre-1977 era of Lord Denning's willingness to advance the law to cure abuse of powers, in contrast to today's more conservative judicial climate); and *Breen v. AEU* [1971] 2 QB 175, 190 (dissenting) ("domestic bodies which control the destinies of thousands").

[47] See and compare *Foster v. British Gas Plc* [1991] QB 405, ECJ; [1991] 2 AC 306, HL (British Gas pre-privatisation: state body); *Doughty v. Rolls-Royce Plc* [1992] ICR 538, CA (Rolls-Royce pre-privatisation; not a state body); and *Griffin v Slough West Water Services Ltd* [1995] IRLR 15, Ch D (post-privatisation water company: state body).

[48] See, however, the retrograde decision in *YL v Birmingham City Council* [2007] UKHL 27; [2008] 1 AC 95 where the minority, in the author's respectful view, were correct to decide that the delegation of the operation of care homes by the Council in discharge of their statutory responsibilities did not mean that the obligations under the Human Rights Act 1998 no longer applied. It is notable that the dissenting minority had a more powerful public law pedigree than the majority.

maker and the affected person. The denial of consensuality, which subjection to market power entails, underlies Article 86 of the Treaty of Rome (as it then was, now Article 102TFEU), a treaty provision entered into between sovereign states and not exclusively private in character. The provision recognises market dominance as contrary to the public interest if abused in a manner that may affect trade between Member States.

I concluded that the law took a wrong turn in 1983 in *Law v NGRC* and, a decade later the opportunity to confine the former to its facts was lost.[49] A too narrow view of public functions now prevailed and would do so unless and until the House of Lords[50] overruled *Aga Khan* and *Law v NGRC* as well. I suggested that their Lordships might draw inspiration from the overseas common law jurisdictions, in which a broader view of public functions had led to successful public law challenges to decisions of sporting bodies and including the Jockey Club of South Africa.[51]

8.4 Does It Matter?

The enactment into English law as from 2 October 2000 of the European Convention on Human Rights through the medium of the Human Rights Act 1998 promoted a new assault on *Aga Khan*. Again it was the fate of a horse which generated the litigation—this time over the sticks not on the flat. In 2002 Be My Royal, trained by Willie Mullins, won the Hennessey Gold Cup at long odds but tested positive for morphine. While the Disciplinary Committee of the Jockey Club acknowledged that the prohibited substance was ingested via contaminated foodstuff, they applied the strict liability rule, as operative in the rules of racing as it is in the regulations of most major sports, and disqualified the horse. An appeal to the Appeal Board failed and, internal remedies having been duly exhausted, Mr Mullins sought judicial review and a declaration of invalidity of the disqualification. Stanley Burnton J held that *Aga Khan* was binding and indistinguishable. None of the jurisprudence on section 6 of the HRA, which obliged public authorities to act in a convention compliant way, had enlarged, in his view the definition of such bodies so as to embrace sporting regulators. The rules of the Jockey Club had no statutory source; they bound those subject to them by contract only.[52] The proceedings were transferred to the Queen's Bench Division. The unfortunate Mr Mullins lost his case there.[53]

49 One commentator, Anderson 2006, described it as "an accident of history".

50 I had not been a prophet of the emergence of the Supreme Court.

51 See Beloff 1989, 105–109; Beloff and Kerr 1995 and Lewis and Taylor 2008, para A3.77, fn 2.

52 *R (o/a Mullins) v Jockey Club Appeal Board* [2006] EWHC 986.

53 *Mullins v McFarlane* [2006] EWHC 986 (QB).

But did the transfer affect the outcome? In all probability not. One of the cases that Stanley Burnton J had to consider in the first action was *Bradley v Jockey Club*,[54] another Jockey Club case, where the ultimate sanction imposed on a jockey for passing racing information to a gambler by the Appeal Board of 5 years (three years shorter than that imposed by the Disciplinary Committee) was challenged on the ground that it was disproportionate and hence in breach of an implied term said to exists between Jockey and Club. Mr Justice Richards, as he then was, propounded two fundamental principles: first; that "even in the absence of contract, the court has a settled jurisdiction to grant declarations and injunctions in respect of the decisions of domestic tribunals that affect a person's right to work"[55]; second, that the principles applied were essentially the same as those which would be applied by the Courts in exercise of its supervisory judicial review jurisdiction,

> …given the difficulties that sometimes arise in drawing the precise boundary between the two, I would consider it surprising and unsatisfactory if a private law claim in relation to the decision of a domestic body required the court to draw adopt a materially different approach from a judicial review claim in relation to the decision of a public body. In each case the essential concern would be with the lawfulness of the decision taken; whether the procedure was fair, whether there was any error of law, whether any exercise of judgement or discretion fell within the limits open to a decision maker and so forth.[56]

The Court of Appeal endorsed his analysis without adding substantiality to it.[57]

It was notable that two out of the three judges in *Aga Khan* expressly reserved their position as to a case in which, unlike the Aga Khan himself, the claimant had no contractual remedy. Sir Thomas Bingham MR concluded his judgment by remarking:

> It is unnecessary for purposes of this appeal to decide whether decisions of the Jockey Club may ever in any circumstances be challenged by judicial review and I do not do so. Cases where the applicant or a plaintiff has no contract on which to rely may raise different considerations and the existence or non-existence of alternative remedies may then be material. I think it better that this court should defer detailed consideration of such a case until it rises. I am, however, satisfied that on the facts of this case the appeal should be dismissed.[58]

Similarly, Farquharson LJ concluded:

> As to Mr Milmo's assertion that the question of the Jockey Club's susceptibility to judicial review must be answered or an all or nothing basis, I can only say as at present advised that I do not agree. In *Reg v Jockey Club, Ex parte R.A.M. Racecourses Ltd* [1993] 2 All ER 225 Simon Brown J. had similar reservations. In both that case and *Reg. v Disciplinary*

---

[54] *Bradley v Jockey Club* [2004] EWHC 2164.

[55] *Bradley v Jockey Club* [2004] EWHC 2164, para 35.

[56] *Bradley v Jockey Club* [2004] EWHC 2164, para 37.

[57] *Bradley v Jockey Club* [2005] EWCA Civ 1056. On this aspect of the public/private law divide as now played out under the Human Rights Act, see further Oliver 2000, 2004.

[58] *Aga Khan* [1993] 1 WLR 909, 924.

> *Committee of the Jockey Club, Ex parte Massingberd-Mundy* [1993] 2 All ER 207, the applicants had no contractual relationship with the Jockey Club. While I do not say that particular circumstances would give a right to judicial review I do not discount the possibility that in some special circumstances the remedy might lie. If for example the Jockey Club failed to fulfil its obligations under the charter by making discriminatory rules, it may be that those affected would have a remedy in public law.[59]

Hoffmann LJ was more sceptical. After adverting to the possibility of a black hole he said, "I do not think one should try to patch up the remedies against domestic bodies by pretending that they are organs of government".[60]

8.5 Conclusion

So the door was left, albeit slightly, ajar. No cases raising this precise issue have come before the Courts hitherto and for three main reasons they are unlikely to do so. First, the Courts are astute, where possible, to identify a contractual relationship between a sports person and a sport regulator even in the context of the usual pyramidical structure of the latter.[61] Second, given the assimilation of the principles governing the exercise of power by public and private bodies the advantage to be gained by use of judicial review would seem more apparent than real. Third, the surviving procedural differences between judicial review and other forms of procedure (the presumptive 3-month limitation period; the greater constraints on the grant of discretionary relief; the absence of automatic disclosure and cross-examination; the absence of any ability to claim damages unless the alleged abuse of power itself equates to a breach of a private law obligation in contract or tort; and the fact that all remedies of judicial review are discretionary) would work to the advantage of the regulated, not the regulated. It is a legal irony that whereas the rule in *O'Reilly v Mackman* has been all but obliterated by a series of powerful decisions at an appellate level, so recording to a claimant a procedural choice denied him by the rule; in the field of sports regulation, the boundary remains intact, but it is now the putative respondent, rather than the claimant who suffers. Law, even sports law, has its little ironies.

References

Anderson J (2006) An accident of history: why the decisions of sports governing bodies are not amenable to judicial review. Common Law World Rev 35:173–196

---

59 *Aga Khan* [1993] 1 WLR 909, 930.

60 *Aga Khan* [1993] 1 WLR 909, 933F.

61 For instance, *Modahl v British Athletic Federation (No 2)* [2001] EWCA Civ 1447; [2002] 1 WLR 1192.

Beloff M (1989) Pitch, pool, rink… court? Judicial review in the sporting world. Public Law 95:95–110
Beloff M (2001) The fate of O'Reilly v Mackman: a cautionary tale. In: Iyer V (ed) Constitutional perspectives: essays in honour of H M Seervai. Universal, Delhi
Beloff M, Kerr T (1995) Judicial control of sporting bodies: the commonwealth jurisprudence. Sport Law J 3:5
Beloff M, Kerr T (1996) Why the Aga Khan is wrong. Judic Rev 1:30–33
Department for Culture, Media and Sport (2011) Football governance: response to the culture, media and sport committee, HC792-1. (Cm 8207)
Fordham M (1994) Judicial review handbook, 1st edn. Wiley, London
Griffith Jones D (1997) Law and business of sport. Butterworths, London
Lewis A, Taylor J (2008) Sport: law and practice, 2nd edn. Tottel, Haywards Heath
Maitland FW (1948) The forms of action at common law: a course of lectures. Cambridge University Press, Cambridge
Oliver D (2000) The frontiers of the state; public authorities and public functions under the Human Rights Act. Public Law Autumn 476–493
Oliver D (2004) Functions of a public nature under the Human Rights Act 1998. Public Law Summer 329–351
Pannick D (1997) Judicial review of sports governing bodies. Judic Rev 2:150–153
Wade W, Forsyth C (2004) Administrative law, 9th edn. Oxford University Press, Oxford
Woolf H, Jowell J, Le Sueur A (eds) (2007) De Smith's judicial review, 6th edn. Sweet & Maxwell, London

Chapter 9
Case C-519/04 P *Meca-Medina* [2006] ECR I-6991

Stephen Weatherill

Abstract The appellants, Mr Meca-Medina and Mr Majcen, both professional long-distance swimmers, asked the European Court of Justice (known since the entry into force of the Lisbon Treaty in December 2009 as the Court of Justice of the European Union or "CJEU") to set aside the judgment of the Court of First Instance of the European Communities (known since December 2009 as the European General Court or "EGC") of 30 September 2004 in Case T-313/02 Meca-Medina and Majcen v Commission [2004] ECR II-3291 by which the EGC had dismissed the appellants' action for annulment of the decision of the European Commission of 1 August 2002 (Case COMP/38158—Meca-Medina and Majcen/IOC). The Commission had rejected the appellant's complaint lodged by them against the International Olympic Committee ("the IOC") and seeking a declaration that certain rules adopted by the IOC and implemented by the Fédération Internationale de Natation (International Swimming Federation; "FINA") and certain practices relating to doping control were incompatible with fundamental principles of European Community law (now, since December 2009, European Union law or "EU law") and including provision on competition law (Case COMP/38158—Meca-Medina and Majcen/IOC). In its ruling the CJEU reiterated that, having regard to the general objectives of the European Union, sport is subject to EU law only in so far as it constitutes an economic activity and where a sporting activity takes the form of gainful employment or the provision of services for remuneration, which is true of the activities of semi-professional or professional sportsmen, it falls, more specifically, within the scope of Article 39 EC et

Stephen Weatherill, Jacques Delors Professor of European Law, Deputy Director for European Law.

S. Weatherill (✉)
Institute of European and Comparative Law, University of Oxford, Oxford, UK
e-mail: stephen.weatherill@law.ox.ac.uk

S. Weatherill
Somerville College, University of Oxford, Oxford, UK

J. Anderson (ed.), *Leading Cases in Sports Law*,
ASSER International Sports Law Series, DOI: 10.1007/978-90-6704-909-2_9,

seq (now Article 45TFEU) or Article 49 EC *et seq* (now Article 56TFEU). These provisions on freedom of movement for persons and freedom to provide services do not, however, affect rules concerning questions which are of "purely sporting interest" and, as such, have nothing to do with economic activity. In assessing the compatibility of the disputed anti-doping regulations with EU competition law, the CJEU noted that, first of all, account had to be taken of the overall context in which the decision of the (sporting) associations was taken or produces its effects and, more specifically, of its objectives. It has then to be considered whether the consequential effects restrictive of competition are inherent in the pursuit of those objectives and are proportionate to them.

Contents

9.1 Introduction

The ruling in *Meca-Medina and Majcen v Commission* ("*Meca-Medina*") in 2006[1] offers a vivid insight into a tension that lies at the heart of EU law in general and a distinct but related tension that lies at the heart of the EU's legal control of sport in particular.

The European Union, as an organisation founded on international Treaties dating back to the 1950s, has no general regulatory or legislative competence. It is, instead, based on a constitutional order of limited material scope. On the other hand, that limited material scope is defined with reference to the scope of economic activity, which promises an extraordinarily broad range of application for EU law. So here is the central tension: *in principle* the EU's reach is limited, *in practice* those limits are drawn in such a manner as to guarantee that little escapes

[1] Full citation: Case C-519/04 P *David Meca-Medina and Igor Majcen v Commission of the European Communities* [2006] ECR I-6991.

the control of the EU's core legal provisions aimed at securing an integrated market spanning the territory of its 27 Member States.

And this central tension in EU law has particular resonance in application to sport. Sport was not even mentioned in the founding Treaties until as late as December 2009, and even since then, the date of entry into force of the Lisbon Treaty, sport has been the subject of only carefully limited and relatively unsophisticated treatment in the Treaty. *In principle*, then, one might suppose that EU lacks the competence to intervene in sport. *In practice*, by contrast, sport has a very significant commercial dimension and EU law has a correspondingly significant influence on sporting practices.

But what should be the nature of EU law's control of the economic aspects of sport? And to what extent should it be conditioned by the plain fact that sport is not simply a commercial activity like any other but rather also engages distinct cultural and social concerns, which typically provide the intellectual energy behind the claims of sporting bodies to an entitlement to autonomy from public regulation? This is what the EU's founding Treaties fail to make clear. The ruling in *Meca-Medina* provides a wonderful contrast between two fundamentally different competing approaches: that which would uphold the virtue of sporting autonomy (the so-called *lex sportiva*) and that which would instead in principle subject sporting practices to orthodox legal regulation, albeit conditioned by contextual appreciation of sporting particularity. The former stance was in essence that preferred in the case by the EGC, whereas the latter was the essence of the choice made on appeal by the EU's senior court, the CJEU. That choice, which favours a more intense and potentially unpredictable application of legal rules, was met with dismay by sports federation. But it has dictated the way in which EU law will apply in future to sport. *Meca-Medina* counts as one of the landmark rulings in EU sports law, while also offering a basis for broader reflection on the extent to which sporting rules and practices deserve autonomy from legal regulation.

9.2 Factual Background

David Meca-Medina and Igor Majcen were professional swimmers. They had failed a drug test administered as part of the control exercised by FINA, swimming's governing body. Consequently they had been deprived of their means of making a living by a ban from competition which, after an appeal, was fixed at two years. The consequential economic detriment to them was plain. But equally plainly this was not *only* a matter of economics. Sport is structured by rules which define the essence of the endeavour. Keeping out drug cheats has an undeniable economic context, but at the same time it is an existential choice: sport is only sport if there is a level drug-free playing field for competitors.

The swimmers complained to the European Commission that their exclusion from the sport constituted a violation of the EU's competition rules. The Commission rejected their complaint and Meca-Medina and Majcen then applied to

EGC for annulment of the Commission's decision to reject their complaint. The EGC rejected their application.[2]

The CJEU subsequently set aside the EGC judgment, though it still ultimately concluded that the swimmers' application for annulment of the Commission decision had to fail.[3] The CJEU's ruling is significant for taking a much less generous approach to the scope of sporting autonomy than had been admitted by the EGC. This is why the litigation is both so illuminating and so important. It captures the choice to be made about the extent to which the law should respect sporting autonomy—and it concludes with that choice having been authoritatively made for the purposes of EU law.

The EGC had begun by adhering to the long-standing and orthodox judicial view that sport is subject to EU Law only in so far as it constitutes an economic activity. It then insisted that anti-doping rules concern exclusively non-economic aspects of sport, designed to preserve "noble competition"[4] and therefore outwith the scope of the Treaty. Such an approach is favourable to sports federations' conventional appeals for sporting autonomy, but it is nonetheless intellectually unstable. At para 41 the EGC refers to "purely sporting rules, that is to say rules concerning questions of purely sporting interest and, as such, having nothing to do with economic activity" and juxtaposes this to a description of "regulations, which relate to the particular nature and context of sporting events, are inherent in the organisation and proper conduct of sporting competition and cannot be regarded as constituting a restriction on the Community rules on the freedom of movement of workers and the freedom to provide services". This, however, is to conflate two different points. Plausibly there exists a (small) category of "purely sporting" rules unassociated with economic activity, but regulations inherent in the organisation and proper conduct of sporting competition form a much larger category in which economic effect is commonly present. Similarly, at para 44, the EGC observes that the "the campaign against doping does not pursue any economic objective". That may not be true, for the EGC itself refers at para 57 to the economic value of a "clean" sport to its organisers, but even if it *is* true, this is not of itself a reason for locating that campaign outside the Treaty. Anti-doping rules certainly have economic effects on those found to have contravened them. Attempts to present such rules as "sporting" and not "economic" are unhelpful. They are both.

The appeal against the CFI's ruling was largely directed at exposing the intellectual inadequacy of the attempt to establish a separation between sporting rules (which escape the scope of application of EU law) and rules of an economic nature (which do not). In this respect it was successful—although this ultimately was of no practical value to the applicant swimmers.

The CJEU, in line with well established case law, began by asserting that sport is subject to EU law "in so far as it constitutes an economic activity". It added that

[2] Case T-313/02 *Meca-Medina* [2004] ECR II-3291.

[3] Case C-519/04 P *Meca-Medina* [2006] ECR I-6991.

[4] Case C-519/04 P *Meca-Medina* [2006] ECR I-6991, para 49.

the Treaty prohibitions against restrictions on free movement "do not affect rules concerning questions which are of purely sporting interest and, as such, have nothing to do with economic activity", citing *Walrave and Koch*, its very first ruling applying EU law to sport.[5] It then referred to "the difficulty of severing the economic aspects from the sporting aspects of a sport", a well-chosen phrase deriving from the famous ruling in 1995 in *Bosman*,[6] confirming its view that the free movement provisions in the Treaty "do not preclude rules or practices justified on non-economic grounds which relate to the particular nature and context of certain sporting events", adding in line with long-standing judicial practice that such a restriction on the scope of the provisions in question must remain limited to its proper objective.

The CJEU then stated that "the mere fact that a rule is purely sporting in nature does not have the effect of removing from the scope of the Treaty the person engaging in the activity governed by that rule or the body which has laid it down".[7] And if the sporting activity in question falls within the scope of the Treaty, the rules which govern that activity must satisfy the requirements of the Treaty "which, in particular, seek to ensure freedom of movement for workers, freedom of establishment, freedom to provide services, or competition".[8] This is of paramount importance. It constitutes a rejection of the notion that a "purely sporting" rule is of itself apt to escape the scope of application of the Treaty. Instead the CJEU appreciates that a practice may be of a sporting nature—and perhaps even "purely sporting" in *intent*—but that it must be tested against the demands of EU law where it exerts economic *effects*.

But the swimmers still lost. The CJEU did not remit the case to the EGC. Instead, in accordance with its Statute, it felt it appropriate to give judgment on the substance of the appellants' claims for annulment of the Commission decision rejecting their complaint. And it rejected their application. It took the view that the general objective of the rules was to combat doping in order for competitive sport to be conducted on a fair basis; and the effect of penalties on athletes' freedom of action must be considered to be inherent in the anti-doping rules. Restrictions must be limited to what is necessary to ensure the proper conduct of competitive sport, and this relates to both defining the crime of doping and selecting penalties.[9] An excessive intervention into an athlete's freedom would generate unlawful adverse effects on competition[10] but in the case the appellants had failed to establish that the Commission made a manifest error of assessment in finding the rules (on quantities of permitted nandrolone) to be justified. Nor did the CJEU treat the penalties imposed as excessive. The judgment displays a proper wariness of

[5] Case 36/74 *Walrave and Koch* v *Union Cycliste Internationale* [1974] ECR 1405.

[6] Case C-415/93 *Bosman* [1995] ECR I-4921.

[7] Case C-415/93 *Bosman* [1995] ECR I-4921, para 27.

[8] Case C-415/93 *Bosman* [1995] ECR I-4921, para 28.

[9] Case C-415/93 *Bosman* [1995] ECR I-4921, para 48.

[10] Case C-415/93 *Bosman* [1995] ECR I-4921, para 47.

questioning the expertise practised by sports federations, but the Court refuses to place such practices beyond the scope of judicial review as a matter of principle.

9.3 The Legal Reasoning: Sport-Sensitive But Not Sport-Specific

In *Meca-Medina* the CJEU was prepared in principle to put sporting practices to the test—but it was also prepared to invest that test with recognition of the particular context in which sport is organised. So EU law overlaps with "internal" sports law (the *lex sportiva*)—but it absorbs, albeit not uncritically, the special expectations of sports governance.

The legal analysis so conducted into the compatibility of sporting practices with EU law is no novelty. The context-specific analysis of sporting practices undertaken in *Meca-Medina* is properly connected to other interpretations of (what is now) Article 101TFEU which have no material association with the sports sector. This is not sports law alone. Insisting that the compatibility of rules with EU competition law cannot be assessed in the abstract, the CJEU in *Meca Medina* stated that in applying Article 101TFEU:

> ...account must first of all be taken of the overall context in which the decision of the association of undertakings was taken or produces its effects and, more specifically, of its objectives. It has then to be considered whether the consequential effects restrictive of competition are inherent in the pursuit of those objectives (*Wouters and Others*, para 97) and are proportionate to them.[11]

The cited ruling in *Wouters* had nothing to do with sport.[12] In that case, the CJEU was asked to consider the compatibility with what is now Article 101TFEU of a Dutch rule forbidding the creation of multi-disciplinary partnerships involving barristers and accountants. The Court took the view that the national rule "has an adverse effect on competition and may affect trade between Member States".[13] A multi-disciplinary partnership could offer a wider range of services, as well as benefiting from economies of scale generating cost reductions. The prohibition was therefore liable to limit production and technical development.

Having found unambiguously that the "rules restrict competition",[14] the CJEU proceeded to state that for the purposes of application of Article 101TFEU account must "be taken of the overall context in which the decision of the association of undertakings was taken or produces its effects. More particularly, account must be

[11] Case C-415/93 *Bosman* [1995] ECR I-4921, paragraph 42.

[12] Full citation: Case C-309/99 *JCJ Wouters, JW Savelbergh, Price Waterhouse Belastingadviseurs BV v Algemene Raad van de Nederlandse Orde van Advocaten* [2002] ECR I-1577.

[13] Case C-309/99 *Wouters* [2002] ECR I-1577, para 86.

[14] Case C-309/99 *Wouters* [2002] ECR I-1577, para 94.

taken of its objectives.... It has then to be considered whether the consequential effects restrictive of competition are inherent in the pursuit of those objectives".[15]

The purpose of the Dutch rules prohibiting partnerships between barristers and accountants was to guarantee the independence and loyalty to the client of members of the Bar as part of a broader concern to secure the sound administration of justice. Though there were—the Court repeated—"effects restrictive of competition"[16] they did not go beyond what was necessary in order to ensure the proper functioning of the legal profession in The Netherlands. There was no breach of EU competition law.

The statement of principle that the notion of a restriction falling within Article 101(1)TFEU must be assessed in context is of general application, and it is the trail followed by the CJEU in *Meca-Medina*. The reasoning in *Wouters*, duly transplanted, invites an argument that the overall context in which sports regulation occurs, built around pursuit of a broad objective of fair competition, produces effects which though apparently restrictive of competition are nonetheless inherent in the pursuit of those objectives and therefore permitted. It is this route that is chosen by the CJEU in *Meca-Medina*. Anti-doping rules cannot simply be excluded from the scope of review by reference to their role in ensuring "fair play". They must be examined in their proper context, including recognition of their economic effect. But placing the rules within the ambit of the Treaty does not mean they will be forbidden by it. The general objective of the rules was to combat doping in order for competitive sport to be conducted on a fair basis; and the effect of penalties on athletes' freedom of action is inherent in the anti-doping rules. This *contextual* examination of the rules was crucial in the Court's conclusion that rules affected the athletes' freedom of action but that they did not constitute a restriction of competition incompatible with EU competition law.

By contrast, the EGC had sidelined *Wouters* for reasons that were logical once it had chosen to analyse the anti-doping rules as "purely sporting". The EGC considered that *Wouters* concerned "market conduct", an "essentially economic activity, that of lawyers". Anti-doping cannot be likened to market conduct without distorting the nature of sport, which "in its very essence... has nothing to do with any economic consideration".[17] This unsuccessful attempt to wall off sport from economic activity was defeated by the CJEU's preference on appeal to accept an overlap between EU law and "internal" sports law, while also accepting that the peculiar demands of the latter may be used to nourish a submission that an apparent restriction is nevertheless an essential element in sports governance. This, following *Wouters*, is the heart of *Meca-Medina*.

What is really at stake is not a group of sporting rules and a separate group of economic rules, but rather a group of sporting rules which carry economic implications and which therefore fall for assessment, but not necessarily

---

[15] Case C-309/99 *Wouters* [2002] ECR I-1577, para 97.

[16] Case C-309/99 *Wouters* [2002] ECR I-1577, para 110.

[17] Case T-313/02 *Meca-Medina* [2004] ECR II-3291, para 65.

condemnation, under EU competition law. Put another way, EU law affords sporting bodies a *conditional* autonomy. The key to EU sports law is: are the economic effects of the rule a necessary consequence of their contribution to the structure of sports governance? And *Meca-Medina* has provided the focus for the elaboration of the debate.

9.4 How *Meca-Medina* Has Come to Frame the Debate About EU Sports Law

The European Commission's White Paper on Sport, issued in July 2007,[18] places heavy reliance for its legal analysis on *Meca-Medina*, which is presented as a landmark ruling. It is the only decision of the CJEU explicitly referred to in the body of the White Paper, which comprises twenty pages. It is stated that:

> …in respect of the regulatory aspects of sport, the assessment whether a certain sporting rule is compatible with EU competition law can only be made on a case-by-case basis, as recently confirmed by the European Court of Justice in its *Meca-Medina* ruling. The Court provided a clarification regarding the impact of EU law on sporting rules. It dismissed the notion of "purely sporting rules" as irrelevant for the question of the applicability of EU competition law to the sport sector.[19]

The *Staff Working Document* which accompanies the White Paper supplies more detailed legal analysis. Annex I of the *Staff Working Document*, entitled *Sport and EU Competition Rules*, is stated to be not legally binding—this is constitutionally obvious—nor even to constitute Commission guidelines. However, it offers a reliable account. It explains that in so far as concessions are made to sporting "specificity" they are made on terms dictated by EU law; and, moreover, a case-by-case analysis of sporting practices is required. A general exemption is "neither possible nor warranted", in the judgement of the Commission.[20] This legal analysis is (quite correctly) heavily dependent on *Meca-Medina*. It concludes that the judgment reveals an interpretation of EU competition law which "provides sufficient flexibility to take account of the specificity of sport and does not impede sporting rules that pursue a legitimate objective (such as the organisation and proper conduct of sport), are indispensable (inherent) to achieve the objective and proportionate in light of the objective pursued".[21] The Annex then surveys existing decision-making practice in order to provide a feel for what may be permitted and what may not. This is largely intended to be descriptive

---

[18] European Commission's White Paper on Sport, COM (2007) 391, 11 July 2007.

[19] European Commission's White Paper on Sport, COM (2007) 391, 11 July 2007, 15.

[20] European Commission's White Paper on Sport, COM (2007) 391, 11 July 2007, Staff Working Document, Annex I, Sport and EU Competition Rules, 69 and 78.

[21] European Commission's White Paper on Sport, COM (2007) 391, 11 July 2007, Staff Working Document, Annex I, Sport and EU Competition Rules, 69.

although, in more ambitious vein, it seeks to explain some pre-existing EU case law on the basis of *Meca-Medina*. It suggests that the *ENIC* decision, concerning rules forbidding multiple ownership of football clubs,[22] is now capable of being understood as a finding that the measure involved no breach of Article 101(1)TFEU "on the basis of the *Wouters* criteria applied in *Meca Medina*".[23] Such a rule dampens demand and therefore restricts competition in the market for clubs, but is required to eliminate suspicions of collusion that would arise were clubs under the same ownership to face each other in matches. *Lehtonen*, a case dealing with transfer windows,[24] is similarly considered with the advantage of post-*Meca-Medina* eyes.[25] Re-interpretation of past practice in this manner is perilous for it may obscure the true course of reasoning adopted at the time, but the landmark significance of *Meca-Medina* justifies such repackaging, and the Commission's analysis is astute.

One could plausibly be more ambitious in such reappraisal of EU sports law prior to *Meca-Medina.* Rules governing selection of individuals for teams participating in high-level international competition are restrictive but necessary: existing case law "fits" the *Meca-Medina* model.[26] Rules limiting ticket sales for major events to particular nationals or residents are restrictive and unnecessary, and so unlawful.[27]

The significance of the approach chosen by the CJEU in *Meca-Medina* is readily appreciated when one glances at the contrasting tone of the "Arnaut Report"—the so-called Independent European Sport Review published in October 2006. The review process that led to the Arnaut Report was initiated by the UK Presidency of the EU in 2005 but dominated by the interests of those who currently control sports governance in Europe. The Arnaut Report almost entirely ignores the *Meca-Medina* ruling and prefers instead to load its analysis on the back of the EGC's judgment which had been set aside some months in advance of the publication of the Arnaut Report. It therefore presents an account of the law which is much more heavily biased in favour of sporting autonomy than the ECJ is willing to accept, and it amounts to little more than propaganda designed to promote the ambition of sports federations to relax the intensity of their subjection to EU law. The political ambition of the Arnaut Report is therefore obvious enough, but its persuasiveness in law is fatally damaged by an unsound inflated assessment of the notion of the "purely sporting rule".[28] The Commission's 2007 White Paper

---

[22] COMP 37.806 *ENIC/UEFA*, IP/02/942, 27 June 2002.

[23] COMP 37.806 *ENIC/UEFA*, IP/02/942, 27 June 2002, 71.

[24] Case C-176/96 *Lehtonen et al . v FRSB* [2000] ECR I-2681.

[25] Case C-176/96 *Lehtonen et al . v FRSB* [2000] ECR I-2681, 72.

[26] Compare to Cases C-51/96 & C-191/97 *Deliege* [2000] ECR I-2549.

[27] Dec. 2000/12 *1998 Football World Cup* [2000] OJ L5/55.

[28] See for example, the following paragraphs of the Arnaut Report: 3.19; 3.26; 3.40-3.41; 3.89; 5.55; 6.28; 6.60; and 6.70. The Arnaut Report is stated to have been prepared with the advice of José Luis da Cruz Vilaca. It seems implausible that such a distinguished jurist could have approved the final text of the Report.

largely ignores the Arnaut Report.[29] The Staff Working Document too shows little enthusiasm for it; for example, at page 28 it dismisses the recommendation that sport enjoys exemption from the state aid rules. And, rejecting suggestions in the "Arnaut Report, it states that the judgment in *Meca-Medina and Majcen* "strongly confirms" that it is not feasible to provide an exhaustive list of rules which do or do not breach the Treaty.

The flawed selectivity found in the Arnaut Report helps to reveal the full implications of the choice on offer when *Meca-Medina* was under consideration: the EGC's approach would have maximised sporting autonomy whereas the CJEU instead insists on a case-by-case examination of whether sporting practices with economic effects apt to bring the matter within the Treaty are compatible with EU law.

9.5 Sporting Uncertainty Before the Law

The *Wouters* formula, absorbed by *Meca-Medina*, ensures that the peculiar features of sport inform the application of the relevant legal rules. Abandoned is an attempt to decide what is "sporting" and what is "commercial", and instead the overlap of the two spheres is embraced. The intersection of EU law and "internal" sports law (the *lex sportiva*) is therefore recognised, and sporting bodies have room to show how and why the rules are necessary to accommodate their particular concerns—fair play, credible competition, national representative sides, and so on. Most positive accounts of the CJEU's ruling have tended to emphasise the scope allowed by the Court for debate about what is truly "special" in the governance of sport, while also appreciating the improved intellectual quality of the analysis, in particular its rejection of the ill-shaped concept of the "purely sporting" rule—which was and is rarely "purely" sporting at all, but rather both sporting and economic in its implications.[30]

On the other hand *Meca-Medina* is, admittedly, troubling for sports bodies, not only because it represents a setback for those who would in principle champion the virtues of sporting autonomy but also for more urgently practical reasons. It asserts the need for case-by-case examination of the compatibility of sporting practices with EU law. This is vulnerable to the criticism that it breeds uncertainty and unpredictability. Such anxieties have been audible for many years, but *Meca-Medina* inflamed the debate. The ruling attracted pained criticism from those close to sports governing bodies.[31] Other sources too have expressed anxieties about

---

[29] See only a bland reference in European Commission's White Paper on Sport, COM (2007) 391, 11 July 2007, 13, fn 7.

[30] See, largely approving of this shift Wathelet 2006 and Weatherill 2006 and, later, Rincon 2007; Szyszczak 2007 and Wathelet 2007.

[31] See Infantino, Director of Legal Affairs at UEFA 2006 and Zylberstein 2007.

inter alia the expertise of the CJEU in Luxembourg to investigate such matters.[32] Similarly the White Paper has been greeted from this perspective with a degree of mistrust from those detecting a diminished concern on the part of the Commission to take full account of the supposed special character of sport.[33]

And sporting bodies have unrivalled expertise at attracting media support for the supposed wounding effect of legal intervention. The *Financial Times* of 18 October 2007 ran the following story on page 11:

> *Olympics chief fears EU grip on doping rules*: The Olympic movement faces the frightening prospect of anti-doping rules coming under the responsibility of the European Union unless the Lisbon summit agrees to exempt sport from EU free market rules, the president of the International Olympic Committee has warned. ... Mr Rogge highlighted the so-called *Meca-Medina* doping case in which the European Court of Justice ruled last year that anti-doping laws contravened EU competition law by taking away freedom to compete from two banned swimmers...

Of course the Court ruled no such thing! That even the *Financial Times*, by far the most (perhaps the only) reliable British newspaper, should publish the very opposite of the truth reveals the remarkable ability of sport to use the media to advance its tendentious claims for autonomy. But, stripped of its inaccuracy, this quote is helpful in capturing the abiding concern of sports federations to keep the law in general and EU law in particular at arm's length—by hook or by crook. This is the more general context within which *Meca-Medina and Majcen* has been attacked for stripping away some of the autonomy to which sports governing bodies regularly lay claim as necessary and appropriate. The vibrant *contestability* of the practice of EU intervention in sport is plain. This paper makes the case that via the *Wouters* formula, absorbed by the Court in *Meca-Medina and Majcen*, EU law accommodates the special concerns of sports governance in the interpretation and application of the law—just as it is open to any sector to seek to persuade the Court that it has particular requirements that are inherent in its operation which are apt for recognition despite their restrictive effect on competition.

9.6 The Lisbon Treaty

With effect from December 2009 the Lisbon Treaty for the first time brought sport explicitly within the scope of EU law. Article 165TFEU provides a limited legislative competence. This is constitutionally significant, since for the first time the EU enjoys an unequivocal basis under its Treaty to legislate in the field of sport. However, Article 6TFEU confines the EU to actions in the field of sport which "support, coordinate or supplement the actions of the Member States" and Article 165TFEU explictly excludes the possibility of harmonisation of laws by the EU.

---

[32] See, for instance, Subiotto 2010.

[33] Hill 2009.

Moreover, there is no likelihood of more than modest budget being allocated for these purposes. So the EU is not about to become a major actor in the field of sports regulation as a result of the insertion of Article 165TFEU into the Treaty.

However, the EU is *already* involved in sports regulation as a result of the application of the Treaty rules on competition law and free movement, and a more interesting question is whether the Lisbon Treaty will adjust the long-standing practice of the CJEU in general and the approach chosen in *Meca-Medina* in particular. And the answer is almost certainly—no. Article 165(1)TFEU provides that "The Union shall contribute to the promotion of European sporting issues, while taking account of the specific nature of sport, its structures based on voluntary activity and its social and educational function". This formula should be understood as a reflection of the failure of sports bodies to extract an exemption from the Treaty in the process of negotiation of what ultimately became the Lisbon Treaty. Denied that prize, sports bodies actively sought the explicit inclusion of sport in the Treaty—precisely in the hope of then using that inclusion as a lever to reduce the intensity of application of EU law.[34] One may readily expect the structure of the argument to be affected by this formula: defence of sporting practices will presented as an appeal to show deference to the "specific nature of sport", thereby to maximise the scope of autonomy from EU law. So in 2010 UEFA stated that "there is now a provision in the Treaty itself recognising that sport cannot simply be treated as another business".[35] But the CJEU already infuses EU law with such sensitivity to sport's peculiar features. Indeed it is possible to interpret the "specific nature of sport" written into Article 165TFEU by the Lisbon Treaty as a codification of the essence of the *Meca-Medina* judgment. The application of EU law to sport should be sensitive to the special (social, economic, cultural) character of sport: this is precisely how the CJEU was able to conclude that the anti-doping rules which it was asked to scrutinise in *Meca-Medina* were compatible with EU law. A landmark on paper, as the dawn of EU sports law explicitly recognised by the Treaty, the Lisbon Treaty's practical transformative effect is likely to be modest.[36]

9.7 After the Lisbon Treaty

In *Olympique Lyonnais* v *Olivier Bernard and Newcastle United*, the CJEU had its first opportunity since the entry into force of the Lisbon Treaty to reflect on its impact.[37] Dealing with French rules requiring that compensation be paid for young

[34] See Garcia and Weatherill 2012.

[35] UEFA 2010.

[36] For discussion see Rangeon 2010 and Weatherill 2010.

[37] Case C-325/08 *Bernard* [2010] ECR I-2177.

players who change club, it repeated its finding in *Bosman*[38] that the objective of encouraging the recruitment and training of young players must be accepted as legitimate in EU law. It then added:

> In considering whether a system which restricts the freedom of movement of such players is suitable to ensure that the said objective is attained and does not go beyond what is necessary to attain it, account must be taken, as the Advocate General states in points 30 and 47 of her Opinion, of the specific characteristics of sport in general, and football in particular, and of their social and educational function. The relevance of those factors is also corroborated by their being mentioned in the second subparagraph of Article 165(1)TFEU.[39]

There is no hint at all that the CJEU is proposing to adjust its approach. Case-by-case inquiry remains necessary; but that inquiry remains informed by sport's special character. *Meca-Medina* retains its significance, unaffected by the Lisbon Treaty's innovations.

The same message emerges in October 2011 from *FA Premier League, Karen Murphy*.[40] This ruling interrogated the compatibility with EU free movement law of British rules imposing penalties on those who transferred decoders allowing decryption of satellite signals from States where prices were low to States where prices were high, thereby undermining the contractual network for the sale of rights to broadcast football matches that was based on territorial exclusivity within a fragmented EU market. The CJEU concluded that such rules could not be applied to sanction private consumers (though resort to copyright law could restrain commercially motivated parties, such as pub landlords, wishing to screen matches in this way). One justification advanced for the restrictions was rooted in the need to protect so-called "closed periods". In the United Kingdom, matches may not be shown on television on Saturday afternoons. Were an English match, played at 3 o'clock on a Saturday afternoon and broadcast in Greece, also then broadcast in England as a result of importation of a decoder, then the "closed period" would be subverted with, it was argued, consequent damage to live attendances at matches. Advocate General Kokott addressed this defence of the fragmented pattern for selling rights throughout Europe from the perspective of Article 165TFEU. Noting that the existence of "closed periods" restricts output and reduces income, she accepted this to be "primarily a sporting interest which is in principle to be recognised in European Union law", citing the Lisbon Treaty's reference to the specific nature of sport and its structures based on voluntary activity. But this was as good as it got for those seeking to defend the rules. She explained that:

> The football associations are required to assess the need for closed periods and they should in principle enjoy a broad margin of discretion in this regard. It cannot be ruled out a priori, however, that the decision by the English Football Association to make use of a

---

38 Case C-415/93 *Bosman* [1995] ECR I-4921.

39 Case C-325/08 *Bernard* [2010] ECR I-2177, para 40.

40 Case C-403/08 *FA Premier League* & C-429/08 *Karen Murphy*, CJEU judgment of 4 October 2011.

> closed period is also based at least in part on safeguarding the economic interest of the most important members of the association in partitioning the internal market for live football transmissions. A particularly strict test is therefore to be applied to the demonstration of the need for closed periods. It is, in fact, doubtful whether closed periods are capable of encouraging attendance at matches and participation in matches.[41]

This is a far cry from interpreting the Lisbon Treaty as granting a wider zone of autonomy to sport. It is, by complete contrast, the most aggressive dismissal of the notion of sporting autonomy that is to be found in the accumulated case law of the Court. The CJEU was not quite so brutal in its subsequent ruling, but it too swept aside the vitality of the justification rooted in attracting fans into stadiums by enforcing closed periods. It simply observed that this could be achieved contractually—by refusing to sell rights to broadcast matches played during the "closed period" in any jurisdiction — which would be less restrictive of trade than the prevailing system (and doubtless less lucrative too). And the CJEU's only reference to Article 165 was a throwaway remark associated with the EU's so-called "protected events" legislation, which was not directly relevant to the matter at hand.[42]

As Advocate General Kokott put it in her Opinion in *Karen Murphy*, citing Article 165TFEU, "whilst European Union law respects the special characteristics of sport, sport does not fall outside the scope of that law".[43] So far the Court's case law seems intent on granting no wider sphere of autonomy to sporting bodies in consequence on the revisions effected by the Lisbon Treaty. So again it seems evident that *Meca-Medina and Majcen* retains centre stage as an authoritative statement of how and why EU law applies to sport.

The low salience of the Lisbon Treaty is emphasised by the sports-related documentation published by the Commission in January 2011. The Commission Communication entitled *Developing the European Dimension in Sport*[44] employs three main themes to structure the analysis: the societal role of sport, the economic dimension of sport and the organisation of sport. This was exactly the model used in the 2007 White Paper on Sport. This is the first significant attempt to shape policy since the entry into force of the Lisbon Treaty in December 2009, but the Lisbon Treaty is the subject of only marginal reference. It is the 2007 White Paper which remains the blueprint—and it, as mentioned, places *Meca-Medina* at the heart of its legal analysis. The ruling is the persisting core of EU sports law.

---

[41] Case C-403/08 *FA Premier League* & C-429/08 *Karen Murphy*, Opinion of the Advocate General of 3 February 2011, para 208.

[42] Case C-403/08 *FA Premier League* & C-429/08 *Karen Murphy*, CJEU judgment of 4 October 2011, paras 101–102.

[43] Case C-403/08 *FA Premier League* & C-429/08 *Karen Murphy*, Opinion of the Advocate General of 3 February 2011, para 165.

[44] Communication from the European Commission to the European Parliament, the Council, the European Economic and Social Committee and the Committee of the Regions, *Developing the European Dimension in Sport* COM (2011) 12, 18 Jan 2011.

9.8 Conclusion

In *Wouters*, the CJEU interpreted EU competition law in the light of concern for values that are developed outside the framework of competition law but which overlap with it. *Meca-Medina* applies this model to sport. The CJEU has taken a broad view of the scope of EU law—but having brought sporting rules within the scope of the Treaty it shows itself readily prepared to draw on the importance of matters not explicitly described as "justifications" in the Treaty in order to permit the continued application of challenged practices which are shown to be necessary to achieve legitimate sporting objectives and/or are inherent in the organisation of sport. And the result of *Meca-Medina* itself demonstrates that the sporting expertise informing (*in casu*) anti-doping inquiries will not lightly be set aside by judges. Sports bodies commonly insist that sport should not be treated like any other business—EU law agrees! The CJEU has shaped EU law so that it allows assessment of the strength of the competing interests at stake when sport intersects with the economic project mapped out by the EU Treaty.

References

Garcia B, Weatherill S (2012) Engaging with the EU in order to minimise its impact: sport and the negotiation of the Treaty of Lisbon. J Eur Public Policy 19:238–256

Hill J (2009) The European commission's white paper on sport: a step backwards for specificity? Int J Sport Policy 1:253–266

Infantino G (2006) Meca-Medina: a step backwards for the European sports model and the specificity of sport? UEFA paper, 2 October. http://www.uefa.com/uefa/stakeholders/europeanunion/index.html. Accessed 31 July 2012

Rangeon F (2010) Le Traité de Lisbonne, Acte de Naissance d'une Politique Européenne du Sport? Revue du Marché commun et de l'Union européenne 538:302–309

Rincon A (2007) EC competition and internal market law: on the existence of a sporting exemption and its withdrawal. J Contemp Eur Res 3:224–237

Subiotto R (2010) The adoption and enforcement of anti-doping rules should not be subject to European competition law. Eur Compet Law Rev 31:323–330

Szyszczak E (2007) Competition and sport. Eur Law Rev 32:95–110

UEFA's position on Article 165 of the Lisbon Treaty (2010) http://www.uefa.com/uefa/stakeholders/europeanunion/index.html. Accessed 31 July 2012

Wathelet M (2006) L'arrêt Meca-Medina et Majcen: plus qu'un coup dans l'eau. Revue de Jurisprudence de Liége, Mon et Bruxelles 41:1799–1809

Wathelet M (2007) Sport governance and EU legal order: the *Wathelet* report. Int Sports Law J 3/4:3–9 and 11–12

Weatherill S (2010) Fairness, openness and the specific nature of sport: does the Lisbon treaty change EU sports law? Int Sports Law J 3/4:11, 14–17

Weatherill S (2006) Anti-doping revisited—the demise of the rule of 'purely sporting' interest? Eur Compet Law Rev 27:645–657

Zylberstein J (2007) Collision entre idéaux sportifs et contingences économiques dans l'arret *Meca-Medina*. Cahiers de Droit Europeen 1/2:213–237

Part IV
Doping and the Spirit of Sports Law

Chapter 10
Modahl v British Athletic Federation (1994–2001)

Hazel Hartley

Abstract In 1994, the claimant, an athlete, was suspended from an international competition by the British Athletic Federation ("BAF") after failing a drugs test. The test was carried out by a Portuguese laboratory accredited by the International Olympic Committee ("IOC"). The relevant testing regime and procedures were governed by world governing body for athletics—the International Amateur Athletics Federation ("IAAF"). The claimant was suspended and prevented from competing at that year's Commonwealth Games. In October 1994, she attended a BAF disciplinary hearing at which she was found to have committed a doping offence, but this finding was subsequently overthrown some months later by an Independent Appeal Panel ("IAP"). In 1996, Modahl instigated legal proceedings based on breach of contract and claiming from the defendant damages and interest for loss and damage suffered during her period of suspension, arguing (i) a breach of contract by allowing her urine sample to be tested at different and unaccredited laboratory premises, and (ii) a breach of contract by way of certain members of the disciplinary panel showing actual or likely bias against her. As it transpired, both limbs proceeded separately. The first, which was ultimately dismissed by the House of Lords, centred on the accreditation status of the laboratory which tested the claimant's sample and whether the BAF should be directly and contractually liable for any maladministration in the drug testing regime carried out under IAAF/IOC regulations. The second limb, which was ultimately dismissed by the Court of Appeal, concerned the issue of bias in sports disciplinary processes and also discussed the contractual nexus between an athlete and their national governing body.

H. Hartley (✉)
Carnegie Faculty, Headingly Campus, Leeds Metropolitan University, Leeds LS6 3QS, UK
e-mail: h.hartley@leedsmet.ac.uk

J. Anderson (ed.), *Leading Cases in Sports Law*,
ASSER International Sports Law Series, DOI: 10.1007/978-90-6704-909-2_10,

Contents

10.1 Introduction

This chapter will devote equal space to the sport disciplinary processes as it does to the legal case in which Diane Modahl sought damages. It will also draw upon comments from some of those who experienced the very challenging sport disciplinary processes at the heart of this case. At the time of the *Modahl* proceedings, anti-doping rules included a presumption of competence in the testing laboratories. They still do so today. From an anti-doping perspective, this high profile "false-positive" case illustrates the harsh reality of strict liability doping rules and an athlete's worst nightmare—"the lab got it wrong". It gives food for thought to those who might be of the view, "So what if we have a few 'false-positives' if, on the whole, the anti-doping system protects sport competition?"

In the area of sport governance, the *Modahl* proceedings provide a very intense and informative education on the challenges facing those who give up their time to volunteer on technical, doping or disciplinary committees in sport. From a sports law perspective, the *Modahl* proceedings were a lengthy and expensive journey for both parties and through the areas of contract law; obligations to act fairly in disciplinary matters; apparent and actual bias; anti-doping rules; laboratory testing procedures; as well as a significant dose of complex medico-legal discourse. It began in June 1994 at a European athletics competition and ended in October 2001 in the Court of Appeal. Debates and questions will no doubt continue around the appropriate legal remedy for athletes in such circumstances, the role of arbitration (if any), the applicability of judicial review to sporting bodies and the ways in which the law views rule-bound sporting relationships.

10.2 Competition Doping Control: Sample "A" and "B" Tests—June to Aug 1994

On 18 June 1994, Diane Modahl, a British athlete, was competing in the 800 m at an international athletics competition in San Antonio, Portugal.[1] She was selected to provide a urine sample, which tested positive for testosterone at a ratio of 42:1.[2] The relevant rules in relation to doping, which were strict liability in nature, were set out in the IAAF Handbook for 1994–1995 ("the IAAF Rules"). IAAF Rule 55 specifically provided that:

> 1. Doping is strictly forbidden and is an offence under IAAF Rules.
> 2. The offence of doping take place when either
>
>   (i) A prohibited substance is found to be present within an athlete's body tissue or fluids…
>
> 4. It is an athlete's duty to ensure that no substance enters his body tissues or fluids which is prohibited under these rules. Athletes are warned that they are responsible for all or any substance detected in samples given by them…[3]

At the time the "A" sample was collected "its pH value was tested and found to be pH5" which was within the normal analytical range.[4] The "A" sample tests began on 17 July and were concluded on 18 July.[5] Under regulation, the IAAF was required to inform the athlete's national federation [the BAF] then arrange for a test on the reserve "B" sample 21 days later. If the B sample tested positive, the procedure was that it would be the responsibility of the BAF to conduct a disciplinary hearing not later than three months after the final laboratory report.[6] There was a significant delay in the notification of the sample "A" result by the PAF. The notification took the form of a fax to the BAF which in turn was passed on to

---

[1] Diane Modahl was competing for the British women's athletics team in a European Amateur Athletics Federation ("EAAA") event under IAAF Rules, organised locally by the Portuguese Athletics Federation ("PAF") with doping control samples being tested by a laboratory in Lisbon—the Labaratorio de Analises de Doping de Bioquimica ("LADB") which was accredited by the IOC.

[2] At the material time, the threshold fail ratio of testosterone to epitestosterone was 6:1. The ratio in Ben Johnson's urine sample, which tested positive for steroids at the 1988 Seoul Olympics following his gold medal in the 100 m final, was 12:1.

[3] The present case took place before the formation of the World Anti-Doping Agency ("WADA") and at that time in 1994 about 20 doping control sample-testing laboratories were accredited by the IOC and were expected to follow IOC guidelines. Now, testing laboratories are accredited by WADA and strict, standardised International Laboratory Standards (ILS) apply. The lastest ISL version (7.0) came into effect on 1 January 2012.

[4] See Modahl 1995, 141.

[5] Modahl 1995, 148.

[6] See Hartley 2004, 61.

Diane Modahl on 24 August when she was just about to defend her 800 m title at the Commonwealth Games in Victoria, Canada. Modahl then had to withdraw from the event. The fax from the PAF to the BAF and then onto the British team management at the Commonwealth Games in Victoria, Canada on 24 August 1994 read as follows:

> We inform you that the results of the doping control performed on Ms. Diane Modahl, from GB in the St. Antonio meeting in Lisbon on June 18 have been positives. The Report of the 'Doping and Biochemistry Analysis Laboratory informs us that the Diane Modahl sample revealed TESTOSTERONE/EPITESTOSTERONE equal to 42.08 –value to consider demonstrative of administration of TESTOSTERONE exogenous. We will contact you in order to agree the date to conduct the test on the reserve 'B' sample.[7]

The IAAF General Secretary subsequently informed Diane Modahl that the opening of the "B" sample would take place on 29 August in Lisbon—it was in fact delayed until Wednesday 31 August 1994. Diane Modahl was represented at the "B" Test by her husband and coach, Vicente Modahl, Dr Malcolm Brown, Head Medical Officer for the BAF and Professor Arnold Beckett, "one of the most respected figures in the world of doping".[8] Dr Peter Radford and Dr David Cowan also represented the BAF. At this event, several serious concerns were raised around the relocation and accreditation of the testing laboratory, the chain of custody documents, the pH level of the "B" sample compared to the "A" sample, the strong smell of ammonia in the sample, indicating bacteria had grown in the sample, and the absence of metabolites.[9]

Chain of custody documents—tracing, contemporaneously, the journey and location of the sample from the moment of the taking of sample "A" until it is tested, analysed and reported—were required both by the then applicable IAAF and IOC regulations.[10] On requesting the chain of custody documents, the Modahl team were told that they were "not available", but would be provided "during the day". Subsequently, Diane Modahl testified that later that day her husband was provided with a two page summary written by the laboratory after the completion of the "B" test but that no contemporaneous chain of custody documents had been produced.[11] She also stated that Dr David Cowan "the head of the only IOC

[7] Modahl 1995, 97.

[8] Modahl 1995, 120.

[9] If testosterone has actually been "exogenous", that is, administered externally and passed through an athlete's body and into the urine sample, the presence of metabolites would be expected in such a sample. See further Modahl 1995, 138–141 and Hartley 2009, 243.

[10] See Modahl 1995, 140–141 citing from a paper given by Professor Manfred Donike, then in charge of worldwide IOC accreditation of laboratories: "The chain of custody which begins with the urine voiding and ends with the analysis result report, must be impeccable before a positive finding can lead to sanctions".

[11] Modahl 1995, 117, 139 and 140.

accredited laboratory in the United Kingdom, gave evidence on behalf of the BAF that he did not consider the chain of custody to be adequate".[12] The significant scientific issues of concern were later summarised by the athlete:

> When the 'B' test was done in front of the observers from the BAF and from my team, it became quite clear from the start that the sample had deteriorated dramatically. When the sample was given in June its pH value was tested and found to be pH5. At the time the sample was opened for testing at the end of August, the pH value was measured in two different ways and showed one of 8.8 and the other was 8.9. Thus the sample was taken to be pH 8.85. The sample also gave off a strong smell of ammonia. This could only mean one thing – bacteria had been growing in the sample and had changed it. Samples deteriorated to a level above pH 7.5 are not generally tested because any results found may not be accurate. Samples allowed to deteriorate to above pH 7.5 are normally thrown away, and Dr. Cowan, in his evidence at the hearing on behalf of the B.A.F. stated that he himself would not have tested the sample.[13]

Diane Modahl noted that both Dr Cowan and Professor Beckett "wanted to stop the ['B'] test" on fear that the sample had been contaminated by bacteria. They took the view that apparent changes to the "characteristics of the sample" raised "serious questions as to the compliance with IAAF Guidelines in relation to storage and treatment of samples pending analysis".[14] On the day in question, however, the IAAF medical representative, a Dr Dolle, insisted that the process continue.[15] The test went ahead and confirmed the results of the "A" sample—that is a positive result, recording a ratio of 42:1 of testosterone to epitestosterone ("T/E ratio").[16] On 6 September 1994, the BAF suspended Diane Modahl, pending a disciplinary hearing. Under IAAF Rules the national sport governing body, in this case the BAF, was responsible for conducting a disciplinary hearing and normally within three months of a positive "B" test result. A BAF Panel was duly convened to hear the case in London on 13 December 1994.

10.3 BAF Disciplinary Panel Hearing: 13 to 14 December 1994, London

The membership of the BAF Disciplinary Panel ("the Panel") displayed a thoughtfully constructed range of backgrounds in terms of gender, ethnicity, experience and expertise. The Panel was chaired by Dr Martin Lucking, a general practitioner and former athlete. He was joined on the Panel by Jocelyn

---

[12] Modahl 1995, 140.

[13] Modahl 1995, 141.

[14] Cited by McArdle 2001, 96.

[15] Modahl 1995, 119.

[16] Modahl 1995, 111 cites from a BBC interview with a contemporary of hers, 110 m hurdler, Tony Jarrett, who observed wryly, "If I had that amount of testosterone in my body I'd have a beard like Barry White".

Hoyte-Smith (a former heptathlete); Chris Carter (a police officer and athletics coach); Walter Nicholls (a solicitor of long standing) and Alan Guy (a member of the IAAF technical committee and an experienced EAAA doping officer). Such a diverse Panel is "quite difficult to achieve, when one considers the voluntary nature of governing body membership, resources, as well as the availability of all the members in one time and place, outside their jobs and a busy athletics calendar".[17] In preparing for the BAF hearing, Modahl recalled that her representatives focussed on seven key points: "there was no proof that the sample was mine or that it hadn't been spiked; the sample was so degraded it should never have been tested; the laboratory staff were not competent; the "B" test should not have gone ahead; the laboratory did not confirm the presence of testosterone; the findings were not consistent with testosterone administration; and the T/E ratio was ambiguous".[18]

Representatives for both Diane Modahl and the BAF attended the Panel hearing on 13 December in London. No one from the Portuguese laboratory was in attendance.[19] Diane Modahl recorded that the approach of the BAF's lawyers on the day was that:

> …the chain of custody, the state of the sample, the disregard of normal doping regulations – none of these things mattered, they said, the only point worthy of attention was that the sample was positive and could only be explained by administering testosterone.[20]

In counter, Modahl's defence attempted to establish reasonable doubt as to the credibility of the test procedure and result. They argued that the key changes in pH could be attributed to the fact that Modahl's samples had lain unrefrigerated for two days in the Lisbon heat. It was also argued that taking testosterone would have produced a reaction in the liver, causing the production of metabolites but that no metabolites were discovered in the sample.[21] Diane Modahl's legal team then went on to highlight concerns regarding the integrity of the chain of custody and the laboratory's procedural behaviour as well as pursuing questions relating to the substantive scientific explanations for the doping result. In response to questions from Diane Modahl's lawyer, Dr David Cowan, the expert called on behalf of the BAF, informed the hearing that there were no contemporaneous chain of custody

---

[17] Hartley 2009, 241.

[18] Modahl 1995, 139–145.

[19] Modahl 1995, 149 explained this absence thusly: "Mark Gay, the I.A.A.F. lawyer, asked them to come over and give evidence in a letter dated 2 December. Professor Mirandela da Costa, said that witnesses could not come over because they were civil servants, the British Press were hostile, and if the B.A.F. wanted, the enquiries could take place in Portugal". Similarly, Grayson 1995, 44 noted that the Technical Director and the Scientific Director of the Lisbon Lab had been invited by the BAF to the hearing but had explained that "as government employees they needed government permission [to attend]" but that that authority had "not been forthcoming".

[20] Modahl 1995, 159.

[21] O'Leary 2012, 379.

documents produced, a fact he found "unacceptable".[22] He further questioned the laboratory's procedural approach.[23] In sum, and at the heart of these lengthy and complex proceedings, was evidence of a medico-legal nature, presented and interpreted by several scientific expert witnesses for both sides, wherein the defence attempted to cast doubt on the validity of the positive test by concentrating on the possibility of bacterial degradation of the urine sample, incorrectly stored at high temperatures, as a satisfactory explanation for the positive, adverse analytical finding of 42:1.

In reflecting on the hearing, Modahl recounted the evidence of one of the scientific experts, Dr. John Honour:

> I felt that the very thing we'd wanted to avoid was happening: the case was becoming very scientific, almost a battle between medical experts. Even though I'd been through it many times, it was hard for me to follow. I knew the panel would also be struggling to understand everything.[24]

The BAF legal team as part of their summing up proposed that there were two realistic possibilities to consider: that the bacteria had affected the sample or that Modahl had administered testosterone. Dr. Honour's explanation—that the bacteria degradation had reacted to create testosterone or something mimicking testosterone—was dismissed as being highly improbable. In contrast, the BAF noted that their medical expert witnesses were at all times dealing with "a practical reality".[25] The BAF further argued that a satisfactory explanation for the positive analytical finding had to be more than a theory or a mere possibility and that there was a distinct lack of published and contemporary scientific research on bacterial degradation in urine samples.[26]

On hearing the evidence, the Panel deliberated and on 14 December 1995 advised the Modahl team of their decision. In short, the Panel was unconvinced that theoretical arguments on the possibility of bacterial degradation altered the balance of probability.[27] The subsequent announcement to the awaiting media and press, by the Panel's chair, Dr Martyn Lucking, read as follows:

> Having heard all the evidence and read all the documents, the committee was satisfied, unanimously, beyond reasonable doubt, that a doping offence had been committed by Mrs.

---

[22] Modahl 1995, 161.

[23] Modahl 1995, 161 recounts that the laboratory technicians present at the "B" test in Lisbon "started to actually open a bottle of pure testosterone.. they actually physically opened it and were going to spoon it out in the laboratory" only for Dr. Cowan to intervene and stop them.

[24] Modahl 1995, 159. In an interview for a BBC TV documentary "On the Line" series, the *Diane Modahl Story*, first transmitted on BBC2 on 3 February 1996), Dr Honour admitted that during his evidence he had, given the complexity of the science in question, thought about whether he was getting his points across in a manner that could be understood by the non-expert.

[25] Modahl 1995, 166.

[26] See Reid 1995, 6 and Hartley 2004, 61.

[27] O'Leary 2012, 379.

> Modahl...Accordingly, she is ineligible to complete in the UK and abroad for four years, from 18 June 1994.[28]

At the press conference in the hotel, following this announcement, Diane Modahl included in her press statement:

> I am horrified at the decision – and the prospect of the nightmare of the last four months continuing. I cannot accept the BAF's decision and will carry on fighting to clear my name because I know I am innocent...I have never taken any banned substance. I have declared my innocence. I shall take my case to the Independent Appeal Panel.[29]

On 15 December 1994, Diane Modahl gave notice of appeal to the BAF. Between January and June 1995, the IAAF refused a request from the BAF to have further tests done at the laboratory in Lisbon. In June 1995, the IAAF appeared at first to relent but in a quick about turn abandoned any proposed re-testing, citing lack of co-operation from Lisbon.

10.4 The Independent Appeal Panel: 24 to 25 July 1995, London

The Independent Appeal Panel ("IAP"), chaired by Robert Reid QC, was presented with five key issues for determination:

(1) Were they satisfied as to the chain of custody relating to the sample, from the time it was given by Mrs. Modahl to its final analysis?
(2) Was the laboratory at which the analysis took place properly accredited, and were its procedures acceptable and staff competent?
(3) Were the "A" and "B" samples analysed (or tested) those given by Mrs. Modahl and if so, should they have been analysed?
(4) Were the tests properly carried out in accordance with relevant guidelines, and what ratio of testosterone to epitestosterone did they reveal?
(5) Could the degradation of the sample have given rise to a false result?[30]

The most significant issue was question five. The IAP accepted that "the low levels of metabolites pointed out by Modahl's representatives, at the 'B' sample test, were not consistent with the presence of *administered* testosterone".[31] The IAP expressed disappointment that the remaining sample was not available, despite requests to the Lisbon laboratory, as "that analysis might (on the evidence

---

[28] BBC TV documentary "On the Line" series, the *Diane Modahl Story*, first transmitted on BBC2 on 3 February 1996.

[29] Modahl 1995, 170. Modahl was aware, at 174, that "no-one had ever won an appeal against the BAF before".

[30] Note the recollections of the chair of the IAP at Reid 1995, 6.

[31] Hartley 2009, 243.

we have heard) have answered definitively some of the questions we have had to consider".[32] Further, new scientific evidence, in the form of experiments carried out by scientific expert witnesses for Diane Modahl showed that "bacterial degradation such as existed in Mrs Modahl's urine, could affect the levels of testosterone in the urine sample".[33] This was crucial. What had been a theoretical possibility (of bacterial degradation) now appeared to be supported by credible scientific evidence. The Modahl team also demonstrated that "the bacterial transformation theory could be replicated under laboratory conditions".[34] The IAP appeared to be impressed in particular by a series of experiments demonstrating that "urine from two female athletes kept for 72 h at 37 °C showed markedly increased levels of testosterone".[35] These experiments, although not thought to "establish any general proposition" did, for the purposes of the IAP appeal, "appear to back up the opinions expressed by three eminent scientists, namely that if urine is degraded by bacterial action, it is possible for the testosterone level to be increased".[36]

The IAP concluded that Diane Modahl was entitled to succeed in her appeal. They could not be sure beyond reasonable doubt that she was guilty of a doping offence. Considering all the evidence presented, they had to acknowledge the possibility that the doping test result in Portugal had "*not been caused by any testosterone being administered*..[but]...by the samples *becoming degraded, owing to them being stored in unrefrigerated conditions*, and that bacterial action has resulted in an increase in the amount of testosterone in the samples".[37] Subsequently, Modahl was formally cleared by the IAAF to compete in athletics, though she remarked ruefully that "it only takes one error in a science like drug testing and the result is the devastation of an innocent athlete's life and career".[38]

10.5 *Modahl v BAF (No 1)*

Three immediate points following the IAP decision are noteworthy. First, the IAAF announced that it would appeal against the IAP's decision to its own quasi-independent arbitration panel. However, in March 1996, the 27-member IAAF Council decided to drop the case on the advice of its Doping Commission Chairman, Professor Arne Ljungvist.[39] Professor Ljungvist agreed with the IAP

32 Hartley 2009, 243.
33 Reid 1995, 6.
34 O'Leary 2012, 379.
35 Reid 1995, 7.
36 Reid 1995, 7.
37 Reid 1995, 6. Emphasis added.
38 Modahl 1995, 192.
39 McArdle 2001, 97.

that the "manifest failures in the testing procedure regarding sample storage and loss of paperwork had effectively relieved Modahl of any obligation to provide an explanation for her testosterone levels".[40] Second, and to reiterate, as it becomes important in the discussion of the accompanying legal proceedings; the only basis for the IAP's decision in the claimant's favour was the new material giving support to what had previously merely been an assertion on the possibility that bacterial contamination could have affected the testosterone reading.[41] Third, on 6 February 1996, Diane Modahl served a writ against the BAF for damages to compensate "the expenses she incurred from fighting the charges (£250,000) and the financial loss she suffered from the wrongful ban from competition for almost a year".[42] This element of the claim was regarded by one commentator as "noteworthy" because it highlights an underlying element of many of these cases, that is:

> …the career of an elite professional athlete is quite short and precarious: rarely will an athlete remain competitive at the lucrative elite level for more than two Olympic cycles i.e., eight years. It follows that a nine-month suspension was, in relative terms, quite lengthy and potentially financially debilitating one for Modahl.[43]

In technical terms, Modahl's action was generally around an alleged breach of contract (claiming damages for expenses and loss of income during the period of her suspension) and specifically on the basis that there had been a breach of an implied contractual term that the disciplinary committee would act fairly and without bias.[44] In fact, the Modahl legal writ focused on two areas. First, it alleged that the laboratory which conducted the urine analysis was not properly accredited and the BAF should not have gone ahead with the disciplinary hearing. Second, it alleged that the rules of the BAF, particularly around anti-doping, formed a contract between the athlete and governing body, which was breached by using an unaccredited laboratory, and by alleged bias against three members of the BAF Disciplinary Panel. Before actually proceeding to trial in the High Court in December 2000, there were several stages of strike out proceedings in the High Court, the Court of Appeal and finally the House of Lords from June 1996 to July 1999.[45]

In response to the writ served by Diane Modahl, the BAF counterclaimed, arguing that as Modahl had ultimately been exonerated by its disciplinary process, her action should be dismissed for disclosing no reasonable cause of action.[46] They

---

[40] McArdle 2001, 97.

[41] *Modahl v BAF (No 2)* [2001] EWCA Civ 1447; [2002] 1 WLR 1192, 1214, Latham LJ. See also Farrell 2001, 110.

[42] Lewis and Taylor 2008, 921.

[43] Anderson 2010, 30.

[44] Gardiner et al. 2012, 106.

[45] See *Modahl v British Athletic Federation Limited (No 1)* Unreported, Queen's Bench Division, 28 June 1996, Popplewell J; *Modahl v British Athletic Federation Limited (No 1)* [1997] EWCA Civ 2209; and *Modahl v British Athletic Federation Limited (No 1)* [1999] UKHL 37.

[46] Anderson 2010, 31.

also argued that a de novo hearing before the IAP meant that any question of alleged bias by individual members of the BAF Disciplinary Committee should be taken to have been cured.[47]

Popplewell J dismissed the striking out application by the BAF and made an important accompanying comment that, although it may be that the actual decision had been cured in one sense by the subsequent hearing, the consequences of it had not necessarily cured.[48] An appeal against this dismissal was heard unsuccessfully in the Court of Appeal in July 1997. The Court of Appeal held that the BAF "had not deliberately chosen an unaccredited laboratory" and the accreditation procedure "did not cast doubt on the substantive reliability of the analysis of the sample".[49] The Court of Appeal did not strike out the matter of alleged bias. Drawing on the authority of *Calvin v Carr,*[50] a matter concerning a disputed decision by racing stewards to disqualify a jockey, the Court of Appeal agreed that there are instances in sports-related disputes where the disciplinary decision has both "serious economic and reputational consequences for the claimant" and "where the defect [in the initial hearing] was so flagrant and the consequences were so severe, that the most perfect of appeals of rehearing will not be sufficient to produce a just results".[51]

The matter was further appealed to House of Lords in July 1999.[52] Their Lordships, upholding the decision of the Court of Appeal, permitted a trial on the bias issue but not on the matter of the alleged unaccredited laboratory. The lack of accreditation was in their view of little merit within the overall context of the BAF's and the IAAF's anti-doping scheme and had no material bearing on the substantive outcome of the matter. The BAF had acted, according to the then House of Lords, "in good faith" and had no choice but to initiate disciplinary proceedings under IAAF Rules.[53]

10.6 *Modahl v BAF* (*No 2*): The High Court

Modahl v BAF (No 2) went to trial in December 2000.[54] By this time the BAF was in administration. The central questions in the High Court were fourfold in nature:

---

[47] Anderson 2010, 32.

[48] *Modahl v British Athletic Federation Limited (No 1)* Unreported, Queen's Bench Division, 28 June 1996, Popplewell J.

[49] Anderson 2010, 33. There was support for this in the IAAF Doping Rules themselves relating to a minor technical error which had no substantive impact on the results of the analysis.

[50] *Calvin v Carr* [1980] AC 574.

[51] Cited by Anderson 2010, 34.

[52] *Modahl v British Athletic Federation Limited (No 1)* [1999] UKHL 37.

[53] See the review by Anderson 2010, 33.

[54] *Modahl v British Athletic Federation Limited (No 2)* Unreported, Queen's Bench Division, 14 December 2000, Douglas Brown J.

1. Was there a contract between Mrs. Modahl and the BAF?
2. If there was a contract was there a duty to act fairly?
3. If there was a contract, with a duty to act fairly, was that duty breached?
4. If there were breaches in the implied term, did these cause loss?

The legal nexus of a contractual relationship was crucial because, simply, if there "was not a contract, then the claim for damages would fail".[55] According to Lewis and Taylor, six sources of contract can be identified in such scenarios:

1. Written contracts between SGBs and commercial partners
2. SBG rules as a contract
3. Side contracts between SGBs and its members
4. Contractual relationships between rules of ISFs and national SBGs
5. Express contracts between individual participants and SGBs
6. Implied contracts between individual participants and SGBs.[56]

In the stated proceedings, Diane Modahl's claim was brought on the basis that "there had been a breach of an implied contractual term that the disciplinary committee would act fairly and without bias".[57] Modahl's legal representative argued that there was a contract could be identified in any of three ways: her membership of Sale Harriers Athletic Club; her participation in athletic events through the permission of the BAF; or her submission to the disciplinary rules and panel along with her right to appeal to the IAP. On the last point, Modhal further submitted that the existence of contractual relations could be drawn by analogy to those relations identified in *Davis v Carew-Pole,*[58] *Mundir v Singapore AAA,*[59] and *Korda v ITF.*[60] Nevertheless, the treatment of these earlier cases was far from straightforward and there were issues of interpretation and relevance. Douglas Brown J pointed to the exhortations of Lord Denning MR in *Nagle v Fielden*[61] and Scott J in *Gasser v Stinson*[62] not to create "fictitious contracts", and concluded that it was artificial to identify a contract between the athlete and the BAF out of either her membership of Sale Harriers, her participation in other meetings

---

[55] Farrell 2001, 110.

[56] Lewis and Taylor 2008, 229.

[57] Gardiner et al. 2012, 106.

[58] *Davis v Carew-Pole* [1956] 1 WLR 833, Pilcher J holding that in submitting to the National Hunt Committee's jurisdiction, the claimant had entered a contractual relationship with the Stewards of the National Hunt Committee.

[59] *Mundir v Singapore AAA* [1992] 1 SLR 18, where a contract was held to have arisen out of the acceptance of an offer to go on a training trip.

[60] *Korda v International Tennis Federation* Unreported, Court of Appeal, Morritt LJ, Auld, LJ and Clarke, LJ, 25 March 1999, accepted by the Court of Appeal that an inferred or implied contract did exist through Korda's submission to the anti-doping programme.

[61] *Nagle v Fielden* [1965] 2 QB 633, 646.

[62] *Gasser v Stinson*, Unreported, Queen's Bench Division, 15 June 1988, Scott J.

organised by the governing bodies or her submission to doping control at a different event abroad run by a different organisation.

Further, Douglas Brown J was unimpressed with *Korda v ITF* as an authority and noted that *Nagle v Fielden* (and its authority on the accompanying concerns surrounding the artificiality of both the contractual nexus and the intention to create legal relations) had not been referred to by the Court of Appeal in *Korda v ITF*.[63] It has been argued that in holding that no contract existed, Douglas Brown J must be seen to have taken a "traditional approach", i.e. a court should not invent a fictitious contract where the standard essentials of a bargain (intent to create legal relations, offer and acceptance of terms and consideration) have not been proven.[64]

In addition to the contractual point, claims were made of actual and apparent bias against members of the BAF Disciplinary Panel and namely, Dr Martyn Lucking, Arthur Gold and Alan Guy. At the material time, the legal authority for apparent bias could be found in the judgment of Lord Goff in *R v Gough*:[65] and thus the test was whether a member of the panel might unfairly regard (or have unfairly regarded) with favour or disfavour, the case of the party under consideration by him. The evidential source of the apparent bias claim was traced to comments made by Dr Lucking in 1990 at an athletics meeting in Gateshead, where Dr Lucking was in charge of doping control testing and when allegedly he made comments to the effect that "all athletes were guilty until proven innocent". Douglas Brown J, although acknowledging that Dr Lucking may have been careless in his phraseology at times in the past, did not believe that Lucking carried into the disciplinary hearing a belief that all athletes were guilty until proven innocent. Douglas Brown J held that there was neither actual nor apparent bias nor had Dr. Lucking unfairly regarded Modahl with disfavour. Finally, the judge regarded the claims of apparent bias against Alan Guy as a "hopeless allegation" and completely rejected the allegation of apparent bias against Sir Arthur Gold.[66] In short, Douglas Brown J was clearly convinced that the constitution of the BAF's disciplinary panel had been carefully and fairly chosen to give a balance of skills and representation and that Modahl had been tried properly and fairly by at least some of her peers.

Finally, the High Court noted that Modahl had ultimately been cleared by the IAP and thus had been granted "a fair [if not necessarily just] deal", reflecting

---

63 For a thorough analysis of this argument see Farrell 2001, 110. In addition, when comparing the *Modahl* case with *Korda*, Douglas Brown J pointed out that Korda had formally signed documents explicitly to enter the International Tennis Federation competitions, whereas there was no evidence of such forms being signed by Diane Modahl.

64 Lewis and Taylor 2008, 229.

65 *R v Gough* [1993] AC 646, 670.

66 As regards Alan Guy, for instance, the claim was based upon Mr Guy being an EAAA Doping Officer at the EAAA competition in 1994 and therefore a "judge in his own cause".

Lord Wilberforce's requirement in *Calvin v Carr* for an examination of hearing process in its totality.[67] Reflecting on these proceedings at the time, Farrell observed presciently:

> There must surely be a better way to deal with such problems. The *Modahl* case may be viewed as one involving a colossal waste of time and money (BAFs and Mrs. Modahl's) particularly as the judge concluded that even if bias had been proved, in the light of all the other evidence; he would have concluded that no loss followed.[68]

10.7 *Modahl v BAF* (*No 2*): The Court of Appeal

On 22 February 2001, Diane Modahl won her right to take her claim to the Court of Appeal. It reached the Court of Appeal in October 2001 where some very complex issues around contract, rule-governed relationships with a sport governing body, fairness, as well as bias and the significance of providing an IAP were considered.[69] The majority held that contractual relations of an implied nature existed between the BAF and the athlete who competed under its rules, i.e. the Court held that, as the athlete accepted the various obligations inherent under the BAF's rules and regulations whenever she entered a competition or underwent out of competition drug testing in order to enter such competitions, the basic structure for a contract was readily identifiable. In so holding, the Court of Appeal displayed a greater preparedness to infer an implied contract out of the circumstances of a governing body/member relationship than it had displayed previously.[70] Nevertheless, the Court of Appeal, and in line with general principles of contract law, was careful to limit the extent of the terms that would be implied into the contract (and consequently the availability of damages).

What then, following on from this rule-bound contractual relationship, was the obligation of the BAF towards Diane Modahl? In the view of Mance LJ it extended at the most, to an obligation to take due care and attention to appoint persons who, as far as it knew or (probably) had good reason to believe were appropriate persons to sit on the relevant disciplinary committee.[71] Similarly, Latham LJ, who was surprised at the lack of cases previously considered by the courts on an athlete in the same circumstances, held that, in considering the ambit of the obligations undertaken by the BAF, an implied element of the contractual nature of the applicability of the BAF rules was a duty to act fairly and that ultimately, thanks to the decision of the IAP, that duty had been discharged. In sum, Latham LJ, as the

---

[67] [1980] AC 574, 593.

[68] Farrell 2001, 115.

[69] *Modahl v British Athletic Federation (No 2)* [2001] EWCA Civ 1447; [2002] 1 WLR 1192.

[70] Lewis and Taylor 2008, 186.

[71] *Modahl v British Athletic Federation (No 2)* [2001] EWCA Civ 1447; [2002] 1 WLR 1192, 1228.

High Court had held, noted that, although a member or members of the disciplinary panel might have been somewhat prejudiced in their approach, this did not, in an overall sense, affect or infect the integrity of that panel's decision based on the facts presented to them. Further, the Court of Appeal concurred that the IAP had reversed the decision of the initial BAF disciplinary panel because, and only because, consistent with its *de novo* status, the IAP had permitted and was convinced by (new) evidence that Modahl's sample might have suffered some sort of bacterial contamination.[72] In sum, the Court of Appeal was satisfied that the BAF's disciplinary processes had eventually concluded in "a fair result".[73]

10.8 Implications and Reflections

10.8.1 Contractual Nexus

The Court of Appeal in *Modahl* reaffirmed the principle of no damages without the existence of a contract. It took a very important step, (despite the paucity and unhelpfulness of previous cases and a lack of factual material on eligibility/entry forms), in recognising the existence of an implied contract. The Court of Appeal displayed a greater preparedness to infer an implied contract from the circumstances of a governing body/member relationship than it had in the past.

> While the courts should avoid inventing contracts, they should not be unduly hesitant about giving contractual effect to a continuous, long-term relationship based on a programme and rules couched in language of a contractual character and purporting to impose mutual rights and obligations.[74]

10.8.2 Fair If Not Just Decision

The ambit of obligations of the implied contract in the present case were very limited and in the end, came down to a duty to be fair in the overall process and in particular, in selecting what was reasonably believed by the BAF to be appropriate persons to sit on its disciplinary committee. There continues to be a debate on the interpretation and application of the "fair" but not necessarily "just" result principle outlined by Lord Wilberforce in *Calvin v Carr.*[75] Blackshaw approves of

---

[72] *Modahl v British Athletic Federation (No 2)* [2001] EWCA Civ 1447; [2002] 1 WLR 1192, 1209–1214.

[73] See further Anderson 2010, 35.

[74] *Modahl v British Athletic Federation (No 2)* [2001] EWCA Civ 1447; [2002] 1 WLR 1192, 1225.

[75] [1980] AC 574, 593.

commentary that suggests that *Calvin v Carr* does not say that all defects can be cured on appeal; the way is open, he says, for the courts to say "fair treatment eventually but not fair treatment overall".[76] It could be argued that the Court of Appeal in *Modahl* took a similar approach to that which, some suggest, can be seen occasionally at the Court of Arbitration for Sport ("CAS"), "which relies on the notion, all's well that ends well…when, in contrast and in fairness]…what should be considered is the impact of the hearing, the time between the hearing and the appeal and the impact on the athlete's career".[77]

The Court of Appeal in *Modahl* used the authority of *R v Gough* on the meaning of bias when, arguably the (refined) test outlined by the Court of Appeal earlier in 2001 in *Re Medicaments and Related Classes of Goods (No 2)*.[78] In that case, Lord Phillips MR, giving the judgment of the court, observed that the precise test to be applied when determining whether a decision should be set aside on account of bias had given rise to difficulty, reflected in judicial decisions that had appeared in conflict, and that the attempt to resolve that conflict in *R v Gough* had not commanded universal approval.[79]

Lord Phillips MR went on to state that an alternative test more closely in line with Strasbourg jurisprudence (which since 2 October 2000 the English courts were required to take into account) meant that it was time to review *R v Gough* to see whether the test it laid down was in conflict with ECHR jurisprudence.[80] Having conducted that review he summarised the court's conclusions and held that a modest adjustment of the test in *R v Gough* was called for, which, no different from the test applied in most of the Commonwealth and in Scotland, meant that in the present circumstances a court should first ascertain all the circumstances which have a bearing on the suggestion that the judge was biased. It must then ask "whether those circumstances would lead a fair-minded and informed observer to conclude that there was a real possibility, or a real danger, the two being the same, that the tribunal was biased".[81]

In *Modahl* the Court of Appeal held that, although the disciplinary chair's previous utterances suggested a bias, there was no remedy because it was decided that even in the absence said bias the result would have been no different. Would this approach, based on its factual matrix, have satisfied the *Medicaments* test?[82] Whatever test applies, the present case also highlights the significance or danger of comments made to the journalists outside of formal disciplinary proceedings by a member of a disciplinary panel.

---

[76] Blackshaw 2001, 1–4.

[77] Gardiner et al. 2012, 381.

[78] *Re Medicaments and Related Classes of Goods (No 2)* [2001] 1 WLR 700.

[79] *Re Medicaments and Related Classes of Goods (No 2)* [2001] 1 WLR 700, 711.

[80] *Re Medicaments and Related Classes of Goods (No 2)* [2001] 1 WLR 700, 711.

[81] *Re Medicaments and Related Classes of Goods (No 2)* [2001] 1 WLR 700, 723–724. Approved by the House of Lords in *Porter v Magill* [2002] 2 AC 357, 494.

[82] Blackshaw 2001, 1–4: "A decision infected by bias is no decision at all".

10.8.3 Judicial Scrutiny

The *Modahl* proceedings appear to have raised more doubts and questions around the public law/private law debate and the applicability of judicial review to sports governing bodies as well as the perception of sport as "work". There is some concern that if contractual relations cannot be identified and the courts persist with the view that governing bodies are not subject to claim for judicial review, the potential is there for the appearance of a legal vacuum in which an individual may find themselves unable to effectively establish their rights and obligations in respect of governing bodies.[83]

Similarly, the proceedings reinforced the consistent reluctance of the courts to intervene in matters where sports governing bodies have expertise, regulatory overview, "unrivalled and practical knowledge" and are better placed to handle such matters.[84] Nevertheless, it confirmed that the courts do have a right to intervene where there is point of law is involved or an alleged breach of natural justice.[85]

10.8.4 The Role of Arbitration

The *Modhal* proceedings have been described as a "colossal waste of time and money".[86] During and after the proceedings, questions were raised about an alternative route through an arbitration process, e.g. CAS.[87]

10.8.5 The Integrity of the Anti-doping Process

Anti-doping rules and the conduct of the laboratory conducting and analysing the "A" and "B" samples were at the heart of this case. Part of what makes this a landmark case is that it was the first challenge against a BAF disciplinary panel on a doping matter and possibly the only successful challenge of the competence of an anti-doping testing laboratory. What issues does the Modahl case raise or illustrate under these themes?

The collection of the "A" sample from Diane Modahl and the contemporaneous testing of among other things, the pH level [found to be normal] at the competition on 18 June 1994, was deemed to be appropriate. What happened next,

---

83 Boyes in Gardiner et al. 2012, 110.

84 For example, see Anderson 2010, 37.

85 O'Leary in Gardiner et al. 2012, 381.

86 Farrell 2001, 115.

87 See, for instance, Blackshaw 2001, 3 and McArdle 2001, 99.

however, in relation to the storage and testing of both samples was a completely different matter. The deviations from IOC guidelines in the areas of pH levels, metabolites, smell of ammonia and chain of custody have been well documented. Such serious concerns were raised not only by the representatives of Diane Modahl at the "B" test in August 1994, but also by BAF experts present at the "B" test. Nevertheless, it is likely that staff at the laboratory in Lisbon felt that the rules gave them no flexibility and that they were compelled to go on to complete the "B" test, despite all the concerns raised at the time, and by more than one party.

In retrospect, the comments of Lord Hoffmann in the House of Lords in July 1999 are quite revealing.

> Although there was no doubt that the IAAF's anti-doping policy was 'draconian' in nature and *carried the risk of a 'grave injustice' to an athlete if the laboratory test was wrong*, in the stated case, the lack of accreditation was of little merit within the overall procedural context of the B.A.F.s and I.A.A.Fs anti-doping scheme (emphasis added).[88]

Lord Hoffmann considered, correctly, in the author's view that, the accreditation argument was weak. More importantly, Lord Hoffmann recognised the serious impact on an athlete's case if *a laboratory test was wrong*. The author is of the view that the this saga could have been stopped at the "B" test stage and the reasons why it did not may revolve around three issues: the unprecedented nature of the circumstances; the possible threat to the integrity of and trust in anti-doping testing procedures, at any level; and the complexity of the medico-legal discourse at the centre of this case.

Consider the comments of Dr Lucking, the chair of the BAF Disciplinary Panel, following the findings of the IAP in July 1995:

> I believe that the IAAF should consider an appeal because the panel decision could have destroyed confidence in our testing procedures. Yet *hundreds of thousands of samples are tested at laboratories here and we have never had an episode like this* (emphasis added).[89]

Fears about such a disciplinary appeal panel decision potentially destroying confidence in the testing procedure was supported by comments made by athletes to a researcher conducting small-scale qualitative research in the perceptions of international athletes following the Diane Modahl case:

> The effect of the Diane Modahl case on athletes cannot be overstated. For some it heralded a fundamental shift in perceptions, while for others it merely reinforced a pre-existing lack of faith in the whole testing procedure. Not one of those interviewed expressed faith in the whole testing procedure.[90]

So, if the BAF had "never seen an episode like this before" in their own accredited laboratories and the staff at the Lisbon laboratory felt compelled to proceed with the "B" test, what kind of intervention at that point in August 1994

---

[88] *Modahl v British Athletic Federation (No 1)* [1999] UKHL 37, discussed by Anderson 2010, 33.

[89] Cited by Mance LJ in *Modahl v British Athletic Federation (No 2)* [2001] EWCA Civ 1447; [2002] 1 WLR 1192, 1200.

[90] McArdle 2001, 108.

might have led to a different outcome? Perhaps the unprecedented situation could have been helped by the provision of an independent roving "crisis management group" of anti-doping testing experts who could be consulted by phone or e-mail by any party present at the "B" test? Such a group would preferably have been experienced experts in IOC [now WADA] accredited laboratories and not just IAAF officers or other governing body doping collection officers.

Finally, the complexity of the medico-legal discourse, in the view of the author, also played a key role from the start of the Diane Modahl case. At crucial stages throughout the internal and court-based proceedings, the lack of contemporary, published, scientific research (on bacterial degradation of urine samples) was commented upon repeatedly. This is not the case in other areas of medico-legal discourse. For example, peer-reviewed sport medicine research has, since the 1970s, played a key role in informing the revision of safety rules on scrums in rugby union.[91] The area of bacterial degradation of urine and other sport doping topics would benefit from multi-disciplinary research and collaborative work across anti-doping agencies, university sports science departments/medical schools/law schools and sport governing bodies.

10.9 Conclusion

In sum, there are at least two significant and enduring points of interest that can be gleaned for the *Modahl* proceedings. First, *Modahl* briefly considered the nature and depth of the contractual relationship between an individual participant in a sport, his or her club and the relevant national and international governing bodies. This legal nexus remains crucial, both in a procedural and substantive sense, because whatever other remedies the sports claimant might have, in the absence of contract, there can be no claim for damages.

Second, the Diane Modahl litigation reveals that the typical means of challenging a decision of a sports body's disciplinary mechanism remains by way of an allegation of procedural unfairness such that the implication of a contractual duty to act fairly has been breached. In *Modahl*, the principal allegation centred on a specific claim of bias against members of the disciplining tribunal but "procedural unfairness" can also encompass allegations that the disciplining body in question either did not have the jurisdiction to hear the case; or did not properly instructed itself to the facts; or denied the participant the right to make representations during the course of the disciplinary hearing; or had, in sanction, acted disproportionately or irrationally. In *Modahl,* the courts held that allegations of procedural irregularity in breach of the principles of natural justice should be discussed in light of the standard expected by the courts of domestic sporting tribunals, namely, that the

[91] See, for example, Silver and Stewart 1994 on the research underpinning the prevention of spinal cord injuries in rugby football.

process as a whole ends in a "fair decision". In short, were the internal proceedings of the sports body designed to produce, and did they in fact produce, a "fair result"?

References

Anderson J (2010) Modern sports law. Hart, Oxford

Blackshaw I (2001) Modahl loses appeal for compensation. Sports Law Bull 4(6):1–4

Boyes S (2012) The legal regulation of sports governing bodies. In: Gardiner S et al (eds) Sports law, 4th edn. Routledge, Abingdon, pp 88–144

Farrell R (2001) Diane Modahl and the law of contract. Sport Law J 9:110–114

Gardiner S et al (2012) Sports law, 4th edn. Routledge, Abingdon

Grayson E (1995) Drugs in sport—chains in custody. New Law J 145:44

Hartley H (2004) An innocent abroad? The Diane Modahl doping case 1994–2001. Int Sports Law J 3/4:61–65

Hartley H (2009) Sport, recreation and the law. Routledge, Abingdon

Lewis A, Taylor J (2008) Sport: law and practice, 2nd edn. Tottel, London

McArdle D (2001) 'Say it ain't so Mo' international performers perceptions of drug use and the Diane Modahl affair. In: O' Leary J (ed) Drugs and doping in sport: socio-legal perspectives. Cavendish, London, pp 91–108

Modahl D (1995) The Diane Modahl story. Hodder and Stoughton, London

O'Leary J (2012) The regulation of doping in sport. In: Gardiner S et al (eds) Sports law, 4th edn. Routledge, Abingdon, pp 363–392

Reid R (1995) The Diane Modahl case. Sport Law J 3(2):6–8

Silver J, Stewart D (1994) The prevention of spinal cord injuries in rugby football. Paraplegia 32:442–453

Chapter 11
CAS 98/211 *B v FINA*

Neville Cox

Abstract In August 1998, B (an Irish swimmer, Michelle Smith de Bruin) was suspended for 4 years by the respondent's (FINA, swimming's world governing body) anti-doping panel, having been found to have committed an offence—the use of substances and methods altering the integrity and validity of urine samples in doping control—contrary to FINA's anti-doping regulations. On 2 September 1998, de Bruin submitted an appeal to CAS in which she challenged the findings of FINA's Anti-doping Panel on various grounds and namely: that FINA's Anti-doping Panel had failed to reach a decision in accordance with the appropriate burden and standard of proof; that the Chairman of FINA's Anti-Doping Panel had exhibited substantial bias against her; that the individual anti-doping testers who had carried out the out-of-competition testing of her at her home, and which led to the stated "manipulation" charges, had lacked the authority to carry out "unannounced" tests; that, in any event, unannounced testing out-of-competition was not permitted under FINA's then anti-doping rules; that the chain of custody of her urine sample had not been properly established by FINA such that CAS ought to have significant doubt as to whether the sample tested was in fact her sample and/or that her sample had been manipulated while on its way to or at the testing laboratory by an unknown third party. CAS dismissed the appeal. The CAS Panel rejected both the "compromised chain of custody" and the "third party manipulation" hypotheses advance by de Bruin. The CAS Panel found that FINA had discharged the burden of proof and met the requisite standard of proof. On the former, the CAS Panel reiterated that there was no doubt that the burden of proof lay upon the sports governing body to establish that a doping infraction had been committed and that the presumption of innocence operated in the athlete's favour until the governing body had discharged that initial burden. On the latter, the CAS Panel reiterated that the requisite standard of proof required of the relevant anti-doping panel was less than the criminal standard but more than the ordinary civil

N. Cox (✉)
Professor of Law, Trinity College, Dublin, Ireland
e-mail: ncox@tcd.ie

J. Anderson (ed.), *Leading Cases in Sports Law*,
ASSER International Sports Law Series, DOI: 10.1007/978-90-6704-909-2_11,

standard, i.e. the "comfortable satisfaction" standard. Moreover, the CAS Panel held that in sitting as an appellate body which formed part of a wider appeals systems and which allowed it to hear the full merits of the dispute before it, that issues such as the fairness of the hearing before the tribunal of first instance "fade to the periphery", i.e. any apparent defects in the hearing before FINA's Anti-doping Panel, were to be considered cured by the *de novo* nature of the CAS hearing.

Contents

11.1 Introduction

From the perspective of an Irish sports fan, the Atlanta Olympic Games of 1996 (even for people with no prior interest in competitive women's swimming) was a genuinely extraordinary occasion as Michelle Smith de Bruin won three gold medals and one bronze—a simply astonishing and entirely unprecedented result for an Irish Olympian. The Irish people hailed a new hero yet only three years later, and despite her ongoing protestations of innocence,[1] her reputation was in tatters at home and abroad as the Court of Arbitration for Sport ("CAS") upheld a decision of the FINA Anti-doping Panel to ban her for four years for a doping offence.[2]

CAS's award in *B v FINA*[3] is an interesting one for a number of reasons. As a result of the very wide ranging defence offered by Ms de Bruin and her lawyer, coupled with the very unusual nature of the case, it was necessary for the CAS

[1] See Ms De Bruin's statement as published in *Irish Times* of 9 June 2009 and also in the same edition Humphries 1999d and Watterson 1999.

[2] See, for example, Hannigan 1999.

[3] CAS 98/211 *B v FINA*. See generally Cox and Schuster 2004, 115–119 and McLaren 2006, 193–212.

Panel to deal with issues which are absolutely basic in so far as the operation of anti-doping policy is concerned—issues such as the rights of athletes in doping cases to fair procedures, the manner in which rules of burden and standard of proof work in doping hearings and specifically the question of the extent to which circumstantial evidence alone can be enough to constitute proof of guilt in doping cases. It is arguably true that the facts of the case were sufficiently unusual (in that the offence at issue was alleged tampering with a sample rather than the more common offence of having the presence of a banned substance within one's system) that the direct impact of what emerged from CAS in this instance will probably be limited. Nonetheless, at a broader level of principle the decision contains important determinations on what fair procedures actually entail for athletes in cases of this kind. Perhaps most importantly, it contains an implicit view as to how anti-doping rules should be regarded—namely as more than just ordinary terms of a contract but less than the terms of a criminal code.

In this chapter we consider the nature of the decision and what it has come to mean for the operation of anti-doping rules. Before doing so, however, it is necessary to look briefly at the precise facts which led, in 1999, to Michelle Smith de Bruin facing a 4-year ban from swimming and the destruction of her reputation.

11.2 Michelle Smith de Bruin as a Sporting Hero

Michelle Smith had been a leading Irish swimmer for some years in the late 1980s and early 1990s. Having retired in 1992, the year in which she met her future coach and husband Erik de Bruin, (at one stage the world number two in discus, but who was the serving a 4-year ban for taking banned substances),[4] she relaunched her career in 1993. At this point her swimming career took off spectacularly. She broke 23 Irish records in a year and did so at an age where, for most swimmers, one would expect their career to be on the wane.[5]

Unsurprisingly, this led to certain rumours about her and specifically about whether she was using performance enhancing substances—not least because her physique was far more muscular than previously.[6] She herself, however, attributed this simply to the fact that she trained extremely hard[7] and she pointed to the fact that she had been tested regularly over a number of years and no traces of banned

---

[4] For background see Humphries 1999c.

[5] See McTeirnan 1996.

[6] On 8 June 1999 the *Irish Times* in an article entitled "De Bruin in Words" quoted a former Irish national coach, Peter Banks, saying in 1996 that "I wish they could pull out a picture of her five years ago because no one would recognise her. I can't imagine how she has gained the muscle mass she has and still swims the 100,000 m a week she is supposedly swimming".

[7] American Pierre La Fontaine, her coach in 1988 and 1990, regarded Michelle Smith as the toughest trainer with whom he had ever worked.

substances had ever been found.[8] Her zenith came in 1996, when she won three gold medals and one bronze at the Atlanta Olympic Games (albeit that there was controversy at the time when certain rival competitors implied that she might be using drugs)[9] and in 1997 when she won two gold and two silver medals at the European Championships in Seville.

As has been mentioned, question marks surrounded her vastly improved levels of performance. She had never failed a drugs test, but nonetheless there were concerns as to her relationship with the anti-doping authorities.[10] In April 1996, for instance, she was required to fill out a standard form announcing where her training facilities would be for the Olympics and simply wrote that she did not know. In 1996 and again in January 1997, FINA complained to her that she had not been available for a random doping test in both 1995 and October 1996, and indeed that the details which she had provided to them in respect of her training schedule in 1997 were overly vague. On 3 February 1997 she narrowly missed another random test, thereby rendering her technically eligible for a ban (as she had received the warning in January 1997). The FINA executive meeting in Lausanne on 23 February 1997, discussed seriously the possibility of imposing such a ban on de Bruin and, in accordance with FINA rules, of stripping the Olympic champion of all medals won and records set over the previous twelve months. It was decided, however, that because she had missed the February 1997 test by as little as one hour, a legal challenge to the validity of imposing such a ban could well be successful. Finally, in early January 1998, she again missed a random test, but instead of it being registered as such, the International Tests and Doping Management testers, husband and wife team Al and Kay Guy[11] were instructed to try again two days later.[12] It was this second test, carried out on an unannounced basis on 10 January 1998, which is at the centre of this case.[13] Moreover, to the extent that the applicant challenged virtually every aspect of the testing process, it is important to give a clear and detailed statement of what happened.

11.3 The Events of January 1998

Mr and Mrs Guy arrived at de Bruin's residence in Co Kilkenny, Ireland at approximately 7:40 am on the day in question and, after a brief delay, at approximately 7:50, a light came on upstairs in the house, at which point Mr. Guy

[8] See Dowling 1999.

[9] See O'Connor 1996.

[10] See Humphries 1997, 1998 and 1999b.

[11] Mr Guy was one of the persons against whom Diane Modahl had alleged bias unsuccessfully arising out of her incorrect positive doping test, as discussed generally in Chap. 10 of this volume.

[12] Cox and Schuster 2004, 116.

[13] Kimmage 1999.

got out of the car and approached the gate. De Bruin was spotted walking to her car and so Mr Guy told her why they were there and asked her to unlock the gate. She did so but then re-entered the house leaving the Guys to follow. They parked their car and unloaded their equipment and then they waited for her to return. The Guys estimated that she was gone from them for between 4 and 7 min (though Ms de Bruin estimated that it was more like 1–2 min—an estimation which, as we will see, CAS rejected) at which point they entered her kitchen and presented the relevant documentation to her to inform her of the test. Ms de Bruin made the point both that she was in a rush to Dublin airport and also that she had been to the toilet just before the Guys arrived, which obviously would impact on her immediate ability to provide a urine sample.

15–20 min passed at which point Ms de Bruin said that she might be able to give a sample. Mrs Guy accompanied Ms de Bruin to the toilet and would later give evidence that Ms de Bruin was wearing a baggy fleece which obscured a view of her vaginal area while the sample was being given. However, from Mrs Guy's perspective this was not a problem in that she could hear the sample being given even if she could not see it. Having urinated into a beaker which she herself (Ms de Bruin) had selected, she held it up, placed it on a shelf, washed her hands and then carried it to the kitchen.

Unfortunately there was insufficient urine for a legitimate sample and so, after another 25 min, the process was repeated. Again (a) Mrs Guy's view of Ms de Bruin's vagina was obscured by the latter's baggy fleece and (b) it was Ms de Bruin only who actually handled the relevant beaker. After the second attempt, Mr Guy informed the client that there was now enough urine for a valid sample. Ms de Bruin then selected one of the Versapak kits on the table containing two plastic containers with a glass bottle in each. She poured the urine from the beaker into both of these bottles and screwed the lids on them and checked for leaks. There was no evidence at any stage that there was any problem with the bottles. Ms de Bruin read out the numbers on the two bottles (which would become her "A" and "B" sample) namely A 074396 and B 074396. She then placed the bottles into the two plastic containers and closed them and indeed then got her husband to ensure that they were closed. Mr Guy placed the two sealed containers in a plastic bag and then placed that bag into a normal carrying bag.

As the CAS Panel emphasised in its determination in the case, what was key here was that at all stages before the containers were placed in the bag, they were in the exclusive custody of Ms de Bruin and neither did anyone else touch them. Naturally this became important during the case, in that as far as CAS was concerned, it would be very difficult to suggest realistically that someone other than Ms de Bruin had tampered with the sample when she was the only person who had the opportunity to do so.

After the containers were placed in the bag, Mr Guy performed a litmus test on the residue of the sample left in the beaker (in order to assess whether the urine was sufficiently concentrated in order for it to be properly analysed). Thereafter, Ms de

Bruin completed the required declaration relating to drugs recently used and signed and verified the doping control form[14] whereupon Mr. Guy handed her the completed doping control form which she verified and signed. Mr Guy then handed her copies (parts 4 and 5) of the completed doping control form and then Mr and Mrs Guy left the house.

One sidebar to these events is worth mentioning, namely that the Guys testified that when in their car, they discussed a strange smell which they had noticed in the kitchen coming from the sample. Mrs Guy suggested that it smelt like Irish Mist whiskey, and Mr Guy suggesting that in fact it smelt like Southern Comfort. This fact was noted on the doping form that was eventually sent to the laboratory in Barcelona.

On leaving de Bruin's house, and having stopped for breakfast (when the bag remained in their sight) the Guys returned home where Mr Guy wrapped the two containers in white polystyrene foam and placed them in the family refrigerator. The containers were due to be sent to the International Olympic Committee ("IOC") laboratory in Barcelona and to be transported by the DHL Courier Service. Mr Guy testified that in his (considerable) experience, the DHL staff working at the weekend tended to be less competent and less experienced than their colleagues who worked during the week and as such he decided to leave the sample in the refrigerator until the following Monday (a point in respect of which much was made by de Bruin at the subsequent CAS hearing). On that Monday (12 January 1998) Mr Guy called a courier from DHL. He wrapped the containers in more foam and strapped it with brown masking tape and then placed them in a DHL shipping bag and sealed the bag which was signed by the courier (who also handed Mr Guy a copy of the relevant form and fixed another copy to the outside of the DHL bag) and thus ended Mr Guy's custody of the samples. On 14 January 1998, the laboratory in Barcelona acknowledged receipt of the two containers A 074396 and B 074396.

No doubt the subsequent hearing at CAS, which involved arguably an unprecedented level of scrutiny being placed on minute aspects of the test collection process, operated as something of a clarion call for the anti-doping authorities to ensure that their rules are complied with to the letter where testing procedures and chain of custody are concerned. Equally (and unsurprisingly given the level of both experience and expertise of the particular testers in this case), it is submitted that procedurally the manner in which the test was conducted did involve a rigorous adherence to all the minutiae required by the FINA rules (and now by the WADA code). As will be submitted throughout this chapter indeed, the real difficulty that de Bruin's legal representatives faced in this case in trying to mount any kind of effective challenge to the finding of the FINA Anti-doping

[14] Counsel for Ms de Bruin would later make much of the fact that the relevant form was only dated after the event (and after Ms De Bruin's copy of the form had been detached from the original). The CAS Panel accepted, however, that there was nothing untoward in this and that Mr Guy had simply forgotten to date the form when originally filling it in. Most importantly, the CAS Panel concluded that there was no improper tampering with the sample.

Panel was that there was nothing that had been done in the case which could ground such a challenge.

Possibly because there was so little straw with which bricks could be made in the case, Ms de Bruin made much of the fact that the urine sample was stored in the family fridge for a weekend. At a rather superficial level this may indeed sound rather odd (and having taught this case to sports law students for a decade I am aware that mention of this fact will inevitably elicit a laugh), but quite apart from the fact that (as the Panel would note), this was a safe place to store it, in addition as a matter of logic this was an entirely sensible thing to do. By refrigerating the sample Mr Guy ensured that its pharmacological integrity was maintained. Moreover, this meant that he could ensure what (in his view) was the safest passage of the containers from Ireland to Barcelona namely through the DHL staff who worked during the week rather than at weekend.

11.4 The Laboratory Report and the Charge Against Ms de Bruin

On 30 January 1998, the Barcelona laboratory sent its anti-doping analysis report to FINA. Pivotally, the report alleged one doping offence (tampering with the sample) and also suggested an explanation (the possible presence of a banned substance). The report recorded:

> Unequivocal signs of adulteration have been found in sample coded A 074396. The content of alcohol of the sample (concentration higher than 100 mg/ml) is in no way compatible with human consumption and the sample shows a very strong whisky odour. Its very low specific gravity (0.983 g/ml) is also compatible with a physical manipulation. Additional laboratory results obtained with the sample (especially, steroid profile and isotope ratio mass spectrometry measurements) suggest the administration of some metabolic precursor of testosterone. Longitudinal follow up is recommended.[15]

In simple terms then, the inference was that Ms de Bruin had deliberately tampered with the sample by attempting to dilute it through the addition of whiskey and that she had done so because there was a precursor to testosterone in her system and she hoped that the presence of the whiskey would mean that that substance would not be discovered. The precursor in question would later be revealed to be androstenedione. This substance, at the time, was not actually named on the FINA banned list and, for example, was used and endorsed by top

[15] See Humphries 1999a who reported that originally there was a degree of controversy in that the specific gravity recorded by the Guys at the time of the test was different to that recorded in the laboratory, which according to the defence indicated that the two urine samples were different. It was later stated by a representative of the Barcelona laboratory, Dr Segura, that the different types of tests used in Kilkenny and Barcelona would explain the differentiation. Indeed, Dr Segura had tested the B sample in Barcelona using *both* methods and the same differential had been found.

baseball players. Having said that, it is submitted that there can be little doubt but that it was a banned substance. After all it will be remembered that the policy of anti-doping authorities (in acceptance of the fact that there are quite clearly more performance enhancing drugs being used than are actually named on the list or within the scientific knowledge of the authorities at any given time) is sensibly to state in the banned list that its terms are not exhaustive, such that substances which are chemically or pharmacologically related to banned substances are themselves banned. For this reason it is surely inconceivable that androstenedione was not a banned substance in 1998. Nonetheless the lack of complete certainty on this point may have been the reason why the offence with which Ms de Bruin was charged was not the relatively simple one of having a banned substance in her system but the far more complex one of having tampered with a sample. This allegation connotes an especially serious offence in that it implies that there was a reason why such tampering had occurred—i.e., to cover up the fact of a second doping offence namely intentionally using performance enhancing drugs.[16]

Critically, in so far as de Bruin's line of reasoning was concerned, it was never specified as to *how* such tampering had occurred and presumably this is something at which FINA could only guess. In other words, whereas theories were advanced, the reality is that this was something which simply could not be known by FINA. It was this fact (which flowed inexorably from the nature of the case and the type of offence which was alleged) which would be seized upon by de Bruin at CAS as the basis for a challenge to the decision of FINA that a doping offence had occurred. Put simply, whereas FINA felt that by presenting the evidence of tampering coupled with a large quantity of circumstantial evidence (the presence of androstenedione in the sample and the relative impossibility of anyone else having tampered with the sample) it had done enough to prove the appellant's guilt; De Bruin on the other hand argued that it was necessary for FINA to prove exactly what happened, which, in practice would mean that it would have to disprove all alternative theories however far fetched or incredible.

In any event, on 27 April 1998, Ms de Bruin was informed by FINA that it was alleged that she had committed an offence deriving from her A sample. On 21 May, her B sample was tested at the laboratory and in the presence of her lawyer and on the same day, the laboratory sent its report to FINA which concluded that the results of the test on the B sample confirmed the results of the test on the A sample. On this basis, a hearing before the FINA Anti-doping Panel was held on 24 July 1998 and on 6 August 1998, the FINA Anti-doping Panel found that de Bruin had committed a doping offence and suspended her for 4 years. It was against this finding that Ms de Bruin appealed to CAS (and very unusually requested that the hearing be heard in public)[17] and it is to the CAS award that we now turn.

---

[16] See Cox and Schuster 2004, 95.

[17] For suggestion that the strategy of having a public hearing may have counted against Ms de Bruin see Ruger 2009, 161.

11.5 The Determination by CAS

To say that the applicant mounted a full and wide-ranging appeal is something of an understatement. Indeed as the CAS Panel noted, (in respect of the fact that Ms de Bruin's legal representative alleged the possibility that everyone from the testers, to the couriers, to FINA might have been responsible for the alleged discrepancies in the sample provided), "the fact that Appellant's counsel was constrained (on instructions) to fire off these volleys in all directions, of itself suggests that he had no single legitimate target for his accusations and implications".[18]

For convenience, it may be suggested that the appellant's focus was ultimately fourfold. First, de Bruin challenged certain procedural aspects of the manner in which the case was dealt with by FINA. Secondly, she questioned whether the taking of the sample by Mr and Mrs Guy on an out-of-competition basis was lawful. Thirdly, she challenged the chain of custody in the case. Fourthly, she alleged that to the extent that FINA had not disproved the possibility that someone else other than de Bruin had tampered with the sample (if in fact it had been tampered with), therefore it could not have been regarded as having satisfied the burden of proof.

The first of these claims was easily rejected. The appellant had claimed that the FINA Anti-doping Panel had not reached a decision in accordance with the appropriate burden of proof, that the Chairman of the FINA Anti-doping Panel had exhibited bias against her and that de Bruin had been misled by the FINA Anti-Doping Panel into believing that before it reached a decision it would hear further oral evidence from the testers, Mr and Mrs Guy. CAS rejected all these claims. It noted the fact that the hearing before it was essentially a *de novo* hearing in which any procedural errors of law that had occurred at the original hearing could be corrected and thereby the appellant's right to a fair hearing could be vindicated.[19] As the CAS Panel put it:

> We did not find it necessary to consider the factual basis for this submission, given that the hearing was a hearing *de novo*. The virtue of an appeal system which allows for a full rehearing before an appellate body is that issues relating to the fairness of the hearing before the tribunal of first instance fade to the periphery...The Appellant's entitlement, which she fully received, was to a system which allowed any defects in the hearing before the Doping Panel to be cured by the hearing before CAS.[20]

It is submitted that (in the case obviously of defects which can be cured on appeal) this is a perfectly fair conclusion and one which has been consistently expressed in the jurisprudence of CAS.[21] Equally and for the avoidance of doubt,

---

[18] CAS 98/211 *B v FINA*, para 44.

[19] See, for example, CAS 98/214 *B v International Judo Federation.*

[20] CAS 98/211 *B v FINA*, para 8.

[21] See Cox and Schuster 2004, 141.

the CAS Panel also stressed that it saw no reason to doubt the good faith of the chairman who had heard the original hearing.[22]

Secondly, the appellant argued both that the particular testers lacked the authority to carry out unannounced doping tests and indeed that out-of-competition testing was not permitted under FINA anti-doping rules. On the first of these points, her argument appears to have been that whereas under FINA Doping Control Rule DC 6.1, FINA had the power to appoint a third party to carry out doping tests and had, in fact, appointed IDTM (a body corporate) for these purposes, but that there was no provision in the FINA rules for that third party to appoint another party (Mr and Mrs Guy) actually to carry out the test. This was a rather optimistic argument and was rejected by CAS which concluded that the relevant rule "necessarily contemplates and permits the third party....itself to appoint servants or agents to perform the actual doping control sampling procedure".[23] Indeed more generally, CAS made the point that the level of technicality in interpretation of the rules which was being suggested by de Bruin was simply inappropriate and thus it held that:

> It seems to us entirely inappropriate to construe a rule of this character with the technicality associated with, for example, a trust deed, when the rule is well capable of being given a purposive construction that respects the practicalities of its subject matter.[24]

More broadly, de Bruin further argued that in fact the rules did not permit out-of-competition testing. Again this conclusion demanded a rather tortuous interpretation of the rules and effectively was based on the fact that the relevant FINA anti-doping rules in dealing with unannounced testing appeared to use the terms "athlete" and "competitor" interchangeably despite the fact that in its guidelines it was provided that the term "athlete" was appropriate for out-of-competition testing, whereas the term "competitor" was appropriate for in-competition controls. It is not completely clear why this logic would necessitate a conclusion that out-of-competition testing was not permitted. In any event, CAS rejected the proposition, noting both that it was absolutely clear under FINA rules that out-of-competition testing was expressly permitted and hence the interpretation suggested by de Bruin would introduce a nonsense into the rules and also that, in any event, the accompanying guidelines expressly provided that in the event of a conflict between them and the rules, such conflict would be determined in favour of the provision contained in the rules.[25]

---

[22] CAS 98/211 *B v FINA*, para 11.

[23] CAS 98/211 *B v FINA*, para 16.

[24] CAS 98/211 *B v FINA*, para 17.

[25] CAS 98/211 *B v FINA*, para 23.

11.6 The Legalistic Challenge

The above were minor aspects of the appeal. The main challenge was more serious and more targeted in that it essentially honed in on the precise nature of both the burden and standard of proof in doping cases and in doing so raised broader questions as to the nature and status of anti-doping rules generally. In practical terms, it focused first on the question of how the chain of custody had been followed in the case and secondly on whether there was a positive obligation on FINA to disprove every other possibility than the appellant's guilt. In reality, however, the two issues blend together and may be treated as such under the broad heading of approaches to the interpretation of doping rules. Before considering this, however, it is necessary to focus on what it was about this precise case which made it so amenable to a highly legalistic style of defence and which could have little useful application in a "run-of-the-mill" doping case.

What was at issue in this case, after all, was the foundational question of whether a doping offence had occurred at all. In general however, (that is to say in the most common kind of doping case where an athlete is accused of having a banned substance in her system) a laboratory report in and of itself tends to close down most serious arguments as to whether or not, as a matter of fact, a doping offence has occurred. In such cases, in other words, whereas the burden of proof rests on the governing body to prove that the offence has occurred, a document from a laboratory demonstrating the presence of a banned substance effective fulfils this obligation—and not least because of the attaching presumption that the results of testing processes within an IOC or now a WADA accredited laboratory are accurate.[26] The options for an athlete (or their legal representatives) who is presented with such a document from a laboratory are therefore twofold. First, if [s]he is rich enough [s]he can hire a scientific expert to analyse the lab report in order to check whether appropriate procedures were followed and whether the results as stated actually flowed from such processes or could be explained in some other way. Alternatively (and possibly following a quick Google-type check to see if there could be some explanation for the positive test result which did not involve the presence of a banned substance) the athlete and his lawyer must simply accept the result (and hence accept that a doping offence has been committed and that the governing body has therefore satisfied the burden of proof) and turn instead to the question of whether there is any evidence which can be adduced to show that there was no fault or negligence on the part of the athlete—evidence which can be adduced in mitigation of sanction.[27]

In the current case, however, there were a number of pivotal ways in which the case differed from the norm. First, and in as much as whiskey is not a banned, out-of-competition substance for a swimmer, the mere fact of whiskey in the sample (that is to say the factual content of the laboratory report) did not in and of itself

[26] See Article 3.2.1 of the World Anti-doping Code 2009.

[27] See generally Article 10 of the World Anti-doping Code 2009.

prove a doping offence. Hence in order to prove the fact of a doping offence it was necessary for FINA not merely to present facts (as would be normal) but also to present analysis in respect of such facts (that is to say the opinion of the Barcelona laboratory, represented by a Dr Segura, that it was an inescapable inference that the density of whiskey in the sample meant that the sample had been tampered with). But because tampering (unlike having a banned substance in one's system) is not a strict liability offence, even the presentation of this analysis would not be sufficient. Put simply, not merely would FINA have to prove that tampering had occurred but also that Ms de Bruin was responsible for it and as outlined above, this is why the question of what precisely this would entail was so pivotal because if de Bruin was correct that FINA essentially needed to prove exactly what happened (in effect by disproving every alternative), then it would simply not have been able to fulfil this burden.

What the entire case turned on, accordingly, was whether a highly legalistic or a more flexible and common sense-based approach should be applied in interpreting doping rules. In order to answer this question it is arguably necessary to consider the nature of anti-doping rules and specifically the question of whether they are merely terms of a contract between sports persons and sports governing bodies or whether they are tantamount to provisions of criminal law (a proposition which de Bruin essentially made) or whether they are something in between.

11.7 Approaches to Interpretation of Doping Rules

Theoretically after all (and I should stress that this is an extreme view which has never, to my knowledge, been reflected in the anti-doping rules of any modern sporting organisation) it can be argued that that the official guidebook or regulations of a governing body or of an organisation like the IOC, and including its anti-doping rules, are merely the terms of a contract between it and its members. To the extent that athletes "sign up" to this contract (through, for example, membership of a relevant organisation) they become bound by these terms and hence are bound by the terms of such anti-doping rules. That being the case, anti-doping rules should be enforced as contractual terms (possibly subject to an implied contractual right of fair procedures). In other words, emphatically, they should not be regarded as tantamount to provisions of the criminal law with all their attendant requirements for strict procedures and so on. On this logic, the terms of the contract (the rules) are all that is important, nor is it relevant that they may appear arbitrary or unfair because the athlete has freely signed up to them. In particular, any dispute in respect of the terms of the contract should be resolved in the normal way—that is through the civil courts or where applicable (and it inevitably will be applicable) through arbitration. Moreover, there would be no need for such contractual terms to be interpreted as rigorously as the terms of a criminal statute or with as much concern with rights of fair procedures as would apply in a criminal trial.

On this logic also, it does not matter whether anti-doping rules cannot be consistently or rationally justified. After all, sport is full of rules which are not, on their face, capable of rational and consistent justification—why, for example are their 18 rather than 20 holes in a golf course or why can one not pass the ball forward in rugby? On the same basis, thus, it might be argued that there is no need for the anti-doping rules of any organisation to be anything other than clear and unambiguous—even if they are clearly and unambiguously harsh on the athlete.

The criticism of this view is based, it is submitted, on three significant propositions.

First, there is the fact that, unlike other playing rules or even disciplinary rules of sport, (that is to say, other relevant terms of the contract between federation and members), anti-doping rules have a unique ability to impact on the rights of athletes. The public, after all, takes a very particular view of the nature of a doping offence, namely that it involves a level of moral turpitude which is not found in any other form of cheating in sport other than possibly match fixing. In a way, this is a somewhat odd proposition. One can think of examples of cheating in sport which have far more propensity to affect the overall result of the sporting contest—diving for a penalty in a football match for example—yet which do not attract the level of public opprobrium which would be reserved for drug cheats. Furthermore, it is notable that the sporting ethic which anti-doping policy seeks to enforce—the idea of sport being a matter of natural ability rather than the skill of a scientist—is routinely violated in a perfectly lawful way in any number of contexts from scientifically designed swimsuits to scientifically designed dietary and nutritional supplements.[28] This is immaterial however. The fact remains that a doping offence carries with it a vast weight of popular moral criticism and this criticism tends not to distinguish between different types of offence and in particular to appreciate the moral significance of the fact that someone accused of using drugs might not have intended to do so. Consequently, the potential for anti-doping policy to impact egregiously on the right to a good name of an athlete is simply enormous.

Secondly there is the issue of sanction. If someone cheats by, for example, diving in a football match [s]he may receive at worst a yellow card for doing so and in turn this will, at worst, lead to him or her being suspended in a subsequent game (and even then this would require other factors to be present—i.e. that [s]he would have picked up another yellow card in the same game or other yellow cards in different games). Yet with doping, the athlete who is found guilty will under WADA rules—and subject only to very rare exceptions which are notoriously difficult to activate—be suspended from all competitive sport for a minimum of two years. This would be bad enough for an amateur athlete given the relationship between sporting competition and personal dreams and ambitions, but for a professional athlete with rights to a livelihood the consequences could be financially disastrous and not least because of the notoriously short careers of most top

[28] See on this: Brown 1980, 1984a, b; Cox 2000, 2004; Cox and Schuster 2004; Fraleigh 1984; Lavin 1987; Marazzo 1997; and Simon 1984a, b.

athletes and the fact that it will be hugely difficult for an athlete who has been banned for a doping offence to retain sponsor links. In other words the financial hit to an athlete (and especially, obviously, an elite athlete) will be simply enormous nor is there anything else in a sports federation's rule book which could impact so significantly on him or her.

The final reason why it is arguably not appropriate to regard doping rules as just another term of a contract is considerably more nebulous, but, it is submitted, no less valid. The financial and popular support for anti-doping policy is based on a clear and unshakeable popular consensus that it is necessary on a "fair play" basis—that is, that doping is bad and hence the fight against doping is, by definition, good. No doubt it can be argued that some of this public support is media driven and its unshakeability is grounded in part on the refusal of anti-doping authorities to engage meaningfully with their critics but again this is immaterial. The point is that such support exists and is vital to underpin the ongoing existence and funding of anti-doping units. But if this is the case then it is obviously necessary that the public continues to believe that anti-doping policy is necessary in the furtherance of a moral ideal connected with broad normative ideals of fair play and justice and hence it would be disastrous if that policy started to be regarded as being itself unjust or immoral. It can be argued, however, that this probably would happen if governing bodies ever imposed an anti-doping policy without any consideration for the interests of athletes accused of doping and on the basis simply that they were entitled to do so as a matter of contract. In other words, quite apart from issues connected with the rights of athletes it actually makes good policy sense in terms of the long-term future of anti-doping policy to ensure that the rules are treated with the seriousness that they deserve, and the rights of athletes are protected as such.

Equally as was observed above, there has never really been any serious question but that WADA and other groups like it do not regard anti-doping rules in a cavalier light, and that provision is made for the rights of athletes to be protected. The question which remains and which faced the CAS Panel in the case under discussion is precisely what this entails, in so far as questions of burden and standard of proof are concerned. In other words, even if we accept that anti-doping rules cannot be characterised as simply terms of a contract but rather are something more than this in so far as the procedural entitlements of athletes are concerned, this does not answer the question of exactly what the nature of these procedural entitlements should be. Specifically, it does not answer the question of whether de Bruin was correct in her contention that the nature of the rules (and their impact on her) meant both that the burden facing FINA was to prove her guilt to the criminal standard of beyond reasonable doubt (using the logic that in as much as the impact on her of such rules was so enormous that they should be regarded as being like of rules of criminal law) and also that it would be appropriate to require FINA, in the admittedly rather unusual circumstances of her case, to prove that a doping offence had been committed by disproving every other possibility at all stages along the chain of causation.

On the first issue, the CAS Panel emphatically rejected the proposition that the standard of proof in doping cases operates at the criminal level and in doing so it implicitly rejected the notion that doping rules were tantamount to provisions of the criminal law. Equally, however, it also stressed that the standard must be higher than the normal civil standard of balance of probabilities and thus it concluded:

> The Panel is in no doubt that the burden of proof lay upon FINA to establish that an offence had been committed. This flows from the language of the doping control provisions as well as general principles of Swiss civil law (Article 8, Swiss Civil Code). The presumption of innocence operates in the Appellant's favour until FINA discharges that initial burden.
>
> The Panel is equally in no doubt that the standard of proof required of FINA is high: less than the criminal standard, but more than the ordinary civil standard. The Panel is content to adopt the test set out in K. and G. v. IOC (see CAS OG 96/003-004) ("K."): "ingredients must be established to the comfortable satisfaction of the Court having in mind the seriousness of the allegation which is made". To adopt a criminal standard (at any rate, where the disciplinary charge is not a criminal offence) is to confuse the public law of the state with the private law of an association (see CAS 98/208).
>
> The Panel further accepts that, in as much as an allegation of manipulation includes an element of mens rea and attributes dishonesty to an athlete (whereas other doping offences may be ones of strict liability), such an allegation bespeaks an extremely high degree of seriousness.[29]

This is a significant conclusion—and one which represents the orthodox view of CAS prior to the coming into being of the World Anti-doping Code[30] and also now the approach that is taken within that Code.[31] To some extent of course, its practical impact is limited—very few cases of this kind will surely arise where the relevant tribunal had a reasonable doubt as to the athlete's guilt but felt that on some legalistic definition it was comfortably satisfied of his or her guilt. Symbolically, however, the approach is significant in that it rejects the two most extreme views of the nature of doping rules (i.e. doping rules as mere terms of the contract and doping rules as quasi criminal law) and instead adopts a middle ground somewhere between the two extremes and ensures that the procedural entitlements of persons accused of doping offences should reflect this fact.

It is further significant that CAS appeared to regard the fact that the offence of which de Bruin stood accused involved an element of *mens rea* and as such "bespeaks an extremely high degree of seriousness" as impacting on the standard of proof that would apply in this case. One can of course appreciate this reasoning—especially in as much as a finding that an athlete was guilty of this offence would mean that her reputation would be in tatters nor could she take refuge in an argument that what had occurred was not her fault morally (as, no doubt, have certain persons who have intentionally used drugs and have been found guilty of

---

[29] CAS 98/211 *B v FINA*, paras 25–27.

[30] CAS 98/222 *B v International Triathlon Union*; CAS 2000/A/281 *H v. International Motorcycling Federation*; and CAS 2002/A/386 *Kabaeva v FIG*.

[31] See Article 3.1 of the World Anti-Doping Code 2009.

the strict liability offence of having a banned substance in their sample). Equally it is submitted that in the present case, the real significance of the nature of the offence was not so much in terms of the standard of proof that should apply but rather in terms of what specifically had to be proved and specifically whether (as she alleged) FINA had to prove how the alleged tampering had occurred and that she was responsible.

11.8 Chain of Custody

Before getting to this point, however, it is necessary briefly to dispose of de Bruin's first argument namely that FINA could not establish the chain of custody in this case and hence that there must remain a doubt as to whether the sample tested was actually the same as that provided by the athlete. This was something of an uphill battle as far as the appellant was concerned, and indeed it is arguable that the "scattergun" nature of the allegations made at this point may even have weakened her defence albeit that it linked with her second argument; namely that it was possible (if the sample tested *was* the sample she had provided) that in fact it had been manipulated by someone other than herself. As has been mentioned above, after all, certainly on the evidence offered, there did not appear to be any flaws in the testing process as it occurred in her case. Nonetheless her first target was the manner in which the Guys looked after the sample before conveying it to DHL. Specifically it was suggested that the family refrigerator was an inappropriate place to leave the sample for a weekend. As has been mentioned above, however, whereas the fact of the sample being in the family fridge is superficially quirky, in reality there is nothing wrong with such an approach. After all, it is necessary for samples to be refrigerated prior to testing and in addition, as the Panel noted,[32] as a matter of security this was actually a highly sensible approach because "Who knew of the sample's whereabouts or could have had access to a private fridge other than the custodians themselves?" Indeed as would become clear in its opinion, the Panel clearly accepted the reliability of the evidence of the Guys and indeed preferred it to that of the appellant.[33]

Secondly, the appellant turned to the role played by DHL and suggested that FINA could not establish the chain of custody for the period between 12 January when the Guys handed the sample over to DHL until 14 January when a sample was received by the laboratory in Barcelona. Again, however, the CAS Panel rejected this proposition noting that DHL "is a carrier of international reputation"[34] and hence there was no reason for it to assume that the sample (which arrived at the laboratory in good time) was not in DHL's custody throughout. No

---

[32] CAS 98/211 *B v FINA*, para 33.

[33] See, in particular, the comments at CAS 98/211 *B v FINA*, para 30.

[34] CAS 98/211 *B v FINA*, para 35.

doubt on the facts this is not an unreasonable conclusion. Equally it is notable that the approach of the Panel appears to have been that the default position for it would be to assume that the approach of DHL was acceptable and that this assumption would only be disturbed on the basis of arguments raised by the appellant. In other words, it does not appear to have required FINA to prove the chain of custody so much as requiring de Bruin to disprove it. It is true that FINA did furnish letters from DHL sent to IDTM to the effect that usual procedures had been followed; nonetheless, the language used by CAS in this regard is perhaps, at least on the face of it, inconsistent with the rules.

That this is the case is best illustrated by the approach of CAS to the appellant's suggestion that there might have been a problem with the chain of custody when the sample reached the laboratory in Barcelona. Such an argument could not really work because under FINA's Anti-Doping Rules (and now the WADA code), there is a "presumption of regularity" in respect of what happens at accredited laboratories nor had de Bruin offered anything to disturb this presumption. Equally, such a presumption does not attach to DHL, and hence for form, it is arguable that the Panel's language in placing a burden on the appellant to prove that DHL had acted inappropriately was inconsistent with the rules. Equally this is legalistic, nor was there any substantive reason which the Panel could see which would prevent it from finding that the chain of custody had been established and that the sample tested was the same as the sample provided by the appellant.

11.9 The Obligation on FINA

The second major claim made by de Bruin was yet more significant; namely that the nature of the case demanded that FINA disprove all possible explanations for the tampered sample other than that she was responsible. In fact such a view of burden of proof requires an approach to anti-doping rules that is even more extreme than the view that they are equivalent to provisions of criminal law in the sense that she was requiring more of FINA than would be required of the prosecution in the context of a criminal case. Hence the CAS panel arguably had two choices on how to proceed namely to determine that such a step was not required of FINA having regarded to the standard of proof in doping cases, or alternatively to assess whether there were any alternative theories which FINA should have had to disprove. In fact, it did both.

In the first instance the CAS Panel rejected the appellant's argument as to what was required of FINA. As we have previously seen, the Panel had already determined that the standard of proof was between the criminal and civil standard (proof to the comfortable satisfaction of the tribunal) and in so far as the Panel was concerned, in order to meet this standard, FINA would merely have to convince it of de Bruin's guilt, and this would not necessarily entail disproving all other theories for the sample being in the condition it was in.[35] Secondly, however, (and, one may submit, for the sake of completeness) the Panel also considered whether there were any other reasonable hypotheses for the whiskey in the sample other than one pointing to the appellant's guilt. In this light it was key that de Bruin had "declined – and ... was unable – to formulate any hypothesis that would point the finger at some such other person, whether identified or not".[36] It is true that she had suggested, in a rather abstract way, that the Guys or some FINA representative might have been guilty of manipulation but the Panel rejected this, and for two reasons. First, the Panel felt that it was ludicrous to suggest that the Guys,[37] or FINA[38] (or, presumably, someone working in the laboratory in Barcelona) would be motivated to conspire against the swimmer. Secondly, all the evidence which was before it, indicated that the relevant Versapak containers could not be opened in a manner which would not leave some detectable markings on the bottle.[39] In other words, even if there was such a conspiracy, and someone was motivated to do her down, then on the basis of such evidence as was available, it would have been impossible for that person to have interfered with the sample without leaving evidence of such interference on the bottle.

Accordingly, in so far as the Panel was concerned, the hypothesis that someone else just might have been responsible for tampering with the sample was unsustainable in that it would have required a combination of circumstances which was simply fantastical.[40] Indeed CAS noted that, even if the criminal standard of "beyond reasonable doubt" applied (which it did not) this would be precisely the kind of doubt which a court would regard as being unreasonable.[41] On the other hand, the appellant clearly had a motivation to try to distort the results of the sample (in that it appeared that the sample did contain a substance which, at the very least, was highly likely to be classifiable as a banned substance) and also there was a clear opportunity for her to have done so (in the period between the Guys arriving at the house and the appellant re-appearing in the kitchen)[42] and evidence of such manipulation would not have been evident during the period when she actually provided the sample because her vaginal region was covered by her baggy fleece top.[43] In other words, from the Panel's perspective not merely was there any

---

[35] CAS 98/211 *B v FINA*, para 41.

[36] CAS 98/211 *B v FINA*, para 42.

[37] CAS 98/211 *B v FINA*, para 43.

[38] CAS 98/211 *B v FINA*, para 44.

[39] CAS 98/211 *B v FINA*, para 45.

[40] CAS 98/211 *B v FINA*, para 49.

[41] CAS 98/211 *B v FINA*, para 50.

[42] The Guys estimated that this was between 4 and 6 min, whereas the appellant suggested that it was one minute. The Panel rejected her testimony in this regard and felt that it was significant that she would make this suggestion, see CAS 98/211 *B v FINA*, para 51.

[43] CAS 98/211 *B v FINA*, para 52.

alternative hypothesis which would work, but the hypothesis proffered by FINA rang true very loudly indeed.

This then enabled the Panel to determine the matter and to uphold the finding of FINA's Anti-doping Panel. It may be submitted moreover, that this is a perfectly reasonable conclusion. The nature of the offence of this kind (where the only hard and fast evidence is the result of a laboratory analysis on a urine sample indicating merely the fact of manipulation) is such that it will be virtually impossible for the governing body to offer direct evidence that the athlete manipulated the sample (unless, of course, the testers actually notice this fact as the process is ongoing). Nonetheless, even in the context of a criminal trial, it will often be possible to prove guilt even in the absence of direct evidence showing that the accused committed the crime. Triers of fact are expected to be able to make reasonable inferential conclusions based on evidence presented and in this case the guilt of the appellant was surely such a conclusion. As the CAS Panel put it: "In short the absence of direct evidence of manipulation (correctly stressed by Respondent's counsel) was in no way fatal to the appellant's case. The substantial circumstantial evidence clearly sufficed".[44]

11.10 Conclusion

It is difficult in some ways to classify *B v FINA*. In one way, it can be regarded as a case of great complexity in that it involved a very rare type of doping offence scenario, which meant that, in terms of satisfying the burden of proof, FINA clearly had more to do in this case than would be the norm. On the other hand, it can also be regarded as an easy case in that so much of the actual factual evidence presented (from the fact that the chain of custody was essentially perfect; to the fact that there was a banned substance in the appellant's system; to the fact that the scientific evidence indicated that there could have been no tampering with the sample from the point from which it was provided) pointed unwaveringly to de Bruin's guilt. From a practitioner's standpoint, and apart from the helpful clarification provided by the CAS Panel on questions of burden and standard of proof, the importance of the decision going forward may well lie in the fact that it indicates clearly that legalistic and rather pedantic propositions from counsel representing persons accused of doping offences will not work unless they are supported by some sort of workable factual hypothesis. In other words, whereas CAS has a strong legal framework to it, this does not mean that it is necessarily blind to the application of common sense and the realisation that, on most occasions, what appears to be the truth actually is the truth. Finally, the decision of CAS in this case confirms that the anti-doing rules, whereas they are more than mere terms of a contract, should not be regarded as being equivalent to provisions

[44] CAS 98/211 *B v FINA*, para 56.

of criminal law. Rather they are sports rules, but rules which have the potential to impact so enormously on athletes that very serious care must be taken in their application.

References

Brown WM (1980) Ethics, drugs and sport. J Philos Sport 7:15–23
Brown WM (1984a) Paternalism, drugs and the nature of sports. J Philos Sport 11:14–22
Brown WM (1984b) Comments on Simon & Fraleigh. J Philos Sport 11:33–35
Cox N (2000) Victory with honour or victory at all costs. Dublin Univ Law J 22:19–49
Cox N (2002) Legalisation of drug use in sport. Int Sports Law Rev 2(Oct) 77–89
Cox N, Schuster A (2004) Sport and the law. First Law, Dublin
Dowling J (1999) De Bruin praised for being helpful in anti-dope checks, Irish Independent, 4 May
Fraleigh W (1984) Performance enhancing drugs in sport; the ethical issue. J Philos Sport 11:23–28
Hannigan M (1999) There's true honour in trailing in last. Irish Times, 12 June
Humphries T (1997) FINA remind Smith on test procedures. Irish Times, 6 Feb
Humphries T (1998) Authorities had long history of difficulty in getting De Bruin to comply with dope-testing procedures. Irish Times, 7 Aug
Humphries T (1999a) FINA ascribe motive and opportunity. Irish Times, 4 May
Humphries T (1999b) High-risk strategy costs dear. Irish Times, 8 June
Humphries T (1999c) The man behind the woman. Irish Times, 8 June
Humphries T (1999d) Time to tackle tainted legacy. The Irish Times, 9 June
Kimmage P (1999) Awaiting the sting. Sunday Independent (Dublin), 2 May
Lavin M (1987) Sports and drugs: are the current bans justified? J Philos Sport 14:34–43
Marazzo D (1997) Athletes and drug testing: why do we care if athletes inhale? Marquette Sports Law J 8:75–91
McLaren R (2006) An overview of non-analytical positive and circumstantial evidence cases in sports. Marquette Sports Law Rev 16:193–212
McTeirnan A (1996) Swimming against tide to olympic success. Irish Times, 22 Nov
O'Connor A (1996) Smith's olympic victories make for a historic week. Irish Times, 27 July
Ruger J (2009) From the trenches: the landscape of sports dispute resolution and athlete representation. Pepperdine Dispute Resolut J 10:157–164
Simon R (1984a) Good competition and drug enhanced performance. J Philos Sport 11:6–13
Simon R (1984b) Responses to Brown & Fraleigh. J Philos Sport 11:30–32
Smith de Bruin M (1999) De Bruin says career is over. The Irish Times, 9 June
Watterson J (1999) Acceptance of guilt. The Irish Times, 9 June

Chapter 12
CAS 2004/O/645 *USADA v Montgomery*

John O'Leary

Abstract The claimant, the United States Anti-Doping Agency ("USADA"), is the independent anti-doping agency for Olympic sports in the United States and is responsible for managing the testing and adjudication process for doping control in that country. The respondent, Tim Montgomery, was an elite and highly successful American track and field athlete. As a sprinter, he had won numerous track and field titles, including World Championship and Olympic gold medals, as well as a world record. In 2004, USADA informed Montgomery that it had received sufficient evidence to indicate that he was a participant in a wide-ranging doping conspiracy implemented by the Californian-based Bay Area Laboratory Cooperative ("BALCO"). USADA sought to ban Montgomery for four years. The legal issue revolved around the fact that USADA had charged Montgomery with the violation of applicable IAAF (athletics' world governing body) anti-doping rules, notwithstanding that Montgomery had never tested positive in any in-competition or out-of-competition doping test. The matter proceeded directly to a single final hearing before the Court of Arbitration for Sport ("CAS"). A CAS Panel held that doping offences can be proved by a variety of means and thus, for instance, in the absence of any adverse analytical finding, other types of evidence can be substantiated. Among these "alternatives" could be uncontroverted testimony of a wholly credible witness, sufficient to establish that the athlete has admitted to the use of prohibited substances in violation of applicable anti-doping rules. In addition, CAS held that USADA bore the burden of proving, by strong evidence commensurate with the serious claims at issue, that the athlete had committed the doping offences. An important aspect of the CAS award was the discussion on whether a "beyond reasonable doubt" or "comfortable satisfaction" standard of proof should apply in determining doping claims against athletes.

J. O'Leary (✉)
Anglia Law School, Anglia Ruskin University, Marconi Building, Chelmsford Campus, Bishop Hall Lane, Chelmsford CM1 1SQ, UK
e-mail: John.O'Leary@anglia.ac.uk

J. Anderson (ed.), *Leading Cases in Sports Law*,
ASSER International Sports Law Series, DOI: 10.1007/978-90-6704-909-2_12,

Contents

12.1 Introduction

The anti-doping regulation of sport is a strange phenomenon. To sports fans across the globe doping is cheating[1]; in the law of England and Wales, it is a breach of contract. As Latham LJ stated in *Modahl v British Athletics Federation (No 2)*, the relationship between athlete and governing body is such that "there is nothing inherently improbable about the concept of a contractual obligation being entered into by an individual athlete which would create a contractual relationship between the athlete and the [governing body]".[2] It is a strange contract for all that[3]; an agreement to which the athlete has no option but to consent if they wish to compete and which excludes them, in most instances, from redress to the courts. Impliedly, athletes agree that, even if they are without culpability, they can be sanctioned and deprived of their livelihood should a doping violation be established by the authorities. This puts the athlete in a vulnerable, relatively powerless position but then there is none so damned in the sporting arena as the doping cheat.

Doping cheats have acquired a status within sport and, by a form of osmosis, to politicians, courts and the public so the fact that their indiscretion is a mere breach of contract has been lost in inquisitorial rhetoric. The courts' position has been relatively simple. Until quite recently they have resisted the temptation to meddle in sports issues which they deemed to be of pure sporting interest. All that changed however in *Meca-Medina and Majcen v Commission*[4] where the Court of Justice of the European Union "collapsed the idea"[5] of "purely sporting interest" by asserting that an anti-doping ban was an economic issue and, therefore, justiciable.

---

[1] See generally Green 2004 and Beloff 2009.

[2] *Modahl v British Athletic Federation (No 2)* [2001] EWCA Civ 1447; [2002] 1 WLR 1192, 1208.

[3] See further Ruijsenaars et al. 2007.

[4] Case C-519/04 P *David Meca-Medina and Igor Majcen v Commission of the European Communities* [2006] ECR I-6991.

[5] Weatherill 2006, 657.

Anti-doping is at last on the legal map.[6] In addition, the Court of Justice of the European Union ("CJEU") in *Meca-Medina* also confirmed that the current doping regime, as represented by the World Anti-Doping Code, was a proportionate administrative response to the issue of doping. Arguably therefore, what started out as a means of providing harmony within sport has thus become a bona fide means of restricting athletes' right to trade.

The anti-doping rules of today are a sophisticated response to the issue but such sophistication was not always de rigueur. The regulations have been refined over the years as part of an organic process of "give and take" involving sports governing bodies, politicians and, most importantly, the courts (although not necessarily with the athletes themselves). Only a decade ago the anti-doping landscape was markedly different. The development of anti-doping regulation may appear incremental but even the smoothest of evolutionary processes are hallmarked by significant incremental leaps. Three critical junctures in anti-doping regulation would surely include the establishment of the Court of Arbitration for Sport ("CAS"), the foundation of the World Anti-doping Agency ("WADA") and the judgment of the CJEU in *Meca-Medina*. This chapter focuses on a fourth pivotal moment—the CAS award of *USADA v Montgomery*.[7]

In 2005, the sprinter Tim Montgomery was banned from competing in athletic events for two years when he lost his case before CAS. His misdemeanour was that he had competed in athletic events whilst using drugs banned under the IAAF's Anti-doping Code of 2002. Montgomery was not unique in having fallen foul of stringent anti-doping regulations but what makes Montgomery's circumstances significant was that he had never failed a drug test. This fact alone would make this a landmark case in the development of anti-doping jurisprudence but given the context of the case—the BALCO enquiry—and CAS's treatment of "non-analytical positives" as they became known, it marked this case out as a marker for the way in which the World Anti-doping Code developed subsequently. The aim of this chapter is to map a discourse in anti-doping that starts with BALCO[8] and ends with the current World Anti-doping Code and which establishes *USADA v Montgomery* at the centre of anti-doping development. For convenience, the chapter is divided into three sections. The first looks at events leading up to the CAS hearing; the second deals with the hearing and its associated issues; and the third looks at the way in which anti-doping has developed post-*Montgomery*.

---

6 See, chronologically, Bailey 2007; Szyszczak 2007; Manville 2008; Pijetlovic 2009; and Subiotto 2010.

7 CAS 2004/O/645 *USADA v Montgomery*.

8 In the early part of this century, Californian-based Bay Area Laboratory Cooperative ("BALCO") was involved in a conspiracy the purpose of which was the distribution and use of sports doping substances and techniques that were either undetectable or difficult to detect in routine drug testing. The affair prompted numerous public and sport-specific investigations, including the stated proceedings. For its origins, see generally Fainaru-Wada and Williams 2006.

12.2 Anti-Doping Before Montgomery

Prior to the hearing, Tim Montgomery had established himself as an important US track and field star. He was a member of the USA 4 × 100 m relay squad for the 1996 Olympics and, in the following year, he won the bronze medal in the 100 m at the world athletics championships in Athens. He was a 4 × 100 m relay squad member at the Olympic Games of 2000 in Sydney and his most significant achievement occurred in 2002 when he set a new world record for the 100 m of 9.78 s. By this time it would be reasonable to conclude that Montgomery was not only a sporting success but also, due to the rewards and appearance money available on the international athletics circuit, a financial success. The significance of Montgomery's financial status is twofold: first, a finding that Montgomery had taken a banned substance[9] would damage future income streams (in addition to the possibility of retrospective cancelling of previous results and winnings); and second that he would be in a position of some strength to challenge any accusation of an anti-doping violation.

Prior to the introduction of the World Anti-doping Code in 2003, anti-doping measures within sports were obscure and discordant. Beloff's oft-quoted remark that "in my experience, rules of domestic or international federations tend to resemble the architecture of an ancient building: a wing added here; a loft there; a buttress elsewhere, without adequate consideration of whether the additional parts affect adversely the symmetry of the whole",[10] remains the most pertinent comment of a system lacking in coherence. One of the most important consequences of such a system is that it was easy prey to lawyers well versed in exploiting the inadequacies of a contradictory system. As a result, around the turn of the century, sport determined to harmonise the doping regulations of the various national and international governing bodies. In the vanguard of this movement is WADA. The rise of WADA can be seen as a response to the inadequacies of earlier regimes and a realisation that successful anti-doping policies come at a price.

---

[9] Under Article 4.3.1 of the 2009 WADA Code, a substance or method shall be considered for inclusion on the Prohibited List if WADA determines that it meets any two of the following three criteria: 4.3.1.1 Medical or other scientific evidence, pharmacological effect or experience that the substance or method, alone or in combination with other substances or methods, has the potential to enhance or enhances sport performance; 4.3.1.2 Medical or other scientific evidence, pharmacological effect or experience that the Use of the substance or method represents an actual or potential health risk to the Athlete; 4.3.1.3 WADA's determination that the Use of the substance or method violates the spirit of sport described in the Introduction to the Code. Under Article 4.3.2 of the 2009 Code, a substance or method shall also be included on the Prohibited List if WADA determines there is medical or other scientific evidence, pharmacological effect or experience that the substance or method has the potential to mask the Use of other Prohibited Substances or Prohibited Methods.

[10] Beloff 2000, 40.

From a jurisprudential perspective WADA might be viewed as one of many quasi-judicial global administrators. De Knop summarises the impact that globalisation has had on sport:

> Today's world is tomorrow's village. As a consequence of increased mobility, new communication technologies, exploring information networks, mass media and the all-embracing economy, we are now experiencing globalisation in numerous areas. We are living in a world where national borders are becoming even more porous and in which different globalisation processes are occurring. Sport, too, is going through this globalisation which has great impact on the way it is managed.[11]

Walker encapsulates the emergence of what is called global administrative law, the characteristics of which are well illustrated by leading world sports governing bodies:

> [to] the extent that they develop a law-like quality, they do so after-the-fact, consequential upon the administrative tasks in which they are engaged. They develop substantive rules of conduct, and also procedural rules for decision-making and decision-accounting, but they lack any constitutive co-ordinates to underpin these substantive and procedural rules. In other words, they are non-autochthonous – unrooted in any state or other stable site of public authority or even at the contested boundaries between different sites of public authority, and instead generate such authority as they have purely out of the regulatory purposes that they pursue and practices that they develop.[12]

Although it can be argued that sport itself was one of the earliest global economies, the same could not be said about the administration of sport. The IAAF may act as the administrator for international athletic events but it shares the global administration with the constituent national governing bodies as well as the International Olympic Committee ("IOC"). The start of this century can be identified as a key stage in the development of the global administration of sport. Not only did WADA assume primary responsibility for the prevention of doping, CAS completed its coup and became the primary dispute resolution body for sport. As doping represents a significant proportion of CAS disputes it is likely that CAS doping cases will provide a focal point for the development of global principles underlying the administration of sport. Anti-doping regulation therefore must be understood as the product of the symbiotic relationship between the WADA and CAS.[13]

The WADA Code however does not have direct application to individual athletes. It exists as a document of minimum standards to be adopted and enhanced as appropriate by the governing bodies of international sports; in this instance the enhanced anti-doping framework of the IAAF. The WADA Code of 2003 specified a number of ways in which a violation may have occurred that covered individual

---

11 De Knop 2000, 20.

12 Walker 2010, 42 and more generally Casini, 2009, 421–446.

13 See generally Oschutz 2002.

offences as well as associated offences such as tampering and trafficking.[14] Rule 60(1) of the IAAF Code of 2002 stated that *inter alia*:

> For the purpose of these Rules, the following shall be regarded as 'doping offences' (see also Rule 55.2): (i) the presence in an athlete's body tissues or fluids of a prohibited substance; (ii) the use or taking advantage of forbidden techniques; (iii) admitting having taken advantage of, or having used, or having attempted to use, a prohibited substance or a prohibited technique...

The rule makes fascinating reading for anti-doping historians. Rule 60(1)(i) is the normal proof of doping rule and finds its correlative in Article 2(1) of the WADA Code. Rule 60(1)(ii) is a relic from the pre-WADA confusion as it depends on the IAAF establishing "use" or "taking advantage"; something difficult to prove. Article 2(2)(1) of the WADA code anticipated this stating, "The success or failure of the use of a prohibited substance or prohibited method is immaterial". The WADA Code is also predicated on the strict liability principle which does away with complications based on use and advantage.[15]

For the purposes of *Montgomery*, however, it is Rule 60(1)(iii) that holds the key. The admission of having used a substance is a logical extension of the positive test in one respect. It would be counterintuitive to hold that an admission of doping to the authorities in the absence of a positive test is not a violation, whereas a denial accompanied by a positive test is a violation. If the athlete is ready to admit their misdemeanour then the authorities should be able to accept it in the spirit of truth and reconciliation. Crucial to this case and what elevates it from the mundane to the significant is to whom must that omission be made? An admission to the governing body is simple to rationalise as an exception to the principle that a violation requires a positive test as proof. An admission to a third party, especially if the admission is later denied, is an entirely different genus of proof for it takes a significant step away from the simple principle that underpinned its application to that juncture. This standard of proof requires the CAS to weigh up conflicting evidence and calls into question the suitability of the "reasonable satisfaction" standard that had been promulgated to that point. To understand this sea change it is necessary to track the development of this genus of proof up to *Montgomery*. Was *Montgomery* "a rabbit pulled from a hat" or was it the product of an identifiable evolution?

---

[14] Under the 2009 WADA Code, the definition of a doping offence under Article 1 is the violation of an anti-doping rule contained in Article 2. They are: the presence of a prohibited substance or its metabolites in an athlete's sample (Article 2.1); use or attempted use by an athlete of a prohibited substance or a prohibited method (Article 2.2); refusing or failing without compelling justification to sample collection (Article 2.3); violation of applicable requirements regarding athlete availability for out-of-competition testing (Article 2.4); tampering or attempted tampering with any part of doping control (Article 2.5); possession of prohibited substances or prohibited methods (Article 2.6); trafficking or attempted trafficking in any prohibited substance or prohibited method (Article 2.7) and administration or attempted administration to any athlete of any prohibited method or prohibited substance (Article 2.8).

[15] For an early discussion and recognition of strict liability in doping-related sports disputes see CAS 94/129 *USA Shooting & Quigley v UIT* and Tarasti 2000.

Evaluating the CAS doping jurisprudence, it is possible to identify an undercurrent of change around this time leading up to *Montgomery*. In *de Bruin*[16] we discover the beginnings of change; that anti-doping infractions cannot be predicated solely on analytical positives. De Bruin was an Irish swimmer. She was accused of adulterating her urine sample with alcohol. The case against de Bruin was based on a relatively simple point. There is very little conceptual difference between a masking agent taken by an athlete to cloak the use of banned substances and a crude masking agent such as alcohol being used in a crude attempt to mask the presence of a banned substance in a urine sample. The difference is simply one of when the masking agent was used. Nevertheless, this was technically a non-analytical finding case as de Bruin did not test positive. Without that positive test the strict liability standard was inappropriate and CAS adopted a "comfortable satisfaction standard" based on its use in *Kerneev & Ghouliev v IOC*.[17]

In *French*,[18] used syringes and other physical evidence of doping were found in a room last occupied by Australian cyclist Mark French. He was charged with using, aiding and abetting and trafficking. This muddies the waters rather, as aiding and abetting and trafficking are, by their nature, non-analytical. On the issue of use, CAS confirmed that the strict liability standard was inappropriate in a non-analytical case such as this and adopted a "higher level of satisfaction than the balance of probabilities". On this basis "there [was] no direct evidence that Mr. French used the material in the sense that no-one saw him use it and he has consistently denied use." The denial in *French* is important as it became a key issue in *Montgomery*. CAS concluded that the evidence against French was "not satisfactory and is totally insufficient" to support a non-analytical finding.[19]

In the context of Montgomery, however, the most significant jurisprudence is contained within the arbitral decision of *Collins*,[20] another athlete embroiled in the BALCO proceedings. The proof against Michelle Collins, an American athlete, was what could best be described as hybrid analytical/non-analytical and based on e-mail evidence between Collins and BALCO in which she admitted anti-doping offences and blood and urine tests, which evidenced a pattern of doping. It should be noted that the arbitral panel were of the view that none of the presented evidence by itself would normally have been sufficient to find doping, but it circumstantially it was consistent with the charges and the other proof presented by USADA. Crucially, this decision was based on the higher standard of beyond

[16] CAS 98/211 *B v FINA*.

[17] CAS OG 96/003-004 *Korneev and Ghouliev v IOC*.

[18] CAS 2004/A/651 *French v Australian Sports Commission and Cycling Australia*.

[19] But see CAS 2004/0/607 *B v IWF*.

[20] Arbitral Award AAA no 30 190 00658 04 *USADA v Collins*. This award was heard before the American Arbitration Association under the auspices of a North American Court of Arbitration for Sport Panel and is available online at: www.usada.org/files/active/arbitration_rulings/AAA%20CAS%20Decision%20-%20Collins.pdf.

reasonable doubt contained in the IAAF rules prior to the IAAF's adoption of the WADA Code. The obvious distinction between these authorities and *Montgomery* is that, prior to *Montgomery*, no pure non-analytical doping violation had been established.

12.3 *Montgomery*: The Hearing

CAS 2004/O/645 *USADA v Montgomery* was heard in parallel to proceedings involving another American athlete under the same scrutiny—Christie Gaines.[21] USADA adopted something of a "shotgun" approach in bringing evidence under seven heads. Effectively, however, there were two grounds. First, that there was a violation based on sufficiency of test abnormality and second that there was a violation based on third party evidence of Montgomery's involvement or admission in anti-doping. Particularly important was the claim that Montgomery had confessed his use of banned substances to a fellow athlete Kelli White. At the time Kelli White was also the subject of a doping ban having confessed to various anti-doping infractions. Cutting through the dense layers of procedure and standards the CAS Panel in *Montgomery* came to a very simple conclusion. On considering, whether it should consider each of the 7 types of evidence presented by USADA as proof of doping by Montgomery,[22] the Panel determined unanimously that, because the athlete had

> in fact admitted his use of prohibited substances to [Kelli White]...on which basis alone the Panel can and does find him guilty of a doping offence. The Panel does not consider it necessary in the circumstances to analyse and comment on the mass of other evidence against the Athlete. Nevertheless, the Panel does not consider that such other evidence could not demonstrate that the Respondent is guilty of doping. Doping offences can be proved by a variety of means; and this is nowhere more true than in "non-analytical positive" cases such as the present.[23]

It is interesting to note that Kelli White's evidence was not challenged by Montgomery's counsel, a point stressed by the CAS:

> It might indeed have affected the Panel's appreciation of Ms. White's evidence had the respondent chosen to provide the Panel with a different explanation of their March 2001 conversation or had he denied that the conversation took place as described by the witness. The fact remains that he did not.[24]

This led to the following deduction by the Panel:

---

21 CAS 2004/0/649 *USADA v Gaines.*

22 CAS 2004/O/645 *USADA v Montgomery*, para 3.

23 CAS 2004/O/645 *USADA v Montgomery*, para 4.

24 CAS 2004/O/645 *USADA v Montgomery*, para 8.

> ...having seen Ms. White and heard her testimony, including in response to questions put to her by counsel and the Panel, the members of the Panel do not doubt the veracity of her evidence. She answered all questions, including in relation to her own record of doping, in a forthright, honest and reasonable manner. She neither exaggerated nor sought to play down any aspect of her evidence. Clearly an intelligent woman, she impressed the Panel with her candour as well as her dispassionate approach to the issues raised in her testimony and regarding which she was questioned by counsel and members of the Panel. In sum, the Panel finds Ms. White's testimony to be wholly credible.[25]

This is indeed ironic considering a differently constituted CAS had recently banned her for two years for being a doping cheat. What remains a mystery is why Montgomery was not called to challenge White's version of events. One might speculate however that it is moot whether a conversation with a third party was an "admission" under the IAAF rule. Unlike White, Montgomery did not confess to the authorities; his "admission" was a less reliable type. The algorithmic route from positive test to doping ban via strict liability was now only one way of proving an anti-doping violation. Another way was one based on preferred evidence and that evidence could be anything that convinced a CAS panel. The next key issue was one with which, up until that point, CAS had not really had to concern itself: what would it take to convince CAS?

In its Statements of Claim, USADA argued that under relevant IAAF Anti-Doping Rules, amended to align with Article 3.1 of the World Anti-Doping Code, the standard of proof in such an instance should be whether USADA could establish an anti-doping rule violation to the "comfortable satisfaction" of the hearing body, bearing mind the seriousness of the allegation at issue. The CAS Panel then had to determine, and in view of the nature and gravity of the allegations at issue in the proceedings, what the appropriate standard of proof is in such instances and, more specifically, whether there was any practical distinction between the standard of proof advocated by USADA (comfortable satisfaction) and that (slightly elevated standard) argued by Montgomery (beyond a reasonable doubt).[26]

CAS concluded:

> ...it makes little, if indeed any difference, whether a 'beyond reasonable doubt' or 'comfortable satisfaction' standard is applied to determine the claims against [Montgomery]. Either way, USADA bears the burden of proving, by strong evidence commensurate with the serious claims it makes that [Montgomery] committed the doping offences in question.
>
> USADA has met this standard. The Panel has no doubt in this case, and is more than comfortably satisfied, that [Montgomery] committed the doping offence in question. It has been presented with strong, indeed uncontroverted, evidence of doping by [Montgomery] in the form of an admission contained in his statements made to [White] and to others while in her presence. On this basis, the Tribunal finds Respondent guilty of a doping offence.

---

[25] CAS 2004/O/645 *USADA v Montgomery*, para 5.

[26] For the sake of accuracy it should be noted that the CAS Panel had addressed the question of the standard of proof applicable in the present case at a preliminary hearing on 4 March 2005, referred to in the final award as the "Decision on Evidentiary and Procedural Issues".

> In particular, the Panel finds [Montgomery] guilty of the offence of admitting having used a prohibited substance under IAAF Rules 55.2(iii) and 60.1(iii).
>
> In the circumstances, the Panel finds that [Montgomery's] admission of his use of prohibited substances merits a period of ineligibility under IAAF Rules of two years.[27]

12.4 *Montgomery*: The Aftermath

In 2009, WADA produced its current version of the World Anti-Doping Code. On the face of it little seems to have changed. The Code remains predicated on positive tests for banned substances, with a strict liability standard, leading to prescribed sanctions. On closer inspection however there are important, subtle changes that implicitly acknowledge the influence of *Montgomery*. The WADA Code 2009 is no longer that basic algorithm flowing naturally from positive test to ban. Article 2 of the 2009 Code explicitly encompasses non-analytical positives. For instance, in the accompanying explanatory notes to the text, the Code elaborates:

> For example, an Anti-Doping Organization may establish an anti-doping rule violation under Article 2.2 (Use or Attempted Use of a Prohibited Substance or Prohibited Method) based on the Athlete's admissions, the credible testimony of third Persons, reliable documentary evidence, reliable analytical data from either an A or B Sample as provided in the Comments to Article 2.2, or conclusions drawn from the profile of a series of the Athlete's blood or urine Samples.

Without question the decision in *Montgomery* has been instrumental in the acceptance that anti-doping violations can be established without a positive test. The influence of Montgomery goes further however for Article 3.2.3 of the WADA Code 2009 states:

> The facts established by a decision of a court or professional disciplinary tribunal of competent jurisdiction which is not the subject of a pending appeal shall be irrebuttable evidence against the Athlete or other Person to whom the decision pertained of those facts unless the Athlete or other Person establishes that the decision violated principles of natural justice.

There is no doubt that BALCO was in the mind of the draftsmen at this point. The conclusions drawn by the Grand Jury investigation into BALCO would satisfy Article 3.2.3.[28] The section effectively short circuits the evidential burden in a CAS hearing but does not preclude a positive doping finding in the event that a court of professional disciplinary body finds no culpability. It is worthy of note

---

[27] CAS 2004/O/645 *USADA v Montgomery*, paras 10–12. USADA requested a doping ban of four years on the basis that IAAF Rule 60 defined the appropriate sanction as being of a *minimum* of two years. CAS, adopting the sanctions prescribed in the WADA Code, imposed a sanction of two years.

[28] See generally Roberts 2007.

that such evidence is irrebuttable and not merely persuasive unless such a conclusion breaches natural justice; an unlikely scenario.[29]

The broadening of the evidential basis on which a doping violation might be proven is effectively counterbalanced in the Code by a more sophisticated, flexible system of sanctions. This product of cause and effect is a more subtle, intangible influence of *Montgomery* but should not be overlooked.

12.5 Conclusion

Anti-doping regulation needs to be analysed as a continuum. Regulation has developed considerably from the naïve, disjointed efforts of yesteryear. Today, it is sophisticated and less dogmatic and attempts to reconcile the desires of sport with legal safeguards of athlete's rights. *Montgomery* sits on the cusp of the old regulation and the new.[30] The ghost of the pre-WADA regulations, that old hotch-potch of conflicting rules, was still evident in *Montgomery* and it is interesting to note that the CAS Panel applied the IAAF rules on burden whilst seemingly relying on the WADA Code for standard. On the other hand, *Montgomery* also hinted at the shape of things to come by moving away from the rigid evidentiary burden of the positive test.

The evolution of anti-doping continues to this day and there will many more landmark cases in its development. Post-*Montgomery*, the UNESCO International Convention Against Doping in Sport of 19 October 2005, has adopted, overtly, the WADA Code and this emphasises how little distinction there is today between law and regulation in this area.[31] There is now a co-operation agreement between WADA and Interpol and an increasing number of countries have now made doping in sport a criminal offence. *Montgomery* is already a relic of history.

At the time of writing Montgomery is serving a prison term for bank fraud and drug dealing. He readily confesses to taking performance enhancing substances because "Maurice [Greene[32]] got in my head real bad…I wanted everything that he had."[33] Arguably therefore, the anti-doping proceedings against Montgomery were justified. Even at the time, however, there seemed to be a degree of trepidation about the findings. Montgomery's coach Steve Riddick echoed those concerns when he said: "This does not make any sense to me based on what Kelli White said. When we start getting athletes suspended based on what somebody

---

[29] Soek 2000, 73.

[30] See further Trasti 2008; Teitler and Ram 2008 and Marshall and Hale 2008.

[31] If there ever was any!

[32] Another American sprinter whose record of five World Champion titles and four Olympic medals eclipses that of Montgomery.

[33] Associated Press 2009.

said, you see what gate that opens up."[34] Such concerns have been largely overlooked since in the development of anti-doping regulation.

Montgomery remains significant, however, not only for the repercussions of the decision itself but also because it provides an insight into an area wrestling with the implications of regulations as quasi-private law. This snapshot illustrates a time of transition, after the first WADA code but before its major re-evaluation in 2009. Most importantly, it shows that however desirable it might be to build a regulatory framework on simple unambiguous principles, reality rarely allows us such a luxury.

References

Associated Press (2009) Montgomery obsessed with Greene. http://sports.espn.go.com/oly/news/story?id=4693099. Accessed 31 July 2012

Bailey D (2007) Taking the governance of sport out of court. Sports Law Adm Pract (June):5–6

BBC Sport Online (2005) Montgomery hit with two-year ban. http://news.bbc.co.uk/sport1/hi/athletics/4521452.stm. Accessed 31 July 2012

Beloff M (2000) Drugs, laws and versapaks. In: O'Leary J (ed) Drugs and doping in sport. Cavendish, London

Beloff M (2009) Fair play—is there still room for the Corinthian spirit in sport? Int Sports Law Rev 3:34–44

Casini L (2009) Global hybrid public-private bodies: the world anti-doping agency. Int Organ Law Rev 6:421–446

De Knop P (2000) Globalisation, Americanization and localization in sport. Int Sports Law J 2:20–21

Fainaru-Wada M, Williams L (2006) Game of shadows. Gotham, New York

Green S (2004) Cheating. Law Philos 23:135–187

Manville A (2008) European Court vs sports organisations—who will win the antitrust competition? Int Sports Law J 3/4:19–26

Marshall J, Hale A (2008) Will the new WADA code plug all the gaps? Will there be by-catch? Int Sports Law J 1/2:37–42

Oschutz F (2002) Harmonisation of anti doping code through arbitration: the case law of the Court of Arbitration for Sport. Marquette Sports Law Rev 12:675–702

Pijetlovic K (2009) Paragraph 31 of C-519/04 *Meca-Medina* reversed. Int Sports Law J 1/2:137–138

Roberts H (2007) BALCO and Beyond: The changing landscape in the fight against doping in sport. Sport Law Adm Pract (August):1–7

Ruijsenaars P et al (2007) Manifesto: stop the doping inquisition! Int Sports Law J 3/4:84–85

Soek J (2000) The fundamental rights of athletes in doping trials. In: O'Leary J (ed) Drugs and doping in sport. Cavendish, London

Subiotto R (2010) The adoption and enforcement of anti-doping rules should not be subject to European competition law. Eur Compet Law Rev 31:323–330

Szyszczak E (2007) Competition and sport. Eur Law Rev 32:95–110

Tarasti L (2000) Legal solutions in international doping cases. SEP Editrice, Milan

Tarasti L (2008) Some juridical question marks in the revised world anti-doping code. Int Sports Law J 2/3:17–23

[34] BBC Sport Online 2005.

Teitler S and Ram H (2008) Analysing the new world anti-doping code: a different perspective. Int Sports Law J 1/2:42–49

Walker N (2010) Out of place and out of time: law's fading co-ordinates. Edinb Law Rev 14:13–46

Weatherill S (2006) Anti-doping revisited—the demise of the rule of 'purely sporting' interest? Eur Compet Law Rev 27:645–657

Chapter 13
CAS 2009/A/1912–1913 *Pechstein v International Skating Union*

David McArdle

Abstract At the material time, Claudia Pechstein was a 37-year-old German speed skater who in a long and distinguished career had taken part in five Olympic Games, where she obtained five gold and two bronze medals, and won several World, European and National championships. In short, Pechstein was one of the most successful winter sports athletes of all time. In the period between 4 February 2000 and 30 April 2009, Pechstein underwent numerous in-competition and out-of competition anti-doping tests. None of these tests resulted in a positive test or an adverse analytical finding. During the same period, the International Skating Union ("ISU") collected more than 90 blood samples from Pechstein as part of its longitudinal blood profiling programme. Towards the end of the period, some of the Pechstein's blood screening results began to show an irregular and abnormal pattern, outside of the accepted ISU-mandated parameters. Consequently, in March 2009, the ISU accused Pechstein of having used some form of blood doping constituting an anti-doping infraction under applicable ISU Anti-doping rules (rules which were said to be in conformity with the World Anti-doping Code). A subsequent ISU Disciplinary Commission found Pechstein guilty as charged and inter alia imposed a two-year period of ineligibility. On 21 July 2009, Pechstein, as supported by her national federation ("DESG"), filed statements of appeal with the Court of Arbitration for Sport ("CAS"), and a hearing took place in Lausanne on 22–23 October 2009. Central to Pechstein's challenge, and to the import of this case as a whole, were arguments surrounding the credibility, reliability and legality of longitudinal blood profiling as a means of anti-doping control. The CAS Panel, bearing in mind the seriousness of the allegations and based on an extensive review of the scientific evidence, found that the ISU had discharged its burden of proving to the comfortable satisfaction of the Panel that the athlete's abnormal blood values could not be reasonably explained by any congenital or subsequently development abnormality but must have derived from the athlete's illicit manipulation of her own blood.

D. McArdle (✉)
School of Law, University of Stirling, Stirling, FK9 4LA, Scotland, UK
e-mail: d.a.mcardle@stir.ac.uk

J. Anderson (ed.), *Leading Cases in Sports Law*,
ASSER International Sports Law Series, DOI: 10.1007/978-90-6704-909-2_13,

Contents

13.1 Introduction

Since 2008, several international sporting federations have required participants in their elite-level events to possess an Athlete Biological Passport, which has been introduced as an indirect means of detecting doping among athletes in accordance with Article 2.2 of the World Anti-doping Code. At the time of writing the IAAF (athletics' world governing body) and the governing bodies for cycling, triathlon, skating, biathlon and swimming have passport schemes and require athletes to provide blood samples, sometimes on average of one a month, and any variations in the key markers that those samples reveal can lead to an athlete being sanctioned for a doping violation if, in the opinion of a panel of scientific experts there is no pathological explanation for those variations and (subsequently) the sports' anti-doping panels and, ultimately, CAS take the view that the variations revealed in the biological passport establishes to its comfortable satisfaction that a doping violation has occurred.

Around the time that the biological passport was being instigated by the stated governing bodies the German speed skater Claudia Pechstein was sanctioned by her international federation on the basis of blood profiles submitted by her, not through an official systematic programme but on the basis of samples provided at particular events. Pechstein thus became the first athlete to be sanctioned for a doping offence on the basis of blood-profiling techniques. In the recent past, she has been joined by five other athletes—all cyclists—who have been similarly sanctioned on the basis of what their biological passports reveal. Consequently, this chapter looks in detail at the background to *Pechstein*, but also makes comparisons with those more recent developments in cycling—particularly the case concerning the Slovenia cyclist Tadej Valjavek—to highlight some of the scientific complexities, and the attendant legal issues, to which blood profiling and, now, biological passports give rise.

13.2 Factual Background

Claudia Pechstein's case centred on blood profiling, which has been developed over the past decade in response to the use of a synthetic version of recombinant human erythropoietin ("rHuEPO"), and which accelerates red blood cell production in bone marrow. This can be beneficial to athletes because rHuEPO can increase the number of red blood cells in circulation and "dramatically improve(s) the oxygen-carrying capacity of the blood and therefore endurance performance".[1] rHuEPO is generally associated with endurance sports (hence the high-profile involvement of cycling's and skiing's governing body in the development of blood profiling), but it has also been shown that "an enhanced oxygen carrying capacity can bestow a marked advantage in events lasting as little as 45 s, as well as recovery from intermittent efforts and general training drills. It is prudent to consider most sports (individual and team) at risk of blood doping".[2]

In the late 1990s, haematologists started to develop ever-more sophisticated procedures that could be used to detect the illicit use of rHuEPO. These procedures focussed on the role of reticulocytes (rather than on other haematological parameters such as haemoglobin) "because of their particular sensitivity in identifying bone marrow stimulation, especially when recombinant human erythropoietin is fraudulently used".[3] Athletes can experience a performance benefit for several weeks after ceasing to use rHuEPO, but upon cessation there will be a significant reduction in reticulocyte count because the body reduces both endogenous erythropoietin production and reticulocyte release until the red cell count returns to normal.[4] In endurance sports, athletes who return an abnormally high red cell mass in hematocrit testing can be prohibited for competing for more than two weeks on medical grounds (high hematocrit levels are particularly associated with an increased risk of deep vein thrombosis); but it is a truism that elite athletes' bodies are not "normal" and up to 5 % of athletes may exceed the "safe" hematocrit threshold because of genetic factors—so there is patently a risk that athletes could be unfairly prevented from competing when their health is not at risk.[5] In turn, this means than any attempt to use hematocrit levels as an evidential basis for a doping offence is necessarily untenable. It had also been noted that testing athletes' urine samples for the presence of rHuEPO is of limited utility because "although a small amount is detectable unchanged in the urine for 24–96 h after each injection, once the red cell mass has been boosted, the athlete

[1] Parisotto 2001, 128.

[2] Ashenden 2002, 225.

[3] Banfi 2008, 188.

[4] See generally Banfi 2008.

[5] See generally Banfi 2008.

can substantially reduce their dosage of rHuEPO. During this maintenance phase, it is difficult to discern the hematologic profile of a maintenance user from that of a non-user".[6]

Establishing an effective test for rHuEPO has thus had to address the entirely legitimate concern that "altitude/training/genetic factors (which) may also be associated with a transient increase in erythropoiesis (albeit of a much smaller magnitude) might lead to mistakenly accusing an athlete when no drug was taken".[7] There was also a clear need to combine any effective in-competition test with reliable out-of-competition random testing, given the need for rHuEPO users to engage in the prohibited activity for several weeks prior to a competition and the concomitant likelihood that in-competition testing would reveal nothing untoward. However, by 2002 the practicality of using a mobile blood testing facility that "could relocate to a remote competition site and would make place-getters subject to blood testing immediately after competition"[8] had been established: the technology to allow many samples to be taken and analysed quickly was in place and a similar facility could be used for random testing too. Moreover, the same machine could be used consistently across all sports to eliminate any technical variations that might skew the results.

Although doubts about the scientific reliability of these new anti-doping strategies remained extant, unproven insinuations that athletes were engaging in doping techniques that could not be detected by traditional methods continued to persist, and on occasion these insinuations were accompanied by revelations which had a much further evidential base. Sport's first mandatory biological passport programme was introduced by cycling's world governing body ("UCI") in October 2007, just three months after the "doping crisis" which had engulfed that year's Tour de France cycle race and threatened to destroy the very credibility of professional cycling by ensuring that what had hitherto remained largely hidden emerged into the public domain. During the Tour the entire Astanta and Cofidis teams were withdrawn after one of their racers was found to have undergone a blood transfusion and tested positive for testosterone respectively; the race leader was withdrawn by his team for lying about his whereabouts prior to the Tour; two German broadcasters ceased televising the race in protest at cycling's "doping culture" and the governing body's apparent complicity in (or at least ignorance of) what was occurring; and two other high-profile riders tested positive in the Tour's later stages.[9] The initial reaction of Pat McQuaid, the UCI President, was to call for the maximum two-year ban for a first doping offence to be increased to a life ban, and, although wiser counsel prevailed in that regard, the UCI's rapid move towards a biological passport thereafter can be regarded as a direct and immediate—perhaps too immediate—response to that summer's activities. Cyclists were

6 Ashenden 2002, 225–226.

7 Ashenden 2002, 228.

8 Ashenden 2002, 229.

9 See generally Hailey 2011, 393–432.

required to give blood samples as part of the regular medical examinations they were obliged to undergo as a condition of their participation in UCI events, and this has became a central aspect of their "biological passport", alongside the results of the urine and other tests.

The difficulty with cycling's scheme, as with all other biological passports, is that they merely provide indirect evidence of doping, and for anyone other than a scientist with particular haematological expertise that evidence will always be far less cogent. Rather than requiring a positive test for a prohibited substance or method, the biological passport records changes in biological variables within the athlete's blood and urine samples. The inferences that scientists can draw from the changes in these variables provides the prima facie evidence of a doping violation, and the anti-doping authority then has the burden of showing that a doping violation has occurred. In the absence of direct evidence garnered in accordance with Article 2.1 of the World Anti-doping Code, reliance on this indirect evidence, or through direct evidence other than a positive analytical finding, will suffice in accordance with Article 2.2 of the Code: Article 2 provides that the use or attempted use of either a prohibited substance or a prohibited method constitutes a doping violation, and whereas an Article 2.1 violation requires a positive analytical finding, Article 2.2 provides that violations can be "established by any reliable means". The comment or annotation accompanying Article 2 stipulates that "conclusions drawn from longitudinal profiling" may suffice for Article 2.2 purposes.

The difficulty is that the weight to be attached to the evidence from non-analytical positive cases is not easy to determine but has always depended on "the value and weight of the circumstantial evidence and the standard of proof that will be applied to evaluate this evidence".[10] Even before the crisis precipitated by the "Tour du Dopage" the "reliable means" that may be advanced before anti-doping panels had been very wide-ranging, and anti-doping panels were not averse to relying upon them. Several significant high-profile non-analytical positive cases arose from the BALCO affair[11] and included *USADA v Collins*,[12] which led to an athlete who had never tested positive being sanctioned on the basis of e-mails sent by her in which she admitted using prohibited substances and techniques. However, the Panel in that case did not rely on her e-mails alone: when considered alongside her test results which indicated fluctuations in her hematocrit and testosterone/epitestosterone ratios, the American Arbitration Association felt able to

[10] McLaren 2006, 194–195.

[11] In the early part of this century, Californian-based Bay Area Laboratory Cooperative ("BALCO") was involved in a conspiracy the purpose of which was the distribution and use of sports doping substances and techniques that were either undetectable or difficult to detect in routine drug testing. The affair prompted numerous public and sport-specific investigations. For its origins, see generally Fainaru-Wada and Williams 2006.

[12] Arbitral Award AAA no 30 190 00658 04 *USADA v Collins*. This award was heard before the American Arbitration Association under the auspices of a North American Court of Arbitration for Sport Panel and is available online at: www.usada.org/files/active/arbitration_rulings/AAA%20CAS%20Decision%20-%20Collins.pdf.

determine that these two pieces of circumstantial evidence, taken together, proved Collins' use of prohibited substances beyond reasonable doubt (which was the mandated standard prior to the coming into operation of the WADA Code's "comfortable satisfaction" test).

Another BALCO case, *USADA v Montgomery*,[13] resulted in the athlete being sanctioned on the basis of fellow athlete Kelli White's testimony to the effect that Montgomery had admitted to her that he had used prohibited substances. On this occasion the athlete chose to bypass the domestic hearing process and proceeded directly to CAS, which declined to consider several other types of evidence (including test results showing an apparent doubling of his testosterone levels in the course of a day, five abnormal blood test results in eight months and incriminating statements from Victor Conte, the head of the BALCO laboratory) and sanctioned him solely on the basis of White's "honest and reasonable" and uncontroverted testimony. Although White's accepting a two-year sanction for her part in the BALCO affair would necessarily give rise to concerns about her own integrity, CAS stressed that Montgomery had not sought to provide a different account of his conversations with White and it was thus content to rely upon her uncorroborated testimony alone. While one can understand why the evidence available in these cases was deemed sufficiently cogent for CAS to feel able to rely on it, the approaches to the evidence which has been available in *Pechstein* and other recent cases concerning blood profiling sits rather less comfortably.

13.3 *Pechstein v International Skating Union*: The Arguments

Pechstein[14] shows that throughout the time of the BALCO affair, sports organisations were investigating the potential benefits of a biological passport system. In the sphere of alpine sports these endeavours were given particular impetus in 2006, when 12 cross-country skiers were suspended at the Winter Olympics in Turin because their blood samples revealed excessive levels of haemoglobin, and in many ways the alacrity of winter sports' response thereafter mirrors the developments that were occurring at the same time within the cycling firmament.

Between 2000 and April 2009, Pechstein underwent many doping control tests both in- and out-of competition and she gave over 90 blood samples under the ISU's blood profiling programme. The last 12 of those were given between January and April 2009. In its charges against her the ISU asserted that "during the months of January and February 2009 the Athlete changed her whereabouts on numerous occasions rendering it especially difficult, if not impossible, to organise

[13] CAS 2004/O/645 *USADA v Montgomery*. Discussed generally in Chap. 12 of this volume.

[14] CAS 2009/A/1912-1913 *Pechstein v International Skating Union*.

any out-of competition testing on her".[15] The implication was that, during those months, Pechstein had changed her whereabouts in order to facilitate her use of rHuEPO and thus artificially stimulate "her body's capacity to produce red blood cells that carry oxygen to muscles and organs, with the evident purpose of reducing fatigue and attaining an unfair advantage over her competitors. In short, blood doping."[16] *Pechstein* is thus significant because, although there are some parallels with the American Arbitration Association's ruling in *USADA v Collins*, it involved sanctioning an athlete who had never returned an adverse analytical finding but was condemned on the basis of her blood values and profile.

The ISU's regulations provide for a blood profile that monitors participants' haemoglobin, hematocrit and percentage of reticulocytes (hereafter "%retics"). The last of these was of particular relevance to this case because it is deemed to be an indicator of potential blood doping,[17] and while the upper end of the "normal" %retics level is deemed to be 2.4; many of Pechstein's readings had been considerably in excess of that level. In particular, on 6 February 2009—the day before a 2009 World Championship event at Hamar, Norway commenced—all participants gave blood samples and Pechstein's %retics value was measured at 3.49. She was tested twice more on 7 February and her readings were 3.54 and 3.38 respectively. These findings were communicated to Pechstein's domestic governing body (the "DEFG"), which took the decision to withdraw her from the competition even though her haemoglobin and haematocrit levels were not so high as to provide a "no-start" situation, where the ISU prohibits the athlete from competing for the next 18 days in order to safeguard their health status.

On 18 February 2009, another test showed that her %retics had declined to 1.37. Such high readings being followed by a much lower level reading ten days later gives rise to a suspicion that the athlete had been engaging in blood doping around the time when the earlier test was taken and, on 5 March 2009 the ISU's Disciplinary Commission duly held that Pechstein has violated its new anti-doping policy (which had come into force on 1 January 2009 and accorded with the terms of the amended World Anti-doping Code) and imposed a two-year ban.[18] In July 2009, the athlete and her governing body appealed to CAS, as they were entitled to do under the ISU's rules.

Pechstein's defences concentrated on sample collection and testing and the propriety of the ISU's regulations—arguments which are the staple fare of athletes' appeals in doping cases but which are almost inevitably doomed to failure unless it can be shown that the established procedures had not been followed, and it is a rare occurrence for an anti-doping agency to fail to follow its own procedures. She contended that because the ISU had only allowed blood profiles to be used as evidence of a doping violation since 1 January 2009 (when its new

---

[15] CAS 2009/A/1912-1913 *Pechstein v International Skating Union Pechstein*, para 68.

[16] CAS 2009/A/1912-1913 *Pechstein v International Skating Union*, para 191.

[17] CAS 2009/A/1912-1913 *Pechstein v International Skating Union*, para 7.

[18] CAS 2009/A/1912-1913 *Pechstein v International Skating Union* paras 12 and 13.

provisions came into effect), only blood samples collected after that date could be used in evidence against her.[19] She also contended that ISU blood profiling rules provided that the blood samples had to be analysed in WADA-accredited laboratories and that WADA's standards governing collection and chain-of-custody applied; that the upper limit of 2.4 %retics was not generally accepted in sports medicine; and that, for several reasons, the blood screening data was unreliable and not appropriate for statistical analysis.

Pechstein also challenged the accuracy of the machine used to analyse her samples, stressed that her haemoglobin and hematocrit levels had always been within ISU limits and asserted that her high %retics values were "likely" due to a hitherto-undiagnosed chronic blood disorder and/or a genetic abnormality. Finally, she argued that, with regard to the burden and standard of proof, the ISU "must convince the Panel to a level very close to 'beyond reasonable doubt' that all alternative causes for the increase in %retics can be excluded and that, additionally, the Athlete had an intention to use blood doping".[20] CAS summarily dealt with this matter by asserting that there was no need to show intent or fault because the strict liability principle applied in doping cases[21] and that the "comfortable satisfaction" test, which applied under the ISU's rules, was well known in CAS practice, had withstood the scrutiny of the Swiss federal tribunal in several previous cases,[22] and would consequently be applied in this case.[23]

Pechstein's domestic governing body, the DESG, "contends that it has a neutral role in the proceedings (but) essentially supports most of the arguments raised by the Athlete".[24] In addition, the DESG argued that any violation must have occurred before 30 January 2009 and, because the ISU made reference to the blood profiling results obtained prior to 6 February 2009 (rather than just relying on the Hamar figures), the ISU had breached its then Rules of Procedure, Article 8.1 of which provided that complaints had to be lodged within 30 days of it learning about the alleged offence (the complaint was lodged with the ISU's Disciplinary Commission on 5 March). The DESG said that, in effect, the ISU had used the Hamar tests as an opportunity to "buy time", and that its case had actually been built upon Pechstein's earlier test results.

In rebuttal of the athlete's arguments, the ISU stated that it had implemented its own procedures for blood profiling in July 2008 and was not obliged to wait for WADA to draft specific rules for blood doping (which it was in the throes of doing at that time and which came into force in December 2009) before it could develop such rules for its own sport; and it drew an important distinction between the blood profiling programme—which, they argued, focused on measuring blood

19 CAS 2009/A/1912-1913 *Pechstein v International Skating Union*, para 47.

20 CAS 2009/A/1912-1913 *Pechstein v International Skating Union*, paras 48–53.

21 CAS 2009/A/1912-1913 *Pechstein v International Skating Union*, para 120.

22 CAS 2009/A/1912-1913 *Pechstein v International Skating Union*, para 124.

23 CAS 2009/A/1912-1913 *Pechstein v International Skating Union*, para 126.

24 CAS 2009/A/1912-1913 *Pechstein v International Skating Union*, paras 55 and 56.

parameters rather than on detecting prohibited substances—and on anti-doping controls, which have far more complex testing and analysis procedures and were accompanied by stringent rules and procedures that were unnecessary in the context of blood profiling. There was no evidence that any of the procedures regulating blood profiling had been departed from, and that "the use of a longitudinal (blood) profile as evidence of doping is legally admissible since it is an evidential/procedural rule to which the prohibition against the retroactive application of the law does not apply".[25] The ISU also said that intent was relevant only in cases of "attempted use" (rather than occasions where use had actually occurred); that it could not provide evidence relating to possible blood diseases because Pechstein had refused to co-operate in its enquiries into that possibility; but that in any event the significant fluctuations in her %retics could not be explained by any known blood disorder.

13.4 The CAS Award

CAS determined that, under the ISU anti-doping rules, the thirty-day period began to run only once the ISU "learned about" the alleged offence—a phrase which must be properly understood as the moment at which the ISU had reasonable suspicion of the alleged offence. Unlike allegations based on an adverse analytical finding, doping charges based on longitudinal (blood) profiling require a series of tests and evaluation of the results by the anti-doping organisations experts. For this reason, the ISU had not "learned" about the offence and was not in a position to raise charges until its medical advisors had determined that Ms Pechstein's blood profile constituted—in their opinion—sufficient proof of the use of a prohibited method.[26]

CAS stated that the Hamar competition tests were "at the core" of the case and there was no evidence of the ISU using them in order to "gain time" as the DESG had suggested.[27] Further, Pechstein's contention that she had never consented to the ISU using her blood profile as evidence of blood doping was summarily rejected on the ground that, under its anti-doping rules, any person taking part in the ISU's "international activities" is bound to comply with all its provisions, and the anti-doping rules cited "conclusions drawn from the profile of the skater's blood or urine samples" as a specific example of a reasonably reliable means by which an anti-doping rule violation could be established.[28] Furthermore, the ISU argued that "in willingly registering for international skating competitions sanctioned by the ISU, she obviously expressed her acceptance of ISU rules and regulations, including the (anti-doping rules).... When they accede to competition,

[25] CAS 2009/A/1912-1913 *Pechstein v International Skating Union*, para 56.

[26] CAS 2009/A/1912-1913 *Pechstein v International Skating Union*, para 91.

[27] CAS 2009/A/1912-1913 *Pechstein v International Skating Union*, para 92.

[28] CAS 2009/A/1912-1913 *Pechstein v International Skating Union*, para 101.

athletes cannot pick and choose the rules they like".[29] This clearly gives rise to concerns about how much credence should be attached to the athletes' putative acceptance of the rules, given that one either signs up to the anti-doping regime or one does not compete at the international level; but if athletes wish to voice their opposition to anti-doping regimes (and there is no evidence that Pechstein or the wider firmament of skaters had opposed them beforehand), this has to be done long before the disciplinary hearing or subsequent application to CAS. In any event, CAS noted that the ISU's rules stated that profiling was just an "evidentiary means" by which a doping offence could be demonstrated, so "the only relevant issue is whether longitudinal blood profiling can be regarded as among the 'reasonably reliable means' to prove the use of a prohibited method… its utilisation for anti-doping purposes does not constitute a retrospective application of a substantive anti-doping rule".[30]

CAS further asserted that "even in cases of adverse analytical findings, departures from WADA international standards do not invalidate *per se* the analytical results, as long as the anti-doping organisation establishes that such departure did not cause the adverse analytical finding".[31] It stated that the WADA draft Biological Passport Guidelines could not be regarded as setting down "minimum standards" (as Pechstein contended), and even when they were finalised (which occurred on 1 December 2009), the Biological Passport Guidelines would not become mandatory. This stands in clear contradiction to WADA's own position: the introduction to the WADA Guidelines states that the Athlete Biological Passport "includes mandatory requirements for collection, transportation, analysis of blood samples and results management that anti-doping organisations wishing to adopt WADA's model will have to following order to ensure consistency of application and to comply with the WADA Code and the International Standards. These mandatory technical documents will be incorporated into WADA's International Standard for Testing and International Standard for Laboratories". For the avoidance of doubt, it is now clear that governing bodies would be very well advised to ensure their blood profiling provisions replicate those laid down by WADA. If they do not, the governing body must be able to advance very strong, clear arguments as to why they have departed from what WADA has laid down; and it ought not be able to expect such a sympathetic hearing from the CAS; it would certainly not be favoured with such sympathy by the courts.

CAS reiterated that Pechstein had been accused of a doping offence in respect of the %retics findings at Hamar in early February 2009 and the sample taken on 18 February 2009. CAS noted that consideration of her earlier results "may help in understanding and interpreting the Athlete's blood values as found on 6, 7 and 18 February 2009 but it is strictly a question of considering the evidence on record

---

[29] CAS 2009/A/1912-1913 *Pechstein v International Skating Union*, paras 98 and 99.

[30] CAS 2009/A/1912-1913 *Pechstein v International Skating Union*, para 108.

[31] CAS 2009/A/1912-1913 *Pechstein v International Skating Union*, para 117.

and its scientific reliability, not involving retrospective application of any new anti-doping rule to old facts".[32] It continued:

> The Panel would have no hesitation in holding that new scientifically sound evidentiary methods, even not specifically mentioned in anti-doping rules, can be used at any time to investigate and discover past anti-doping rule violations that went undetected, with the only constraint deriving from the eight-year time limitation and the timely initiation of disciplinary proceedings. As long as the substantive rule sanctioning a given conduct as doping is in force prior to the conduct, the resort to a new evidentiary method does not constitute a case of retrospective application of the law.[33]

With regard to the athlete's allegations that the collection, administration and storage of her blood samples had not complied with the provisions of the World Anti-doping Code, CAS asserted that, because this was not a case of adverse analytical finding, the ISU was not obliged to follow WADA's provisions on those matters. Instead, "in the Panel's opinion, any reasonably reliable practice of sample collection, post-test administration, transport of samples, analytical process and documentation would suffice".[34] With that in mind, CAS engaged in a long analysis of the collection, storage and sampling procedures that had been adopted by the ISU in July 2008 and utilised at the Hamar event. It found that Pechstein had never challenged the procedure or asserted her right to have the samples taken by her own doctor rather than an ISU official, and that she had never protested against any of the sampling procedures or been able to point out any of the material flaws in the process as applied to her.[35] It highlighted the distinction between the procedures for blood testing for screening purposes and those for post-event anti-doping control[36] and stressed that:

> The analytical process followed by the (testing) laboratories does not require any person from the laboratory personnel to open the (sample), since it is placed directly... into the analysing machine... Unlike in anti-doping where the laboratory (by means of a complex and costly investigation) looks for prohibited substances yielding an adverse analytical finding, in blood screening the laboratory simply measures (by means of an automated machine) certain hematological parameters.[37]

CAS had no reservations about the chain of custody ("the Panel has heard and examined evidence that does not leave any reasonable doubts as to the transportation conditions").[38] Pechstein further contended that physical stress due to cold temperatures, altitude, intense exercise, pressure on the foot cause by her skates and blades, menstrual bleeding, infection or the fact that the tests were unequally

---

[32] CAS 2009/A/1912-1913 *Pechstein v International Skating Union*, para 107.

[33] CAS 2009/A/1912-1913 *Pechstein v International Skating Union*, para 109.

[34] CAS 2009/A/1912-1913 *Pechstein v International Skating Union Pechstein*, para 116.

[35] CAS 2009/A/1912-1913 *Pechstein v International Skating Union Pechstein*, para 137.

[36] CAS 2009/A/1912-1913 *Pechstein v International Skating Union Pechstein*, paras 133 and 134.

[37] CAS 2009/A/1912-1913 *Pechstein v International Skating Union Pechstein*, para 146.

[38] CAS 2009/A/1912-1913 *Pechstein v International Skating Union Pechstein*, para 144.

distributed throughout the year could have caused her adverse profile. Nevertheless, the Panel was not swayed:

> The Panel has not found the above-mentioned justifications, nor the few others that the Appellants have thrown in during the course of the proceedings, to be convincing…The athlete's multifarious explanations imply that all of a sudden a perfectly fit athlete incurred all sorts of unlikely situations and misfortunes that in some way affected her blood values; it appears to the Panel to be too astonishing a coincidence to be reasonably credible.[39]

Medical tests carried out in advance of the hearing had returned no untoward results, and the Panel was comfortably satisfied that Pechstein's abnormal %retics values "must derive from the athlete's illicit manipulation of her own blood, which remains the only reasonable alternative source of such abnormal values".[40] It upheld the ISU's original sanction of a two-year ban.

13.5 Future Developments?

It is argued that, had she been minded to pursue the matter at an EU level, the conduct of the *Pechstein* case before CAS indicates that her strongest arguments would have been to the effect that the CAS Panel erred in either adopting a "comfortable satisfaction" test at all, or in its application of it, or that it had erred in departing from WADA Guidelines, for *Meca-Medina* illustrates the difficulty in persuading the courts that the scientific basis that underpins any aspect of the anti-doping regime is so flawed as to amount to a breach of competition (or free movement) law.[41] Doubtless, the scientific complexities of longitudinal profiling demand a far more robust legal scrutiny than has occurred hitherto; but Pechstein's problem was that her arguments were weak, the totality of the evidence against her was strong and (to adopt a maxim of equity) she failed to give the impression that she was coming with clean hands. The ISU had little difficulty in rebutting her arguments to the comfortable satisfaction of the CAS; but when a challenge through the courts arises in the future (as it surely will) legal advisers may well decide that there is little merit in revisiting the *Pechstein* approach and will choose instead to advance the proper legal arguments, while preparing their client for a long haul through the domestic or European courts, if their overtures are rejected by CAS. Those stronger potential arguments can be discerned in the almost contemporaneous blood doping cases that arose in professional cycling.

The UCI was the first international federation to implement a biological passport programme, incorporating it into its anti-doping rules in June 2008 and thus requiring professional cycling to submit themselves to blood as well as urine tests at any time. In the five months prior to June 2008 the UCI took nearly 3,200

---

[39] CAS 2009/A/1912-1913 *Pechstein v International Skating Union*, para 197.

[40] CAS 2009/A/1912-1913 *Pechstein v International Skating Union*, para 210.

[41] Discussed generally in Chap. 9 of this volume.

blood samples from over 850 professional cyclists in order to create the longitudinal profiles for each biological passport by establishing the individual's parameters for reticulocytes, haemoglobin and haematocrit. As is the case with the ISU, if there are fluctuations in an individual cyclist's parameters which exceed the thresholds set by a statistical model there is a perception that a doping violation is likely to have occurred because the cyclist's profile is now different to that which would be expected of athletes who were not doping.[42] The cyclist's data is then submitted to three members of the UCI's nine-member panel of anti-doping experts, and it is their task to determine whether these variables do indeed amount to indirect evidence of an anti-doping violation, and if so whether to advise the UCI to use its discretion to instigate disciplinary proceedings. If it does so, at that stage the athlete is provisionally sanctioned and the domestic federation (not the UCI) is requested to instigate disciplinary proceedings and impose sanctions if necessary. However the UCI, like the athlete, has the right to appeal the domestic federation's decision to CAS.[43]

In the first two years that cycling's biological passport was in operation, proceedings were commenced against eight cyclists on the basis of the fluctuations in their data. The first five cases revealed a degree of support for the system on the part of the governing bodies for cycling in Spain and Italy, which sanctioned all athletes involved in the course of 2009. Then in May 2010 the UCI provisionally suspended another Italian, another Spaniard and a Slovenian, Tadej Valjavec. Valjavec has the distinction of being the first cyclist to not be banned by his domestic federation on the basis of an abnormal biological passport result,[44] and the Italian federation followed suit in the case of Franco Pellizotti.[45] Accordingly it was now the case that not all biological passport suspensions have subsequently resulted in the imposition of bans by the domestic federations—but in the five cases that have been appealed to CAS (*Pechstein* and those involving four cyclists) CAS has either upheld the doping sanctions that were imposed in three of them or, in the cases of Valjavec[46] and Pelizotti,[47] has overturned the domestic federation's initial determination that no offence has occurred and has proceeded to impose a sanction on the athlete.

Although the athlete did not consent to the CAS award being made public, it is possible to discern sufficient information about Valjavec's case from what is publicly available (especially in the cycling media) to at least highlight some of the potential concerns around cycling's biological passport regime, and to make valid

---

[42] For more details see www.doping.chuv.ch/en/lad_home-prestations-laboratoire/lad-prestations-laboratoire-passeport.htm. Accessed 31 July 2012.

[43] Details on UCI's variation of the biological passport can be accessed under the "anti-doping" tab at http://www.uci.ch/. Accessed 31 July 2012.

[44] Slovenian Press Agency 2010.

[45] Velonews 2010.

[46] *Guardian* Online 2011.

[47] CAS Press Release 2011.

comparisons with the *Pechstein* award. First, it is a matter of record that the Slovenian Anti-doping Authority had been unconvinced by the evidence presented in relation to the biological passport and held that his profile did not provide evidence of blood doping. Contrary to the CAS Panel's approach in *Pechstein*, it accepted that Valjavec's abnormal profile could indeed have been the consequence of other factors, including bleeding due to a stomach ulcer, training at high altitude, medical treatment for a wasp sting and training at altitude and in a hypobaric chamber. The domestic hearing decided that there was "a lack of irrefutable proof" that his increased oxygen levels were a consequence of blood doping and said the statistical methods adopted for the biological passport could not ever demonstrate the use of doping techniques but could only be evidence of the presence of unusual values, which in turn could carry physiological explanations such as those advanced by Valjavec.

It further found that UCI had "failed to prove that the model of the biological passport had been used correctly and that it factored in variables, such as the type of instrument and the altitude at which (he) had trained", and that "the UCI had not sufficiently investigated the possibilities that the obtained blood readings were a result of factors that Valjavec stated in his defence".[48] If the media report is an accurate one, it seems the domestic Commission was operating to a quasi-criminal standard of proof, so that in every respect the burden lay on the cycling authorities to show beyond reasonable doubt that doping had occurred. This was never going to be a tenable position to defend before CAS, but the concerns arising from the award go much deeper than the domestic body's decision as to the requisite standard of proof.

In March 2011, shortly before hearing the UCI's appeal in Valjavec, CAS had overturned the Italian anti-doping tribunal's finding in the Pelozzi case and imposed a two-year suspension and €115,000 fine, holding that the fluctuations in Pelozzi's biological passport were sufficient evidence, to its comfortable satisfaction, that he had engaged in blood doping. For those involved, it probably occasioned little surprise when, the following month, CAS also overturned the initial decision in the Valjavec case and reversed the National Anti-doping Committee's decision, banned the cyclist for two years and fined him €52,500. Although he gave blood samples on over 20 occasions between March 2008 and September 2009, CAS must have taken the view that abnormalities which were revealed in just two tests—conducted in April and September 2009—were entirely consistent with blood manipulation, for any other approach would have been entirely inconsistent with its earlier assertions (in *Pechstein*, *Caucchioli* and *Pellizotti*) that blood profiles as a reliable means of indirectly detecting doping offences. One assumes that the CAS Panel was critical of the Slovenian Commission's insistence upon a "reasonable doubt" standard of proof, and that the potential alternative explanations for Valjavec's abnormal profile, such as his various medical conditions and his engagement in high-altitude training for some

---

[48] Slovenian Press Agency 2010.

of the time, were not sufficiently credible to undermine the evidence to such an extent that it fell below the "comfortable satisfaction" standard.

13.6 Conclusion

The biological passport as adopted by the cycling authorities, and now consistently upheld by CAS, thus gives rise to issues which might come to be regarded as distinguishing features between *Pechstein* and those of *Valjavec* and the other cyclists. First, while the fact that the UCI review process requires the cyclist's data to be submitted to just three of the nine scientific panel members does not of itself raise pressing legal concerns, it does become an issue when each of those three panel members is then vested with a wide discretion to decide which scientific markers to examine and which to ignore. If one of the cycling cases were to become "*Meca-Medina* mark II" and be challenged through the European courts, the UCI would need to be able to explain why only some, rather than all, of the nine panel members are involved in any particular case, how the three are selected in respect of any particular case and—most importantly—why there are so few limits on the extent of the discretion they seem to have in determining which parameters to examine have. It is evident from *Meca-Medina* that the European courts are properly willing to defer to scientific expertise in doping cases where appropriate[49]—but in the same way that the governing body in that case still needed to be able to explain why the permissible levels of nandrolone were what they were; in relation to biological passports they would equally need to be able to explain why it was appropriate to look at some markers but not at others and whether this gave rise to risks that important information might be overlooked simply on the basis of the scientific panel members' subjective decisions. Given that there are a finite number of panel members and a finite number of scientific markers, it would be entirely reasonable for a court to seek convincing evidence as to why all panel members should not all be looking at all the markers, and given that the stakes are so high the obvious answers of cost and timeliness have little to commend them. In such a case, it might also be moved to ask whether it would not then be appropriate for the opinions of those experts to be peer-reviewed by other experts who are entirely independent of the biological passport industry, the cycling fraternity and the wider CAS-WADA anti-doping triad.

Second, UCI's willingness to proceed with a case solely on the indirect evidence yielded by the biological passport, and CAS's willingness to uphold that approach, raises particularly glaring concerns. UCI's fundamental, and potentially terminal, difficulties in this regard mirrors those which arose in *Pechstein* in relation to the desirability of following WADA's own guidelines—namely, that those operating guidelines clearly envisage that it will be used as a "complementary strategy" to

[49] See generally McArdle and Callery 2011.

traditional anti-doping methods, with its objective being to integrate "the Athlete Biological Passport into the larger framework of a robust anti-doping program" and including the identification and targeting of athletes "for specific analytical testing by intelligent and timely interpretation of blood passport data".[50] The strength of the athlete biological passport system lies in its utility as a "screening test" which can form a basis for closer scrutiny and greater testing of an athlete whose profile gives rise to suspicion. Nevertheless, it was never envisaged by WADA as being, and should not now be used by the UCI as, sufficiently cogent evidence to justify, by itself, a finding that a doping violation has occurred. Indeed, shortly after the 2010 Tour de France, WADA was highly critical of UCI's failure to supplement the indirect biological passport data with dedicated and targeted anti-doping controls.[51] In December 2010, UCI announced plans to increase target-testing under the biological passport programme in direct response to that criticism,[52] but it still felt able to pursue its cases before CAS against Pellizotti and Valjavec four months after that change was made. Consequently, a situation arose where, on the one hand, UCI implicitly accepted that its system was flawed and was thus moved to increase target-testing but, on the other hand, CAS willingly accepted UCI's argument that it should indeed rely solely on the evidence of the biological passport. Arguably, this renders the cycling line of cases particularly open to challenge.

Regardless of what Valjavec or Pechste*in* may or may not have done, one rather hopes that at least one of them can find the support and the resources to challenge their ban through the European courts. While the desire to rid sport of doping is a laudable and widely accepted goal, European sports organisations' adherence to European law and the principles of natural justice are infinitely more important; and certainly too important to be subjected to the tender mercies of what is, after all, no more than a private arbitral body which is otherwise subject to little more than the very light-touch supervisory jurisdiction of the Swiss courts.

References

Ashenden M (2002) A strategy to deter blood doping in sport. Haematologica 87:225–232

Banfi G (2008) Reticulocytes in sports medicine. Sports Med 38(3):187–211

CAS Press Release (2011) CAS imposes a two-year ban on the Italian cyclists Pietro Caucchioli and Franco Pellizotti http://www.tas-cas.org/d2wfiles/document/4615/5048/0/press20release 20ANG_201020032008_.pdf. Accessed 31 July 2012

Cycling News (2011) Testa and BMC weigh in behind biological passport, http://www.cyclingnews.com/news/testa-and-bmc-weigh-in-behind-biological-passport. Accessed 31 July 2012

Fainaru-Wada M, Williams L (2006) Game of shadows. Gotham, New York

50 World Anti-doping Code Athlete Biological Passport Operating Guidelines 2012, 5.

51 Cycling News 2011.

52 See further Hailey 2011.

Guardian Online (2011) Biological passport pays off as Tadej Valjavec receives two-year ban, http://www.guardian.co.uk/sport/2011/apr/22/biological-passport-tadaj-valjavec-ban Accessed 31 July 2012

Hailey N (2011) A false start in the race against doping in sport: Concerns with cycling's biological passport. Duke Law J 61:393–432

McArdle D, Callery C (2011) Doping, European law and the implications of *Meca-Medina*. Int J Sports Pol Polit 3(2):163–174

McLaren R (2006) An overview of non-analytical positive and circumstantial evidence cases in sports. Marq Sports Law Rev 16:193–212

Parisotto R et al (2001) Detection of recombinant huma erhthropoietin abuse in athletes using markers of altered erythropoiesis. Haematologica 86:128–137

Slovenia Press Agency (2010) Cyclist Valjavec cleared of doping charges. http://www.sta.si/en/vest.php?s=a&t=0&id=1539082. Accessed 31 July 2012

Velonews (2010) Italian Panel clears Franco Pellizotti of doping charges. http://velonews.competitor.com/2010/10/news/italian-panel-clears-franco-pellizotti-of-doping-charges_147208. Accessed 31 July 2012

World Anti-doping Code Athlete Biological Passport Operating Guidelines (2012) Available through http://www.wada-ama.org/en/Science-Medicine/. Accessed 31 July 2012

Part V
Contemporary Issues in Sports Law

Chapter 14
CAS 2008/A/1480 *Pistorius v IAAF*

Steve Cornelius

Abstract The appellant in this award is Oscar Pistorius, a professional athlete from South Africa competing internationally in 100, 200 and 400 m sprints. The respondent, the International Association of Athletics Federations (the "IAAF"), governs the sport of athletics throughout the world. Broadly, the dispute concerned the eligibility of an athlete with disabilities to compete in IAAF-sanctioned events alongside able-bodied athlete. More specifically, in this arbitration, Mr Pistorius appealed Decision No. 2008/01 of the IAAF Council dated 14 January 2008 which held that the "Cheetah" prosthetic legs worn by Pistorius, who has been a double amputee since he was eleven months old, constituted a technical device and provided him with an advantage over an able-bodied athlete in violation of IAAF Competition Rule 144.2(e). At the material time, IAAF Rule 144.2(e) stated that "For the purposes of this Rule, the following shall be considered assistance, and are therefore not allowed:...(e) Use of any technical device that incorporates springs, wheels, or any other element that provides the user with an advantage over another athlete not using such a device". The appeal centred principally on whether there was sufficient evidence of any metabolic advantage in favour of a disabled athlete. The appellant argued successfully that (a) due to the fact that he used the same oxygen amounts as able-bodied runners at a sub-maximal running speed and (b) there was no evidence that the biomechanical effects of using his particular prosthetic device gave him an advantage over other athletes not using the device; he, as a disabled athlete, should not have been banned from competeing in international IAAF-sanctioned events alongside able-bodied athlete. The CAS Panel held that there were glaring due process flaws in the process that led to the decision by the IAAF Council to ban Pistorius from IAAF sanctioned events alongside able-bodies athletes. It further held that when it related to the eligibility of an athlete to participate, convincing scientific proof was required to show that the athlete gained an unfair overall net competitive advantage over other athletes.

S. Cornelius (✉)
Department of Private Law, Centre for Intellectual Property Law, University of Pretoria, Law Building, Hatfield Campus, Lynnwood Rd, Pretoria, South Africa
e-mail: steve.cornelius@up.ac.za

J. Anderson (ed.), *Leading Cases in Sports Law*,
ASSER International Sports Law Series, DOI: 10.1007/978-90-6704-909-2_14,

A secondary element to the appeal was the CAS Panel's holding that where an appeal to the Court of Arbitration for Sport does not concern any disciplinary element, it is not the "beyond reasonable doubt" standard applicable in criminal cases which is applicable nor can it be any of the possible intermediate standards that are discussed from time to time in connection with the disciplinary processes, e.g. the "comfortable satisfaction" approach. In such a case, the applicable standard is the "balance of probability".

Contents

14.1 Introduction

On the evening of 3 September 2011, a group of athletes—twelve in all—lined up to receive medals at the thirteenth World Athletics Championships hosted by the IAAF in Daegu, South Korea. The previous night, the men's 4 × 400 m relay team from the United States of America took first place in the final, with the team from South Africa finishing second and the Jamaican team finishing third. However, the group of athletes which stepped onto the podium to receive the respective medals did not present the full picture. Under the IAAF's Competition Rules (rule 170.10 IAAF), a relay team consists of four athletes who must each run one leg of the relay race. The rule, however, also provides that up to two additional athletes may be used as substitutes in the course of the elimination and final rounds. However, regulation 108.2.1 of the *Technical Regulations for IAAF World Series* provides that, in the case of relay events, only the four athletes who competed in the final, may represent the team at the medal ceremony, and that substitutes are to receive their medals afterwards. Because of this, when the medal ceremony took place, there were athletes sitting in the crowd, who had made a major contribution during the heats to ensure that their respective teams made it to the finals. One of them was a remarkable young South African sprinter called Oscar Pistorius. At first glance, he looked like any other track athlete, smartly dressed in his South African colours and watching with pride (and probably a tinge of disappointment) as his team received their medals, knowing that he too would receive his silver medal afterwards.

But six days earlier, as he prepared to walk onto the track to participate in the individual 400 m race, there was something patently different about Pistorius. Instead of putting on his sprinter's spikes like all the other athletes around him, Pistorius promptly removed his lower limbs and fitted prosthetic blades designed for sprinting. On 28 August 2011, Pistorius became the first amputee to participate in the regular IAAF World Championships. He finished third in his heat and qualified for the semi-final where he finished last and was thus eliminated from the competition. On 1 September 2011, Pistorius ran the first leg of the 4 × 400 m relay race for the South African team which set a new national record of 2:59.21 at the World Championships. This meant that Pistorius also had become the first amputee to set a national record in an event for able-bodied athletes. The following evening Pistorius, who made way for 400 m hurdler, LJ van Zyl, on the relay team, had to watch from the sidelines as his team finished second in the final of the 4 × 400 m race. In the process, Pistorius became the first amputee to win a medal at the World Championships. The 2011 IAAF World Athletics Championships in Daegu turned out to be a historic occasion for Pistorius. But his record breaking performances did not come easily and, because of a ruling by the IAAF Council, almost did not happen at all.

Pistorius was born on 22 November 1986 in Johannesburg, South Africa. He was born without fibula bones in both his legs and at the age of eleven months, after his parents had consulted some of the leading orthopaedic surgeons across the globe, his legs were amputated below his knees. His parents were advised that if his legs were amputated before he could learn to walk, it would greatly improve his chances of mobility in later life. He soon received his first prosthetic limbs and mastered them within a few days. Pistorius was an active child and, with the aid of his prosthetic limbs, has managed to do pretty much everything that other young boys his age would do. As a result, he has never thought of himself as disabled and participated in sport like all other children of his age. He attended the prestigious Pretoria Boys' High School where he played rugby, tennis, cricket and water polo and participated in triathlons and Olympic style wrestling! In 2003, Pistorius shattered his knee during a rugby match and, on medical advice, took up track running to aid his rehabilitation. In 2004, on the insistence of a teacher, Pistorius entered the 100 m race at a school athletics meeting. He won the race in 11.72 s and only learned later that his time was markedly faster than the existing world record for the T43 (double amputees) class.

His incredible talent was immediately evident a few months later when Pistorius won the gold medal in the 200-m event and the bronze medal in the 100-m event in the T43/T44 class at the 2004 Paralympic Games in Athens and he went on to set various world records at 100, 200 and 400 m in the T43 class. For Pistorius, who had always played all kinds of sport with able-bodied athletes, it was only natural that he would also compete alongside able-bodied athletes and in 2005 he participated in the South African Athletics Championship, in which he finished sixth in the 400 m event. His exploits did not go unnoticed and Pistorius was invited to participate in a Grand Prix meeting in Helsinki, but had to decline the invitation due to school commitments. In 2007, he finished second in the 400 m race at the South African championships.[1]

14.2 Factual Background

Oscar Pistorius was invited to participate at an athletics' meet at Glasgow in June 2007 but this invitation was subsequently withdrawn following intervention by the IAAF. In March 2007, the IAAF Council had introduced an amendment to IAAF Rule 144.2 to regulate the use of technical devices. Subsection (e) of the new rule prohibited the "Use of any technical device that incorporates springs, wheels or any other element that provides the user with an advantage over another athlete not using such a device". Pistorious eventually got his opportunity to participate in an international athletics meeting in July 2007, when he took part in the 400 m "B" race at the Golden Gala meeting in Rome. During this period, the IAAF asked Dr Elio Locatelli to evaluate whether the prostheses used by Pistorius contravened rule 144.2(e). The IAAF arranged to have the Rome race videotaped by an Italian sports laboratory using several high-definition cameras from different angles.

Analysis of the video revealed that Pistorius was slower than other runners off the starting blocks, during the acceleration phase and running around the first bend, but faster over the back straight. The split times of the race confirmed that able-bodied sprinters ran their fastest 100 m splits in the first and second 100 m, while Pistorius ran his fastest 100 m splits in the second and third 100 m. The scientific analysis of the videotapes by the Italian laboratory indicated that neither Pistorius' stride-length, nor the length of time that his prosthesis was in contact with the ground, were significantly different from those of the other runners. In short the results of the study were inconclusive.[2]

Locatelli then instructed Professor Peter Brüggemann at the Institute of Biomechanics and Orthopaedics at the German Sport University in Cologne to conduct a biomechanical study to demonstrate whether or not Pistorius' prosthetic limbs gave him an advantage over other athletes. Brüggemann prepared a testing protocol based on instructions given to him by the IAAF. The tests were mainly designed to evaluate Pistorius' sprint movement using an inverse dynamic approach and also to study Pistorius' oxygen intake and blood lactate metabolism over a 400-m race simulation. Crucially, the IAAF instructed Brüggemann to carry out the testing only when Pistorius was running in a straight line after the

[1] The sources for this introduction are taken from an interview conducted by the author with Oscar Pistorius on 11 January 2012 at the Sports Science Institute, University of Pretoria, South Africa and from www.oscarpistorius.com/about. Accessed on 31 July 2012.

[2] CAS 2008/A/1480 *Pistorius v IAAF*, p. 3.

acceleration phase. The tests were conducted in November 2007 and involved Pistorius and five control athletes of similar sprinting ability as him.[3] Dr Robert Gailey, a scientist nominated by Pistorius to participate in the Cologne testing, set out a number of questions and suggestions directly relating to the testing protocol, but this was ignored by the IAAF and not shown to Brüggemann. Gailey was allowed to attend the tests only as an observer and was allowed no input on the testing protocol or on the analysis that would be made subsequently by Brüggemann's team.[4]

Brüggemann and his colleagues issued their report in December 2007 (the "Brüggemann Report"). They concluded that, when compared to the control athletes, Pistorius displayed a lower aerobic capacity and his VO2 uptake was 25 % lower than the oxygen consumption of the control athletes. They also found that the prostheses displayed significantly different joint kinetics when compared to the ankle, knee and hip joints of the control athletes and energy return was higher in the prostheses than in the human ankle joints. They concluded that Pistorius received significant biomechanical advantages by the prosthesis in comparison to sprinting with natural human legs.[5] Pistorius indicated that it would take time to produce a considered scientific response to the Brüggemann Report, but was given less than a month to respond.[6] In January 2008, the IAAF Council was provided with a summary of the Brüggemann Report prepared by the IAAF, the report itself and the reply by Pistorius. The IAAF's brief summary of the Brüggemann Report was not approved by Brüggemann, nor was it wholly accurate.[7]

As a result of the Brüggemann Report, the IAAF Council concluded that running with prostheses required a less-important vertical movement associated with a lesser mechanical effort to raise the body, and the energy loss resulting from the use of prostheses was significantly lower than that resulting from a human ankle joint at a maximal sprint speed. In January 2008, and based on these findings, the IAAF held that the prosthetics used by Pistorius were to be considered as a technical device providing the user with an advantage over other athletes in contravention of Rule 144.2(e) IAAF—IAAF Council decision no 2008/01 of 14 January 2008 ("the IAAF Decision"). Pistorius was thus declared ineligible to compete in IAAF-sanctioned events with immediate effect.[8]

In February 2008 Pistorius commissioned his own series of tests against able-bodied athletes as controls at a laboratory in Houston, Texas (the "Houston Report"). The Houston Report measured elements which the Brüggemann Report did not measure and found that Pistorius fatigued normally: he used the same

[3] CAS 2008/A/1480 *Pistorius v IAAF*, pp. 3–4.

[4] CAS 2008/A/1480 *Pistorius v IAAF*, paras 14–15.

[5] CAS 2008/A/1480 *Pistorius v IAAF*, p. 4.

[6] CAS 2008/A/1480 *Pistorius v IAAF*, para 16.

[7] CAS 2008/A/1480 *Pistorius v IAAF*, para 17.

[8] CAS 2008/A/1480 *Pistorius v IAAF*, p. 5.

oxygen amounts as able-bodied runners at a sub-maximal running speed, and thus did not have a metabolic advantage. The Houston Report also found a greater amount of energy loss from the prosthesis against the intact human leg.[9]

On the basis of this report and other evidence, Pistorius then appealed to the Court of Arbitration for Sport ("CAS") to have the IAAF Decision quashed. Pistorius raised four basic issues in his appeal: the IAAF Council exceeded its jurisdiction in taking the IAAF Decision; the process leading to the IAAF Decision was procedurally unsound; the IAAF Decision was unlawfully discriminatory; the IAAF Decision in determining that the use of the prosthetic devices contravenes Rule 144.2(e) was wrong.[10] On hearing, Pistorius abandoned his challenge to the IAAF Council's jurisdiction and the CAS Panel was left to determine the remaining three issues.[11]

14.3 Determination at CAS

The CAS Panel determined that the IAAF Decision had first to be traced in form and context to the adoption of Rule 144.2(e) IAAF in March 2007. They rejected testimony that the introduction of this rule was aimed primarily at the use of "spring" technology in running shoes and found it more likely that the new rule was aimed specifically at Pistorius by, for example, enabling the IAAF to subject Pistorius to the various tests.[12] The CAS Panel did acknowledge that the event in Rome, where Pistorius was filmed, was a *bona fide* attempt to determine whether his stride-length was greater than that of other athletes who ran comparable times in competition.[13] However, when this proved inconclusive, the CAS Panel noted that the IAAF had made some crucial procedural and due process errors when it commissioned further tests by Brüggemann.[14] In this, the CAS Panel highlighted that the instructions to carry out the testing only when Pistorius was running in a straight line (and thus not considering the effect of the prostheses over the entire race) was probably taken after the analysis of the Rome tests and was presumably designed to create a distorted view of any advantages Pistorius may have.[15] Consequently, the CAS Panel questioned the scientific basis, validity and relevance of the Brüggemann Report. The CAS Panel further concluded that Brüggemann was briefed to determine whether or not the prostheses provided an

[9] CAS 2008/A/1480 *Pistorius v IAAF*, para 43.
[10] CAS 2008/A/1480 *Pistorius v IAAF*, para 5.
[11] CAS 2008/A/1480 *Pistorius v IAAF*, para 7.
[12] CAS 2008/A/1480 *Pistorius v IAAF*, paras 5–6.
[13] CAS 2008/A/1480 *Pistorius v IAAF*, para 10.
[14] CAS 2008/A/1480 *Pistorius v IAAF*, para 11.
[15] CAS 2008/A/1480 *Pistorius v IAAF*, paras 12–13.

advantage in certain determined respects only and the Brüggemann Report therefore did not address all the questions which had to be determined.[16]

The CAS Panel also questioned the voting procedure followed by the IAAF Council. It noted that the documents were sent to IAAF Council members on a Friday with a request that the votes should be returned by the following Monday morning, while abstentions would be counted as positive votes to declare Pistorius ineligible. As a result, the IAAF press statement to the effect that the decision was made by the IAAF Council unanimously was misleading.[17] The CAS Panel found clear evidence of "prejudgment" in that Locatelli and other IAAF officials told the press before the vote was taken that Pistorius would be banned from IAAF-sanctioned events.[18] The Panel held that the manner in which the IAAF handled the case fell short of the high standards that the international sporting community is entitled to expect from a leading federation.[19]

The CAS Panel then went on to dismiss the submission by Pistorius that the IAAF Decision was in breach of its obligation of non-discrimination. It held that disability laws only require that an athlete be permitted to compete on the same footing as others. It followed that if the CAS Panel found that Pistorius gained no advantage from using the prostheses, he would be able to compete on an equal basis with other athletes. On the other hand, if the CAS Panel concluded that Pistorius did gain an advantage, he could not claim to participate on an equal footing.[20]

Lastly, the Panel had to determine whether the IAAF Decision was wrong in determining that Pistorius' use of the prostheses contravened Rule 144.2(e)IAAF which prohibited the use of any technical device that incorporates springs, wheels, or any other element that provides the user with an advantage over another athlete not using such a device. The CAS Panel identified the critical question as relating to the meaning of the expression "an advantage … over another athlete".[21] The CAS Panel rejected the IAAF's argument that the rule referred to any advantage, however small, in any part of a competition regardless of any disadvantages.[22] The Panel held that convincing scientific proof was required to show that the prostheses provide Pistorius with an overall net advantage over other athletes. If the use of the prostheses provided more disadvantages than advantages, then it could not reasonably be said to provide an advantage over other athletes, because the user was, in scientific and sporting fact, at a competitive disadvantage.[23] Crucially, the IAAF did not brief Brüggemann to make that "net" determination and the testing

16 CAS 2008/A/1480 *Pistorius v IAAF*, para 13.

17 CAS 2008/A/1480 *Pistorius v IAAF*, para 19.

18 CAS 2008/A/1480 *Pistorius v IAAF*, para 20.

19 CAS 2008/A/1480 *Pistorius v IAAF*, para 22.

20 CAS 2008/A/1480 *Pistorius v IAAF*, paras 24–30.

21 CAS 2008/A/1480 *Pistorius v IAAF*, para 34.

22 CAS 2008/A/1480 *Pistorius v IAAF*, para 34.

23 CAS 2008/A/1480 *Pistorius v IAAF*, para 36.

protocol that Brüggemann prepared was not designed to provide an authoritative scientific opinion as to whether the prostheses provided an overall net advantage over other athletes not using such devices. The Panel also found insufficient evidence that the prostheses provided any metabolic or biomechanical advantage over other athletes not using the device.[24]

Finally, although the CAS Panel upheld Pistorius' appeal, it nevertheless found it necessary to stress that its ruling applies only to Pistorius while using the particular model of (Cheetah Flex-Foot) prosthesis that was the subject of the various tests. It did not relate to any further developments of prostheses. Furthermore, the Panel did not exclude the possibility that advances in scientific knowledge might in the future prove on the balance of probabilities[25] that the existing prostheses provide an overall net advantage. In sum, the Panel explained that its decision did not apply to any other athlete and each case must be considered by the IAAF on its own merits under Rule 144.2(e) as interpreted by the Panel.[26]

14.4 Discussion and Analysis

At first glance, this case seems to have dealt a major blow for the benefit and recognition of the fundamental rights of disabled athletes, and in particular their right to be adequately accommodated, to have genuinely equal opportunity to participate in sport and to be treated with personal dignity. And in many ways, this holds true. The misguided attempts of the IAAF to amend its rules, hide behind ill-conceived "scientific" reports and exclude Pistorius from participation against able-bodied athletes was exposed for the sham it was.[27] The CAS Panel sent a clear message to international federations that they must address the participation criteria surrounding disabled athlete in a transparent and impartial manner. In this, credit should go the IAAF, though, for the dignified way in which it accepted the CAS award and welcomed Pistorius into events sanctioned by the IAAF including the London Olympics of 2012, where, on 4 August 2012 Pistorius became the first amputee to take part in the Olympic Games.

---

[24] CAS 2008/A/1480 *Pistorius v IAAF*, para 36.

[25] CAS 2008/A/1480 *Pistorius v IAAF*, paras 38–39. The IAAF accepted the burden of proof. The parties disagreed on the applicable standard of proof. The CAS Panel determined that where an appeal to it does not concern any disciplinary element (as was the case here) it is not the "beyond reasonable doubt" standard applicable in criminal cases which is applicable nor can it be any of the possible intermediate standards that are discussed from time to time in connection with the disciplinary processes, e.g. the "comfortable satisfaction" approach in doping cases. Accordingly, in this case, the applicable standard was the "balance of probabilities".

[26] CAS 2008/A/1480 *Pistorius v IAAF*, paras 53–56.

[27] See CAS 2008/A/1480 *Pistorius v IAAF*, para 12 where the Panel uses the phrase "off the rails" to describe the IAAF's testing of Pistorius.

As with all aspects of this case, all is not, however, quite what it seems. It is ironic that a case which signals a clear victory for the rights of disable athletes to participate equally with able-bodied athletes was not decided on the basis of unlawful discrimination. In fact, the arguments in this regard were clearly dismissed by the Panel.[28] But perhaps this is also fitting as Pistorius has never considered himself to be disabled. As he put it, there are "no disabilities, only hurdles".[29] Instead, the CAS Panel focussed on the question of what constitutes an unfair advantage and the scientific evidence presented in this regard. In addition, while the award was based mainly on the proper interpretation of Rule 144.2(e) IAAF, the CAS Panel's view that "advantage" referred to an overall "net" advantage is significant as it demands that both the benefits and burdens have to be taken into consideration in determining whether a device provides an advantage to an athlete who uses it.[30] In this respect, this case is also a landmark case that will undoubtedly be cited in future cases which involve other sports rules that seek to ensure fair competition and prevent a competitor from obtaining an unfair advantage over other competitors.

It must be noted that, in any event, this "net" approach is how this concept of "advantage" has been applied in some other sports. For instance, in Formula 1 motor racing, racing regulations have long provided that if a car leaves the race track, the driver may rejoin the race if it is safe and the driver does not gain an advantage. Where a driver leaves the track and rejoins the track in such a way that he passes the car in front or avoids being passed by the car behind (and thus gains an advantage), the driver is generally not penalised if he immediately relinquishes his place to the driver then behind him (and effectively gains no "net" advantage). In the end, this is a simple common sense interpretation of the expression "advantage". In application to the Pistorius affair, the CAS Panel explained, again in a commonsense manner, that if a device (or incident) provides more disadvantages than advantages, then it cannot reasonably be said to provide an advantage over other athletes, because the user is in a factual, scientific and sporting sense at a competitive disadvantage.[31]

This interpretation does however beg one final question. In determining whether an athlete gains a net advantage, should only the advantages and disadvantages that manifest themselves during actual competition be considered, or should overall advantages and disadvantages, such as those that impact on training, also be considered? For instance, one matter that was not even put before the CAS Panel relates to the impact which the use of prosthetic devices have on Pistorius' ability to train to the same extent that able-bodied athletes do. The prostheses do not always fit snugly on his legs and from time to time he suffers from such severe

---

[28] CAS 2008/A/1480 *Pistorius v IAAF*, para 30.

[29] Interview conducted by the author with Oscar Pistorius on 11 January 2012 at the Sports Science Institute, University of Pretoria, South Africa.

[30] CAS 2008/A/1480 *Pistorius v IAAF*, para 36.

[31] CAS 2008/A/1480 *Pistorius v IAAF*, para 36.

chafing to the skin on his legs that he has to cut back on his training.[32] Able-bodied athletes wearing running shoes may suffer some blisters, but this occurs less frequently and usually heals much quicker. In addition, even with any kind of prosthesis, Pistorius is unable to perform many of the typical weight training exercises that able-bodied sprinters take for granted, especially those exercises that strengthen the leg muscles.[33] A disadvantage during training must surely also result in a competitive disadvantage during competition.

14.5 Conclusion

Pistorius' selection to participate at the 2012 Olympic Gems in London continues to arouse controversy and even some hostility.[34] The bigger picture and the one in which Oscar Pistorius, and not his critics, will stand prominently must however be about how sport at the Olympics and elsewhere is based fundamentally around a celebration of the human body and mind and the physical and psychological prowess of the participants. It is about training and turning the human body into something capable of incredible feats of speed, strength, endurance and skill. CAS 2008/A/1480 *Pistorius v IAAF*, which allowed one of the most remarkable athletes of our time, who has had to overcome adversity from the day he was born, to exhibit his incredible talent on the world stage alongside able-bodied athletes, is a clear affirmation of the spirit of sport and, possibly more importantly still, an inspiration to millions of people across the globe who face daily struggles of their own.

References

McRae D (2011) Blade runner aims to take his inspiring tale to olympian heights. The Guardian, Sport, 26 May, p 8

www.guardian.co.uk/sport/oscar-pistorius. Accessed 31 July 2012

www.oscarpistorius.com. Accessed 31 July 2012

[32] Interview conducted by the author with Oscar Pistorius on 11 January 2012 at the Sports Science Institute, University of Pretoria, South Africa.

[33] Interview conducted by the author with Oscar Pistorius on 11 January 2012 at the Sports Science Institute, University of Pretoria, South Africa.

[34] An archive of material and commentary relating to Pistorius at the Olympics can be found at www.guardian.co.uk/sport/oscar-pistorius. Accessed 31 July 2012. See, in particular, the interview with Pistorius by McRae 2011.

Chapter 15
American Needle Inc v NFL 130 S Ct 2201 (2010)

Matthew J. Mitten

Abstract The National Football League ("NFL") is an unincorporated association of 32 separately owned professional football teams. The teams each own their name, colours, logos, trademarks and associated intellectual property. The teams formed National Football League Properties (NFLP) to exploit this intellectual property. Initially, NFLP granted non-exclusive licences to various sports manufactures (including American Needle) to manufacture and sell NFL team labelled sportswear. In December 2000, the teams authorised NFLP to grant exclusive licences, one of which was granted to Reebok International Ltd to produce and sell trademarked head wear for all 32 teams. American Needle Inc, whose licence had not been renewed at the material time, challenged the NFLP's use of an exclusive licence as contrary to section 1 of the Sherman Act 1890 which makes "every contract, combination…or, conspiracy, in restraint of trade" illegal. The respondents argued that the nature of section 1 of the Sherman Act is that it requires two or more parties to participate in the stated manner and thus, given that the NFLP was a "single entity" a claim of anti-competitive activity could not be brought, save under section 2 of the Sherman Act (which addressed monopolisation or conspiracy to monopolise). American Needle Inc countered that the NFLP was not in form a "single entity"—noting that the courts have long been alert to sports leagues' efforts to label various collective commercial arrangements as single entity; but rather it was in substance an arrangement that sought to veil ongoing concerted actions by separate and multiple parties with different corporate and economic interests. Guided by its decision in Copperweld Corp v Independence Tube Corp 467 US 752 (1984), the US Supreme Court held against the single entity argument and remitted the matter to the lower courts to determine whether a section 1 violation had occurred. Importantly, the US Supreme Court also acknowledged, as guided by NCAA v Board of Regents 468 US 85 (1984, that in order to have and maintain a sports league many forms of coordination and

M. J. Mitten (✉)
National Sports Law Institute, Marquette University Law School, Milwaukee, WI, USA
e-mail: matt.mitten@marquette.edu

J. Anderson (ed.), *Leading Cases in Sports Law*,
ASSER International Sports Law Series, DOI: 10.1007/978-90-6704-909-2_15,

cooperation between and among competitors would have to take place. Whether such "coordination" might necessarily entail a violation of the Sherman Act would have to be assessed in light of the Rule of Reason i.e., only contracts or combinations that unreasonably restrain trade should be subject to antitrust law.

Contents

15.1 Introduction

One of the most difficult issues affecting legal regulation of the United States professional sports industry is whether (and, if so, how) section 1 of the Sherman Act 1890,[1] a provision of the U.S. antitrust laws prohibiting concerted action that unreasonably restrains interstate trade or commerce, applies to professional sports league rules and internal governance decisions. In other words, are league clubs separate economic entities whose collective action is subject to section 1, or is a sports league and its clubs an economically integrated single business enterprise whose conduct is not covered by section 1 (the basis of the "single entity defence")?[2] If the latter, what is the appropriate standard for determining if the challenged concerted action unreasonably restrains trade?

In *American Needle Inc v NFL*[3] a 2010 case, the United States Supreme Court unanimously held that the National Football League ("NFL") clubs' centralised and exclusive licensing of their individual trademarks through a wholly owned league subsidiary is not immune from judicial scrutiny under section 1 of the Sherman Act. This landmark decision has broad implications because its rationale suggests that all collective decisions by a US professional sports league's member clubs that reduce intrabrand economic competition among themselves (e.g., joint decisions regarding the ownership, number, and geographical location of teams,

---

[1] 15 USC § 1.

[2] There is a rich body of scholarly commentary debating the merits of the single-entity defence. See, for example, Feldman 2009; Goldman 1989; Grauer 1983; Jacobs 1991; Lazaroff 1988; McCann 2010; Piraino 1999; Roberts 1984; Waxman 2001.

[3] *American Needle Inc v NFL* 130 S Ct 2201 (2010).

restrictions on the sale of broadcasting rights, labour relations issues, etc.) are subject to section 1 of the Sherman Act.[4] Nevertheless, and acknowledging that a sport's league's member clubs must cooperate to produce on-field athletic competition, the Court reaffirmed: "When 'restraints on competition are essential if the product is to be available at all,' *per se* rules of illegality are inapplicable, and instead the restraint must be judged according to the flexible Rule of Reason.'"[5]

Before describing and analysing *American Needle*, this chapter explains how US major professional sports leagues are structured and governed and briefly surveys the rulings of lower courts, which generally rejected the single entity defence. It concludes by reviewing how lower courts have applied *American Needle* to subsequent sports antitrust litigation and scholarly commentary regarding any potentially open questions concerning its application to professional sports leagues.

15.2 Structure and Internal Governance of US Professional Sports Leagues

The NFL, Major League Baseball ("MLB"), the National Basketball Association ("NBA"), and the National Hockey League ("NHL") are each comprised of separate, independently owned and operated for-profit member clubs, which collectively produce their respective brands of athletic competition. Each league was formed in the late 1800s or early 1900s when a group of existing independent clubs banded together to play games against each other and govern their business affairs in an agreed centralised manner. Each league is autonomously governed,[6] and each of their respective member clubs has a voice and vote concerning the league's constitution and bylaws, selection of the league commissioner, and significant internal league governance decisions.

In the words of the late George Halas, one of the NFL's founders who owned the Chicago Bears club:

> Our league for me was then – and still is – best exemplified as a wheel.... In 1920 [before the NFL was formed], we were 12 independent spokes. But spokes, if they are to serve a useful purpose and make a contribution, must have a rim. A spoke may weaken, even break, but the rim prevents collapse. Our league was and is our rim.[7]

---

4 With the exception of professional baseball, the business activities of other U.S. professional sports leagues generally are subject to the federal antitrust laws. For a detailed discussion of the origins and scope of professional baseball's common law antitrust exemption, see Chap. 2 of this volume.

5 *American Needle Inc v NFL* 130 S Ct 2201, 2216 (2010).

6 In the US there is no government body that directly regulates professional sports. Unlike the prevailing hierarchical model of sports governance prevalent in Europe, there is no national federation that exercises plenary governing authority over all levels of professional and amateur competition for each sport within the US.

7 Harry 2002, C1.

The member clubs of the NFL, NBA, NHL and MLB are geographically dispersed throughout the United States.; some NBA (Toronto), NHL (Calgary, Edmonton, Ottawa, Montreal, Toronto, Vancouver) and MLB (Toronto) clubs are in Canada.[8] Most of each league's respective clubs are given an exclusive home geographical territory (i.e., generally there is only one league club in a city or its 75-mile radius). However, some clubs in the same league share a large metropolitan area (for example, the NFL's New York Giants and New York Jets). Major league clubs are located in cities with significantly different populations and economic bases; for example, large metropolitan areas such as New York City, Los Angeles and Chicago as well as much smaller cities like Cleveland, Milwaukee and Pittsburgh. Thus, league clubs' respective revenue-generating potential from ticket sales, concessions, parking fees, sponsorships, merchandising rights and game broadcasts within differing local markets varies considerably and significantly impacts their individual finances.

As a means of preventing significant disparities in local revenue streams from inhibiting or destroying on-field competitive balance among their teams by adversely affecting a small market club's ability to afford the multi-million dollar salaries to attract the best players to its team, the NFL, MLB, NBA and NHL have implemented varying degrees of revenue sharing among their member clubs.[9] The NFL currently has the most significant degree of revenue sharing among its member clubs (approximately 80 %), which provides the Green Bay Packers, located in a small city of approximately 100,000 people, with the financial resources to compete effectively on the field with large market clubs such as its rival the Chicago Bears, which is based in a metropolitan area of almost 10 million people. In 1982 testimony before Congress, former NFL commissioner Pete Rozelle stated "revenue sharing is the key to maintaining geographic and competitive balance in professional football and ensure[s] that each club, irrespective of the size of its community, stadium, or television market, has a comparable opportunity to field a championship team."[10]

As another means of maintaining league-wide competitive balance and ensuring the financial stability of all teams, league clubs also seek to limit intrabrand economic competition with each other by agreements concerning exclusive geographical territories as well as restrictions on club relocations, the sale and licensing of broadcast rights and the acquisition of and payment for players' services.

---

8 Currently, the NFL has 32 member clubs; the NBA, NHL and MLB each have 30 clubs.

9 This has been particularly important for the financial stability of Canadian MLB, NBA and NHL clubs that earn local revenues in Canadian dollars while paying player salaries in relatively more valuable US dollars, based on historical exchange rates for these currencies.

10 See Hoffman 1997, 262.

15.3 Lower Courts' Differing Views Regarding the Single Entity Defence

Some early cases simply assumed without deciding that professional sports league rules or agreements that allegedly reduce or eliminate intrabrand economic competition among league clubs are subject to section 1 of the Sherman Act.[11] Ironically, the single entity defence was not raised by the NHL in a 1973 case alleging that the NHL's then-existing centralised exclusive trademark licensing agreement violated section 1 of the Sherman Act by preventing its clubs from individually licensing their respective trademarks. In *Boston Professional Hockey Association Inc v Dallas Cap & Emblem Manufacturing Inc*,[12] a Texas federal district court rejected this antitrust claim without considering whether this restraint should be immune from section 1 scrutiny because league clubs function as a single economic entity that collectively produces one product (e.g., NHL hockey) whose trademarks symbolise the associated goodwill generated by all clubs—an important threshold issue not decided by the US Supreme Court until almost 40 years later in *American Needle*.

In a 1975 case, *San Francisco Seals Ltd v National Hockey League*,[13] a California federal district court implicitly accepted the single entity defence in ruling that the NHL's refusal to permit one of its clubs to relocate from San Francisco to Vancouver, British Columbia did not violate section 1 of the Sherman Act. Observing that "it is fundamental in a section 1 violation that there must be at least two independent business entities accused of combining or conspiring to restrain trade," the court concluded that, when producing NHL hockey, NHL clubs are "acting together as one single business enterprise, competing against other similarly organized professional leagues." Because NHL clubs collectively produced hockey games, the court held that the league's refusal to permit the relocation was not a conspiracy to restrain trade as a matter of law. However, it recognised league clubs may "compete economically, to a greater or lesser degree" among themselves in some other markets in which two or more exist (for example, New York City).

In the 1980s and 1990s most federal appellate courts rejected the single entity defence when directly raised by professional sports leagues in antitrust litigation. In *North American Soccer League v. National Football League*,[14] the United States for of Appeals for the Second Circuit reversed the trial court's ruling that the NFL and its clubs constitute a single economic entity. Rather than focusing on

---

[11] *Mid-South Grizzlies v NFL* 720 F 2d 772 (3d Cir 1983) ("In this case there is no dispute about the requisite concert of action among the defendants.").

[12] *Boston Professional Hockey Association Inc v Dallas Cap & Emblem Manufacturing Inc* 360 F Supp 459 (ND Tex 1973). The defendant did not appeal the district court's ruling on its antitrust defence, so this issue was not considered by the Fifth Circuit in 510 F 2d 1014.

[13] *San Francisco Seals Ltd v National Hockey League* 379 F Supp 966 (CD Cal 1974).

[14] *North American Soccer League v National Football League* 670 F 2d 1249 (2d Cir 1981), *cert denied*, 459 US 1074 (1982).

whether the NFL clubs are in fact economic competitors in the alleged relevant market that is restrained (e.g., professional sports capital and entrepreneurial skill), the Second Circuit found they were separately owned and operated legal entities that did not share expenses, capital expenditures, profits or all revenues with each other. It held that NFL teams are ''separate economic entities engaged in a joint venture'' and that the NFL's cross-ownership rule, which prohibited NFL club owners from having a controlling interest in any other major league professional sports team, could be subject to antitrust challenge under section 1 of the Sherman Act. In a vigorous dissent from the US Supreme Court's denial of certiorari (i.e., refusal to accept this case for review), Justice Rehnquist strongly suggested that a professional sports league is a single economic entity: "The NFL owners are joint ventures who produce a product, professional football, which competes with other sports and other forms of entertainment in the entertainment market. Although individual NFL teams compete with one another on the playing field, they rarely compete in the market place."[15]

Similarly, in *Los Angeles Memorial Coliseum v NFL*,[16] the United States Court of Appeals for the Ninth Circuit rejected the NFL's argument that the league "is in essence a single entity, akin to a partnership or joint venture," which is not subject to section 1 of the Sherman Act, on the ground that "NFL policies are not set by one individual or parent corporation, but by the separate teams acting jointly," which are "separate business entities whose products have an independent value." Consequently, the court determined that the league's rules and conduct are covered by section 1 of the Sherman Act. Although the clubs must cooperate to produce NFL football, it ruled they are "sufficiently independent and competitive with one another to warrant rule of reason scrutiny under § 1" rather than judicial immunity from this provision of the federal antitrust laws.[17]

In a 1984 case, *Copperweld Corp v Independence Tube Corp*,[18] the Supreme Court held that legally separate business entities with a "complete unity of interest," such as a parent corporation and its wholly owned subsidiary, are not subject to section 1 of the Sherman Act. The Court explained that the Sherman Act contains a "basic distinction between concerted and independent action," and that anticompetitive independent conduct by a single economic entity does not violate section 1. The Court explained that the business relationship between a parent corporation and its wholly owned subsidiary is "like a multiple team of horses drawing a vehicle under the control of a single driver;" therefore, there is no sudden joining of previously diverse economic forces raising the prospect of

---

[15] *North American Soccer League v National Football League* 459 US 1074, 1077 (1982).

[16] *Los Angeles Memorial Coliseum v NFL* 726 F 2d 1381 (9th Cir), *cert denied*, 469 US 990 (1984).

[17] Even if courts accepted the single entity defence, US professional sports leagues (with the exception of professional baseball) would be subject to section 2 of the Sherman Act, which prohibits monopolisation, attempted monopolisation, and conspiracies to monopolise interstate trade or commerce.

[18] *Copperweld Corp v Independence Tube Corp* 467 US 752 (1984).

collusive anticompetitive conduct. The court observed that internal coordination within a single business enterprise is often necessary for effective competition and that its internal organisational structure is irrelevant regarding any resulting anti-competitive consequences in the marketplace.[19]

Although there is no complete unity of interest in economic terms between a professional sports league's member clubs, some of *Copperweld's* reasoning provided support for the single economic entity defence. However, in *Sullivan v NFL*,[20] the United States Court of Appeals for the First Circuit concluded that league clubs do not satisfy *Copperweld's* "complete unity of interest" standard because they often act in furtherance of their own individual economic interests rather than the league's collective economic interests. Subsequently, in *Fraser v Major League Soccer LLC*,[21] the First Circuit observed that "if ordinary investors decided to set up a company that would own and manage all of the teams in a league, it is hard to see why this arrangement would fall outside *Copperweld's* safe harbor." When it was formed in 1996, Major League Soccer (MLS), the only Division 1 professional outdoor soccer league in the United States, sought to structure itself as a single economic entity to avoid any potential section 1 antitrust liability arising out of its player labour relations.[22]

Unlike the NFL, NBA, MLB and NHL, whose member clubs are independently owned and operated, MLS developed a unique structure and operated as a limited liability company that effectively functioned as a corporation. MLS owned all league clubs, and its management committee (consisting of representatives of each

---

[19] In *Brown v Pro Football Inc* 518 US 231 (1996), the Supreme Court observed "that the clubs that make up a professional sports league are not completely independent economic competitors, as they depend upon a degree of cooperation for economic survival." But its resolution of the dispositive issue in *Brown*, the scope of the non-statutory labour exemption's bar to the use of antitrust law to resolve labour disputes, did not require the Court to determine how *Copperweld* applied to a professional sports league's internal governance. Thus, *Brown*, one of the Supreme Court's few cases considering the application of antitrust law to professional sports, did not provide any definitive guidance to lower courts regarding the applicability of the single entity defence.

[20] *Sullivan v NFL* 34 F 3d 1091 (1st Cir 1994).

[21] *Fraser v Major League Soccer LLC* 284 F 3d 47, 56 (1st Cir 2002), *cert denied*, 537 US 885 (2002).

[22] Courts have ruled that agreements among league clubs to reduce competition for player services (for example, restrictions on the ability of a player whose contract with his current club has expired to agree to play for other league clubs) are subject to section 1 of the Sherman Act. See *Chicago Professional Sports Ltd Partnership v. NBA*, 95 F 3d 593, 599 (7th Cir 1996) (''[From the perspective of college basketball players who seek to sell their skills, the teams are distinct, and because the human capital of players is not readily transferable to other sports (as even Michael Jordan learned) the league looks more like a group of firms acting as a monopoly''). See also *McNeil v. NFL* 790 F Supp 871 (D Minn 1992) where there is a recognition that some player restraints may be necessary to ensure on-field competitive balance among league clubs and to produce close, exciting games attractive to consumers, courts have held that the need for intraleague competitive balance is a relevant factor in assessing the reasonableness of particular player restraint rather than a justification for providing blanket immunity from section 1.

of its investors) exercised significant centralised control over both league and individual team operations. Several investors individually operated league teams, and were paid a management fee based largely on the team's locally generated revenues. The MLS itself operated some clubs. Team operators could not transfer their operational rights without the MLS management committee's approval. These rights could be terminated if a team operator violated the MLS operating agreement or failed to act consistently with the league's best interests. All revenues generated by the league belonged to MLS, which paid most expenses associated with league operations, including all player acquisition costs, salaries and benefits. Individual team operator/investors were responsible for paying certain operating expenses, none of which were player-related expenses. All MLS investors shared equally in the league's net profits and losses.

A Massachusetts federal court rejected a section 1 antitrust claim by a group of professional soccer players challenging MLS's centralised system of contracting for player services, pursuant to which all players were hired by MLS as league employees, with ''marquee players'' allocated to particular league teams and others assigned to various league teams selected by individual team operator/investors through a player draft. Relying on *Copperweld*, the court characterised MLS as a single corporation and its team operator/investors as essentially its officers and shareholders. It concluded that "each operator-investor's personal stake is not independent of the success of MLS as a whole enterprise'' and that MLS investors "surrendered the degree of autonomy that team owners in 'plural entity' leagues typically enjoy." The court held that "MLS's policy of contracting centrally for player services is unilateral activity of a single firm. Since section 1 does not apply to unilateral activity—even unilateral activity that tends to restrain trade—the claim...cannot succeed as a matter of law.''

On appeal, the First Circuit stated "that the case for applying single entity status to MLS and its operator/investors has not been established." The court did not definitively resolve this issue because the jury found that the MLS's system of contracting centrally for player services did not unreasonably restrain trade. Nevertheless, the First Circuit strongly suggested that MLS's operations, including its unilaterally imposed player restraints, should be subject to section 1 scrutiny:

> ...there is a diversity of entrepreneurial interests that goes well beyond the ordinary company. MLS and its operator/investors have separate contractual relationships giving the operator/investors rights that take them part way along the path to ordinary sports team owners: they do some independent hiring and make out-of-pocket investments in their own teams; they retain a large portion of the revenues from the activities of their teams; and each has limited sale rights in its own team that relate to specific assets and not just shares in the common enterprise. One might well ask why the formal difference in corporate structure should warrant treating MLS differently than the National Football League or other traditionally structured sports leagues....[23]

[23] *Fraser v Major League Soccer LLC* 284 F 3d 47, 57 (1st Cir 2002).

By contrast, in *Chicago Professional Sports Limited Partnership v National Basketball Association,*[24] the United States Court of Appeals for the Seventh Circuit suggested the single entity defence should not be rejected based on how professional sports leagues are structured and governed. Some of the court's judges proposed that a functional approach, which analyses whether league clubs are economic competitors in the alleged relevant market that is restrained (as *San Francisco Seals* did), be used to determine the appropriateness of applying section 1 of the Sherman Act on a case by case basis. In other words, whether the particular challenged conduct has the requisite degree of economic integration to be considered that of a single economic entity requires facet by facet analysis of each league's operations.

Judge Easterbrook observed that the NBA is closer to a single firm than a group of independent firms when acting in the broadcast market:

> Whether the NBA itself is more like a single firm, which would be analyzed only under § 2 of the Sherman Act [which prohibits monopolization or attempted monopolization], or like a joint venture, which would be subject to the Rule of Reason under § 1, is a tough question under *Copperweld.* It has characteristics of both. Unlike the colleges and universities that belong to the National Collegiate Athletic Association...the NBA has no existence independent of sports. It makes professional basketball; only it can make "NBA Basketball" games...From the perspective of fans and advertisers (who use sports telecasts to reach fans), "NBA Basketball" is one product from a single source even though the Chicago Bulls and Seattle Supersonics [two of the NBA's clubs] are highly distinguishable...[25]

Judge Cudahy, however, disagreed:

> As long as teams are individually owned and [all] revenue is not shared in fixed proportion, the teams both retain independent economic interests and make decisions in concert. Where this is the case, there is a strong argument that sports leagues should be treated as joint ventures rather than single entities because there remains a potential that league policy will be made to satisfy the independent economic interests of some group of teams, rather than to maximize the overall performance of the league...[26]

15.4 *American Needle Inc v National Football League*

In *American Needle,* a headwear manufacturer alleged that the NFL clubs' grant of an exclusive 10-year license to manufacture and sell trademarked headwear for all 32 teams to Reebok International, through NFL Properties ("NFLP"), their wholly owned trademark marketing and licensing subsidiary, violated section 1 of the Sherman Act. In defence, the NFL argued that its member clubs function as a

[24] *Chicago Professional Sports Limited Partnership v. NBA* 95 F 3d 593 (7th Cir 1996).

[25] *Chicago Professional Sports Limited Partnership v. NBA* 95 F 3d 593, 599 (7th Cir 1996).

[26] *Chicago Professional Sports Limited Partnership v. NBA* 95 F 3d 593, 606 (7th Cir 1996).

single economic entity in jointly producing NFL football and collectively licensing their intellectual property, which does not constitute the requisite concerted action under section 1. A Chicago federal district court held that "with regard to the facet of their operations respecting exploitation of intellectual property rights, the NFL and its 32 teams are, in the jargon of antitrust law, acting as a single entity."[27] The Seventh Circuit affirmed, concluding that "the record amply establishes that since 1963, the NFL teams have acted as one source of economic power-under the auspices of NFL Properties-to license their intellectual property collectively and to promote NFL football."[28]

A unanimous US Supreme Court reversed the Seventh Circuit and ruled that "the NFL's licensing activities constitute concerted action that is not categorically beyond the coverage of § 1." The Court explained that the key inquiry was whether there was an agreement "amongst separate economic actors pursuing separate economic interests."[29] In other words, "the question is whether the agreement joins together 'independent centers of decisionmaking.'"[30]

Rejecting the NFL's argument that NFLP's trademark licensing decisions constitute unilateral conduct, the Court noted that, although the NFL clubs jointly control NFLP,[31] they have individual economic interests distinct from NFLP. It explained:

> Although NFL teams have common interests such as promoting the NFL brand, they are still separate, profit-maximizing entities, and their interests in licensing team trademarks are not necessarily aligned. Common interests in the NFL brand '*partially* unit[e] the economic interests of the parent firms, but the teams still have distinct, potentially competing interests.[32]

---

[27] *American Needle Inc v New Orleans Louisiana Saints* 496 F Supp 2d 941, 943 (ND Ill 2007).

[28] *American Needle Inc v NFL* 538 F3d 736, 744 (7th Cir 2008). Contrary to the Seventh Circuit, other federal courts appeared unwilling to accept the single entity defence in antitrust litigation challenging centralised league licensing or sale of its clubs' intellectual property rights. See for instance: *Madison Square Garden LP v NHL* US Dist LEXIS 80475, 38–42 (SDNY 2008) (observing, at 40, that most courts have concluded that a professional sports league is not a separate economic entity, but declining "to resolve the question at this juncture" because "arguments advanced by the NHL in favor of single entity status require examining facts outside the pleadings."); *Pecover v. Electronic Arts Inc* 633 F Supp 976, 982 (ND Cal 2009) (even if the single entity defence is "persuasive in the context of [the] NFL's role as a competitor in the entertainment business" because "[an] individual team can offer no entertainment value without the other teams in the league," it is "somewhat less persuasive (to the undersigned, at least) when it comes to licensing NFL team logos on headwear (after all, individual teams could make their own license agreements)."; *Shaw v Dallas Cowboys Football Club Ltd* 1998 US Dist LEXIS 9896, 1–2 (ED Pa 1998), *aff'd on other grounds*, 172 F 3d 299 (3d Cir 1999) (allegation that NFL Sunday Ticket satellite television package of all weekly games broadcast nationwide constitutes an agreement among the NFL's member clubs sufficiently alleges concerted action under section 1 of the Sherman Act).

[29] *American Needle Inc v NFL* 130 S Ct 2201, 2212 (2010).

[30] *American Needle Inc v NFL* 130 S Ct 2201, 2212 (2010).

[31] NFLP is a separate corporation that is independently managed and most of its revenues are distributed to NFL clubs on a pro rata basis.

[32] *American Needle Inc v NFL* 130 S Ct 2201, 2213 (2010).

Because each NFL club is an independently owned and operated business that owns its individual trademarks, the Court concluded:

> To a firm making hats, the Saints and the Colts are two potentially competing suppliers of valuable trademarks. When each NFL team licenses its intellectual property, it is not pursuing the 'common interests of the whole' league but is instead pursuing [its own individual] interests.[33]

Acknowledging that NFL clubs must cooperate to produce and market NFL football, the Supreme Court determined that their joint conduct satisfies section 1 of the Sherman Act's concerted action requirement:

> Any joint venture involves multiple sources of economic power cooperating to produce a product. And for many such ventures, the participation of others is necessary. But that does not mean that necessity of cooperation transforms concerted action into independent action; a nut and a bolt can only operate together, but an agreement between nut and bolt manufacturers is still subject to § 1 analysis. Nor does it mean that once a group of firms agree to produce a joint product, cooperation amongst those firms must be treated as independent conduct. The mere fact that the teams operate jointly in some sense does not mean that they are immune.[34]

The Supreme Court held that the legality of collectively licensing league clubs' trademarks is covered by section 1 of the Sherman Act and "must be judged under the Rule of Reason."[35] The Court recognised that a professional sports league has a "legitimate and important interest" in maintaining competitive balance among its clubs, which is "unquestionably an interest that may well justify a variety of collective decisions made by the teams."[36] It remanded the case for determination of "what role it properly plays in applying the Rule of Reason,"[37] which requires judicial analysis of a restraint's competitive effects in economic terms. Acknowledging that "teams that need to cooperate are not trapped by antitrust law," the Court noted that the "special characteristics" of the sports industry may justify "a host of collective decisions" necessary to make "the entire league successful and profitable"[38] under Rule of Reason analysis.

Although there are reasonable legal and economic arguments on both sides of this issue, the Supreme Court correctly held that a professional sports league comprised of separate, independently owned and operated for-profit member clubs is not a single economic entity immune from section 1 of the Sherman Act as a matter of law, which is consistent with the rulings of the majority of federal lower courts pre-*American Needle*. Although the league's member clubs jointly produce a single product and are economically interdependent, they have diverse economic interests (rather than a complete unity of economic interest), which provide a

---

33 *American Needle Inc v NFL* 130 S Ct 2201, 2213 (2010).

34 *American Needle Inc v NFL* 130 S Ct 2201, 2214 (2010).

35 *American Needle Inc v NFL* 130 S Ct 2201, 2207 (2010).

36 *American Needle Inc v NFL* 130 S Ct 2201, 2217 (2010).

37 *American Needle Inc v NFL* 130 S Ct 2201, 2217 (2010).

38 *American Needle Inc v NFL* 130 S Ct 2201, 2216 (2010).

corresponding incentive to make business decisions reflecting their respective individual self-interests rather than the best interests of the league as a whole. Although there is legitimate concern about subjecting all of the myriad agreements among league clubs to judicial scrutiny under section 1, the difficulty of identifying a principled basis for characterising their collective conduct as that of a single economic entity suggests that being under inclusive in determining the reach of section 1 of the Sherman Act is a greater evil from a consumer welfare perspective. It is better to characterise a lawfully integrated professional sports league governed by separate and independently owned clubs as a joint venture whose alleged collective anti-competitive conduct is subject to section 1 antitrust scrutiny under the Rule of Reason.[39] This will enable courts to use section 1 to invalidate anti-competitive conduct by a professional sports league's member clubs that harms consumers, while permitting them to make predominantly pro-competitive joint decisions that enhance the league's ability to compete in the US entertainment market or do not have any significant anticompetitive market effects (e.g., rules of the game, scheduling of games, the number of teams qualifying for the playoffs, selection of a commissioner).

On the other hand, if a professional sports league is governed by a separate economic entity that wholly owns and controls all of its member clubs,[40] or by an independent company with separate ownership and control from its clubs (similar to the National Association for Stock Car Auto Racing's ("NASCAR's") business model),[41] there would be the requisite complete unity of interest under *American Needle* and *Copperweld* to justify characterising it as a single economic entity.

15.5 Conclusion: Post-*American Needle* Cases and Scholarly Debate

Construing *American Needle* soon after it was decided by the Supreme Court, the United States Court of Appeals for the Third Circuit suggested an agreement

[39] See, by analogy, *Texaco Inc v Dagher* 547 US 1 (2006).

[40] *Fraser v Major League Soccer LLC* 284 F 3d 47, 56 (1st Cir 2002): ("…if ordinary investors decided to set up a company that would own and manage all of the teams in a league, it is hard to see why this arrangement would fall outside *Copperweld's* safe harbor."). See also Werden 2011, 403: ("A professional sports league entirely owned and operated by a single person undoubtedly would be treated as a single economic entity, even though the teams compete on the field of play, and even though the teams have separate identities and fan loyalties.").

[41] See generally Szymanski and Ross 2008, 70–107. However, *American Needle* suggests that affiliated companies such as NASCAR, which sanctions stock car races, and International Speedway Corporation, a partially owned affiliate that owns race tracks, may be capable of conspiring for purposes of section 1 of the Sherman Act, which was an issue raised but not judicially resolved in *Ky Speedway LLC v. NASCAR* 588 F 3d 908 (6th Cir 2009) because of the Sixth Circuit's ruling that section 1 was not violated because the plaintiff had failed to prove that the defendants had reduced competition in the relevant market.

among the Association of Tennis Professionals' ("ATP's") member tournaments regarding the stratification of ATP tennis tournaments is not immune from section 1 scrutiny. The court stated:

> At trial, ATP contended it constitutes a single enterprise, and under *Copperweld,* its internal decisions cannot violate § 1 of the Sherman Act. It asserted each of its tournament members is dependent on the others to produce a common product-a marketable annual professional tennis tour that competes with other forms of entertainment, within and without the sports arena. ATP maintained its members do not compete but instead cooperate to produce the Tour, and its adoption of the Brave New World plan was the core activity of producing this product. For their part, the Federations contended ATP operates in the market for top tier men's professional tennis players, and individual tournaments compete to attract top players. They asserted the Brave New World plan was an agreement unreasonably restraining trade in this alleged market...The agreement among the ATP's tournament members in the Brave New World Plan might have deprived the marketplace of potential competition. Professional sports teams or tournaments always have an interest in obtaining the best players possible. *Brown v. Pro Football, Inc.,* 518 U.S. 231, 116 S.Ct. 2116, 135 L.Ed.2d 521 (1996). The record in this case indicates that the individual tennis tournaments traditionally compete for player talent. An agreement restricting this competition should not necessarily be immune from § 1 scrutiny merely because the tournaments cooperate in various aspects of producing the ATP Tour. "The justification for cooperation is not relevant to whether that cooperation is concerted or independent action." *Am. Needle,* — U.S. —, at —, 130 S.Ct. 2201, —L.Ed.2d —, at —, 2010 WL 2025207, at * 11. The necessity of cooperation does not 'transform[ ] concerted action into independent action.' 'The mere fact that the teams operate jointly in some sense does not mean that they are immune.[42]

In contrast, in *Minnesota Made Hockey Inc v Minnesota Hockey Inc*,[43] a Minnesota federal district court ruled that a statewide amateur hockey governing body and its local associations and their respective directors constitute a single economic entity under *Copperweld*, whose joint conduct is not subject to section 1 of the Sherman Act. Although the court did not cite *American Needle* in its opinion (presumably because the operative facts were dissimilar), its ruling is consistent with this Supreme Court precedent. In *Washington v. National Football League*,[44] a Minnesota federal district court rejected a group of former NFL players' allegations that the NFL's refusal to pay them royalties for the use of their images in game films for promotional purposes violated section 1 of the Sherman Act. Distinguishing *American Needle*'s facts, the court explained: "Here, unlike in *American Needle*, the intellectual property involved is historical football game footage, something that the individual teams do not separately own, and never have separately owned. Rather, the NFL owns the game footage, either alone or in conjunction with the teams involved in the game being filmed." It rejected the plaintiffs' assertion that *American Needle* "determined that the NFL and its teams can 'act in concert for the purpose of marketing their collective intellectual property.'" The court concluded that the

---

[42] *Deutscher Tennis Bund v ATP Tour Inc* 610 F 3d 820, 835–837 (3d Cir 2010).

[43] *Minnesota Made Hockey Inc v Minnesota Hockey Inc* 789 F. Supp 2d 1133 (D Minn 2011).

[44] *Washington v. National Football League* Civil No. 11-3354 (PAM/AJB) (D Minn, 13 June 2012) (unpublished opinion).

"NFL and its teams can conspire to market each teams' individually owned property, but not property the teams and NFL can only collectively own."

Scholarly commentary regarding the post-*American Needle* application of the single entity defence to the joint conduct of US professional sports league clubs outside of the context of intellectual property licensing and other restrictions is divided. One commentator has stated "because differences do exist between the various leagues' structures, *American Needle* should not be read to automatically foreclose the possibility that another league could assert a colorable case for single entity status."[45] Another one has observed: "*American Needle* is unclear… whether a court should treat a league pooling all of the teams' revenues and costs as single economic entity or as a cartel. By stressing the potential for competition, *American Needle* suggests treatment as a cartel, but by focusing on incentives to maximize league profits, the decision suggests single-entity treatment."[46] Another has suggested *American Needle* leaves open the possibility that any "core activity" of a professional sports league (e.g., the rules of the game; equipment, club ownership, club relocation and broadcast restrictions; player restraints)[47] may be effectively immune from section 1 scrutiny. Others, however, assert that *American Needle* "put[s] an end to the argument that a sports league [as currently structured] is a single entity immune from antitrust scrutiny" and "reinforces the need to view sceptically any argument purporting to define a zone of conduct as automatically lawful without regard to its competitive effects."[48]

References

Feder M (2011) Is there life after death for sports league immunity? *American Needle* and beyond. Villanova Sports Entertain Law J 18:407–428

Feldman G (2009) The puzzling persistence of the single-entity argument for sports leagues: American needle and the supreme court's opportunity to reject a flawed defense. Wis Law Rev 4:835–916

Goldman L (1989) Sports, antitrust, and the single entity theory. Tulane Law Rev 63:751–797

Grauer M (1983) Recognition of the national football league as a single entity under section 1 of the Sherman Act: implications of the consumer welfare model. Mich Law Rev 82:1–59

Grow N (2011) *American Needle* and the future of the single entity defense under section one of the Sherman Act. Am Bus Law J 48:449–501

Harry C (2002) NFL owners in a league of their own. *The Orlando Sentinel*, 17 March, C1

Hoffman W (1997) Comment: Dallas' head cowboy emerges victorious in a licensing showdown with the NFL: *National football league properties v. dallas cowboys football club*. Seton Hall J Sports Law 7:255–289

Jacobs M (1991) Professional sports leagues, antitrust, and the single entity theory: a defense of the status quo. Indiana Law J 67:25–58

[45] Grow 2011, 497.

[46] Werden 2011, 404–406.

[47] Keyte 2010, 51–52.

[48] Feder 2011, 428.

Keyte J (2010) *American Needle*: a new quick look for joint ventures. Antitrust 25:48–54
Lazaroff D (1988) The antitrust implications of franchise relocation restrictions in professional sports. Fordham Law Rev 53:157–220
McCann M (2010) American needle v NFL: an opportunity to reshape sports law. Yale Law J 119:726–781
Piraino T (1999) A proposal for the antitrust regulation of professional sports. Boston Univ Law Rev 79:889–957
Roberts G (1984) Sports leagues and the Sherman Act: The use and abuse of section 1 to regulate restraints on intraleague rivalry. UCLA Law Rev 32:219–301
Szymanski S, Ross S (2008) Fans of the world, unite! A (capitalist) manifesto for sports Consumers. Stanford University Press, Palo Alto
Waxman P (2001) *Fraser v. MLS, LLC:* is there a sham exception to the copperweld single entity immunity? Marq Sports Law Rev 12:487–499
Werden G (2011) *American Needle* and the application of the Sherman Act to professional sports leagues. Villanova Sports & Entertain Law J 18:395–406

Chapter 16
Cases T-385/07, T-55/08 and T68/08 *FIFA* and *UEFA v Commission*

Katrien Lefever and An Vermeersch

Abstract Under EU law Member States have the right to designate sporting and cultural events said to be of major importance for broadcast on free-to-air TV channels. Member States have to notify the European Commission of their list of designated events and the Commission then verifies the compatibility of the Member State's list with the relevant provisions of EU law. The United Kingdom under the umbrella of its Broadcasting Act 1996 designated the entire tournament stages of the FIFA World Cup and the UEFA European Football Championships as a "listed event" and thus mandating that every match therein be broadcast on free-to-air TV channels. The EU Commission verified the UK's list. FIFA and UEFA sought to challenge the Commission's decision arguing that there were certain procedural irregularities in the manner in which it had been reached but, more relevantly, in contrast to the approach of other Member States, where only "prime" or "gala" or "knockout" matches were listed, the UK approach unfairly and illegitimately resulted in all matches at the named tournaments being protected as listed events. FIFA and UEFA's challenge was unsuccessful, as was a parallel challenge made against the Commission's verification of Belgium's approach to the TV broadcasting designation of sporting or cultural events of only major importance.

Katrien Lefever, affiliated researcher at the Interdisciplinary Centre for Law and ICT, Faculty of Law, KU Leuven, Belgium and a company lawyer at VMMa (English: Flemish Media Company), the parent company of the first Flemish commercial television station. An Vermeersch, Visiting Professor of Sports Law and Legal Advisor at the cabinet of the Flemish Minister for Sports. The authors are writing in a personal capacity only and their opinion is not necessarily that of their employers.

K. Lefever (✉)
Faculty of Law, Interdisciplinary Centre for Law and ICT, Leuven, KU, Belgium
e-mail: katrien.lefever@vmma.be

A. Vermeersch
Department of Penal Law and Criminology, University of Ghent, Ghent, Belgium
e-mail: An.Vermeersch@ugent.be

J. Anderson (ed.), *Leading Cases in Sports Law*,
ASSER International Sports Law Series, DOI: 10.1007/978-90-6704-909-2_16,

Contents

16.1 Introduction

It is often recognised that sport is characterised by a social dimension promoting a shared sense of belonging and creating social cohesion. However, a necessary pre-condition for the achievement of these goals is that sport is available to and affordable for all citizens. With the development of pay-television, a concern has arisen that sports events could disappear behind a decoder.[1] In order to deal with this issue, Member States can list events of major importance for society which should only be shown in an exclusive way on free-to-air television. Belgium and UK decided to list all matches at the tournament stages of the FIFA World Cup and the UEFA European Football Championships. According to the European Commission, these long lists are compatible with EU law. However, FIFA and UEFA decided to seek annulments of these decisions. In this article, the three General Court's ("GCE") decisions dealing with this question will be dealt with in detail. Furthermore, these decisions will be analysed from the perspective of the public's right to information and the specificity of sport. Finally, the implications for the selling of football media rights will be briefly touched upon.

16.2 The "Listing" of Events of Major Importance for Society

Directive 89/552/EEC is known as the Television without Frontiers ("TWF") Directive.[2] An amendment to the TWF Directive in the mid-1990s introduced a

[1] See generally Iosifidis and Smith 2011.

[2] Directive 89/552/EEC, *The Television without Frontiers Directive* [1989] OJ L 298/23.

"list of major events" mechanism.[3] The newly inserted Article 3a permitted Member States to draw up a list with events, being of major importance for society and that can only be broadcast exclusively on a free-to-air television in order to ensure that a substantial proportion of the public would not be deprived of the possibility of following such events. Currently, this mechanism is included in Article 14 of the Audiovisual Media Services ("AVMS") Directive.[4] So far, only a relatively limited number of Member States have followed this procedure. What follows here is an outline of the key elements, substantive and procedural, to the list of major events mechanism.

16.2.1 Events of Major Importance for Society

The AVMS Directive does not contain a definition of "events of major importance for society". Recitals 49 and 52 of the AVMS Directive provide some guidance in this regard. Events of major importance for society should be outstanding events which are of interest to the general public, such as the Olympic Games, the FIFA World Cup and the UEFA European Football Championships. The events included in the national lists differ from Member State to Member State depending on their national traditions. As a result, the Belgian list—which is in fact a consolidated version of both the "Flemish" and the "Walloon" list—contains the World Cyclo-Cross championship[5]; while the Irish list contains a show jumping event (the Nations Cup at the Dublin horse show)[6] as a major event. As indicated by Weatherhill, there is even a wide variation in connection with events which one would suppose would be of a more or less equally powerful interest.[7] The final

---

[3] Directive 97/36/EC of the European Parliament and of the Council [1997] OJ L 202/60.

[4] Directive 2010/13EU, *Audiovisual Media Services Directive* [2010] OJ L 95/1.

[5] Article 1, section 1(6) of the Order of the Flemish Government of 28 May 2004 establishing the list of events of major importance to society, *Belgian State Gazette*, 19 August 2004 ("Order of the Flemish Government establishing the list of events of major importance to society").

[6] Broadcasting (Major Events Television Coverage) Act 1999 (Designation of Major Events) Order 2003, S.I. 99/2003.

[7] Weatherill 2004, 134.

tournament stages of the FIFA World Cup and UEFA European Football Championships are listed in their entirety in the UK[8] and Belgium,[9] while in Germany[10] and Austria[11] only the final, semi-finals, opening match and matches of the respective national team are listed. In Italy,[12] only the final and those matches involving the *Azzurri* are listed.

16.2.2 Free-to-Air Television Reaching a Substantial Proportion of the Public

According to Article 14(1) of the AVMS Directive, it should be ensured that events of major importance for society will not be broadcast on an exclusive basis with the result that "a substantial proportion of the public" cannot follow those events on "free television". Recital 53 of the AVMS Directive defines free-to-air television as "broadcasting on a channel, either public or commercial, of programmes which are accessible to the public without payment in addition to the modes of funding of broadcasting that are widely prevailing in each Member State (such as licence fee and/or the basic tier subscription fee to a cable network)". It follows that pay-television broadcasters are not categorised as free-to-air television, because the public has to make an additional payment, i.e., an extra subscription fee, to watch the events offered by the pay-television operator. The bar on pay-television providers does not always imply that pay-television operators are not permitted to acquire the exclusive broadcasting rights on those listed events. The aim of the "list of major events" mechanism is to prohibit exclusive coverage on pay-television, and not the acquisition of the broadcasting rights by those pay-television operators.[13]

---

[8] In the UK, the Broadcasting Act 1996 as amended by the Television Broadcasting Regulations 2000 and the Communications Act 2003, requires the independent regulator for the UK communications industry ("Ofcom") to draw up, and from time to time review, a code giving guidance on certain matters relating to the televising of sports and other events of national interest which have been listed by the UK Secretary of State for Culture Media and Sport. The current code is available online at: http://stakeholders.ofcom.org.uk/binaries/broadcast/other-codes/ofcom_code_on_sport.pdf.

[9] Article 1, section 1(2) of the Order of the Flemish Government establishing the list of events of major importance to society.

[10] Section 5(a) of the Interstate Treaty on Broadcasting of 31 August 1991, last amended by the Twelfth Interstate Treaty for Amending the Interstate Treaties of 18 December 2008, *German Federal Law Gazette* 27 March 2009.

[11] Section 1(2) of the Ordinance on events of substantial social interest, *Austrian Federal Law Gazette* II No 305/2001.

[12] Article 2 of Decision No 8/1999 of 9 March 1999, *Italian Official Gazette* No 119 of 24 May 1999, as amended by Decision No 172/1999 of 28 July 1999, *Italian Official Gazette* No 192 of 17 August 1999.

[13] Scheuer and Schoenthal 2008, 414.

Furthermore, the "list of major events" mechanism requires only that "a substantial proportion of the public" have "free" broadcasting access to the listed events. It is therefore left to the individual Member States freely to interpret this concept. In the UK, for example, the listed events must be seen on a television channel accessible to at least 95 % of households.[14] In the Flemish Community "a large part of the population of the Flemish Community is considered to be able to follow an event of major importance to society on free-access television when the event...and can be received by at least 90 % of the population".[15]

16.2.3 Procedure

Article 14(1) of the AVMS Directive holds that if a Member State decides to create a list of major events, it must do so in a clear, transparent manner[16] and with due notification to the Commission.[17] The Commission then has three months in which to verify whether the list is compatible with EU law and publish that verification in the Official Journal of the European Union.[18] The formality of this process (instead of, for example, a letter sent to each Member State by a Commission official, such as Director-General of the Education and Culture DG) is rooted in the fact that the decision on a list's compatibility with EU law can produce legal effects for the Member States and thus is open to challenge before the European Courts.[19]

Currently, eight countries have formally notified their list to the Commission: Austria, Belgium; Finland; France; Germany; Ireland; Italy and the UK.[20] It must be noted that other Member States do also have lists of major events. In the Netherlands, for example, a list is attached to the Dutch Media Decree.[21] However, the list was not sent to the European Commission because initial soundings from

---

14 Section 98(2)(b) of the Broadcasting Act 1996.

15 Article 2 of the Order of the Flemish Government establishing the list of events of major importance to society.

16 So, for instance, in the UK, and for the purpose of fulfilling the statutory duty under section 104 of the Broadcasting Act, the Ofcom list is produced after consultation with broadcasters, sports bodies, the holders of sports rights and other interested parties.

17 Article 14(1) of the AVMS Directive.

18 Article 14(2) of the AVMS Directive.

19 See further Case T-33/01 *Infront WM AG v Commission of the European Communities* [2005] ECR II-5897 and Case C-125/06 P *Commission v Infront WM AG* [2008] ECR I-1457.

20 National measures taken pursuant to Article 14(1) of the AVMS Directive, verified by the Commission for their compatibility with EU law, and published in the Official Journal of the European Union, in accordance with Article 14(2) of the Directive can be found online at http://ec.europa.eu/avpolicy/reg/tvwf/implementation/events_list/index_en.htm.

21 Articles 5.1–5.3 of the Media Act of 29 December 2008, *State Gazette of the Kingdom of the Netherlands* 2008/583 and Articles 18–21 of the Media Decree of 29 December 2008, *State Gazette of the Kingdom of the Netherlands* 2008-585.

Brussels had indicated that the Commission had found the list too lengthy. The major difference between the notified and non-notified lists is that if a Member State notifies its list to the Commission, broadcasters from other Member States have an obligation to comply with the published list irrespective of whether it has drawn up such a list itself, i.e. a principle of mutual recognition operates.[22]

Both Belgium and the UK decided to draw up such a list and formally notify them to the Commission. In its decisions of 16 October 2007 and 25 June 2007, the Commission found, respectively, the lists of the UK and Belgium compatible with EU law.[23] FIFA and UEFA sought to annul the 2007 decisions.

16.3 FIFA and UEFA Versus the "List of Major Events" Mechanism

FIFA[24] and UEFA[25] sought annulments of the Commission's decisions on a number of grounds. These grounds are distilled and discussed as follows.

16.3.1 Prime Matches Versus Non-prime Matches

First and broadly, the sports organisations involved claimed that the European Commission had failed to state reasons for approving the inclusion on the list of major events of all matches, including matches not involving any home nation team in the UEFA European Football Championships or the FIFA World Cup.[26] Although FIFA and UEFA accepted that "prime matches", i.e. games involving

---

[22] On the principle of mutual recognition in broadcasting see further *R v Independent Television Commission, ex parte TV Danmark 1* [2001] UKHL 42; [2001] 1 WLR 74 and Valcke et al. 2010, 296.

[23] Commission decision of 16 October 2007 on the compatibility with Community law of measures taken by the United Kingdom pursuant to Article 3a(1) of Council Directive 89/552/EEC on the coordination of certain provisions laid down by law, regulation or administrative action in Member States concerning the pursuit of television broadcasting activities. [2007] OJ L 295/12; Commission decision of 25 June 2007 on the compatibility with Community law of measures taken by Belgium pursuant to Article 3a(1) of Council Directive 89/552/EEC on the coordination of certain provisions laid down by law, regulation or administrative action in Member States concerning the pursuit of television broadcasting activities. [2007] OJ L 180/24.

[24] Case T-68/08 *FIFA v European Commission* 17 February 2011 and Case T-385/07 *FIFA v European Commission* 17 February 2011.

[25] Case T-55/08 *UEFA v European Commission* 17 February 2011.

[26] Case T-68/08 *FIFA v European Commission* 17 February 2011, para 59; Case T-385/07 *FIFA v European Commission* 17 February 2011, para 64; and Case T-55/08 *UEFA v European Commission* 17 February 2011, para 74.

the national teams[27] should remain on free-to-air television, along with the final, the knock-out rounds and the opening game; "non-prime" matches[28] should be made available for pay-television broadcasters.[29] Although Recital 49 of the AVMS Directive makes specific reference to the FIFA World Cup and the UEFA European Football Championships, both FIFA and UEFA argued that this did not necessarily imply that all the matches in those tournaments must automatically be included on the list, and that, at the very least, the Member States in question should have provided explicit reasoning justifying the all-inclusive nature of their lists.[30] In this regard, FIFA argued that this arbitrary method of composition of the list did not satisfy the requirements of clarity and transparency.[31] So, for example, is a match between Norway and Czech Republic of such cultural or social importance for citizens (other than the Norwegian or Czech people) that it must be broadcast on free-to-air television in the UK or Belgium? In sum, FIFA indicated that in its opinion the Commission had disregarded its obligation to conduct a detailed, as opposed to a superficial or "rubberstamp" review, of the compatibility of the lists with EU law.[32]

The GCE agreed that, although the FIFA World Cup and UEFA European Football Championships are mentioned in Recital 49 of the AVMS Directive, it does not mean that the inclusion of these events as a whole is automatically compatible with EU law.[33] The GCE indicated that the recital implies that "when a Member State includes World Cup matches [or/and EURO matches] in the list it has decided to draw up, it does not need to include in its notification to the Commission specific grounds concerning their nature as an event of major importance for society".[34] Given that the FIFA World Cup and UEFA European Football Championships should be seen as a single event rather than as a series of

---

[27] UEFA labels these matches as "gala" matches, see Case T-55/08 *UEFA v European Commission* 17 February 2011, para 95.

[28] UEFA labels these matches as "non-gala", see Case T-55/08 *UEFA v European Commission* 17 February 2011, para 95.

[29] Case T-68/08 *FIFA v European Commission* 17 February 2011, para 59; Case T-385/07 *FIFA v European Commission* 17 February 2011, para 64; and Case T-55/08 *UEFA v European Commission* 17 February 2011, para 116.

[30] Case T-68/08 *FIFA v European Commission* 17 February 2011, para 59; Case T-385/07 *FIFA v European Commission* 17 February 2011, para 76; and Case T-55/08 *UEFA v European Commission* 17 February 2011, paras 53–54.

[31] Case T-68/08 *FIFA v European Commission* 17 February 2011, paras 79–81 and Case T-385/07 *FIFA v European Commission* 17 February 2011, paras 144–148.

[32] Case T-68/08 *FIFA v European Commission* 17 February 2011, para 60.

[33] Case T-68/08 *FIFA v European Commission* 17 February 2011, para 56; Case T-385/07 *FIFA v European Commission* 17 February 2011, para 60; and Case T-55/08 *UEFA v European Commission* 17 February 2011, para 52.

[34] Case T-68/08 *FIFA v European Commission* 17 February 2011, para 61 and Case T-55/08 *UEFA v European Commission* 17 February 2011, para 53.

individual events divided into "prime" matches and "non-prime" matches,[35] the GCE stated that "there is no valid consideration leading to the conclusion that, in principle, only 'prime' ['gala'] matches may be thus categorised and therefore included in such a list".[36] The GCE even indicated that not all "non-prime" matches must be necessarily and directly of major importance for society in order to be legitimately viewed as a listed event.[37] For example, other "group stage" matches that could have an influence on the fate of the national team in the tournaments in question (such as determining whether the national team might make the knockout phase of the competition and/or even who they might meet at that stage),[38] might because of that "influence" justify inclusion on the list.[39]

The fact that such "non-prime" matches would attract less viewers or that broadcasters might decide not to broadcast those matches did not in the GCE's view necessarily imply that those matches could not be included on the list of major events.[40] Additionally, the GCE stated that the importance of these "non-prime" matches arises "from the simple fact that they are part of the World Cup tournament [EURO tournament], just like other sports for which interest, usually low, is heightened when they take place in the Olympic Games".[41] As a result, the GCE held that the Commission, in not questioning the view that it is not appropriate to distinguish between "prime" and "non-prime" matches for the purpose of determining the importance of the FIFA World Cup and UEFA European Championships for Belgian and UK citizens, did not make any error.[42]

Furthermore, the GCE highlighted that Article 14(1) of the AVMS Directive "does not set out specific matters which must feature in the procedures put in place at national level for the purposes of drawing up the list of events of major

[35] Case T-68/08 *FIFA v European Commission* 17 February 2011, para 72 and Case T-55/08 *UEFA v European Commission* 17 February 2011, para 103.

[36] Case T-68/08 *FIFA v European Commission* 17 February 2011, para 69; Case T-385/07 *FIFA v European Commission* 17 February 2011, para 71; and Case T-55/08 *UEFA v European Commission* 17 February 2011, para 103.

[37] Case T-385/07 *FIFA v European Commission* 17 February 2011, para 102.

[38] Case T-68/08 *FIFA v European Commission* 17 February 2011, para 70; Case T-385/07 *FIFA v European Commission* 17 February 2011, para 72; and Case T-55/08 *UEFA v European Commission* 17 February 2011, para 103.

[39] Case T-68/08 *FIFA v European Commission* 17 February 2011, para 120; Case T-385/07 *FIFA v European Commission* 17 February 2011, para 102; and Case T-55/08 *UEFA v European Commission* 17 February 2011, para 136.

[40] Case T-68/08 *FIFA v European Commission* 17 February 2011, para 123; Case T-385/07 *FIFA v European Commission* 17 February 2011, paras 103 and 105; and Case T-55/08 *UEFA v European Commission* 17 February 2011, para 127.

[41] Case T-68/08 *FIFA v European Commission* 17 February 2011, para 117; Case T-385/07 *FIFA v European Commission* 17 February 2011, para 99; and Case T-55/08 *UEFA v European Commission* 17 February 2011, 124.

[42] Case T-68/08 *FIFA v European Commission* 17 February 2011, para 118; Case T-385/07 *FIFA v European Commission* 17 February 2011, para 100; and Case T-55/08 *UEFA v European Commission* 17 February 2011, para 125.

importance for society. That provision leaves the Member States a margin of discretion for organising the procedures in question as regards their stages, possible consultation of parties concerned and allocation of administrative competence, whilst stating that they must be clear and transparent as a whole". According to the GCE, the procedures should be clear and transparent, in the sense that "they must be based on objective criteria which are known in advance by the parties concerned, so as to prevent the Member States' discretion for deciding on the specific events to include in their lists from being exercised in an arbitrary manner". Although the formulation of specific criteria to assess the importance of a certain event is an important element in order for lists to be drawn up in a transparent manner, the GCE concluded by saying "that the requirement of clarity and transparency does not...oblige the competent national authority to set out the reasons why it did not follow the opinions or observations put forward during the consultation procedure."[43]

16.3.2 Distortion of Competition

The general thrust of the argument here, made principally by UEFA, was that the decisions of the Commission at issue contained no proper analysis of the competition law or the free movement of services implications.[44] On the former, UEFA contended that the Commission should have undertaken a deeper analysis given that the "list of major events" mechanism represents, in effect, a significant intervention in the market for the acquisition of sports rights. On the latter, the applicants, UEFA and FIFA, submitted that the listing mechanism restricted the freedom to provide services by preventing them from licensing foreign broadcasters (and indeed from licensing national audiovisual media providers outside the traditional TV-platform providers) in a manner that was not justified, proportionate or necessary.[45] FIFA also contended that the mechanism at issue restricted freedom of establishment by preventing them from licensing new media entrants who might wish to use premium sports broadcasting to establish themselves in the national markets at issue. In sum, both sports governing bodies submitted that by inter alia depriving them of exclusivity in respect of the exploitation of their broadcasting-related intellectual property

---

[43] Case T-68/08 *FIFA v European Commission* 17 February 2011, paras 84–96; Case T-385/07 *FIFA v European Commission* 17 February 2011, paras 150–158; and Case T-55/08 *UEFA v European Commission* 17 February 2011, paras 87–107.

[44] Note the "pleas in law and main arguments" in the notification of the action brought on 5 February 2008, *UEFA v. Commission*, Case T-55/08, [2008] OJ C 107/28.

[45] See also the "pleas in law and main arguments" in the notification of the action brought on 4 October 2007, *FIFA v Commission*, Case T-385/07 [2007] OJ C 315/41.

rights in the stated tournaments, the "list of major events" mechanism adversely affected their earnings and thus disadvantaged FIFA and UEFA compared to other rights holders.[46]

Although at first instance the idea that this system affects the bidding process and prevents new media operators and pay-television operators from acquiring broadcasting rights and from establishing themselves on the broadcasting market seems reasonable, this way of thinking is not entirely correct. This is because the exclusive rights to listed events may nevertheless still be attributed to the highest bidder, being a free-to-air television, a pay-television operator or even a new media provider not reaching the required penetration rate, or as the GCE put it: "the 'list of major events' mechanism does not prohibit any broadcasters from acquiring the broadcasting rights for the World Cup or EURO, but only provides that some broadcasters are not allowed to broadcast those events on an exclusive basis".[47] The only requisite is that the broadcasters, not fulfilling the two criteria of "free-to-air television" and "reaching a substantial proportion of the public", cannot broadcast those events exclusively and, thus, have to offer or sub-license these rights to free-to-air broadcasters. In this, it must be acknowledged, of course, that the fact that these providers cannot broadcast the stated events exclusively almost certainly reduces their willingness to pay or likely deters them from bidding at all and thus leaving the free-to-air broadcasters to negotiate a lower price.[48] Logically, the GCE recognised that the "list of major events" mechanism affected FIFA's and UEFA's property rights, but that the restriction of such rights may be justified by the social (broadcasting accessibility) function underpinning the listing mechanism.[49]

That being said, the matter of the value of "listed" broadcasting rights, which it would be presumed would always remain below free market value, has not proven as straightforward as the above paragraph might at first suggest. In the UK, for example, the Jockey Club argued that the BBC was placed in an overwhelmingly beneficial position given that both the Grand National and Derby horse races are listed events and that over the last five years the rights to both the Grand National and the Derby have declined steadily in value by nearly 70 %. However, the assumption that this was wholly because of the listed events status of both races, and that its removal would thereby lead to fiercer competition and a higher price for their rights, was undermined by BSkyB, the leading sports subscription provider. BSkyB contended

[46] See, for instance, Case T-68/08 *FIFA v European Commission* 17 February 2011, para 165.

[47] Case T-68/08 *FIFA v European Commission* 17 February 2011, paras 84–96 General Court, Case T-68/08, para 178.

[48] See Craufurd Smith and Bottcher 2002, 126; Weatherill 2004, 136 and Gratton and Solberg 2007, 213.

[49] General Court, Case T-68/08, paras 141–145; General Court, Case T-385/07, paras 137–141; General Court, Case T-55/08, paras 178–182.

that one-off sporting events of whatever magnitude were of much lower priority for them than series of race meetings over a year that enabled them to build up a subscriber base.[50]

Moreover, Kesenne has argued that, given the wider audience "reach" of free-to-air providers, and depending on the demand level and the price advertisers are willing to pay per viewer, free-to-air coverage of sports events could in fact generate more revenues for sports organisations.[51] Not only are advertisers willing to pay more for advertising spots during the commercial breaks, they are also willing to pay more for shirt and board advertising and thus maximising exposure of sport via free-to-air television could increase the popularity of the sport and stadium attendance. Using Formula 1 as an example, the argument is that in order for a pay-television broadcaster to win the exclusive rights to the sport, it would need to offer a significantly higher price than a free-to-air channel, so as to make up for any shortfall in sponsorship revenues associated with its smaller audiences.[52] As late as 2011, the commercial owner of Formula 1, Bernie Ecclestone, was claiming that a shift from free-to-air television to pay-television for F1 would be "suicidal"[53]; nevertheless, one year later and until 2018 in the UK, Sky Sports and the BBC will share F1 rights.[54]

16.3.3 Article 10 of the European Convention on Human Rights

Recital 49 of the AVMS Directive explicitly states that a key element underpinning the "list of major events" mechanism is the protection of the general public's right to information. The principle of freedom of expression and the public's right to information has been enshrined in different documents at the European level and notably Article 10 of the European Convention on Human Rights ("ECHR") and Article 11 of the Charter of Fundamental Rights of the European Union, as well as at the international level pursuant to Article 19 of the Universal Declaration of Human Rights and Article 19 of the International Covenant on Civil and Political Rights.

In 1996, the then chair of the Parliament's Committee on Culture, Youth, Education and Media, Luciana Castellina, was quoted as stating that "watching a football match on television is a human right".[55] Leaving aside the hyperbole of

---

[50] Independent Advisory Panel to the Secretary of State for Culture, Media and Sport 2009, para 76.

[51] See generally Kesenne 2011.

[52] See generally Zeffman 2009.

[53] Sportsbusiness International 2011a.

[54] Sportsbusiness International 2011b. Sky Sports will show every race, qualifying session and practice session live, while the BBC will air half the races live as well as the qualifying and practice sessions from those events.

[55] Lewis and Taylor 2003, 325.

such a statement, the more fundamental question is the material relevance of the right to information, included in Article 10 ECHR, to any legal claims surrounding the broadcasting of "live" or "highlight" or "short news" packages of and reporting on sporting events.[56] There is no doubt that the broadcast of highlights or short news reports of sports events (as included in Article 15 of the AVMS Directive) is protected under Article 10 ECHR. The aim of such short reports about sports events is to provide information about those events for the people unable to watch the live coverage. In short, the right to short news reporting obliges all Member States to ensure the possibility for non-rights holding broadcasters to report about events of high interest to the public which are transmitted on an exclusive basis. Member States must clearly define the modalities and conditions regarding the provision of such short news extracts—compensation arrangements; the maximum length of short extracts; and time limits regarding their transmission. With regard to the compensation arrangements, the Austrian Bundeskommunikationssenat has asked the Court of Justice of the European Union to interpret Article 15(6) of the AVMS Directive, which holds simply that "where compensation is provided for, it shall not exceed the additional costs directly incurred in providing access".[57]

The question is whether Article 15(6) of the AVMS Directive is compatible with the property rights of the broadcaster who purchased the exclusive broadcasting rights and its freedom to conduct business, pursuant to Article 1 of the First Protocol to the ECHR and Articles 16 and 17 of the Charter of the Fundamental Rights of the European Union and Article 1 of the first protocol. This question arose in a dispute between ORF, the Austrian public broadcaster, and Sky Austria, the holder of exclusive broadcasting rights for a number of UEFA European League games. The Austrian broadcasting regulator had allowed ORF to use the Sky satellite signal for making short extracts for news programmes and decided that Sky could not ask for any compensation. This case provides another opportunity for the judges in Luxemburg to give guidance on the interpretation and the application of the right to information in the AVMS Directive. In June 2012, the Advocate General Bot decided that the limitation of the compensation payable by a television channel for the use of short extract of high-interest events to the public, such as football matches, is justified.[58]

Given that live and full coverage exceeds a purely informative objective, in this view, Article 10 ECHR seems only to provide a legal basis to the right to watch highlights of sports events. Arguably, however, the concept of "information" does not only refer to knowledge communicated or received concerning a particular fact or circumstance or to the mere transfer of data. Pointedly, the European Court of

---

[56] See generally Scheuer and Strothmann 2004.

[57] Case C-283/11 Reference for a preliminary ruling from the Bundeskommunikationssenat lodged on 8 June 2011—Sky Österreich GmbH v Österreichischer Rundfunk [2011] OJ C269/25.

[58] Case C-283/11 Sky Österreich GmbH v Österreichischer Rundfunk, Opinion of Advocate General Bot, 12 June 2012.

Human Rights uses a broader definition with regard to the information and the right to information: the right to information embraces everything that can play an important role in the development of a democratic society and the development of the citizens.[59] Can and does sport fulfil such a role in the sense of having the capacity to generate a sense of belonging and a strengthening of national identity? In this vein, full and direct access to sports events, as experienced by a large number of people simultaneously and live,[60] may be seen as a means of promoting civil participation in our democratic society, by enabling citizens to participate fully in public discourse about these events. In other words, is there also an identifiable "political" discourse at play here that might merit enhanced protection by the law?[61] There might be and as Weinstein holds, public discourse (in the sense of discourse in the public interest) is, elementally, discourse on the culture of society.[62] In sum, it is argued that the "live" experience of important sports events contributes to public discourse to such a significant degree that it merits the suggested protection of human rights law.[63]

16.4 Specific Nature of Sport

The question might arise as to why the GCE did not refer to Article 165 TFEU, and in particular to the specific nature of sport. Such a reference could have emphasised the link between the right to information and sport. Admittedly, the actions for annulment were lodged before the entering into force of the Lisbon Treaty. However, the *Bernard* case was also initiated before the entering into force of the Lisbon Treaty and yet, in that case, the CJEU explicitly referred to Article 165 TFEU.[64] The difference between *Bernard* and the proceedings at issue lies in the two different sets of interests that are taken into consideration. The latter cases entail a balancing exercise between free movement and competition rules on the one hand and the right to information on the other hand, whereas the *Bernard* case entailed a balancing exercise between the free movement provisions and the specific nature of sport. In this respect, it seems that the specificity of sport was already taken into account at the moment of drafting the AVMS Directive. By confirming the Commission's finding that both lists were compatible with EU law and by emphasising the discretion of the Member States in this matter, the GCE seems to have taken into account a number of aspects that relate to the specificity

[59] *Handyside v the United Kingdom* (1976) 1 EHRR 737, para 49; ECHR and *Perna v Italy* (2004) 39 EHRR 28, para 39.

[60] See, for example, Saltzman 2000, 2 and Gratton and Solberg 2007, 208.

[61] Barendt 2005, 25–26.

[62] See generally Weinstein 2009, 23–62.

[63] See further Lefever et al. 2010, 396–407.

[64] Case C-325/08 *Bernard* [2010] ECR I-2177, para 40.

of football competitions, such as the influence of non-prime matches on the fate of the national team in these tournaments.

16.5 Conclusion

Sport and television is an interdependent and never ending story. In fact, the next chapter in this story has already begun: in April 2011, FIFA and UEFA decided to appeal the rulings of the GCE.[65] The nature of the appeals is such that these sports governing bodies cannot simply repeat the arguments that were already set out and heard by the GCE and expect the decision to be overturned. They must overcome the high threshold of demonstrating that the GCE either breached procedure or made an error in EU law in their initial ruling or that the GCE lacked competence, e.g. that the GCE erred in law by deeming the football tournaments in question "by nature, a single event". If the CJEU were to overrule the GCE on this matter, non-prime matches during said tournaments could be broadcast on pay-television, though, to reiterate, it must be doubted whether pay-television operators would be willing to pay FIFA or UEFA substantial sums for such one-off and "non-gala" matches. More generally, an overruling of the GCE on this matter would most likely not undermine the "list of major events" regulatory scheme and would, at most, have a cautionary influence both on the Member States' discretion to draft their lists and on the Commission's supervisory role in the verification of said lists. Whatever the CJEU decides, matches involving a Member State's national team will remain "free-to-air". Moreover, FIFA and UEFA have also labelled the semi-finals and finals of their respective tournaments as prime or gala matches. The pay-per-view revolution in the broadcasting of major international football tournaments will not be televised, at least not yet.

References

Barendt E (2005) Freedom of speech. Oxford University Press, Oxford

Craufurd Smith R, Bottcher B (2002) Football and fundamental rights: regulating access to major sporting events on television. Eur Public Law 8:107–133

Gratton C, Solberg HA (2007) The economics of sports broadcasting. Routledge, London

Independent Advisory Panel to the Secretary of State for Culture, Media and Sport (2009) Review of free-to-air listed events. http://webarchive.nationalarchives.gov.uk/+/http:/www.culture.gov.uk/images/consultations/independentpanelreport-to-SoS-Free-to-air-Nov2009.pdf. Accessed on 31 July 2012

---

[65] Case C-201/11 P Appeal brought on 27 April 2011 by UEFA [2011] OJ C 204/30; Case 204/11 P Appeal brought on 27 April 2011 by FIFA [2011] OJ C 232/12 and Case C-205/11 P Appeal brought on 27 April 2011 by FIFA [2011] OJ C 232/13.

Iosifidis P and Smith P (2011) The European television sports rights market: balancing culture and commerce, 20 Years of private television in Europe conference, Brussels, Belgium, 28–29 April. http://openaccess.city.ac.uk/1237. Accessed 31 July 2012

Kesenne S (2011) Private television and sports broadcasting, 20 years of private television in Europe conference, Brussels, Belgium, 28–29 April. http://ideas.repec.org/e/pke26.html. Accessed 31 July 2012

Lefever K (2010) Watching live sport on television: a human right? Eur Hum Rights Law Rev 4:396–407

Lewis A, Taylor J (2003) Sport: law and practice. Butterworths, London

Saltzman R (2000) Television news access to exclusively owned sporting events: a comparative study. Sports Lawyers J 7:1–28

Scheuer A, Schoenthal M (2008) Article 3a TWFD. In: Castendyk O, Dommering E, Scheuer A, Böttcher K (eds) European media law. Kluwer Law International, Alphen aan den Rijn, pp 407–428

Scheuer A and Strothmann P (2004) Sports as reflected in European media law part I. *Iris Plus* (4) Online http://www.obs.coe.int/oea_publ/iris/iris_plus/iplus4_2004.pdf.en. Accessed on 31 July 2012

Sportsbusiness International (2011a) Pay-TV shift for F1 would be 'suicidal', claims Ecclestone, Sportsbusiness, 10 May. www.sportbusiness.com/news/183591/pay-tv-shift-for-f1-would-be-suicidal-claims-ecclestone. Accessed on 31 July 2012

Sportsbusiness International (2011b) Sky Sports and BBC to share F1 rights Sportsbusiness, 29 July. www.sportbusiness.com/news/184058/sky-sports-and-bbc-to-share-f1-rights. Accessed on 31 July 2012

Valcke P et al (2010) The EU regulatory framework applicable to broadcasting. In: Garzaniti L, O'Regan M (eds) Telecommunications, broadcasting and the internet: EU competition law & regulation, 3rd edn. Thomson Sweet & Maxwell, London, pp 263–330

Weatherhill S (2004) Sport as culture in EC law. In: Craufurd Smith R (ed) Culture in European Union law. Oxford University Press, Oxford, pp 113–152

Weinstein J (2009) Extreme speech, public order, and democracy: Lessons from *The Masses*. In: Hare I, Weinstein J (eds) Extreme speech and democracy. Oxford University Press, Oxford, pp 23–62

Zeffman D (2009) The future for broadcast sports and free-to-air events, Westminster Media Forum Keynote Seminar, London, 27 Oct

Chapter 17
Cases C-403/08 and C-429/08 *FA Premier League Ltd and Others v QC Leisure and Others; and Karen Murphy v Media Protection Services Ltd*, 4 Oct 2011

Johan Lindholm and Anastasios Kaburakis

Abstract The FA Premier League ("FAPL") runs Premier League football in England. FAPL's activities include commercially exploiting the associated broadcasting rights. In maximising the value of the broadcasting rights to its member clubs, FAPL grants licences in respect of these rights for live transmission on a territorial basis and for three-year terms. In order to protect the territorial exclusivity of all broadcasters, they each undertake, in their licence agreement with FAPL, not to supply decoding devices that allow their broadcasts to be decrypted for the purpose of being used outside the territory for which they hold the licence. In the UK, certain restaurants and bars began to use foreign decoding devices to access Premier League matches. FAPL took the view that such activities were harmful to its interests because they undermined the exclusivity of the rights granted by licence in a given territory and hence the value of those rights. Consequently, FAPL and others brought, in Case C-403/08, what they consider to be three test cases before the High Court in England and Wales. Two of the actions were against suppliers (QC Leisure, AV Station etc.) to public houses of equipment and satellite decoder cards that enabled the reception of programmes of foreign broadcasters, including NOVA. The third action was brought against the operators of four public houses that screened live Premier League matches by using a foreign decoding device. In Case C-429/08, Ms Murphy, the manager of a public house in Portsmouth, procured a NOVA decoder card to screen Premier League matches. Ms Murphy was subsequently convicted of two offences under the Copyright, Designs and Patents Act 1988. Ms Murphy brought an appeal by way of case stated before the High Court of Justice, taking a position similar to that adopted by QC Leisure. In both proceedings, the High Court in England and Wales

J. Lindholm (✉)
Department of Law, Umeå universitet, SE-901 87 Umeå, Sweden
e-mail: johan.lindholm@jus.umu.se

A. Kaburakis
John Cook School of Business, Saint Louis University, Davis-Shaughnessy Hall, 407 3674 Lindell Blvd, St. Louis, MO 63108, USA
e-mail: kaburakis@slu.edu

J. Anderson (ed.), *Leading Cases in Sports Law*,
ASSER International Sports Law Series, DOI: 10.1007/978-90-6704-909-2_17,

decided to stay proceedings and to refer a series of questions to the CJEU for preliminary ruling. The referred questions, the ruling of the CJEU and its implications are discussed below.

Contents

17.1 Introduction

On 4 October 2011, the Court of Justice of the European Union ("CJEU") delivered a highly anticipated decision in *Murphy*[1] a consolidated case dealing with free movement, competition law and intellectual property issues pertaining to the exploitation of broadcasting rights. For years, UK pub owners such as Karen Murphy, acting in conjunction with equipment providers, circumvented the steep license fees required to commercially display games from the elite level of England's most popular sport, i.e. Premier League football matches ("PL"). These pub owners were able to procure licenses intended for private viewing of PL games in Greece and the decoding equipment necessary to provide their customers with PL games at a fraction of the cost.

In a decision that is likely to reshape broadcast licensing practices in Europe within and beyond sports, the CJEU in *Murphy* examined the practice of media rights holders, such as the FAPL, licensing their rights to broadcasters on a nation-by-nation basis and in principle declared it unlawful within the European Union. Considering how fundamental this practice is to the way that broadcasts are currently licensed, *Murphy* will have a substantial impact on how sports are broadcasted and, by extension, on sport itself. Accordingly, this chapter outlines key elements of the decision and attempts to forecast its potential ramifications for international sport business and media organisations, and most importantly its enduring appeal in the process of sport law development in the area of media rights, in particular intellectual property and competition law.

[1] Cases C-403/08 and C-429/08 *FA Premier League and others v QC Leisure and others; and Karen Murphy v Media Protection Services Ltd*, 4 October 2011.

17.2 Factual Background

The case stemmed from the practices of several pub owners in the UK to circumvent FAPL's licensing scheme that divides and upholds broadcasting rights on a national exclusivity basis. FAPL's primary reason for this scheme is to maximise profits: the public appeal for PL games varies among nations and broadcasting companies, which normally and primarily broadcast only within single nations. These broadcasting companies can charge their customers different fees and are therefore, in turn, able and willing to pay different amounts for the broadcasting rights. By dividing the broadcasting rights along national borders, FAPL is able to maximise the total price of its media rights.[2] The primary means for creating and upholding this national division of markets are the broadcasting agreements between FAPL and the broadcasting company under which the latter is granted an exclusive right to broadcast matches in one nation but undertakes a corresponding duty not to provide access to these broadcasts to viewers in other nations. It is then left to the broadcasting companies to capitalise from this right and fulfil this obligation through their customer agreements.[3]

The UK pub owners in *Murphy* sought to avoid paying between £500 and £1,500 per month that Sky, the exclusive broadcaster of PL matches in Britain, required for a public viewing license.[4] Through the services of intermediaries, such as the co-defendants QC Leisure and AV Station, and by providing false names and addresses, the pub owners were able to purchase Greek private viewing licenses,[5] satellite decoders and decoding cards allowing them to access and display Premiership matches through EPL's Greek broadcasting partner, NOVA, at a fraction of the cost, i.e. approximately £70 per month.

FAPL responded to these practices by filing civil claims in the English courts against the publicans and their enablers, relying on the Copyright, Designs and Patents Act 1988 more specifically its provisions establishing FAPL's general rights under copyright law and a specific provision criminalising the import, sale

[2] Cases C-403/08 and C-429/08 *FA Premier League and others v QC Leisure and others; and Karen Murphy v Media Protection Services Ltd*, 4 October 2011, paras 32–34. It should be noted that EPL invited broadcasters to tender on other territorial basis, including regional or global, but that broadcasting rights were in practice sold on a national basis since broadcasters normally operate on the market of a single market.

[3] Cases C-403/08 and C-429/08 *FA Premier League and others v QC Leisure and others; and Karen Murphy v Media Protection Services Ltd*, 4 October 2011, paras 34–35.

[4] The BSkyB/ESPN-partnership had paid the substantial sum of £1.78 billion for the exclusive UK broadcasting rights from 2010 to 2013.

[5] It is important to note that the remarkably high fees were only set for places of public viewing, whereas the private subscriptions were much more reasonable and closer to individual subscriptions in mainland Europe. Per Cases C-403/08 and C-429/08 *FA Premier League and others v QC Leisure and others; and Karen Murphy v Media Protection Services Ltd*, 4 October 2011, paras 129–130, rights holders may differentiate between public viewing subscriptions and private purposes' viewing. Indeed, the public viewing fees were a considerable revenue-generator for Sky, and partly allowed for the billion-pound FAPL license. See generally Harris 2011.

and use of foreign decoding equipment procured through "dishonest" means.[6] The plaintiffs responded by questioning the compatibility of the licensing scheme and of the British law with European Union law, and namely Articles 56 and 101TFEU—that establish the right to free movement of services and the ban on anti-competitive agreements, respectively—and various EU legislative acts governing intellectual property rights. Uncertain about the proper interpretation of these provisions, the English High Court referred a number of questions for a preliminary ruling by the CJEU.

The full consequences of the Court's lengthy reply to these questions in *Murphy* are yet to be determined. A characteristic of the proceedings is that the parties had manifestly different views on what the law now requires; and this divergence of opinion even extended after the English High Court applied the CJEU's decisions in *Murphy* to the matter at hand.[7] The confusion is hardly surprising considering how *Murphy* turned on the complex relationship of intellectual property, free movement of services and competition law. However, by considering these issues in order below it is possible to make some conclusions regarding the impact of *Murphy* in the long-term.

17.3 Much Ado About Nothing? Copyright and Free Movement of Services

While it is interesting, stimulating and intellectually challenging to apply copyright law and the right to free movement of services to the particular facts in *Murphy*, it is probably not primarily the sections addressing these issues that will have a substantial, long-term impact on sports or most frequently cause lawyers to revisit the judgment. In this, much has been made of the CJEU's conclusion that live sport is not protected under European Union copyright law.[8] However, the conclusion is neither particularly controversial—why would a match as such be the result of a creative process and, if so, who would be its creator?[9]—nor particularly

[6] Sections 297 and 298 of the Copyright, Designs and Patents Act 1988.

[7] On delivery of the judgment in Case C-403/08, the resumption of the hearing of the trial occured on 3 February 2012 in *FA Premier League and others v QC Leisure and others* [2012] EWHC 108 (Ch). On the delivery by the CJEU of its judgment in C-429/08, the resumption of Murphy's appeal occurred on 24 February 2012 in *Murphy v Media Protection Services Ltd* [2012] EWHC 466 (Admin).

[8] Cases C-403/08 and C-429/08 *FA Premier League and others v QC Leisure and others; and Karen Murphy v Media Protection Services Ltd*, 4 October 2011, paras 96 and 98. See generally Szyszczak 2012.

[9] The CJEU pontificates at Cases C-403/08 and C-429/08 *FA Premier League and others v QC Leisure and others; and Karen Murphy v Media Protection Services Ltd*, 4 October 2011, para 96 that "[FAPL] cannot claim copyright in the Premier League matches themselves, as they cannot be classified as works". Two paragraphs later the CJEU declares that football matches are

significant.[10] As Szyszczak points out, right holders can easily create a copyrighted work by branding their feeds with logos or graphics,[11] and then use the ordinary rules under copyright law to pursue unlawful use of that work. This is supported by the English High Court, which confirmed that *Murphy* does not prevent a rights holder from relying upon national copyright law to prevent unauthorised use of the final broadcast to the extent the particular use includes elements protected by copyright.[12] It follows that the FAPL could and probably will ensure that its proprietary marks appear continuously in every conceivable satellite feed originating from a match by way of, simply, embedding its own logos into the transmissions that reach viewers. Put simply, this "marking" of transmissions gives the recipient little scope plausibly to deny the proprietary interests of the copyright owner to the transmissions in question i.e., in effect, the transmissions are "branded".

For the technically minded, the CJEU's conclusions regarding legislative EU acts in the field of copyright law may be of interest. These were, in principle, that unmodified decoders such as those in question are not "illicit devices"[13] and the operation that takes place inside a decoder for the purpose of viewing the feed on a screen does not constitute "reproduction".[14] Of slightly greater general relevance is the CJEU's analysis of the right to free movement of services as expressed in Article 56TFEU. The CJEU began by observing that this provision, rather than the Treaty provision establishing the free movement of goods, was applicable since the singular use for the goods in question, the decoders, was to receive a service.[15] National legislation that thwarts the freedom to provide services by securing legal

(Footnote 9 continued)
"subject to rules of the game, leaving no room for creative freedom for the purposes of copyright".

[10] The CJEU recognised that *domestic* law may deem it appropriate to afford intellectual property protection over such sporting competitions, triggering perhaps cases where national intellectual property laws will conflict with EU Law. Concurrently, the CJEU still allows for EU-wide copyright protection over sections of matches, which refer to select video sequencing, the Premier League Anthem, highlights, and various graphics. And it is exactly for those protectable rights that a public viewing operator needs to seek permission prior to use/public viewing from the right owner, who may approve the expansion of such communication to a new public for a price. See further Cases C-403/08 and C-429/08 *FA Premier League and others v QC Leisure and others; and Karen Murphy v Media Protection Services Ltd*, 4 October 2011, paras 149 and 197.

[11] Szyszczak 2012, 174.

[12] *FA Premier League and others v QC Leisure and others* [2012] EWHC 108 (Ch), paras 56–90.

[13] Cases C-403/08 and C-429/08 *FA Premier League and others v QC Leisure and others; and Karen Murphy v Media Protection Services Ltd*, 4 October 2011, paras 68–74, interpreting Directive 98/84/EC, *Conditional Access Directive* [1998] OJ L 320/54.

[14] Cases C-403/08 and C-429/08 *FA Premier League and others v QC Leisure and others; and Karen Murphy v Media Protection Services Ltd*, 4 October 2011, paras 208–210, interpreting Directive 93/83/EEC, *Satellite Broadcasting Directive* [1993] OJ L 248/15.

[15] Cases C-403/08 and C-429/08 *FA Premier League and others v QC Leisure and others; and Karen Murphy v Media Protection Services Ltd*, 4 October 2011, para 82.

protection over such contractual relations, which exclude foreign service providers from the supply of services in the territory of a Member State, is consistently found in violation of EU law. It follows from established case law that in accordance with the "transmitting state principle", the Member State in which the broadcaster is based is primarily responsible for regulating the broadcast and that the receiving state is in principle forbidden from interfering with the reception of the broadcast.[16] The CJEU did not sway from this course in *Murphy*, declaring the British legislation banning the import of decoding equipment and, by extension, banning individuals in Britain from subscribing to foreign broadcasting services, to be contrary to Article 56TFEU.[17] Much like the conclusion regarding what constitutes a "work" for copyright purposes, this conclusion is hardly surprising.

The enduring relevance of this part of the decision is lessened by the fact that the Treaty provision, as far as we currently know, cannot be relied upon directly against a physical or legal person.[18] That is, an individual in Karen Murphy's situation cannot invoke the free movement of services to challenge either her agreement with the broadcaster or the broadcaster's agreement with the rights holder, which lies at the root of the restrictive practice. However, the fact that such restrictive policies are declared unlawful per Article 56TFEU will in practice have a limited impact as it has no bearing on the Court's conclusion that right holders can actively pursue unauthorised use of protected works.

17.4 Competition Law Limits to Exploitation of Media Rights

Many of the initial responses to *Murphy* focused on the case's aspects concerning the right to free movement of services and copyright law whereas its competition law aspects were undeservedly overlooked.[19] As concluded above, it follows from the CJEU's interpretation of copyright law in *Murphy* that organisers of sporting events have an exclusive right to exploit those events commercially which *inter*

[16] See for example Case 352/85 *Bond van Adverteerders* et al. *v Netherlands* [1988] ECR 2085, paras 21–22 and Case C-288/89 *Stichting Collectieve Antennevoorziening Gouda* et al. *v Commissariaat voor de Media* [1991] ECR I-4007, paras 17–18. *See also* Joined Cases C-34–36/95, Konsumentombudsmannen v. De Agostini et al. [1997] ECR I-3843, paras 28–36 (regarding the protection of the"transmitting state principle" through legislative acts).

[17] Cases C-403/08 and C-429/08 *FA Premier League and others v QC Leisure and others; and Karen Murphy v Media Protection Services Ltd*, 4 October 2011, paras 85–89.

[18] The CJEU has established that an individual can rely upon the free movement of services against a private entity when it "collectively regulates" the market; see Case C-341/05 *Laval un Partneri Ltd v Svenska Byggnadsarbetareförbundet* et al. [2007] ECR I-11767, paras 97–98. It is, however, yet unclear whether Article 56TFEU can also be relied upon in other situations, i.e. whether it enjoys" full horizontal direct effect". See generally Barnard 2010, 234–235.

[19] Szyszczak 2012, 169.

alia includes the rights to copy, rent, lend, perform, show, play and communicate the work.[20] Moreover, under copyright law, the copyright holder may enforce that right against infringement—which occurs if a person commits one of these acts without license by the copyright holder.[21] This conclusion is not affected by the CJEU's analysis of the right to free movement of services described above. However, contrary to how it may appear at first glance, this does not mean that *Murphy* was an outright win for FAPL and other media right holders.

The situation in *Murphy* turned on how the work was "used" in this context and whether this was "authorised" or "unauthorised" for purpose of copyright law. Considering what was stated above, this is a contractual issue that can normally be answered by examining the existence of a proper license. However, that precise matter of FAPL broadcasting licenses to regionally restricted broadcasters turned out to be somewhat more complicated.

To begin with, it must be remembered that multiple license agreements existed: a broadcasting agreement between FAPL and NOVA and a customer agreement between NOVA and its prospective subscriber.[22] This contractual structure is normal business practice and does not regularly complicate the legal analysis but is of great and particular relevance in *Murphy*. The situation in *Murphy* was further complicated by the fact that the identity of the latter licensee was somewhat unclear; Murphy received her license from NOVA using misleading information and acting through an intermediary. It is also questionable whether Murphy's license covered her use; the license with NOVA only covered personal viewing and not public viewing. However, the CJEU paid limited attention to the validity and terms of the consumer license and, instead, considered whether the underlying broadcasting agreement between FAPL and NOVA constituted an anti-competitive agreement contrary to Article 101TFEU.[23] This, in our humble opinion, is the issue in *Murphy* most likely to have a great impact on sports in the long-term. The

---

[20] Note the comments of Hyland 2012, 12: "While the [*Murphy*] ruling has been interpreted by some commentators as being firmly in favour of the defendants, it is probably fairer to say that the copyright component...of the judgment went in FAPL's/licence holders' favour. In essence, following the Court of Justice's ruling, pub owners still require the consent of the rightholder before they broadcast copyright works to customers on their premises."

[21] See, for instance, s16(1) and (2) of the Copyright, Designs and Patents Act 1988, (the national law applicable to the facts in *Murphy*). Moreover, copyright holders may attempt to engage in all-encompassing enforcement action and introduce new means of monitoring potential infringers. This could be pursued via random visits, e.g. by Media Protection Services staff, at places of public accommodation or via contractual agreements with broadcasters, which may be able to introduce GPS technology or other means to identify the decoder receiving the satellite feed, and whether it reaches a location of public viewing or personal use.

[22] Described in Cases C-403/08 and C-429/08 *FA Premier League and others v QC Leisure and others; and Karen Murphy v Media Protection Services Ltd*, 4 October 2011, paras 32–41.

[23] The attention given this matter was "limited" but not "undue" and was mainly down to the manner in which the English High Court of Justice had framed the referred questions referred. See Cases C-403/08 and C-429/08 *FA Premier League and others v QC Leisure and others; and Karen Murphy v Media Protection Services Ltd*, 4 October 2011, para 54. However, it would not have been out of character for the CJEU to take the liberty of addressing the validity and

importance of the competition law section of the judgment is perhaps not immediately obvious to the reader since it is the shortest and least technical.

Applying Article 101TFEU to the situation in *Murphy* is, at least in retrospect, expected as it is the provision primarily capable of setting aside restrictive individual agreements such as those in question[24] The CJEU concluded that exclusive broadcasting licenses are not per se contrary to Article 101.[25] Indeed, the validity of the provision granting exclusive rights was not even called in question.[26] The CJEU did, however, take issue with the closely related provisions obliging broadcasters not to provide their services in other Member States.[27] According to the CJEU, "an agreement which might tend to restore the divisions between national markets is liable to frustrate the Treaty's objective of achieving the integration of those markets through the establishment of a single market [and they] must be regarded, in principle, as agreements whose object is to restrict competition within the meaning of Article 101(1)TFEU."[28] When an agreement, such as FAPL's broadcasting agreements, prevents or limits the supply of services across the national borders of the Member States, it is assumed to have an anticompetitive objective contrary to Article 101TFEU,[29] and the FAPL-aligned parties failed to rebut this assumption.[30]

The CJEU's conclusion that the agreement did not qualify under the exception in Article 101(3)TFEU[31] is hardly surprising. Its broad reference to its analysis on whether the restriction of free movement of services was justified[32] is, however,

(Footnote 23 continued)
interpretation of the consumer contract, notwithstanding that it had not being asked to do so by the referring national court. See further Anderson and Demetriou 2002, 312–314.

[24] To reiterate, Article 56TFEU does not in principle apply to individual agreements.

[25] Cases C-403/08 and C-429/08 *FA Premier League and others v QC Leisure and others; and Karen Murphy v Media Protection Services Ltd*, 4 October 2011, paras 137–138, citing Case 262/81 *Coditel SA* et al. *v Ciné-Vog Films SA* et al. *(Coditel II)* [1982] ECR 3381, para 15 and Article 1(2)(b) of the Satellite Broadcasting Directive.

[26] Cases C-403/08 and C-429/08 *FA Premier League and others v QC Leisure and others; and Karen Murphy v Media Protection Services Ltd*, 4 October 2011, para 141.

[27] Cases C-403/08 and C-429/08 *FA Premier League and others v QC Leisure and others; and Karen Murphy v Media Protection Services Ltd*, 4 October 2011, paras 141–142.

[28] Cases C-403/08 and C-429/08 *FA Premier League and others v QC Leisure and others; and Karen Murphy v Media Protection Services Ltd*, 4 October 2011, para 139, citing Joined Cases C-468/06 to C-478/06 *Sot Lélos kai Sia* et al. *v GlaxoSmithKline AEVE Farmakeftikon Proionton* [2008] ECR I-7139, para 65 and Joined Cases C-501/06 P, C-513/06 P, C-515/06 P and C-519/06 P. *GlaxoSmithKline Services* et al. *v. Commission* et al. [2009] ECR I-9291, paras 59 and 61.

[29] Cases C-403/08 and C-429/08 *FA Premier League and others v QC Leisure and others; and Karen Murphy v Media Protection Services Ltd*, 4 October 2011, para 140.

[30] Cases C-403/08 and C-429/08 *FA Premier League and others v QC Leisure and others; and Karen Murphy v Media Protection Services Ltd*, 4 October 2011, para 143.

[31] Cases C-403/08 and C-429/08 *FA Premier League and others v QC Leisure and others; and Karen Murphy v Media Protection Services Ltd*, 4 October 2011, para 145.

[32] Cases C-403/08 and C-429/08 *FA Premier League and others v QC Leisure and others; and Karen Murphy v Media Protection Services Ltd*, 4 October 2011, paras 105–124 and 145.

somewhat perplexing. Presumably, the CJEU meant that the ultimate objective behind this provision—to maximise FAPL's profits—does not fall within the objectives described in Article 101(3), that it restricts broadcasters more than necessary to attain that objective, or possibly both. Further, the CJEU did not address whether the provision in *Murphy* qualified for the exception from Article 101 for restrictions necessary to achieve "a legitimate objective" that it established in *Wouters*[33] and applied to sporting situations in *Meca-Medina*.[34] However, had it addressed the issue, the CJEU would in all likelihood have concluded that the provision did not qualify for the aforementioned exception, given its conclusion that the measures did not qualify under the rather similar exception to free movement of services[35] Thus, the conclusion of the CJEU in *Murphy* was that the broadcasters' contractual obligation not to provide their services across national borders constituted an indefensible restriction of competition contrary to EU law.[36]

17.5 *Murphy* and the Specificity of Sport

Whether EU law should be applied differently to sports due to the special characteristics of the sector has been a hot topic for quite some time,[37] and it is thus worth addressing whether and, if so, in what way the "specificity of sport" came into play in *Murphy*. Notably, the CJEU in *Murphy* did not consider whether the characteristics of sports could warrant the measures falling outside of Article 101TFEU. The CJEU did, however, address sport's specificity with regard to the application of free movement of services. It is in this context interesting to note that the CJEU Grand Chamber reached a milestone as it marked the second time ever that the CJEU has referred to Article 165(1)TFEU,[38] which after the Lisbon Treaty refers to the "specific nature of sport". The CJEU's reference to Article 165 in the first case, (*Bernard*)[39] was primarily symbolic,[40] and the same can largely be

[33] Case C-309/99 *Wouters* [2002] ECR I-577.

[34] Case C-519/04 P *Meca-Medina* [2006] ECR I-6991, paras 41–42 (more precisely to anti-doping rules), citing Case C-309/99 *Wouters* [2002] ECR I-577, para 97.

[35] Cases C-403/08 and C-429/08 *FA Premier League and others v QC Leisure and others; and Karen Murphy v Media Protection Services Ltd*, 4 October 2011, paras 105–124.

[36] Cases C-403/08 and C-429/08 *FA Premier League and others v QC Leisure and others; and Karen Murphy v Media Protection Services Ltd*, 4 October 2011, para 146.

[37] See generally Parrish and Miettinen 2008.

[38] Cases C-403/08 and C-429/08 *FA Premier League and others v QC Leisure and others; and Karen Murphy v Media Protection Services Ltd*, 4 October 2011, para 101.

[39] Case C-325/08 *Bernard* [2010] ECR I-2177, para 40.

[40] Pijetlovic 2010, 858: (characterising the first utilisation of the Lisbon Treaty-acknowledged EU competency in sport as symbolic and unnecessary, yet significant of an important potential trend to consider the specificity of sport as dispositive ("...could prove just enough to influence the outcome in certain cases...") towards resolution of entangled cases in the sport industry

said for its reference in *Murphy*. The CJEU relied upon the provision to conclude that it is permissible under EU law for Member States to extend legal protection to make possible the commercial exploitation of sporting events through broadcasts. It appears, however, from the judgment that the "unique and original characteristics" of sporting events would allow this even in the absence of the language in Article 165.[41]

Accordingly, and by means of affording intellectual property protection to sport governing bodies, such as the English FA, national legislation may accomplish the goal of Article 165TFEU. In this, however, it must be reiterated that (a) the CJEU recognises that restrictive practices in favour of sport organisations should not go beyond what is necessary to accomplish the goals pursued and (b) in any event the CJEU will assume a position where the balance generally should lean in favour of upholding fundamental EU law principles.[42] Indeed, in *Murphy* the CJEU advised that:

> …the specific subject-matter of the intellectual property does not guarantee the right holders concerned the opportunity to demand the highest possible remuneration [but] must be reasonable in relation to the actual or potential number of persons who enjoy or wish to enjoy the service…and the language version.[43]

The potential audience and interest in sporting competitions have also been a major objective of the Television Without Frontiers Directive's provisions on "outstanding events of major importance for society",[44] which are reserved for free on-air broadcasters rather than pay-per-view subscription providers, and may be arranged by lists of importance for each Member State.[45]

(Footnote 40 continued)
where fundamental principles of EU Law will continue to conflict with sport (business) considerations).

[41] Cases C-403/08 and C-429/08 *FA Premier League and others v QC Leisure and others; and Karen Murphy v Media Protection Services Ltd*, 4 October 2011, paras 100–102.

[42] Cases C-403/08 and C-429/08 *FA Premier League and others v QC Leisure and others; and Karen Murphy v Media Protection Services Ltd*, 4 October 2011, para 115: ("…here such a premium is paid to the right holders concerned in order to guarantee absolute territorial exclusivity…to result in artificial price differences between the partitioned national markets. Such partitioning and such an artificial price difference…are irreconcilable with the fundamental aim of the Treaty, which is completion of the internal market…").

[43] Cases C-403/08 and C-429/08 *FA Premier League and others v QC Leisure and others; and Karen Murphy v Media Protection Services Ltd*, 4 October 2011, paras 108–110.

[44] Directive 89/552/EEC, *The Television without Frontiers Directive* [1989] OJ L 298/23.

[45] Note the discussion at Chap. 16 of this volume.

17.6 Where Do We Go from Here? *Murphy*'s Law

It follows from the CJEU's conclusion that the obligation in the broadcasting agreement not to supply the broadcast in other Member States constitutes a violation of Article 101TFEU,[46] and thus it is automatically void.[47] Because of the fundamental importance that such clauses hold in the current licensing practice, this means that copyright holders such as FAPL must reconsider how they commercially exploit their rights. Thus, while the long-term consequences of *Murphy* are still uncertain, the judgment has changed the conditions under which broadcasting rights to sporting events are commercially exploited and right holders will be forced to respond.[48] In this section, we explore the options legally available to right holders after *Murphy*. The full impact of the case on both the UK market and overall in Europe, as well as international markets, can only be understood through careful economic analysis. One may for example forecast that fees for the UK viewership may dip, while EU-wide negotiations may lead to an increase of rights fees.[49]

The narrower holding of *Murphy*—that organisers of sporting events are pre-empted from commercially exploiting the associated intellectual property rights on a country-by-country basis—will affect such organisers differently. In this regard, three categories of organisers are broadly discernible and *Murphy* affects each differently. First, for "small leagues"—organising competitions with little or no public interest outside the state in which they are held—*Murphy* means little, as they have few economic opportunities for broadcasting their events in other Member States and will accordingly largely lack incentives for dividing up the market. Consequently, it does not affect such organisers negatively if *Murphy* leads to broadcasters attracting a few, foreign subscribers.

Second, "large leagues", for whose events there is extensive public interest in several Member States, have several options. Some of them could largely circumvent the restrictive effects of *Murphy* by self-broadcasting and luring subscribers to their own league and sport-specific channels or nascent Pan-European sport networks as funded by these leagues or with which they would be affiliated.[50] There are, however, very few leagues that attract sufficient public interest to sustain this model and have the considerable resources necessary to invest in infrastructure and staffing. In reality only the Premier League and maybe a handful

---

[46] See generally Cases C-403/08 and C-429/08 *FA Premier League and others v QC Leisure and others; and Karen Murphy v Media Protection Services Ltd*, 4 October 2011, paras 134–144.

[47] See generally Cases C-403/08 and C-429/08 *FA Premier League and others v QC Leisure and others; and Karen Murphy v Media Protection Services Ltd*, 4 October 2011, paras 145–146.

[48] See generally Kaburakis et al. 2012 and Szyszczak 2012.

[49] See further Stothers 2012.

[50] In addition, there is the comparative of the Dutch *Eredivisie*, where the subscription channel is available on every platform on a non-discriminatory basis. In the UK, that would mean a subscription PL TV channel being available on each of the Sky, Virgin, BT Vision, Top Up TV and FreeView platforms.

of other European football leagues[51] could create and sustain a TV, radio or Internet-based media network for subscribers to consider. Moreover, one may see at some point further competition law analysis of ensuing agreements between leagues attempting to fully exploit their attractive sports' products. Alternatively, organisers may find it imprudent to keep licensing to small markets, given the risk of such licenses driving down the fees in larger markets.[52]An alternative for small European markets with limited revenue generation potential would be for "large leagues" to license the foreign language broadcasts evaluating the total subscribers' potential target market.[53] For example, the NOVA license was geared toward Greek subscribers; however, there are approximately eleven million Greeks in Greece, and approximately eight million Greek language speaking residents of countries outside Greece; as a matter of fact NOVA currently affords commentary in both Greek and English).[54]

An alternative that was extensively discussed during the first few weeks subsequent to the decision[55] was that major media conglomerates would bid for EU-wide rights. We believe, however, that this may encounter competition law scrutiny.[56] Absent a sports broadcasting rights' exemption allowing leagues and professional associations to pool broadcasting rights into one outlet or a group of providers, there may be competition law scrutiny forthcoming, for example in the conceivable scenario that selected broadcasters such as Sky/ESPN or Al Jazeera[57] make a strong push to exclude competitors.

Third and finally, there are "medium-size leagues" for whose competitions there is some pan-European interest but it is not sufficiently great to support a pan-European broadcasting model. In their case, one may forecast regional interest packages[58] and possibly the advent of mid-size leagues' media conglomerates of regional focus, as in the case of powerful media partners in each region. Another business model worth considering is the one suggested by the CJEU in *Murphy*:

---

[51] Such as the Bundesliga, Premiera Division/La Liga, Dutch League, Il Campionato, and the French League.

[52] See the blog opinion of Geey 2011.

[53] As suggested by Moody-Stuart 2011.

[54] Note further Demetriou 2011: Demetriou, who represented Karen Murphy in the CJEU case, agreed that there probably would not be a competition law issue to sole licensing according to language market targets and stated: "...what happens at the moment is that Nova provides commentary in both English and Greek. That's why it's so attractive to people like Karen Murphy. I don't think there would be a competition objection to removing that service." It was explained that Murphy held a domestic license with Greek broadcaster Nova as opposed to a commercial one, as commercial licenses in the Greek market required an assessment of the premises in which the license was to be used. This could not be carried out in Murphy's case since her pub was in Southsea, near Portsmouth.

[55] See, for example Geey 2011 and Harris 2011.

[56] Cf Szyszczak 2012.

[57] Note Daily Mail 2011.

[58] For example Balkan leagues, Northern European Leagues, Central or Eastern European Leagues.

rights holders should conduct auctions where broadcasters bid for the right to broadcast and remuneration is based on actual and potential viewers.[59] Such auctions could be for the exclusive pan-European broadcasting rights. However, it may be difficult to find competitive buyers interested in such rights for many works. If the auctioned broadcasting rights were divided on the basis of geographical territory, it is clear from *Murphy* that this would not be lawful, at least if this division were to be enforced vis-à-vis the different broadcasters.

The only suggestion for a lawful division of broadcasting rights given by *Murphy*, and which was made only in passing, is by language version.[60] Thus, rights holders could possibly employ a licensing system lawfully based on language exclusivity. This would somewhat alleviate FAPL's problems, as it would presumably make Karen Murphy less interested in subscribing to the Greek broadcast of Premier League games.[61] Such auctions could also be for non-exclusive broadcasting rights. That could mean a combination of economies of scale[62] or economies of scope.[63] Any loss from the fees' structure for UK broadcasting rights might possibly be recouped through higher fees across the EU, Asia, and America as well. One could also envision the potential movement by the leading clubs in terms of popularity and viewership potential to exploit club-based broadcasting rights and subscription alternatives and current discussions have, for instance, been initiated by Liverpool and Manchester United.[64]

A technical issue that has been mostly missed from the post-October 4th discourse is *Murphy*'s impact on "geo-blocking",[65] that is technology preventing

---

[59] See generally Cases C-403/08 and C-429/08 *FA Premier League and others v QC Leisure and others; and Karen Murphy v Media Protection Services Ltd*, 4 October 2011, paras 112–113.

[60] Cases C-403/08 and C-429/08 *FA Premier League and others v QC Leisure and others; and Karen Murphy v Media Protection Services Ltd*, 4 October 2011, para 110. See also Advocate General Kokott's opinion in *Murphy*, delivered on 3 February 2011, paras 160, 186 and 202.

[61] Naturally, pub owners may subscribe to a foreign-language operator (NOVA provided commentary in both Greek and English), if the price is reasonable, and simply mute the broadcast for their pubs' clientele. Some may even complement the foreign live video feed with live radio broadcast of the same match, if available in their region. Any video-audio discrepancies and signal delays may be well recompensed by the pub manager's savings.

[62] Where, for example, the FAPL might attempt to go for maximisation of European media operators' outreach through regional broadcasters wishing to expand, such as NOVA. Whilst the overall cost of broadcasting fees would initially decrease, the fess might possibly increase progressively to yield a higher profit margin for FAPL.

[63] Where, for example, FAPL and other leagues/sports and entertainment organisations might seek to offer more customised packages, languages' combinations, regular and postseason competitions, different delivery systems, etc. so that the partnership between FAPL and broadcasting networks may lead to attracting more subscribers.

[64] See further Sports Business Daily 2011b. It is useful to note that in the same issue, FAPL club Wigan Athletic Chair Dave Whelan, was quoted commenting on Liverpool discussing the possibility of clubs individually selling overseas television rights: "If this happened, it would lead to the destruction of the Premier League, I have no doubt about that". As quoted in Sports Business Daily 2011a.

[65] One exception has been Szyszczak 2012.

users from certain countries accessing Internet content.[66] Presumably such practices—or, more precisely, the contractual obligation forcing broadcasters to employ geo-blocking—are rendered unlawful according to *Murphy* since they serve to set up the artificial trade barriers and national borders the EU abolished.[67] Finally, it is worth noting that *Murphy* can perhaps be viewed as a win in the short term from a sport fan's perspective, supporting viewers' right to "parallel import" broadcasts. However, most of the possible future business model outlined in this section would in the long term be to consumers' detriment as *Murphy*'s ban on territorial restraints leads rights holders to adopt more restrictive business practices.[68]

17.7 Conclusion

The *Murphy* case tackled many taboos and thus far unresolved legal questions, particularly in the realm of global media and sports organisations' relations, intellectual property rights and competition. The CJEU's reasoning was on some points of law fairly elaborate, leaving comparatively little room for national courts.[69] For the purpose of protecting the internal market, the CJEU interpreted Article 56TFEU in a way severely restricting Member States' ability to discourage "parallel import" of broadcasting services,[70] finding that such restrictions cannot be justified on either intellectual property or sporting interests' grounds. Similarly, under the competition law lens, the CJEU did not engage in an elaborate analysis weighing pro-competitive and anti-competitive effects, instead concluding that compartmentalisation of the internal market for the purpose of maximum exploitation is inherently anti-competitive.

Despite being an unusually long and detailed judgment, *Murphy* leaves many important questions unanswered. UEFA, the film industry, and TV production entities have expressed fears over *Murphy*'s consequences for them as right holders.[71] Right holders in non-Member States who consider promoting their works within the European Union face similar concerns. The most pressing concern for right holders following *Murphy* is that they cannot contractually grant

---

66 See generally Svantesson 2004.

67 See generally Guerrero 2011.

68 Note the comments of Fejø 2012.

69 Consider, alternatively, a more than twenty-year case law history on gambling services and state monopolies, during which the CJEU consistently deferred the most crucial aspects of protectionism and preservation of monopoly power over state-aided gaming operators to national courts. See generally Kaburakis and Rodenberg 2011, 2012.

70 Cases C-403/08 and C-429/08 *FA Premier League and others v QC Leisure and others; and Karen Murphy v Media Protection Services Ltd*, 4 October 2011, paras 90–133 (revolving around the key finding of such legislation as incompatible with EU law in para 125).

71 See Garrett 2011 and White 2011.

broadcasters territorial exclusivity. Some of these questions left by *Murphy* will be answered as rights holders adapt; some will be answered by national courts as they apply the lessons in *Murphy*; and some are for the CJEU to answer in a future case.[72] *Murphy*'s Law will be re-visited.

References

Anderson D, Demetriou M (2002) References to the European Court, 2nd edn. Sweet & Maxwell, London

Barnard C (2010) The substantive law of the EU, 3rd edn. Oxford University Press, Oxford

Daily Mail (2011) Sky face premier league TV rights battle as Al Jazeera ponders rival mega deal, 23 Oct. http://www.dailymail.co.uk/sport/football/article-2052402/Sky-face-Premier-League-TV-rights-battle-Al-Jazeera.html. Accessed 31 July

Demetriou M (2011) Emergency briefing: CJEU ruling on sport, IP & broadcasting rights. World sports law report conference, London, 20 Oct

Fejø J (2012) It's not all about football. In: Derlén M, Lindholm J (eds) Festskrift till Pär Hallström. Iustus, Uppsala, pp 129–140

Garrett S (2011) One football result could be the end for Spooks. The times, 4 Oct

Geey D (2011) 4th October Premier League Broadcasting D-Day. The tomkins times, 22 Sep. http://tomkinstimes.com/2011/09/4th-october-premier-league-broadcasting-d-day/. Accessed 31 July 2012

Guerrero E (2011) Networks in the digital television age: new context, new roles. The case of the Spanish industry. J Span Lang Media 4:102–124

Harris N (2011) Murphy's law: Why the sky isn't about to fall in on the premier league. Sporting intelligence, 3 Oct. http://www.sportingintelligence.com/2011/10/03/murphys-law-why-the-sky-isnt-about-to-fall-in-on-the-premier-league-031004. Accessed 18 Feb 2012

Hyland M (2012) The football association premier league ruling—the Bosman of exclusive broadcasting rights? Commun Law 17:7–13

Kaburakis A, Rodenberg R (2011) European union gambling at the intersection of policy and litigation. J Gambl Bus Econ 5:1–9

Kaburakis A, Rodenberg R (2012) Odds, gambling, law, and strategy in the European union. Bus Law Int 13:63–96

Kaburakis A, Lindholm J, Rodenberg R (2012) British pubs, decoder cards, and the future of intellectual property licensing in the EU after *murphy*. Columbia J Eur Law 18:307–322

Moody-Stuart T (2011) Emergency briefing: CJEU ruling on sport, IP & broadcasting rights. World sports law report conference, London, 20 Oct

Parrish R, Miettinen S (2008) The sporting exception in European Union law. TMC Asser Press, The Hague

Pijetlovic K (2010) Another classic of EU sports jurisprudence: legal implications of *Olympique Lyonnais SASP v Olivier Bernard and Newcastle United FC*. Eur Law Rev 35:857–868

Sports Business Daily (2011a) Liverpool finds little support among EPL clubs for TV rights proposal. http://www.sportsbusinessdaily.com/Daily/Closing-Bell/2011/10/12/ManU-Liverpool-plan.aspx?hl=ManU%20AND%20Liverpool&sc=0. Accessed 31 July 2012

Sports Business Daily (2011b) Liverpool reportedly talked with ManU about television plan before going public, 13 Oct. http://www.sportsbusinessdaily.com/Daily/Issues/2011/10/13/Media/Liverpool.aspx?hl=ManU%20AND%20Liverpool&sc=0. Accessed 31 July 2012

---

[72] A point made consistently in Kaburakis, Lindholm and Rodenberg 2012.

Stothers C (2012) Copyright owners cannot require satellite broadcasters to impose territorial restrictions on the use of decoder cards. J Eur Compet Law Pract 3:265–268

Svantesson D (2004) Geo-location technologies and other means of placing borders on the 'borderless' internet. John Marshall J Comput Inf Law 23:101–139

Szyszczak E (2012) *Karen Murphy*: decoding licences and territorial exclusivity. J Eur Compet Law Pract 3:169–174

White D (2011) What you need to know about the premier league TV ruling. The daily telegraph, 4 Oct. http://www.telegraph.co.uk/sport/football/competitions/premier-league/8807377/What-you-need-to-know-about-the-Premier-League-TV-ruling.html. Accessed 31 July 2012

Chapter 18
R v Amir & Butt [2011] EWCA Civ 2914

Simon Gardiner

Abstract The Court of Appeal's decision opened with the following paragraph: "This is a notorious and essentially simple case." Three men who had the represented Pakistan in test match cricket took bribes. Mohammad Amir and Salman Butt were two of those players. Butt, in his mid-twenties at the material time, was the captain of the Pakistan team which toured Britain during the summer of 2010. Mohammad Amir, in his late teens, was described as "a prodigious young cricket talent with huge potential." The third cricketer was Mohammad Asif. The three cricketers agreed with a fourth man, Mazhar Majeed, who was resident in England and was the agent for Butt and Asif, that "no balls" would be bowled at specific identified moments in a test match against England at Lords which took place at the end of August 2010. As agreed, three "no balls" were bowled, two by Amir and one by Asif, in a betting scam called "spot fixing". The cricketers were corruptly paid for their actions. These events were first revealed in the context of an investigation by a newspaper, the News of the World, into possible corruption in international cricket and the profits to be made by criminals involved in arranging, and gambling on, "spot-fixes". On 16 September 2011, in the Crown Court trial before Cooke J, Amir pleaded guilty to conspiracy to accept corrupt payments and conspiracy to cheat. On 1 November 2011, Butt was convicted by a jury of the same offences. On 3 November they were sentenced as follows: Butt, to two years six months' imprisonment for the first offence and two years' imprisonment for the second, to run concurrently; and Amir, to six months' detention in a young offender institution on each count, to run concurrently. Asif was convicted by the jury on the same day as Butt and was sentenced to one year's imprisonment on each count, to run concurrently. On 16 September 2011, Mazhar Majeed had pleaded guilty to conspiracy to give corrupt payments—that is the corrupt payments accepted by Butt, Amir and Asif—and to conspiracy to cheat. He too was

S. Gardiner (✉)
Leeds Metropolitan University, Cloth Hall Court, Quebec Street, Leeds LS1 2HA, UK
e-mail: s.gardiner@leedsmet.ac.uk

J. Anderson (ed.), *Leading Cases in Sports Law*,
ASSER International Sports Law Series, DOI: 10.1007/978-90-6704-909-2_18,

sentenced on 3 November to two years eight months' imprisonment and 16 months' imprisonment, the sentences to run concurrently. Butt and Amir appealed against sentence. Both appeals were dismissed, as discussed below.

Contents

18.1 Introduction

During the summer of 2010 the Pakistan cricket team played four test matches in England against the England team. In the context of suspicion about members of the Pakistan team having been involved in "match fixing" activities over many years, a journalist with the now defunct newspaper, the *News of the World*, Masher Mahmood, commenced an investigation into suspected corruption. He did so by pretending to be a businessman. He gave himself the identity of "Mohsin Khan" and suggested that he wished to set up a cricket competition in the Middle East. As a result, a number of meetings and telephone calls took place with Mazhar Majeed, an agent of a number of the Pakistan international cricketers. All these communications were carefully recorded.

In mid-August, the two men met at a series of meetings in central London. During the course of the first meeting the question of match fixing was raised. At a subsequent meeting, there was conversation about a variety of different events that might occur or be arranged to occur. Majeed said that he had been doing this with the Pakistan team for about two-and-a-half years. Mahmood asked Majeed to show that the system worked by arranging for the pre-determined bowling of "no balls"[1] during the test match at the Oval cricket ground played between 18 and the 21

[1] The reason that these deliveries are called "no balls" is that the back of the bowler's front foot lands beyond the line marking the crease, which is a line four feet up the pitch from the stumps. Under the rules, a no ball is deemed an illegitimate delivery by the bowler and a run is awarded to the other side and the delivery needs to be bowled again. There are other ways that a delivery by a bowler may be called a no ball but ultimately it is the umpire makes the determination of whether it is a no ball. See generally The Laws of Cricket 2000, Law 24.

August 2010. For this he agreed to pay £10,000. Majeed agreed. However, this did not happened during the match. Subsequently, and the day before the next test match to be played at Lords cricket ground from Thursday 26 August, Mahmood gave Majeed £140,000 in cash. Majeed told Mahmood that three no balls would be bowled on the first day of the Lords Test, and he identified the exact moment when each of the no balls would be bowled. Majeed had extensive communication with the Pakistan team captain, Salman Butt, acting as an intermediary with the bowlers.

On the first morning of the match, a no ball was bowled by Mohammad Amir in accordance with the arrangement i.e., that this no ball would occur on the first ball of the third over. On the sixth ball of the tenth over, a no ball was bowled by Mohammad Asif, again in accordance with the arrangement. However, due to the intervention of bad weather the agreed third no ball could not be bowled on the Thursday. The next day as had been re-arranged, the third no ball was bowled in the third over by Amir. His two pre-determined no balls were exaggerated so as to guarantee the attention of, and the determination as a no ball by, the Umpire. Commentating for TV, the ex-international fast bowler Michael Holding exclaimed: "No ball is the call … how far is that – wow."

On that Saturday police officers went to the Pakistan team hotel near Regent's Park, London. In Butt's room, officers found money including £2,500 in £50 notes which were marked and had come from the bundle of cash paid by Majeed to Mahmood. In Amir's room, police officers found £1,500 in £50 notes which had come from the same bundle of cash. At the home address of Majeed, the police found £50 notes which had come from the same bundle. No money was found in the accommodation occupied by Asif.

Allegations were made in that Sunday's *News of the World* newspaper concerning "spot fixing" against the three Pakistani players, with claims that they were secretly paid deliberately to bowl no balls in order to allow gambling syndicates to make money from betting on them. The world of international cricket was in turmoil. This chapter outlines the two specific procedures that have been applied against the principals in this alleged corruption. First, the three players, Butt, Asif and Amir were charged under Article 2 of the International Cricket Council's Anti-Corruption Code for Players and Player Support Personnel.[2] Initially, this included allegations concerning both the Oval and Lords Test matches between Pakistan and England. However at the disciplinary tribunal hearing in Doha in January 2011, charges concerning the Oval test were dropped and the focus was on the Lord's test, and notably against (a) Butt for instigating the events and (b) Asif's and Amir's purported agreement to bowl three no balls at particular times. The second procedure was a criminal prosecution. The Crown Prosecution Service in England and Wales determined that charges should be brought for

[2] Accessible online at www.icc-cricket.com/rules_and_regulations.php. Accessed 31 July 2012. The International Cricket Council ("ICC") is the sport's world governing body.

conspiracy to cheat and conspiracy to accept corrupt payments against the three players and Majeed.

As stated, this chapter will provide an analysis of these two separate actions, one essentially sporting, the other a legal prosecution that arose in the context to these events. An evaluation of which process works best in engaging with this type of conduct, which is universally acknowledged as striking at the heart of the integrity of sport, will be made. This event will also be located within the context of the wider problem of corruption of sporting competition through match fixing and spot fixing in the past in cricket generally and specifically involving the Pakistan team.

18.2 Context

There have been incidents of match fixing in sport over many years. The true extent of the problem however remains unknown. Using terminology developed in criminology, there is an unknown "dark figure" of match fixing based on suspicions, allegations and undetected incidents. There are reasonably few official determinations or measures of match fixing. Those that do exist come from official investigations by sporting authorities and/or by law enforcement agencies.[3] The common theme is that most elite sporting competitions have complex interstices with the gambling industry. Where a sport becomes tainted with allegations of fixing, fundamental concerns are raised, principally relating to the potential commercial fall out. Where the essential sporting value of "uncertainty of outcome" is compromised, the risk is that core financial stakeholders such as sponsors and media companies may withdraw. Two sports where this problem has been identified internationally have been cricket and tennis.[4] They both share the

[3] See generally Gardiner et al. 2012, Chap. 6.

[4] In May 2008, the International Tennis Federations, the sports' global governing body, commissioned an independent review of the betting-related corruption challenges that faced the game. The comprehensive review concluded that while corruption had not taken a serious hold on the sport, the threat to the game's reputation posed by the huge and ever-increasing sums of money bet on it demanded that swift action be taken to protect the integrity of the game for all stakeholders, from players, support staff and officials through to commercial partners and fans around the word. The establishment of a permanent Tennis Integrity Unit ("TIU") for world tennis was the major recommendation to come out of the independent review, which was entitled "Environmental Review of Integrity in Professional Tennis". In September 2008, the TIU came into being and has a global remit covering the investigation of suspicious betting patterns and allegations of corrupt practice for all professional tennis; enforcement of the stringent rules contained in the Uniform Tennis Anti-Corruption Programme (effective from 1 January 2009) and player education initiatives to ensure all participants in the professional game are fully aware of their responsibilities with regard to potential corruption issues. For further details on the TIU and related codes and programmes see www.tennisintegrityunit.com. Accessed 31 July 2012.

potential problem of players being vulnerable to being influenced to partake in corrupt activity when elite players are "on the road" away from home for significant periods of their professional life and particularly susceptible to external, nefarious manipulation.

What is true is that the opportunities for gambling around sporting events have become generally easier, culturally more acceptable and certainly more sophisticated in the products that are available such as spread betting and on-line betting exchanges. The latter gambling product facilitates person-to-person betting with no traditional bookmaker taking a profit and also allowing the gambler be the bookmaker and make and "lay" bets. In the former, not only is the bet itself but also the size of the stake won or lost determined by events during the sports event. For example, in a cricket match, a bookmaker may make a forecast on the number of runs scored in an over and gamblers bet on whether that prediction is too high or low. Their winnings or losses will correspond with the difference between the runs actually scored and the bookmakers' forecast.

The form of gambling involved here is known as "spot-betting" and is a type of gambling on a market created around the occurrence of a specific event or events that occur during the game e.g., when or against whom will the first corner be conceded in a football match. The focus on manipulation of sporting events has moved from being primarily on the end result of a game ("match fixing"), that is the manipulation of the result of a sporting competition, to the more sophisticated and focused manipulation of an event or occurrence within a match, ("spot fixing"). In this incident, it was the bowling of a number of "no-balls" at pre-determined times during the cricket match which provide the opportunity to illegitimately bet on this specific happening. A range of sports have a myriad of such variables events that can be brought about by a player or players in unison. The sophistication of gambling opportunities available mean that illegitimate bets can be placed around these events and the unpredictability of sporting competition is desecrated.

Although there are different cultural and jurisdictional controls on gambling in countries around the world, these are increasingly difficult to enforce due to the technological nature of gambling, primarily via the internet. The regulation of the gambling industry on the Indian sub-continent—gambling is to a large part prohibited in law—creates a criminal black market, which provides the environment for potential manipulation of matches and betting patterns. Huge amounts of money can be involved. For instance, it in the International Cricket Council's Annual Report, 2004–2005, it was acknowledged by the then Chairman of the ICC Anti-Corruption and Security Unit, Lord Condon, that during each one day international cricket match of India's home series against Pakistan in 2004 around US$500 million changed hands through the illegal betting market.

18.3 It's Just Not Cricket

International cricket has involved suspicions around fixing over the last twenty years or so. National cricket boards brought a number of internal disciplinary cases during the 1990s but the emphasis was on obfuscation and keeping the issue away from the public gaze. A number of these involved cricket in Pakistan. The following is what is now public knowledge about some of these events. From the mid-1990s onwards investigations had taken place in Pakistan, India and Australia concerning allegations of match fixing. A number of international players reported being approached by bookmakers seeking information on issues such as pitch conditions, team selection and current form of players.

During the "World Series" of one-day internationals in Sri Lanka in September 1994, it subsequently transpired that Australian players Mark Waugh and Shane Warne had accepted money from an Indian bookmaker, known to them as "John". Information was provided on a match between Pakistan and Australia in Colombo. In the subsequent series in Pakistan in October 1994, Warne and Tim May later claimed that the Pakistan captain, Salim Malik, approached them offering money if they bowled badly. A subsequent inquiry reported that a Lahore bookmaker had paid a total of US$100,000 to Malik and leg spinner Mushtaq Ahmed to ensure that Australia won a further one-day international later in October 1994. In the match, the Pakistanis, batting second, collapsed dramatically when victory seemed to be easily in their grasp. Warne, Waugh and May waited a number of months before they reported what had happened in Sri Lanka and Pakistan.

In February 1995, after an internal report by the Australian Cricket Board ("ACB"), Waugh was fined a sum of Aus$10,000 and Warne, Aus$8,000. The ICC agreed at the time to the ACB's request to keep the details of the players' actions and penalties confidential. In December 1998, the ACB admitted that it had secretly fined Waugh and Warne in 1995. It stated that both players agreed that they "were stupid and naïve" but denied they gave information concerning team line-ups or tactics. The ACB convened an independent inquiry into any other possible involvement of players headed by former Chairman of the Queensland Criminal Justice Commission, Rob O'Regan (the "O'Regan Inquiry"). In February 1999, the O'Regan Inquiry pronounced no evidence of Australian players' involvement in the practice of match fixing and reported that players had always played to their optimum potential. The O'Regan Inquiry was critical of the ACB's handling of the Waugh/Warne affair.

In March 1995, Salim Malik was sacked as Pakistani captain and, although initially suspended from all first class cricket, was reinstated pending a Pakistan Cricket Board ("PCB") investigation. In October 1995 the inquiry, headed by Justice Fakhruddin Ebrahim concluded that Malik had no case to answer and stated that the allegations made by Waugh, Warne and May were concocted. In April 1997, the Pakistan international Amil Sohail was banned from international cricket by a PCB disciplinary committee for allegations he had made against fellow team mates concerning match fixing. It seems that in the world of cricket, whistle blowing has not been encouraged.[5] In August 1998, a further PCB appointed panel headed by Justice Ijaz Yousuf investigated match fixing and concluded that the conduct of Malik, Wasim Akram and Ijaz Ahmed had been suspicious. It recommended a further detailed investigation to take place. A new government initiated a commission of inquiry headed by Lahore High Court Judge, Malik Mohammad Qayyum (the "Qayyum Inquiry"). In October 1998, Mark Taylor, the Australian captain and Mark Waugh gave evidence to the commission. In October 1999, the Qayyum Inquiry was concluded and the findings handed to the Pakistani Government.

For the next six months or so immense (media-led) pressure came upon the PCB to publish the Qayyum Inquiry and this finally happened in late May 2000. Judge Qayyum had conducted the inquiry from September 1998 to October 1999 and about 70 players, officials and alleged bookies testified. The Qayyum Inquiry's finding was that there was neither planned betting nor match fixing as a whole by the players of the Pakistan cricket team. However, doubt, of varying intensity, was cast on the integrity of some members of the team. Judge Qayyum's main recommendation was a life ban on former captain Salim Malik:

> In the light of evidence to support allegations made by Shane Warne and Mark Waugh, the commission recommends that a life ban be imposed on Salim Malik and he be not allowed to play cricket at any level... He should not be allowed to even associate himself with any cricketing affairs as he may be able to influence the new generation.[6]

It was recommended that former captain Wasim Akram be fined US$6,000 with the Qayyum Inquiry observing: "He cannot be said to be above suspicion. It is, therefore, recommended that he be censured and be kept under strict vigilance".[7] In the end, Wasim Akram was given the benefit of the doubt by the authorities and suffered no sanction.

The above notwithstanding, it was not until after the well-publicised Conjé affair in 2000, that the general sporting public became cognizance of the fact that there was a real and identifiable problem. The then South Africa captain Hansie Cronjé admitted taking money for match fixing during his country's series against India in March 2000 (the "Cronjé Affair").[8] The Cronjé Affair highlighted, particularly in the sport's English speaking countries, the problems facing international cricket. The Qayyum Inquiry highlighted that in parts of the international

---

[5] In yet another example an investigation by a magazine in India called *Outlook* published revelations made in June 1997 by former Indian international Manoj Prabhakar concerning match fixing and Indian players. The Board of Control for Cricket in India ("BCCI") asked the former Chief Justice of India, Mr YV Chandrachud, to conduct a wide-ranging inquiry. In November 1997, he concluded his investigation. His views were not publicly released for a further two-and-a-half years. He revealed that, although there is a great deal of cricket-related betting occurring in India, his investigation had failed to find that any Indian player or official has been involved in betting activities. For further background see generally Magazine 2000.

[6] Qayyum Inquiry 2000, para 61.

[7] Qayyum Inquiry 2000, para 11.

[8] For a recent review of the Cronjé Affair see Chapman 2012.

cricket world, in this case Pakistan, the problem was in fact chronic and long-standing. The ICC recognised it had a serious problem relating to the perceived integrity of international cricket and in late June 2000 former Commissioner of the London Metropolitan Police, Sir Paul Condon (now Lord Condon), became the head of the ICC's new anti-corruption unit (now the Anti-Corruption and Security Unit, "ACSU"), with a brief to investigate match fixing allegations worldwide. It published an Interim Report (on Corruption in International Cricket) in April 2001 (the "Condon Report").[9]

In the intervening years between the Cronjé Affair and the 2010 events, there have been a number of investigations by the ACSU leading to bans for players. The dominant rhetoric concerning corrupt activities within both domestic and international professional cricket has been that the problem is under control but there continues to be a need to be vigilant. The ICC has stressed that the problem is not solely sporting in nature and that there is also a need for increasingly extensive criminal provisions to engage with an activity that has close connections to organised crime and money laundering.[10] A number of investigations and disciplinary actions have been completed by the ACSU.[11] However, concern and suspicion has continued within international cricket as to match manipulation and connections to illegal gambling and organised crime. It is also clear that domestic professional cricket is vulnerable, as illustrated by the recent criminal conviction and custodial sentence for ex-Essex player Mervyn Westfield for conspiracy to defraud by allowing the scoring of a certain number of runs off his bowling during a one-day match between Durham and Essex in September 2009.[12]

18.4 The Independent Tribunal Determination, Doha, January 2010

On foot of what had occurred during the British summer of 2010, Butt, Asif and Amir were charged under a variety of provisions under Article 2 of the ICC Anti-Corruption Code for Players and Player Support Personnel, notably:

> Article 2.1.1 - Fixing or contriving in any way or otherwise influencing improperly, or being a party to any effort to fix or contrive in any way or otherwise influence improperly, the result, progress, conduct or any other aspect of any International Match or ICC Event....

---

[9] The Condon Report can be read in full at www.icc-cricket.com/anti_corruption/condon-report.php. Accessed 31 July 2012.

[10] See generally Gardiner and Naidoo 2007.

[11] For example, Kenya player, Maurice Odumbe, was banned for five years in 2005 and a West Indies player was banned for two years in 2007.

[12] See Wilson 2012.

> Article 2.4.2 - Failing to disclose to the ACSU (without undue delay) full details of any approaches or invitations received by the Player or Player Support Personnel to engage in conduct that would amount to a breach of the Anti-Corruption Code.

The disciplinary hearing which took place in Doha between 6 and 11 January 2011 under the chairmanship of Michael Beloff QC used the nomenclature of being "an independent international arbitral" tribunal ("the Tribunal"). The 100 pages or so of the Tribunal's Determination were released (in redacted form) on 5 February 2011.[13] The functions of the Tribunal were articulated clearly in that "jurisdiction extends only to determining whether there have been breaches of the [ICC Anti-Corruption] Code and in relation to the particular charges".[14] The media speculation surrounding the players and even the fact that they faced criminal charges in Britain at the time, were not, the Tribunal observed, to distract it from the focus and terms of reference of its investigation:

> ...as an independent international arbitral tribunal, we approach the evidence without any predisposition and *"pay no heed to media hyperbole"* as it was put in *N.J.Y.W. v FINA* CAS 98/208 para 8. The residue of previous enquiries in relation to match-fixing by other Pakistani cricketers, aggravated by unsubstantiated rumour, has played no part at all in our deliberations. The decision of the Tribunal is based solely on the evidence placed before us.[15]

In addition, the Tribunal noted that not only it would carry out a careful scrutiny of the evidence but also that any determination on the liability of each player under the ICC Anti-Corruption Code for Players and Player Support Personnel would be done with "the required degree of certainty".[16] The ICC plainly had the burden of proof, but it was however not so certain what was the relevant standard of proof. Article 3 of the ICC Anti-Corruption Code for Players and Player Support Personnel indicated that the Tribunal must be:

> ...comfortably satisfied bearing in mind the seriousness of the allegation that is being made, that the alleged offence has been committed. This standard of proof in all cases shall be determined on a sliding scale from, at a minimum, a mere balance of probability (for the least serious offence) up to proof beyond a reasonable doubt (for the most serious offences).

Given the gravity of the charges and the implications for the players, the Tribunal considered it appropriate to adopt the criminal standard of proof i.e., beyond reasonable doubt.[17] The Tribunal explained:

---

[13] ICC Independent Tribunal's Determination 2011.

[14] ICC Independent Tribunal's Determination 2011, para 15 and citing CAS 98/211 *B v FINA*, para 57. The chair of the ICC Tribunal had also been an arbitrator on *B v FINA*, which itself discussed fully at Chap. 11 of this volume.

[15] ICC Independent Tribunal's Determination 2011, para 16.

[16] ICC Independent Tribunal's Determination 2011, para 20.

[17] On the standard of proof used in sports disciplinary procedures from (typically) the balance of probabilities; to the comfortable satisfaction approach (found in doping cases heard under the

> While a lesser standard might in principle be utilised if the charges were only of non-disclosure of another's wrongdoing, in this case the linkage between the charges [in effect, charges of conspiracy] makes such dissection unfruitful.[18]

As to what constituted "beyond reasonable doubt" the Tribunal stated that it found useful guidance in the dictum of an English case from the mid-1940s where Denning J spoke about a degree of cogency that, although not needing to reach "certainty", must nevertheless "carry a high degree of probability".[19]

The ICC Anti-Corruption Code for Players and Player Support Personnel provides that the consideration of evidence in the tribunal should not be "bound by judicial rules governing the admissibility of evidence… facts relating to an offence … may be established by any reliable means including admissions".[20] The Tribunal stressed that evidence would be evaluated on the basis of "weight rather than admissibility".[21] This therefore provided an inclusive approach to the available evidence, including circumstantial evidence, and the Tribunal found support for this approach in other comparable cases before CAS.[22] The actual evidential basis of the ICC's investigation was founded largely on the video and tape recordings made by the *News of the World* journalist Mazhar Mahmood. This was supplemented by the transcripts of the subsequent interviews with the London Metropolitan Police and the records from the various phone calls and texts between the Majeed and the three cricketers. TV coverage of the no balls was reviewed.

The bulk of the deliberation focused on the testing of the evidence presented against the three players and including discussions about the nature of the no balls and the alleged contrivance between Majeed and the players. What was established immediately was that Majeed's knowledge of the timing of the no balls was based on insider knowledge and not coincidence or as the Tribunal termed his "unique prophetic gifts".[23] In fact, the likelihood of a guesstimate in this instance was calculated at odds of 1.5 million to one. The Tribunal was clear that in "a choice between fluke or fix"—it was clear that there was a fix.[24]

(Footnote 17 continued)
World Anti-doping Code); to beyond a reasonable doubt, see generally Lewis and Taylor 2008, 75.

[18] ICC Independent Tribunal's Determination 2011, para 26.

[19] ICC Independent Tribunal's Determination 2011, para 27 citing *Miller v Minister of Pensions* [1947] 2 All ER 372, 373, Denning J. It must be noted that pursuant to Article 11.5, the ICC Anti-Corruption Code for Players and Player Support Personnel is generally governed by and construed in accordance with English law.

[20] ICC Anti-Corruption Code for Players and Player Support Personnel, Article 3.2.

[21] ICC Independent Tribunal's Determination 2011, para 29. It followed that evidence given directly would be weighted heavier that hearsay evidence, though the latter would remain admissible.

[22] See, for instance, CAS 98/211 *B v FINA*, para 57.

[23] ICC Independent Tribunal's Determination 2011, para 39.

[24] ICC Independent Tribunal's Determination 2011, paras 36–41.

All three players denied liability to the charges. The explanations of the players as far as the ability of Majeed to predict the three no balls and the timing of the incidents were somewhat contradictory. Butt accepted that Majeed must have had insider information but that it did not come from him. Amir's only explanation was 'fortuity' on Majeed's part. Asif also accepted Majeed must have possessed insider information but that it came from Butt.

In February 2011, the Tribunal findings were announced and a written award or "determination" published.[25] All three players were found liable. Butt was found liable under Articles 2.4.2 and 2.1.1 of the ICC Anti-Corruption Code for Players and Player Support Personnel. He was identified as the instigator of the corrupt incidents. Asif and Amir were found liable under Article 2.1.1 only. Essentially the players were found guilty of "spot fixing" in relation to the three no balls bowled at Lords. Butt was banned from cricket for ten years; five were suspended on condition that he committed no further breach of the ICC's Anti-Corruption Code for Players and Player Support Personnel and that he participated in programmes of public education and rehabilitation under the auspices of the Pakistan Cricket Board. Asif was banned for seven years with two suspended on the same basis. Amir was banned from cricket for five years, of which two were suspended. The nature of the bans is that the cricketers cannot play or coach in any form of international, first-class or club cricket anywhere in the world. Considerations were made concerning Amir's youth and immaturity (he was eighteen at the time), but his five-year ban was justified under the ICC Anti-Corruption Code for Players and Player Support Personnel as not being "so severe as in his case to take it into the realms of gross disproportion or oppression such as might enable us to misapply the Code".[26] The Tribunal was concerned however that the lack of discretion in imposing a minimum five-year ban on a finding of liability under the ICC's Anti-Corruption Code could lead to cases "where a minimum 5 year ban would be palpably unfair".[27]

18.5 Trial, Southwark Crown Court, London, October 2011

The protagonists in this "spot fixing" affair also faced a criminal trial with a judge and jury. The Crown Prosecution Service in the UK ("CPS") determined that sufficient evidence existed to sustain charges (against cricketers Butt, Asif, Amir and agent Majeed) for conspiracy to cheat at gambling and conspiracy to accept corrupt payments connected to offences under the UK Gambling Act 2005 and

[25] The ICC Independent Tribunal's Determination was not available in the UK in expectancy of the criminal trial and was only available on the ICC website from January 2012 onwards.

[26] ICC Independent Tribunal's Determination 2011, para 237.

[27] ICC Independent Tribunal's Determination 2011, para 242.

other provisions.[28] The prosecution case was based on the newspaper revelations and the police evidence accumulated through the interviews and searches carried out with the defendants together with the evidence complied by the ICC. In considering whether to exercise its prosecutorial discretion, the CPS utilises a two-part test: first, is there enough evidence to provide a "realistic prospect of conviction" against each defendant on each charge ("the evidential test"); and second, whether the prosecution is needed in the public interest ("the public interest test"). Both parts of the test would appear to have been straightforwardly fulfilled and the fact that the three cricketers were awarded playing bans by the ICC's Independent Tribunal was strongly persuasive particularly in the context of the standard of proof used in Doha.

Butt and Asif pleaded not guilty—Amir and Majeed pleaded guilty at an early stage before the trial. Butt was convicted of conspiracy to accept corrupt payments and conspiracy to cheat of the same offences and sentenced to two years six months imprisonment for the first offence and two years imprisonment for the second, to run concurrently. Asif was convicted and sentenced to one year's imprisonment on each count, to run concurrently. In the context of his guilty plea, Amir was sentenced to six months' detention in a young offender institution on each count, to run concurrently. Majeed pleaded guilty to conspiracy to give corrupt payments—that is the corrupt payments accepted by Butt, Amir and Asif—and to conspiracy to cheat. He was sentenced to two years eight months' imprisonment on the first count and 16 months' imprisonment on the second count, the sentences to run concurrently. All three players and Majeed were ordered to make contributions to the costs of the prosecution.

The judge at Southwark Crown Court, Mr Justice Cooke, somewhat unusually, published written "Sentencing Remarks" to substantiate the sentences given to the defendants. Cooke J was unambiguously of the view that Majeed, as the initiator of the fix, and Butt as captain, were central to the conspiracy. They had had a lengthy relationship, one, which the Cooke J highlighted, was likely to have involved previous corrupt activities. Speaking directly on Butt, Cooke J commented:

> You bear the major responsibility for the corrupt activities, along with Majeed. The evidence of the text exchange between you and Majeed in the West Indies in May 2010 shows your involvement in such activities outside the scope of the period covered by the indictment.[29]

---

[28] In the criminal law of England and Wales, conspiracy to commit an offence is defined under section 1 of the Criminal Law Act 1977. Section 3 of that Act specifies that the maximum sentence for an offence also applies to a conspiracy to commit that offence. Obtaining and accepting corrupt payments is an offence contrary to section 1 of the Prevention of Corruption Act 1906. It carries a maximum sentence of seven years' imprisonment and/or an unlimited fine at the Crown Court. Cheating is an offence contrary to section 42 of the Gambling Act 2005. It carries a maximum sentence of two years' imprisonment and/or an unlimited fine at the Crown Court.

[29] Sentencing Remarks of Mr Justice Cooke 2011, para 20.

Further, Butt's role in including and encouraging the other two players to participate was highlighted by Cooke J: "Not only were you involved but you involved others and abused your position as captain and leader in doing so, bringing to bear your considerable influence on Amir at the very least."[30]

This "undue influence" by Butt over the other players, particularly Amir who was eighteen and new to the Pakistan side, can be compared with the co-conspirators who Hansie Cronjé chose to include within his match fixing plans, notably Herschel Gibbs and Henry Williams. These players were the non-white players in the South African side who were likely to be the least empowered to resist this inducement. Asif and Amir were included as they were bowlers able to bowl the required no balls. Amir was plainly particularly susceptible to such an approach.

18.6 Court of Appeal, Criminal Division, London, November 2011

There were appeals to the Court of Appeal Criminal Division as far as the length of sentence by both Butt and Amir. Mohammad Asif did not appeal and was released in May 2012 after serving six months of his 12 month prison term. The Lord Chief Justice (Judge J) as part of a three-person court delivered judgment. The conclusion was that Mr Justice Cooke at the trial had provided a clear and detailed justification of the relative sentences the two should receive. The Court of Appeal agreed that Butt was clearly:

> ...the orchestrator of the corrupt activity by the three players. Because of his status as the captain, with many advantages which the other two cricketers lacked in the context of education and so on, he was the most culpable of the three. He was directly involved with Majeed and, more important, he had involved Amir. Butt was undoubtedly the most deeply involved of these cricketers. He was the captain and a malign influence on both Amir and Asif. Without him the corruption would not have occurred. When there was the faintest whiff of corruption, his duty as Captain was to step in, to stop it, and to see that the young members of his team in particular, but every member of his team, was helped to resist it. Without him the corruption could not have occurred. The judge said that he had orchestrated it. The judge was fully entitled to reach that conclusion.[31]

Butt's appeal was dismissed. In June 2012, Butt was freed seven months into his 30 month prison sentence and immediately returned to Pakistan. He was most likely released early under the UK government's early prisoner release scheme which for foreign nationals usually involves them agreeing both to be formally deported and not to return to the UK for 10 years.[32]

---

30 Sentencing Remarks of Mr Justice Cooke 2011, para 24.

31 *R v Amir & Butt* [2011] EWCA Civ 2914, paras 28 and 33.

32 See Hoult 2012.

Amir's sentence was more troubling for the Court of Appeal (it must be remembered that the ICC Tribunal expressed similar reservations in its comments on its lack of sentencing discretion to vary the minimum five-year playing ban). At the trial hearing, Amir's counsel had argued that "significant punishment had already been imposed on Amir by the ICC decision, given that he was on the threshold of his career."[33] Indeed, Amir's counsel made a strong pitch in mitigation of sentence drawing the trial judge's attention to the "difficulties of [Amir's] background, his youth, his lack of experience, his naivety, and the fact that as an impressionable young man he would have come under the influence…of his Captain."[34] Further, in the related written submissions of mitigation to the trial judge emphasis was placed by counsel on the length of Amir's involvement in the conspiracy, the circumstances in which it all came about and the fact that Amir had "courageously" (in the context of the intimidation and duress he must have been under) pleaded guilty. Accordingly, Amir's counsel concluded that "the custodial sentence was wrong in principle; alternatively, if a custodial sentence was appropriate, this was an exceptional case in which the sentence should be suspended."[35]

The Lord Chief Justice again thoroughly reviewed the trial judge's reasoning statement in this specific regard and commended it by observing:

> Although Amir's situation is much less culpable, try as we might we cannot reach the conclusion that his culpability was any more than reduced. It was not extinguished. He was young and open to the malign influence exerted by Butt. However, he can have been in no doubt about the risks, the dangers and the problems of corrupt approaches and how they should be dealt with. That was an elementary part of his education as a potential Test cricketer. He was not so young that he did not fully appreciate what he was doing. He appreciated perfectly well that he was responsible for delivering the two no balls at the crucial moments. Indeed, he made absolutely sure that there was no way the umpire could miss the no balls that he bowled. No reluctance was apparent then, and he happily took his financial reward for what he had done. Thereafter, he fully contested the allegation before the ICC when all this came to light, before he eventually and courageously accepted that he was criminally involved in the corrupt processes.[36]

The Lord Chief Justice then went on to make remarks which go to the heart of current concerns about spot-fixing in sport.

> This prodigious talent has been lost to cricket for some years. The reality is that if he cannot play cricket at any level for some years, his talent may be irreparably damaged. That is his own loss and cricket will be the poorer for the loss. But in the long term the game would be utterly impoverished if the court failed to make it clear that conduct like

[33] *R v Amir & Butt* [2011] EWCA Civ 2914, para 31.

[34] *R v Amir & Butt* [2011] EWCA Civ 2914, para 31.

[35] *R v Amir & Butt* [2011] EWCA Civ 2914, para 31.

[36] *R v Amir & Butt* [2011] EWCA Civ 2914, para 34.

> this is not simply a matter of breaking the rules of the game and therefore subject to internal regulation and discipline by the ICC, but that it is also criminal conduct of a very serious kind which must be marked with a criminal sanction.[37]

In sum, and even allowing for all the matters of personal mitigation, the Court of Appeal agreed that "a short, immediate prison sentence was necessary and appropriate".[38] Amir was released from a young offenders' institution on 1 February 2012 after serving half of his sentence.

18.7 Conclusion

Amir's playing ban and custodial sentence are perhaps the most troubling element of these events. It will be of interest that if an appeal is made to CAS regarding the lengthy ICC-imposed playing bans on the players—and in January 2012 Asif asserted that he would lodge an appeal to CAS—issues of proportionality will no doubt be examined.[39] More generally, Amir's criminal sentence seems to embody an unmistakable retributive element together with a strong deterrent message to similar young cricketers. It would be wrong to identify him as an "innocent cheater",[40] but equally and rightly he was characterised as naïve and vulnerable to manipulation. In the technical language of the law, Amir was subject to "undue influence" from others but not to an extent that it would amount to a defence of duress.[41] The sadness is that a potentially great sporting career appears prematurely ended.

More generally there would seem to be no "double jeopardy" concerns that the players were wrongly subject to both the internal sporting disciplinary sporting jurisdiction and the legal jurisdiction of the criminal justice system. Clearly, and in addition to whatever sporting punishment results, there is an accepted public interest in prosecuting evident and conspiratorial criminal fraud. Moreover, the ICC Tribunal's determination was underpinned by the authority of its membership: three experienced individuals, the Honourable Michael Beloff QC, Mr Justice Albie Sachs and Mr Sharad Rae, all with considerable experiences as both "sporting judges" and adjudicators in wider judicial roles. Their published determination suggests a rigorous and forensic examination of these matters and

[37] *R v Amir & Butt* [2011] EWCA Civ 2914, para 35.

[38] *R v Amir & Butt* [2011] EWCA Civ 2914, para 36.

[39] At CAS the issue of proportionality of sentence is usually argued in the context of doping appeals. See, for instance, CAS 2009/A/2012 *Doping Authority Netherlands v N* [39]–[53]. In English (sports) law some guidance on the proportionality of sporting sanctions can be found in *Bradley v Jockey Club* [2005] EWCA Civ 1056 [17]-[27], Lord Phillips MR endorsing the approach of Richards J in *Bradley v Jockey Club* [2004] EWHC 2164.

[40] The term has been used in the context of athletes such as sixteen-year-old Andreea Raducan, who failed an anti-doping test at the Sydney Olympics for use of a prescribed flu remedy, see CAS OG 2000/011 *Raducan v IOC*.

[41] See generally Hudson and Findley 2010.

good exemplar of a transparent disciplinary process. The criminal court proceedings at both the trial court and appeal court were adjudicated upon with the objectivity of the legal judge. Unlike earlier criminal trials in England for alleged match fixing in football and horse racing where problems of reliability of evidence and particularly expert witnesses led to failed prosecutions; here there was a strong evidential case supported by an earlier and thorough disciplinary tribunal applying the highest standard of proof.[42]

The ICC Tribunal Determination interestingly is not as censorial as to the conduct of the players compared to the criminal courts but provides liability and appropriate sanctions in the context of the ICC Anti-Corruption Code. Perhaps some uneasiness is visible over the fact that this wrongdoing was not exposed by the ICC and its own anti-corruption machinery but by investigative journalism. Conversely, the criminal courts were unambiguous that this conduct was not simply a matter of breaking the rules of the game and therefore subject to internal regulation and discipline but also criminal conduct of a very serious kind which had to be marked with a criminal sanction. The Lord Chief Justice emphasised that:

> …the corruption was carefully prepared… the criminality was that these three cricketers betrayed their team, betrayed the country which they had the honour to represent, betrayed the sport that had given them their distinction, and betrayed the very many followers of the game throughout the world.[43]

It is universally accepted that financially induced manipulation of sporting competitions is inherently wrong and strikes at the heart of sporting integrity. This chapter has focused on the various adjudications of the wrong doing of three Pakistan cricketers. This has been located within an historical context of members of the Pakistan cricket team having been implicated in match and spot fixing in matches over a period of time. The phenomenon can also been explained variously due to ineffective sports administration in Pakistan, the relatively low remuneration levels of Pakistan international cricketers compared with other countries and the chronic problems of corruption and disorder that generally pervades the Pakistan state. Certainly, improved sports governance is the key to addressing this problem of financial corruption both nationally and internationally. More effective internal regulations are important—more important is effective policing and enforcement of these regulations.

This case highlights the role that the criminal law has in reinforcing the internal sports mechanisms. As the threat from gambling-led corruption increases, greater multi-agency co-operation between sport, the licensed gambling industry and law enforcement agencies is required. The form that this co-operation might take—for example a World Anti-Corruption Agency based on the model of the World

---

[42] See prosecutions based on allegations of match fixing brought against Premier League footballers, Bruce Grobbelaar, Hans Segers and John Fashanu in 1995 and against champion flat race jockey, Keiren Fallon in 2007. Discussed by Gardiner et al. 2012, Chap. 6.

[43] *R v Amir and Butt Court of Appeal* [2011] 11 EWCA Crim 2914, para 32.

Anti-Doping Agency—remains unclear for now. What is evident however from the legal proceedings and arbitral adjudication discussed in this chapter is that while tough sanctions should be imposed on those who fix; of equal importance is that sports governing bodies both nationally and internationally need, not only to have widespread education programmes and effective anti-corruption regulations in place, they also need to have more robust and independent compliance and integrity units that are more active in policing and uncovering corrupt activities. Crucial as its role is, the identification of spot fixing as in this case, should not be left to investigative journalism alone.

References

Chapman M (2012) Hansie Cronje: 10 years on, the independent (London) 2 June http://www.independent.co.uk/sport/cricket/hansie-cronje-10-years-on-7811732.html. Accessed 31 July 2012

Hudson K, Findley R (2010) Corruption: agreeing to match fixing under duress: analysis. World Sports Law Rep 8(6):14–16

Gardiner S et al (2012) Sports law, 4th edn. Routledge, Oxford

Gardiner S, Naidoo U (2007) On the front foot against corruption. Sport Law J 15:16–27

Hoult N (2012) Salman Butt released seven months into his 30 month prison sentence for spot fixing and returns to Pakistan. The daily telegraph (London) 21 June http://www.telegraph.co.uk/sport/cricket/international/pakistan/9346263/Salman-Butt-released-seven-months-in-to-his-30-month-prison-sentence-for-spot-fixing-and-returns-to-Pakistan.html. Accessed 31 July 2012

ICC Independent Tribunal's Determination (2011) International Cricket Council v Salman Butt, Mohammad Asif and Mohammad Amir. 5 February. http://static.icc-cricket.com/ugc/documents/DOC_CF78CCD3836520E24F2D2D68A6B28766_1326261335095_886.pdf. Accessed 31 July 2012

Laws of Cricket (2000 Code 4th Edition—2010) www.lords.org/data/files/laws-of-cricket-2000-code-4th-edition-final-10422.pdf. Accessed 31 July 2012

Lewis A, Taylor J (2008) Sport: law and practice. Butterworths LexisNexis, London

Magazine P (2000) Not quite cricket: the explosive story of how bookmakers influence the game today. Penguin, London

Qayyum Inquiry (2000) http://static.cricinfo.com/db/NATIONAL/PAK/NEWS/qayyumreport/qayyum_report.html. Accessed 31 July 2012

Sentencing Remarks of Mr Justice Cooke (2011) R v Mazhar Majeed, Salman Butt, Mohammad Asif and Mohammad Amir, Southwark Crown Court, 3 Nov. http://www.judiciary.gov.uk/Resources/JCO/Documents/Judgments/butt-others-sentencing-remarks-03112011.pdf. Accessed 31 July 2012

Wilson A (2012) Mervyn Westfield released from jail but awaits fate over playing future. The Guardian, 19 April, p 38

Part VI
Enduring Themes in Sports Law

Chapter 19
Football and Crowds: *Gough and Smith v Chief Constable of Derbyshire* [2002] QB 1213

Geoff Pearson

Abstract In 2000, the Chief Constable of Derbyshire applied to a Magistrates' Court for banning orders against Gough and Smith under section 14B of the Football Spectators Act 1989. The Chief Constable adduced evidence that Gough had been convicted of common assault in March 1998 and that Smith had been convicted of assault with intent to resist arrest in November 1990. The Chief Constable also adduced in evidence "profiles" gathered by the police from information supplied by informant "spotters" at football matches. The spotters purportedly described incidents at domestic football matches involving Derby County FC between September 1996 and June 2000 in which Gough and Smith had participated. On the balance of probabilities the district judge was satisfied that the preconditions for making an order pursuant to section 14B(4)(a) and (b) of the Football Spectators Act 1989 were met, and namely that Gough and Smith had caused or contributed to violence or disorder in the United Kingdom or elsewhere and that there were reasonable grounds to believe that making a banning order would help to prevent violence or disorder at or in connection with any regulated football match. The district judge accordingly made banning orders against Gough and Smith for the minimum period of two years. Gough and Smith appealed to the High Court (and on dismissal there to the Court of Appeal) inter alia on three grounds: (i) whether the restrictions on their freedom of movement were compatible with EU law; (ii) whether the restrictions on their movement were otherwise at odds with the principle of proportionality and (iii) whether the procedural and evidential rules in section 14B, including its low standard of proof, violated the requirements of procedural fairness applicable to criminal charges contained in Article 6 ECHR. A decade or so after the judgment, this chapter reviews the Court

---

Director of Studies for the MBA (Football Industries) programme and Lecturer in Law.

G. Pearson (✉)
University of Liverpool Management School, University of Liverpool, Chatham Street, Liverpool L69 7ZH, UK
e-mail: pearsong@liv.ac.uk

J. Anderson (ed.), *Leading Cases in Sports Law*,
ASSER International Sports Law Series, DOI: 10.1007/978-90-6704-909-2_19,

of Appeal's decision and looks at its impact upon the human rights of football fans and policing tactics to prevent football crowd disorder.

Contents

19.1 Introduction

In the summer of 2000, I was carrying out crowd observations amongst England fans in Charleroi town square shortly before England beat Germany in a UEFA European Championships Group Stage match. The crowd in that square, around 2,000 England fans interspersed with tourists and locals, had just been subjected to water-cannon and baton-charge dispersal by the Belgian riot police. This show of force had been a response to a very minor incident of disorder in one corner of the square and, although some England fans retaliated to the draconian police response by throwing chairs, the vast majority of those who were subjected to it had not been involved in any disorder.[1] Around 1,500 England fans including myself were subsequently corralled by Belgian police and detained in the square until shortly before the match when those with tickets were allowed through the police cordon. Corralled with me that day was a Derby County FC fan called Gary Smith, and the evidence of this containment was subsequently used to help obtain a Football Banning Order ("FBO") under section 14B of the Football Spectators Act 1989 (as amended by the Football Disorder Act 2000). The disorder in the square that resulted from the ill-advised intervention by the Belgian riot police was to be a key factor in the introduction of that amending legislation.

Smith, and another Derby fan Carl Gough, appealed against their bans and the case reached the Court of Appeal in 2002. Lord Phillips MR's judgment in that case was to set the precedent for the imposition of s14B FBOs, ruling them lawful under the EU law and the European Convention of Human Rights ("ECHR"), but setting down strict standards about under what circumstances they could be

[1] For background see generally Crabbe 2003; Stott and Pearson 2007 and Weed 2001.

granted.[2] This chapter returns to *Gough and Smith v Chief Constable of Derbyshire*[3] ten years after the judgment and looks at the impact of the case upon the human rights of football fans and policing tactics to prevent football crowd disorder.

19.2 The Football Disorder Act and the Football Banning Order Scheme

It is clear that the Charleroi incident was pivotal in justifying the introduction of the legislation amending the Football Spectators Act 1989 by way of the Football (Disorder) Act 2000,[4] though, arguably, enough political momentum had already been gathered following the more serious disorder involving England fans in Marseilles at the 1998 FIFA World Cup to ensure that the changes brought about to the FBO scheme would have occurred at some point that decade.[5] The media response to the disorder, and the arrest of 965 England fans in Belgium that week, was to place immediate pressure on the New Labour government to find a way to ban "known hooligans" who had not previously been convicted of a football-related offence and could at the time therefore not be subjected to a FBO. Within a month of Charleroi, the Football (Disorder) Act 2000 had entered the statute book.[6] The 2000 Act radically extended the existing FBO regime, introducing FBOs "on complaint" and thus enabling magistrates and judges to impose orders on fans who did not possess a previous "football-related" conviction, as had previously been required under the scheme initiated by the Public Order Act 1986 and the Football Spectators Act 1989. For the purposes of this review, the key amendment to the Football Spectators Act was the insertion of a new section 14B:

---

[2] See further Pearson 2002.

[3] *Gough and Smith v Chief Constable of Derbyshire* [2002] QB 1213.

[4] See the House of Lords Debate on the Football Disorder Bill, HL Deb, 20 July 2000, vol 615, cols 1182–1262.

[5] In November 1998, the British Government issued a consultation document, entitled the *Review of Football-Related Legislation*, which set out suggested changes to improve and strengthen the existing legislation relating to football. The measures proposed included recourse to the law to prevent a range of offenders from attending matches domestically and travelling to and attending designated matches abroad. Subsequently, a private members bill led to the enactment of the Football (Offences and Disorder) Act 1999, though the provisions on banning orders were very much a "watered down" version of what was to follow.

[6] FBOs on complaint can be seen as part of New Labour's wider policy of introducing "hybrid" measures to deal with low-level criminality and most notably Anti-Social Behaviour Orders. See generally Ashworth 2004; Brownlee 1998; Crawford 2008, 2009 and Duff and Marshall 2006. Note in particular Von Hirsch and Simester 2006 who refer to such "hybrid" provisions as "two-step prohibitions" and launch a strong criticism on the constitutional legitimacy of Anti-Social Behaviour Orders in particular.

Banning orders made on a complaint.

(1) An application for a banning order in respect of any person may be made by the chief officer of police for the area in which the person resides or appears to reside, if it appears to the officer that the condition in subsection (2) below is met.
(2) That condition is that the respondent has at any time caused or contributed to any violence or disorder in the United Kingdom or elsewhere.
(3) The application is to be made by complaint to a magistrates' court.
(4) If—(a) it is proved on the application that the condition in subsection (2) above is met, and (b) the court is satisfied that there are reasonable grounds to believe that making a banning order would help to prevent violence or disorder at or in connection with any regulated football matches, the court must make a banning order in respect of the respondent.

This meant that rather than FBOs being imposed upon those proven to have committed football-related offences, the police could now also pursue orders against those they suspected were involved in football-related violence or disorder but against whom they had insufficient evidence to gain a criminal conviction. Once banned, fans would be prevented from attending matches, or the immediate geographical area around matches, for between two and three years[7] and would have to surrender their passports to the police when England or their club side played abroad, preventing them from travelling. It was claimed that the legislation would have prevented the disorder seen at Marseilles and Charleroi, but this was not supported by the evidence as to why that disorder occurred or who was involved. In both incidents, UK Football Intelligence Officers ("FIOs") present at the scene noted that "known" (but not banned) hooligans were typically *not* involved, and in Belgium only 3 % of those arrested were known to the UK authorities as potential troublemakers.[8] In short, there was no evidence that FBOs on complaint would have prevented or reduced the disorder that was used to justify the introduction of the provision.

19.3 *Gough and Smith* at the Court of Appeal

The Chief Constable of Derbyshire applied to a magistrates' court for the imposition of FBOs on Gough and Smith. In order to satisfy the requirements of section 14B of the Football Spectators Act 1989, the Chief Constable as the applicant needed to demonstrate that Gough and Smith had first been involved in previous disorder or violence. The Chief Constable adduced evidence that Gough had been convicted of common assault in March 1998 and that Smith had been convicted of assault with intent to resist arrest in November 1990. More

[7] This was increased to three to five years by the Violent Crime Reduction Act 2006. See in particular s52 and Schedule 3 of that Act.

[8] See generally Stott and Pearson 2007.

problematic was the need to prove, pursuant to section 14B(4)(b) of the 1989 Act, that there were "reasonable grounds to believe that making a banning order would help to prevent violence or disorder at or in connection with any regulated football matches". Here, the applicant relied upon police "profiles" gathered on the defendants, noting their presence in groups that were considered by the police to be "risk", and their association with others who had been involved in football-related disorder. In fact, the local FIOs believed that Gough and Smith were "prominent" in a group calling itself the "Derby Lunatic Fringe". This "risk" group had been under observation at and around football matches for some time, but, although the group and some of the defendants' "associates" had been involved in disorder with rival risk groups during this period, neither defendant had been seen directly involved in violence or disorder.

The FBO was granted and an appeal by Gough and Smith was dismissed by the High Court.[9] The Court of Appeal, which ultimately also dismissed Gough and Smith's appeal, did not identify as problematic the fact that the magistrates' court and, later the High Court, had failed to take an objective and impartial stance on the nature and seriousness of the phenomenon of football-related disorder and the so-called "Derby Lunatic Fringe" in particular. As with the High Court, Lord Phillips MR in the Court of Appeal uncritically accepted evidence adduced by the Home Office about the organisation and seriousness of football-disorder and deemed that "the word 'warfare' is hardly too strong" to describe what took place in these confrontations.[10] The Master of the Rolls also paid particular attention to the profile noting that "Smith was seen in the square in Charleroi after the disorder had occurred corralled by the Belgium police with around 15 other Derby prominents and 1,500 other England supporters",[11] despite the fact that this proved nothing in terms of propensity to having been involved in the disorder that took place in that square. Overall, Lord Phillips MR was of the opinion: "In each case the cumulative effect of the individual observations pointed unequivocally to the appellant being one of the Derby County football 'prominents'."[12]

The appeal focussed primarily upon two arguments. First, that a consequence of the imposition of the FBOs was that they had to surrender their passports during certain "control periods" around matches abroad involving Derby County FC and England. In doing so, they contended, the FBO scheme equated to a de facto restriction on both their freedom of movement and their right to leave a member state enshrined in EU law. Lord Phillips MR felt that this restriction was only lawful if it satisfied the test of proportionality, which he identified from the case of *de Freitas v Permanent Secretary of Ministry of Agriculture, Fisheries, Lands and*

---

[9] *Gough and Smith v Chief Constable of Derbyshire* [2002] QB 459.

[10] *Gough and Smith v Chief Constable of Derbyshire* [2002] QB 1213, 1224, Lord Phillips MR.

[11] *Gough and Smith v Chief Constable of Derbyshire* [2002] QB 1213, 1229, Lord Phillips MR.

[12] *Gough and Smith v Chief Constable of Derbyshire* [2002] QB 1213, 1245, Lord Phillips MR.

Housing.[13] This test required the court to determine whether: (i) the legislative objective is sufficiently important to justify limiting a fundamental right; (ii) the measures designed to meet the legislative objective are rationally connected to it and (iii) the means used to impair the right or freedom are no more than are necessary to accomplish the objective. In applying the *de Freitas* test on proportionality, the Court of Appeal concluded:

> …it is proportionate that those who have been shown to constitute a real risk of participation in football hooliganism should be required to obtain permission to travel abroad during periods when prescribed matches are taking place and to demonstrate that the purpose of doing so is other than attendance at the prescribed match or matches. We are not able to envisage a scheme which would achieve the public policy objective that involves a lesser degree of restraint.[14]

The second key argument was that the restrictions upon liberty imposed by the orders (most notably the exclusion zones around stadia and city centres around matches and the requirement that they surrender their passports when relevant matches took place abroad) took the form of a criminal penalty and therefore, according to European Court of Human Rights' ("ECtHR") jurisprudence, could only be imposed following the correct criminal procedure.[15] In contrast, the FBO scheme under section 14B of the Football Spectators Act 1989 operated under a civil procedure providing fewer rights and protections for defendants. This argument also failed. Lord Phillips MR ruled that the purpose of the orders was preventative rather than punitive, meaning that the civil procedure did not breach article 6ECHR (right to a fair trial).[16] As a result, the appeal was dismissed and the FBOs remained in place on both defendants.

However, in reaching this decision on the second limb of the *Gough* appeal, Lord Phillips MR made what should have been a vital change to the way in which FBOs "on complaint" are awarded. The Court of Appeal observed that because FBOs "impose serious restraints on freedoms that the citizen normally enjoys" the civil standard of proof "must reflect the consequences that will follow if the case for a banning order is made out. This should lead the justices to apply an exacting standard of proof that will, in practice, be hard to distinguish from the criminal

---

[13] *Gough and Smith v Chief Constable of Derbyshire* [2002] QB 1213, 1237, Lord Phillips MR citing *de Freitas v Permanent Secretary of Ministry of Agriculture, Fisheries, Lands and Housing* [1999] 1 AC 69, 80, Lord Clyde.

[14] *Gough and Smith v Chief Constable of Derbyshire* [2002] QB 1213, 1242, Lord Phillips MR.

[15] Note the comments of the ECtHR in *Engel v The Netherlands (No. 1)* (1976) 1 EHRR 647, *Garyfallou AEBE v Greece* (1997) 28 EHRR 344 and *Lauko v Slovakia* (1998) 33 EHRR 439 where it indicated a willingness to look beyond the domestic clarification of analogous measures and instead focus on the impact of the provision upon the defendant.

[16] See the "conclusions" in *Gough and Smith v Chief Constable of Derbyshire* [2002] QB 1213, 1240–1242, Lord Phillips MR.

standard".[17] According to the Court of Appeal, this higher standard of proof should be applied to both the requirement for proof of involvement in previous disorder or violence, and evidence of past conduct and likely future conduct that could lead to disorder at or around football matches.

Construing section 14B(4) of the Football Spectators Act 1989, the Court of Appeal noted that a magistrates' court in such instances must be "satisfied that there are reasonable grounds to believe that making a banning order would help to prevent violence or disorder at or in connection with any regulated football matches". In practice, the Court of Appeal went on:

> ...the "reasonable grounds" will almost inevitably consist of evidence of past conduct. That conduct must be such as to make it reasonable to conclude that if the respondent is not made subject to a banning order he is likely to contribute to football violence or disorder in the future. The past conduct may or may not consist of or include the causing or contributing to violence or disorder that has to be proved under section 14B(4)(a), for that violence or disorder is not required to be football related. It must, however, be proved to the same strict standard of proof. Furthermore it must be conduct that gives rise to the likelihood that, if the respondent is not banned from attending prescribed football matches, he will attend such matches, or the environs of them, and take part in violence or disorder.[18]

In contrast to the pre-existing belief that section 14B orders required only the normal civil standard of proof (balance of probabilities), this concession appeared to provide significant protections against the risk of innocent football supporters receiving banning orders on relatively flimsy evidence.

This author has been critical of the Court of Appeal's approach in *Gough* on a number of grounds, of which two are of note. First and with reference to the article 6ECHR argument, this author believes that the Court of Appeal concentrated too much on the legislative *intention* rather than the statutory *effect* when it determined that the orders were preventative rather than punitive.[19] Second, I have also been critical of the application of the *de Freitas* proportionality test, arguing that the court did not apply it in any meaningful way, and that if it had done, Lord Phillips MR would have found the justification for section 14B wanting under point (iii) and arguably (ii) of the *de Freitas* test.[20] My view on this second point has in fact strengthened in the years that have followed as I have witnessed, researched and written about a number of "least restrictive alternatives", most notably through changes in police tactics, which have led to the successful supervision and policing of large crowds of English football supporters home and abroad.[21]

---

[17] *Gough and Smith v Chief Constable of Derbyshire* [2002] QB 1213, 1242–1243, Lord Phillips MR and citing *B v Chief Constable of Avon and Somerset Constabulary* [2001] 1 WLR 340, 354 and *R (McCann) v Crown Court at Manchester* [2001] 1WLR 1084, 1102.

[18] *Gough and Smith v Chief Constable of Derbyshire* [2002] QB 1213, 1243, Lord Phillips MR.

[19] See generally Pearson 2006.

[20] See generally Pearson 2005 and Stott and Pearson 2006.

[21] See generally Stott and Pearson 2007 and Stott et al. 2012.

Nevertheless, it must be acknowledged that, in contrast to the hard-line stance taken by both the Home Office and the High Court, the Court of Appeal's approach was much more mindful of the argued principles of EU and human rights law. Moreover, the requirements for a standard of proof akin to beyond reasonable doubt in determining whether a defendant was causing or contributing to football-related disorder and would do so in the future, should have ensured a greater onus on the police to provide evidence of actual involvement in instances of disorder on behalf of defendants, rather than mere evidence of association in "risk groups" or with "known hooligans". Per force, this should, in theory at least, have also obliged magistrates to more carefully scrutinise applications for FBOs.[22] In the remainder of this chapter, the extent to which this requirement from *Gough* has been followed in magistrates' and Crown Court will be reviewed. The analysis is based upon court observations of contested section 14B hearings and correspondence with pressure groups such as *The Football Supporters Federation* and *Liberty*.

19.4 Impact of *Gough* Upon the Lower Courts and the Football Banning Order Scheme

Establishing, even against a criminal standard of proof, that a "risk supporter" has been engaged in past disorderly or violent conduct at or around football matches should not, one would think, be difficult. Football-matches are highly regulated areas. All major UK stadia are saturated with CCTV cameras and there is a heavy presence of police at and around the stadia environs, at train stations and on popular routes to the stadium.[23] FIOs from the host police force and that of the visiting team are present in addition to the normal officers charged with maintaining order. FIOs monitor groups of "risk supporters" on match days and are usually able to prevent groups confronting each other. The movements of supporters are recorded by CCTV, static and handheld video cameras and sometimes police helicopters with infrared capability. When this level of regulation and evidence-gathering capability is combined with laws prohibiting behaviour

[22] See further *Doyle and Others v R* [2012] EWCA Crim 995, where the Court of Appeal ruled that the definition of violence or disorder "in connection with" football should not include behaviour that merely happened to occur at or around a match event. In *Doyle*, three defendants who assaulted a train passenger who had objected to their behaviour as they returned from a football match had their FBO revoked because the offence was not football related and no evidence had been provided that the order would prevent disorder at football in the future. *Doyle* was used successfully to contest the imposition of a s14B FBO in the observed case of *Commissioner of Police for the Metropolis v Melody*, Unreported, Tower Bridge Magistrates Court, 9 July 2012.

[23] In the 2009 football season, the Association of Chief Police Officers estimated that policing of designated matches in England and Wales cost around £25million per year. See further Stott et al. 2012.

considered to be breach of the peace, or disorderly or threatening behaviour[24] and making it an offence to be drunk upon entering a football stadium[25] or to engage in "indecent" chanting[26]; it is very difficult for any supporter who wishes to engage in disorderly or violent conduct to do so without committing a criminal offence and leaving a pursuable trail of hard evidence.

However, if a supporter commits any of these offences, then pursing a banning order under section 14B is unnecessary, as a banning order can be obtained upon conviction of a relevant offence under the amended section 14A of the Football Spectators Act 1989. In other words, the targets of section 14B were those who, despite being under intensive surveillance at football matches, have *not* become involved in observed football-related disorder or violence. It follows from this that being able to obtain evidence approaching the criminal standard of such violence or disorderly conduct should be exceptionally difficult without also gaining evidence that should lead to a criminal conviction and a section 14A FBO. In reality what has happened is that the police have almost always only pursued section 14B applications against fans who already possess a non-football-related conviction (and thereby fulfilling the requirement in section 14B(2)). Then, as we will see magistrates and judges have accepted evidence of little more than guilt by association as being capable of satisfying the *Gough* standard on whether an individual is likely to commit acts of violence and disorder around football matches in the future.

Even in *Gough* itself it can be argued that the evidence of football-related activity engaged in by the appellants should not have been sufficient to lead to the conclusion that it was beyond reasonable doubt that they would engage in disorder or violence around football matches in the future. The evidence suggested that Gough and Smith were seen in the same groups as other supporters considered by the police to be "risk", and that they sometimes travelled on the same coaches as fans who took weapons and hooligan "calling cards" to matches. However, all the evidence suggested that neither had actually engaged in any violence or disorder at matches. The more this evidence accumulated, the harder it should have been to reach the conclusion that their observed (non-violent) actions of the appellants were atypical. Instead, the evidence of continual non-engagement in disorder was put together to build a profile to suggest that their engagement in future disorder was *more*, rather than less, likely.

Observations carried out at Magistrates and Crown Courts in Manchester, Trafford, Leeds and Bristol and London between 2006 and 2012 suggest that this pattern of application and judicial interpretation was not atypical. A more detailed account of section 14B hearings in the first two locations has been published previously by this author in the *Journal of Criminal Law* (2006 with Dr Mark James). Its findings, combined with later observations, reveal a pattern of application, interpretation and imposition of section 14B FBOs that suggest a

[24] Sections 4 and 5 of the Public Order Act 1986.

[25] Section 2(2) of the Sporting Events (Control of Alcohol etc.) Act 1985.

[26] Section 3 of the Football (Offences) Act 1991.

significant short-fall between Lords Phillips MR's ruling on the standard of proof and the reality of its application in the lower courts. It was not that the judiciary in these observed hearings were unaware of the standard of proof necessary—in all observed cases explicit reference was made to Lord Phillips's ruling in this regard; however, the following, and usually a combination of more than one of these factors, have been used by judges and magistrates in observed cases as proof to the *Gough* standard of a likelihood of engagement in future disorder and violence.

In all observed cases the key evidence of conduct indicative of engagement in violence or disorder at matches came from guilt by association. It was typical for the defendant to be identified as being part of a group that was labelled by the police as a "risk group". Sometimes this "association" went no further than evidence that they had been drinking in the same public house. The reason this group was considered "risk" was usually because the police identified some individuals within it as being "risk supporters". On a few occasions this was because a (usually unidentified) individual in that group (never the defendant) had tried to confront rival supporters or had thrown a missile. Occasionally, it was because those individuals had previous convictions or had previously served banning orders. Usually, however, it was because they had been identified in absence of conviction as being believed to engage in violence or disorder at and around matches.

Here a certain amount of circular reasoning came into play. Evidence was provided that defendants were "associating" with "risk supporters", but the very definition of what constituted a risk supporter was in most cases reached by way of their association with others labelled in the same way. When a number of section 14B cases were observed at Trafford Magistrates' Court in 2006 over the period of a week one part of the accepted evidence in a later case was that the defendant had been "associating" with a defendant given an FBO earlier that week. Furthermore, since those defined as "risk supporters" were typically not informed of this categorisation prior to the section 14B application, it was impossible for fans to avoid associating with these individuals on this basis.[27]

The importance placed upon "association" with those categorised in an extra-judicial way as "risk supporters" was also underpinned by fundamental misunderstandings of contemporary English fan culture by magistrates and judges in observed cases. At Leeds Magistrates' and Crown Courts, evidence provided by the applicant to prove that the football supporter was likely to engage in disorder at matches included the fact that they (a) attended pubs many hours in advance of kick-off; (b) did not wear their team's colours or (c) did not always possess match tickets. However, a long-term ethnographic study of English football fan behaviour at away matches by this author indicates that the first two modes of behaviour were typical of a large proportion of non-violent travelling supporters.[28] Heavy alcohol consumption and social drinking with friends formed an integral part of the match-day

[27] Again, see generally James and Pearson 2006.

[28] Pearson 2012.

"experience" for this subculture of "carnival fans". At away matches the non-wearing, or covering-up, of "colours" was essential in order to achieve this aim safely as many pubs would not grant access to visiting supporters, and visiting supporters at some venues also believed that wearing colours would invite confrontation. Indeed at some clubs, the ethos or culture of fans is expressly *not* to wear colours.

It was rare that fans would travel without tickets, but some did, especially to the most important games where tickets were scarce and the "craic" around the match would be at its best (and high-risk and high-popularity matches also often went hand-in-hand). At these matches, the best chance to find spare tickets would be in the pub beforehand, and the more time spent in the establishment surrounded by fans, the higher the chance of obtaining a ticket. Finally, it was not always possible for fans generally to be aware of which supporters had been specifically categorised as "risk" by the police, and where only one pub was open to visiting fans (or where the police corralled visiting fans in one establishment), fans were not always given the chance to disassociate with risk supporters even if they had that knowledge and inclination. In short, being in a pub hours before kick-off, not wearing colours, not having a ticket and "associating" with those characterised as "risk supporters" was not as unlikely a combination as many applicants and judges believed. In sum, even on "achieving" all of these "risk" factors, this still should not be sufficient to prove an individual's propensity to become involved in disorder at and around football matches to Lord Phillips MR's standard of proof.

In addition to the problems about whether the totality of such circumstantial evidence could lead to a belief beyond reasonable doubt that an individual was involved in football-related disorder, observations have also consistently raised concerns about the admissibility and validity of individual elements of the police profile. Whilst magistrates and judges were sometimes observed to discount evidence that purely indicated attendance at pubs or stadia when no disorder occurred; nevertheless, facets of the evidence relied upon in the imposition of section 14B FBOs was clearly and highly unreliable. In *Chief Constable of Greater Manchester v Davies*, a hearing observed by the author at Trafford Magistrates' Court on 16 February 2006, the defendant was served with a section 14B banning order primarily as a result of being identified by a FIO as an individual who had led an attack on a group of rival supporters. Police officers on the ground did not identify the defendant at the time of the incident but video footage captured a blurred individual that the FIO subsequently alleged was the defendant. The footage was relayed on the court monitor. The judge could not identify, even on a balance of probabilities, that the individual was the defendant. However, the FIO's retrospective opinion that the blurred image was the defendant was held to be sufficient.

Another example comes from *Chief Constable of West Yorkshire Police v Ford and others*, a hearing observed by the author at Leeds Magistrates' Court on 21 June 2010. Here, a number of Leeds United fans were gathered in a pub in Manchester ahead of a high-risk match. The pub was surrounded by police and all those who did not have tickets were served with an "Alcohol Dispersal Order" pursuant to section 27 of the Violent Crime Reduction Act 2006. Those fans served with section 27 orders and who had previous relevant convictions were then all subjected to section 14B FBO applications. One crucial piece of evidence in the awarding of these FBOs came from a number of anonymous "posts" on internet fan forums read by FIOs suggesting that some of the fans in the pubs were there with the intention of confronting rival fans. The evidence was accepted as relevant and influential despite the fact that (a) the identity and reliability of the poster(s) were unknown; (b) exaggeration and posturing to gain "reputation" for a club's hooligan firm (whether real or imagined) is a common feature of such discussions[29]; and (c) no confrontation actually occurred. Indeed, on a number of occasions it was observed that the mere serving of a section 27 order was accepted as evidence of involvement in football-related disorder even in the absence of such disorder even though there is some evidence that the orders are sometimes used unlawfully and indiscriminately by certain police forces.[30]

Finally, court observations cast doubt upon the Court of Appeal's opinion in *Gough* that section 14B orders are purely preventative and do not therefore need to satisfy criminal rules of procedure in order to satisfy article 6ECHR. Observations by this author and Dr Mark James in 2006 at Trafford Magistrates' Court in 2006 indicated that a high level of costs were imposed upon those given section 14B orders, rising from £800 for uncontested cases to £1,447 for contested ones. Regardless of the intention of the orders, associated costs clearly have a significant punitive effect. Additionally, the observed hearings revealed that the length of section 14B orders varied, not in line with the risk of disorder posed by the defendant, but instead with whether the defendant chose to contest the application. This led to the absurd result that those who posed a higher risk of disorder (and against whom more evidence was available) received shorter bans than those apparently posing lesser risk (because there was little evidence and a greater chance of successfully contesting the FBO). Across the board there was a general lack of individualised consideration of the risk posed by a defendant when determining the conditions of the FBO, with courts ordering the surrendering of passports even for defendants who had never travelled abroad for football or did not even possess a passport.

19.5 Impact of *Gough* Upon Levels of Football-Related Disorder

The Court of Appeal's endorsement (at common, EU and ECHR law) of the FBO scheme under the section 14B of the Football Spectators Act 1989 meant that a

---

[29] Pearson 2012.

[30] See, for example, *R (on application of Lyndon) v Chief Constable of Greater Manchester Police*, Unreported, Queen's Bench Division, 15 Nov 2008.

"green light" was given to police forces to apply for FBOs against those who, although not previously convicted of a football-related offence, they believe might currently, or at some point in the future, be involved, even tangentially, in football-related disorder. Different constabularies have availed of this opportunity with varying enthusiasm. Numerous interviews with officers by the author over the period 2002–2010, have indicated that many officers involved in football crowd management are of the opinion that section 14B orders have contributed to the controlling of football-related disorder. However, this anecdotal evidence has not been supported with anything more concrete or of a validated empirical nature. Indeed, statistics of arrest for "football-related" offences have remained largely static during the period 2001–2012 and—as far as it is possible to ascertain—what might be described broadly as hooligan-related incidents have continued at largely the same rate. It may be that section 14B FBOs are helping to manage the problem, but they have certainly not stopped it. From reported and observed cases it is also clear that those being served with FBOs are not typically the "ringleaders" against whom, it was suggested during the debates on the Football (Disorder) Act 2000, these orders would be specifically targeting and excluding.[31] Anecdotally and from ethnographic study of football supporters,[32] it appears that levels of disorder tend to fluctuate at different clubs irrespective of the numbers of section 14B FBOs imposed (although increasing levels of disorder may lead to increased resources being dedicated to the obtaining of FBOs "on complaint").

Additionally, research by the Elaborated Social Identity School of social psychology contends very strongly that excluding suspected "hooligans" from football matches will not in and of itself prevent crowd disorder.[33] Proponents of this model have argued that serious crowd disorder and "rioting" is best understood as the result of the unchecked development of inter-group identities whereby even those who do not attend matches with the intention of becoming involved in disorder may engage in such actions when they feel that, as part of a group, their rights or legitimate intentions have been infringed. Conversely, this School also contends that this fact means that by managing the development of these group identities, crowd disorder can be limited even when those wishing to become involved in confrontation are present. In football crowds, it is argued that it is primarily the police who hold the power to mould this "social identity" to make disorder either more or less likely to occur. The most powerful evidence supporting the Elaborated Social Identity Model came from its application in the

---

[31] Note the comments of the then Parliamentary Under Secretary of State for the Home Department (Kate Hoey) during the House of Commons Standing Committee D Debate on the Football (Offences and Disorder) Bill of 5 May 1999, SC Deb (D) 5 May 1998, available online www.publications.parliament.uk/pa/cm/stand.htmcol: "The power to make banning orders in respect of people without conviction is necessary…because from football intelligence we know that some people commit offences or are involved in organising violence but cleverly manage not to be where they may be arrested. We need to find a way of dealing with those people".

[32] See in chronological order, Rookwood 2009; Stott et al. 2012 and Pearson, 2012.

[33] See generally Stott and Reicher 1998; Stott et al. 2001 and Stott and Pearson 2007.

training of the Portuguese Public Security Police ("PSP") prior to the 2004 UEFA European Football Championships. There, the PSP, applying this model to large crowds of drunken England fans (some of whom were identified as "risk supporters") successfully avoided any large-scale disorder and made only one arrest for a violent offence. In contrast, similar fan groups rioted at the tournament in areas controlled by the Portuguese National Republican Guard ("GNR"), a gendarmerie police force, adopting a more confrontational style of policing.[34]

My own ethnographic research with fans of Blackpool FC, England and Manchester United revealed findings supporting the model. Whilst there were a significant number of fans who attended matches with the intention of involvement in disorder; mass crowd disorder was rare and often involved both men and women who did not possess this predisposition. This was particularly notable abroad, where large crowds of English fans gathered and were confronted with styles of policing more similar to the GNRs—relying on tactics of avoiding interaction with fans followed by large numbers in riot gear attempting to disperse areas or make arrests by force. This should be no surprise, as during the instances of disorder involving England fans in Marseilles (1998) and Charleroi (2000) both the opinions of the UK FIOs at the scene and statistics of arrest demonstrated that the vast majority of those involved in the rioting were not known or suspected "hooligans".[35] Furthermore, post-*Gough*, several serious instances of disorder have occurred involving English football fans abroad, including Albufeira (2004, England); Stuttgart and Cologne (2006, England); Rome (2007, Manchester United); Seville (2007, Tottenham Hotspur) and Athens (2007, Liverpool), indicating that section 14B FBOs have certainly not been the panacea to the problem of England fans engaging in disorder abroad.

19.6 Conclusion

As with many statutory provisions rushed through Parliament on a wave of moral panic, the Football Disorder Act 2000 can be seen as a fundamentally flawed and inevitably reactionary piece of legislation. Not only was the 2000 Act, and the FBO scheme that it established, based on a false premise concerning the cause of crowd disorder abroad involving England fans, but, as was subsequently stated by the Court of Appeal in *R v Boggild and others*,[36] the relevant provisions of the amended Football Spectators Act 1989 are "rather complex"[37] and even unfairly inconsistent and uncertain in application. In *Boggild*, which concerned an

[34] Stott et al. 2007, 84–85.

[35] Stott and Pearson 2007.

[36] *R v Boggild and others* [2012] 1 Cr App R (S) 81; [2011] EWCA Crim 1928.

[37] *R v Boggild and others* [2012] 1 Cr App R (S) 81; [2011] EWCA Crim 1928, para 23, Hughes LJ.

unsuccessful application for leave to appeal brought by the prosecution that a Crown Court judge was wrong not to make a football banning order following the conviction of seven defendants for an affray which was committed in the aftermath of a football match, the Court of Appeal remarked that the FBO scheme places significant demands of proper statutory interpretation on magistrates and district judges and that the Court of Appeal's judicial colleagues "who are addressing the test of whether making an [FBO] would help to prevent violence or disorder ought…to have in mind the extent of the regime as well of course as its potentially draconian effect".[38] Moreover, and in a contemporaneous case note on *Boggild*, Thomas noted the statutory provisions relating to football banning orders "have now been amended many times and as a result have reached a point of near incomprehensibility" and that in any event, as shown by the sentencing judge in *Boggild*, alternative means, based on extant criminal law provisions, such as prevention of harassment and youth rehabilitation orders, may be more effective than the FBO scheme.[39]

Finally, a decade prior to *Boggild*, the Court of Appeal in *Gough* had been provided an opportunity to clarify some of these problems in relation to section 14B orders, but instead, through Lord Phillips MR's ruling on the standard of proof, it merely added another layer of complexity to the issue. Although Lord Phillips MR's ruling on this matter should be welcomed in tempering some of the harsher aspects of section 14B, observations of section 14B hearings have suggested that in reality *Gough* has done little to protect the rights of fans who have not been convicted of football-related offences but who are suspected by the police of being active in "risk groups". Magistrates and district judges appear confused about when section 14B orders can be imposed, and their interpretations of both the legislation and Lord Phillips MR's guidance vary widely. As a result, it seems inevitable that we will see either another case reach the Court of Appeal, or, following the prompting of the Court of Appeal in *Boggild*, that the legislation itself will be further amended to provide further clarification and guidance to judges in the lower courts, and protection against a challenge under EU and human rights law. It is hoped that should such a substantial amendment come to pass, a genuine assessment of current football fan culture and the utility of football banning orders in controlling football-related violence and disorder will also form part of the debate.

References

Ashworth A (2004) Social control and anti-social behaviour: the subversion of human rights. Law Q Rev 120:263–291

Brownlee I (1998) New labour—new penology? punitive rhetoric and the limits of managerialism in criminal justice policy. J Law Soc 25:313–335

---

[38] *R v Boggild and others* [2012] 1 Cr App R (S) 81; [2011] EWCA Crim 1928, para 24, Hughes LJ.

[39] Thomas 2012, 51–52.

Crabbe T (2003) The public gets what the public wants: England football fans, 'truth' claims and mediated realities. Int Rev Sociol Sport 38:413–425

Crawford A (2008) Dispersal powers and the symbolic role of anti-social behaviour legislation. The Mod Law Rev 71:753–784

Crawford A (2009) Governing through anti-social behaviour: regulatory challenges to criminal justice. Brit J Criminol 49:810–831

Duff R, Marshall S (2006) How offensive can you get? In: von Hirsch A, Simester A (eds) Incivilities: regulating offensive behaviour. Hart, Oxford, pp 57–90

James M, Pearson G (2006) Football banning orders: analysing their use in court. J Crim Law 70:509–530

Pearson G (2002) A cure worse than the disease? reflections on *Gough and Smith v Chief Constable of* Derbyshire. Entertain Law 1:92–102

Pearson G (2005) Qualifying for Europe? The legitimacy of football banning orders 'on complaint' under the principle of proportionality. Entertain Sports Law J 3(1). Online: www2.warwick.ac.uk/fac/soc/law/elj/eslj/issues/volume3/number1/pearson. Accessed 31 July 2012

Pearson G (2006) Hybrid law and human rights: quasi-criminal banning and behaviour orders in the appeal courts. Liverp Law Rev 27:125–145

Pearson G (2012) An ethnography of english football fans: Cans, cops and carnival. Manchester University Press, Manchester

Rookwood J (2009) Fan Perspectives of Football Hooliganism: defining, analysing and responding to the British phenomenon. VDM Publishing House, Saarbrucken

Stott C, Pearson G (2006) Football banning orders, proportionality and public order. Howard J Crim Justice 45:241–254

Stott C, Pearson G (2007) Football hooliganism: policing and the war on the english disease. Pennant Books, London

Stott C, Reicher S (1998) How conflict escalates: the inter-group dynamics of collective football crowd 'violence'. Sociology 32:353–377

Stott C, Hutchinson P, Drury J (2001) 'Hooligans' abroad? inter-group dynamics, social identity and participation in collective 'disorder' at the 1998 world cup finals. Brit J Soc-Psychol 40:359–384

Stott C et al (2007) Variability in the collective behaviour of England fans at Euro 2004: 'Hooliganism', public order policing and social change. Eur J Soc Psychol 37:75–100

Stott C, Hoggett J, Pearson G (2012) 'Keeping the peace': social identity, procedural justice and the policing of football crowds. Brit J Criminol 52:381–399

Thomas D (2012) Sentencing: banning orders—football Spectators Act 1989—appeal by prosecutor against refusal of crown court to make order. *Criml Law Rev* (1):48–52

Von Hirsch A, Simester A (2006) Regulating offensive conduct through two-step prohibitions. In: von Hirsch A, Simester A (eds) Incivilities: regulating offensive behaviour. Hart, Oxford, pp 173–194

Weed M (2001) Ing-Ger-Land at Euro 2000: how "handbags at 20 paces" was portrayed as a full-scale riot. Int Rev Sociol Sport 34:407–424

Chapter 20
Player Violence and Compensation for Injury: *R v Barnes* [2005] 1 Cr App Rep 507

Mark James

Abstract Barnes appealed against his conviction for unlawfully and maliciously inflicting grievous bodily harm, contrary to section 20 of the Offences against the Person Act 1861. The victim had sustained a serious leg injury as a result of a tackle by Barnes during an amateur football match. Barnes's appeal, which was upheld, was essentially threefold in nature. First, he argued that, although the tackle was "hard", it was "fair", and that the resulting injury was accidental and incidental to what could be expected in a game of football. Second, he argued that the trial judge's summing up had been inadequate on the application of the criminal law to "sporting assault". Third, and an underlying element of the appeal as a whole, was the general issue of when it might be appropriate for criminal proceedings to be instituted after an injury had been caused to one player by another during a sporting event. The Court of Appeal reiterated the long held view that where injuries are sustained in the course of a contact sport the defence of implied consent, to a threshold set in public policy, applies. In this instance, the Court of Appeal held that the threshold of that defence depended on all the circumstances and including an acknowledgement that, in highly competitive sports, where conduct outside the rules could be expected to occur in the "heat of the moment", such conduct might not reach the threshold level required for it to be criminal. Further, the Court of Appeal held that the threshold level of consent to injury in a contact sport should be viewed objectively as determined by the type of sport; the level at which it was played; the nature of the act; the degree of force used; the extent of the risk of injury; and the state of mind of the defendant. As regards the summing up by the judge, the Court of Appeal agreed that it had been inadequate in that the trial judge had, crucially, failed to explain to the jury the fact that, although the tackle was a foul, this did not necessarily mean that the threshold of criminal conduct had been reached or, indeed, breached. Overall, the Court of Appeal held that the criminal prosecution of those who had inflicted injury on

M. James (✉)
Salford Law School, University of Salford, Lady Hale Building, Salford M5 4WT, UK
e-mail: M.D.James@salford.ac.uk

J. Anderson (ed.), *Leading Cases in Sports Law*,
ASSER International Sports Law Series, DOI: 10.1007/978-90-6704-909-2_20,

another in the course of a sporting event was reserved for those situations where the conduct was sufficiently grave to be properly categorised as criminal.

Contents

20.1 Introduction

The use of the criminal law to regulate the conduct of sports participants is one of the oldest categories of sports law litigation and one that can be located in Victorian era determinations on the legality of sparring, prize-fighting and boxing[1] and the criminal behaviour of footballers making challenges for the ball.[2] Indeed, with the possible exception of Canada, the jurisdictions of the UK remain unique in the use of the criminal law as a means of governing player behaviour with any significant degree of regularity.[3] Despite this longevity,[4] judicial reasoning on this issue has often been characterised by vague, inconsistent and contradictory pronouncements. About the only consistency is the view that the principles and procedures of the criminal law as applied to on-field violence during contact sports should be resorted to only in exceptional circumstances and when other mechanisms appear to be inadequate.[5] Even *Barnes*, in which the Court of Appeal (Criminal Division) attempted to provide the definitive judicial guidance on the subject, has left a number of questions unanswered and a fuller application of the criminal law can only be appreciated when *Barnes* is read alongside developments in the law of torts, and particularly those emanating from the Court of Appeal

[1] See, for example, *R v Coney* (1881–82) 8 QBD 534.

[2] See, for example, *R v Bradshaw* (1878) 14 Cox CC 83 and *R v Moore* (1898) 15 TLR 229.

[3] See generally James 2010, Chap. 6.

[4] In the UK, the criminal law's long and complex relationship with sport and in particular with contact sports predates the use of the (civil) law of negligence in similar circumstances by over 100 years. See, for example *Condon v Basi* [1985] 1 WLR 866.

[5] See generally Anderson 2005 and Gasser and Schweizer 2008.

(Civil Division) in cases such as *Caldwell v Maguire and Fitzgerald*[6] and *Gravil v Carroll and Redruth RFC*.[7]

Outside of the confines of a strict case analysis of *Barnes*, this chapter will attempt to illustrate that the use of the criminal law of assault and its application to sports participants remains an important aspect of any analysis of the underlying purpose of sports law more generally.[8] This is because the topic is one of the few areas of sports law that applies across all sports and to all levels of sport, rather than being of application only to elite performers and professional sports. The topic also highlights the ongoing and often entrenched arguments about the appropriateness of the use of the law as a means of regulating sports disputes, as opposed to the alternative paradigm of self-regulation. Accordingly, the development of the law of assault and its application to sports disputes provides an ideal context for discussions on whether or not the law of the land should stop "at the touchline"[9] and whether the debate's modern incarnation, the "specificity of sport",[10] can provide a justification for an interpretation and application of the law that differs from the norm.

20.2 The Legal Context of *R v Barnes*

The key to an understanding of the importance of *Barnes* is an appreciation of the role of consent in the law of non-fatal offences against the person. In most legal systems, a fundamental principle of the criminal law is that a person's bodily integrity is protected by the law and each individual has the right to choose who touches them and in what circumstances and, therefore, any contact made with a person without either their express or implied consent is a criminal assault.[11] However, the simple fact that consent is present is not an absolute guarantee that the contact is lawful; it is a necessary, though not always a sufficient, requirement. In addition, the criminal law has long placed limits on a person's ability to consent to their being injured to ensure that bodily harm is not inflicted without "good reason".[12] Sport is considered to be an activity that provides the necessary "good reasons" by promoting a healthy lifestyle and attributes considered important by society such as fair play and teamwork. It follows that the contacts required by participation in contact sports, and the resultant injuries caused by them, can be consented to by the athletes. The criminal cases arising out of assaults in contact

6 *Caldwell v Maguire and Fitzgerald* [2001] EWCA Civ 1054.

7 *Gravil v Carroll and Redruth RFC* [2008] EWCA Civ 689.

8 See also Anderson 2008.

9 One of the first uses of that phrase can be found in Grayson and Bond 1993, 693.

10 See generally Parrish and Miettinen 2008.

11 See generally Simester et al. 2010, Chap. 11.

12 *Attorney-General's Reference (No.6 of 1980)* [1981] QB 715 and *R v Brown* [1994] 1 AC 212.

and fighting sports thus provide an interesting perspective on both the scope of the law of consent and the limits of the conduct to which a person's consent can extend.

The nineteenth century cases on the legality of the various early forms of boxing provide the basis upon which the law of assault as it applies to contact sports has developed. That series of cases determined that fighting for sport was lawful where the contest was a test of skill and where there were sufficient rules in place in order to determine, objectively, who was the better fighter. In contrast, unlawful fights were those where the test was more of endurance, not skill, where there was inadequate sporting and/or safety regulation governing the fight and where the nature of the event could provoke public disorder.[13] Although developed to regulate the deliberate assaulting of one person by another, similarities of approach can be seen in the first reported case involving contact, as opposed to combat, sport. In *R v Bradshaw*, the defendant had barged an opponent when attempting to make a challenge for the ball during a game of football. The victim fell awkwardly and died later from his injuries, resulting in the defendant being prosecuted for manslaughter. Bramwell LJ's direction to the jury required them to consider whether this was an accident that had occurred during the course of a lawfully conducted sport or whether it was a criminal assault that had gone beyond what could be considered to be lawful play:

> No rules or practice of any game whatever can make that lawful which is unlawful by the law of the land…[If] a man is playing according to the rules and practice of the game and not going beyond it, it may be reasonable to infer…that he is not acting in a manner which he knows will be likely to be productive of death or injury. But…if the [defendant] intended to cause serious hurt to the deceased, or…was indifferent or reckless as to whether he would produce serious injury or not, then the act would be unlawful.[14]

This gives rise to three specific issues. First, the rules of the game must not facilitate illegality on the part of the players. In this context, that appears to mean that contact sports, as opposed to fighting sports, should not have as their object the causing of serious injury or death. Contact sports, therefore, can be seen in a general sense to be activities "tolerated" by society that carry with them a risk of harm being inflicted unintentionally on their participants.[15] Secondly, it should be inferred that those who are playing in accordance with the rules of the game are acting lawfully because they do not intend to cause serious injury or death to their opponents, whilst those who are acting outside of those rules and with the intention to cause serious injury and/or death, or are reckless as to whether such harm will be caused, are committing a criminal assault. Thirdly, it should also be inferred that those who are playing a sport in accordance with its accepted practices, including commonly occurring incidents of foul play, are acting lawfully and that those who are acting outside of those accepted norms by intending to cause serious

[13] See *R v Roberts*, Unreported, Central Criminal Court (London), 28 June 1901.

[14] *R v Bradshaw* (1878) 14 Cox CC 83, 85 Bramwell LJ. See further Williams 1962, 80.

[15] See Cooper and James 2012 on other "tolerated activities".

injury, or being reckless as to whether serious injury will be caused, are committing a criminal assault.

The *Bradshaw* direction appeared to mean that contact sports are lawful provided that their aim or purpose is not the intentional or reckless infliction of serious injury or death and participation in them according to their rules is a lawful activity. Further, though without any explanation of why or how this is to be determined, it was taken from *Bradshaw* that conduct that is part of the accepted practices of the sport, though not necessarily within the rules of the game, is also lawful provided that there is no intention to cause death or serious injury. This lack of elaboration as to what exactly could and could not be consented to caused much of the confusion that plagued this area of the law throughout the twentieth century.

When almost a century later in *R v Billinghurst*, a court in England and Wales was given the opportunity to provide clarification on the *Bradshaw* direction, an alternative phrasing emerged: "conduct that could reasonably be expected to occur during a game".[16] This test was then used by the court to determine that fighting "off-the-ball" in rugby union was "unreasonable" at law, and therefore criminal, even if it was accepted as normal and reasonable by those actually playing the game. Thus, a further complicating factor was added; even if violent and injury-causing conduct was within the playing norms of the sport in question, the judiciary would now stand as final arbiters of whether such play was lawful, not the players, match officials and governing bodies of sport.

This confusion reached its apogee in two Law Commission Consultation Papers published in the mid-1990s.[17] In attempting to define the then state of the law, the Law Commission of England and Wales initially stated:

> The best that we can do, therefore, is to say that the present broad rules for sports and games appear to be: (i) the intentional infliction of injury enjoys no immunity; (ii) a decision as to whether the reckless infliction of injury is criminal is likely to be strongly influenced by whether the injury occurs during actual play, or in a moment of temper or over-excitement when play has ceased, or is 'off the ball'; (iii)...principle demands that even during play injury that results from risk-taking by a player that is unreasonable, in the light of the conduct necessary to play the game properly, should also be criminal.[18]

By focusing on the causing of injury, rather than the making of the initial contact, the Law Commission confused itself in much the same way as many courts had. If the injury-causing contact is part of the playing of the game, then it is consented to and there is no question of an assault having been committed, no matter how grave the harm caused. Instead of attempting to define the legality of the contact, the Law Commission proposed that the reasonableness of a defendant's conduct be taken into account when determining whether or not he had

---

[16] *R v Billinghurst* [1978] Crim LR 553.

[17] Law Commission 1994, 1995.

[18] Law Commission 1994, para 10.18.

acted with subjective recklessness when injuring his opponent, potentially leaving the law with yet another incomplete and unworkable set of guidelines.[19]

When returning to the subject of consent following the publication of the initial consultation, the Law Commission created yet further confusion. First, each of its recommendations were made using the terminology of a Criminal Law Bill and Draft Criminal Code, which it had previously proposed,[20] rather than being directed at the law then, and still now, in force. The dramatic overhaul of the law on offences against the person contained in the proposed Bill and Code rendered meaningless much of what the Law Commission had to say in respect of sport. Further, the Law Commission proposed that an appropriate body, such as what is now UK Sport, determine which sports are lawful activities but that the courts should reserve the right to review the reasonableness of a sport's rules if it was felt that that body allowed for too great a risk of injury. Thus the legality of an athlete's conduct was subsumed within a discussion of whether or not the sport in which they participate was of itself "lawful".[21]

In short, there was little meaningful discussion, and much considerable confusion, about what type of conduct might be an inherent risk of participation, which contacts could be consented to and which constituted unlawful criminal assaults. A promised final report by the Law Commission, following the above consultations, never materialised. In contrast, the reported cases from the time were demonstrating some clarity and certainty on the matter: defendants who had punched,[22] kicked,[23] head-butted[24] or bitten[25] their victims/opponents in circumstances that were very clearly unconnected with the playing of the sports in which they were participating were acting unlawfully and were guilty of a criminal assault. However, as injured sports participants made increasing use of the Criminal Injuries Compensation Scheme[26] to secure compensation for the injuries received at the hands, feet, heads and mouths of their opponents, sports' governing bodies began voicing their concern about the "juridification" of an aspect of their regulatory powers over which they sought sole jurisdiction.

---

[19] Law Commission 1994, paras 41–47.

[20] See, for instance, Law Commission 1995, Part 1 and Appendix A.

[21] See, for instance, Law Commission 1995, Part 12.

[22] *R v Birkin* (1988) 10 Cr App R (S) 303.

[23] *R v Garfield* [2008] EWCA Crim 130.

[24] *R v Piff* (1994) 15 Cr App R (S) 737.

[25] *R v Johnson* (1986) 8 Cr App R (S) 343.

[26] The Criminal Injuries Compensation Scheme is a government funded scheme that allows blameless victims of violent crime to get a financial award. The Criminal Injuries Compensation Authority is the government body responsible for administering the Criminal Injuries Compensation Scheme (latest version, 2008) in England, Scotland and Wales. On how the scheme operates see further www.justice.gov.uk/about/criminal-injuries-compensation-authority.

20.3 Guidance from Elsewhere

Some guidance, as to what both the criminal law and sports bodies in England and Wales might agree as "acceptable conduct" during a contact sport, was found in Canadian jurisprudence. There, a series of cases based on assaults with ice hockey sticks (*R v Cey*[27] and *R v Ciccarelli*,[28] for example) began to provide a much clearer explanation on how best to determine whether or not a player's conduct was an acceptable part of the game and therefore lawful. In *Cey*, the defendant had used the stick in order to push his opponent into the boards surrounding the edge of the rink whilst in *Ciccarelli*, the defendant had hit his victim repeatedly over the head with his stick. In both cases, the defendants were found guilty of assault. In coming to its conclusions in *Cey*, the court held that not only are contacts and resultant injuries that are permitted by the rules of the game lawful, but so are such contacts and resultant injuries that follow from breaches of the rules that fall within the accepted standards by which the game is played.[29] In *Ciccarelli*, the court refined and added to the other factors found to be important in *Cey* by stating that the following must be taken into account in order to determine the acceptability, and therefore the legality of an injury-causing blow: the nature of the game being played; the level at which the game was being played, for example, whether it was an amateur or professional match; the nature of the injury-causing act and its surrounding circumstances; the degree of force employed; the degree of risk of injury; and the state of mind of the accused.[30]

Alongside these developments in Canadian criminal law, in England the law of tort, in particular the tort of negligence, was developing at a significantly more rapid pace following its first intervention in an athlete-against-athlete case in *Condon v Basi* in 1985.[31] In one of the shortest judgments handed down by the Court of Appeal, Donaldson MR held that negligence applies to sport as it does to any other field of activity. Thus, where a tackle in a football match drops below the standard of care expected of the defendant-athlete, there is no reason why they should not be held liable in negligence for the injuries caused. The brevity of this judgment, however, led to some confusion over the circumstances in which the duty of care owed by an athlete could be breached by conduct associated with playing sport and in particular whether "reckless disregard" should replace the normal standard of "negligence in all the relevant circumstances" as it has in a number of states in the United States.[32]

---

27 *R v Cey* (1989) 48 CCC (3d) 480.

28 *R v Ciccarelli* (1989) 54 CCC (3d) 121.

29 *R v Cey* (1989) 48 CCC (3d) 480 490, Gerwing JA.

30 *R v Ciccarelli* (1989) 54 CCC (3d) 121, 126, Corbett DCJ.

31 *Condon v Basi* [1985] 1 WLR 866.

32 For a general review see McArdle 2005.

Clarity was eventually provided by the Court of Appeal in *Caldwell v Maguire and Fitzgerald*.[33] In determining whether one jockey's interference with a competitor was negligent, where an unintentional contact between horses had resulted in the claimant's horse falling and causing him career-ending injuries, it was held that a generally identifiable approach had evolved from the previous 16 years' of litigation. First, it was confirmed that each contestant in a lawful sporting contest owes a duty of care to all other contestants. Secondly, the applicable duty is to exercise in the course of the contest all care that is objectively reasonable in the prevailing circumstances for the avoidance of infliction of injury to those other contestants. Thirdly, the relevant prevailing circumstances include the object of the contest; the demands inevitably made upon its contestants; its inherent dangers; its rules; conventions and customs; and the standards, skills and judgement reasonably to be expected of a contestant. Fourthly, proof of something more than an error of judgement or lapse of skill would be required as these aspects of a contestant's conduct are an integral part of playing sport. Finally, proof that a contestant had acted with reckless disregard for an opponent's safety would be a sufficient, but not a necessary, condition of liability.

It must be reiterated here that the test for negligence in sporting cases remains as it is throughout English law; whether the defendant has dropped below the standard of conduct reasonably expected of him in the circumstances in which he is acting, not that he has acted with recklessness as to the safety of the claimant-victim.[34] The evidential burden of proof may in reality be a difficult one to discharge in the context of contact sports where mistakes and errors of judgement, as opposed to culpable negligence, can result in catastrophic injuries to the athletes. The object of the third stage of the test outlined above is to provide an understandable, coherent and workable approach in determining whether or not an athlete has breached the duty of care owed to their co-participants, leaving recklessness relevant only to criminal, not tortious, liability.

Thus, *Caldwell v Maguire and Fitzgerald* provides the detail on how to determine liability in negligence that had been missing in the criminal law for well over a century. In particular, the third point provides a framework for determining the acceptability or otherwise of an athlete's conduct reminiscent of the approach in Canadian criminal law but absent from the English jurisprudence. As consent cannot be individually or subjectively defined by each participant, as would ordinarily be the case in other situations attracting the attention of the criminal law, it is essential that a coherent and universally applicable test is available for determining the scope of a sportsperson's consent to potentially injury-causing contacts. Instead, the approaches developed in Canadian criminal cases and English negligence litigation were ignored and the aphorism that "hard cases make bad law" was epitomised by the application in the pre-*Barnes* era of the law of assault to contact sports.

---

[33] *Caldwell v Maguire and Fitzgerald* [2001] EWCA Civ 1054.

[34] *Caldwell v Maguire and Fitzgerald* [2001] EWCA Civ 1054, para 11, Tuckey LJ.

20.4 *R v Barnes*

Three summarising points can be made of the context in which *Barnes* must be read: there was confusion over the application of the law to contact sports; jurisdiction over these disputes was contested by the various governing bodies of contact sports; and the evolution of a more sophisticated and far-reaching law of negligence was taking shape.[35] In addition, and as has often been the case in sports law, *Barnes* was a simple sporting scenario that has had far-reaching consequences. Barnes was charged with assault following a challenge on an opponent during an amateur football game. He had been angered by the conduct of his victim/opponent, who he considered to have been time-wasting, and had been warned by the referee to calm down having pushed the victim off the pitch in an earlier incident. Some minutes later, the victim was through on goal in the penalty area, shot and scored. After the victim had kicked the ball, the defendant performed a sliding tackle which was described by himself as a hard but fair challenge and the prosecution as a crushing tackle that was late, unnecessary, reckless, high up the leg and more like a stamp. Evidence was also put forward that the defendant had said something along the lines of, "have that", before walking off the pitch. The referee sent him off for violent conduct.

In directing the jury, the judge attempted to describe how to determine whether or not a particular challenge was a criminal assault. In doing so, he stated that if the challenge was, "so reckless that it could not have been in legitimate sport",[36] or that if it was, "over and above what is generally acceptable in a football game,"[37] or "criminally reckless…and therefore beyond what is acceptable in the game of football,"[38] then the charge of unlawfully inflicting grievous bodily harm under section 20 of the Offences Against the Person Act 1861 was made out. On the basis of these explanations, the jury returned a verdict of guilty.

Despite the language of the direction being of a similar nature to that used in previous criminal cases, the defendant appealed on the grounds that the judge had misdirected the jury. Lord Woolf CJ, giving judgment at the Court of Appeal, held that, although the concept of "legitimate sport" was not unhelpful, it had been inadequately explained to the jury. In particular, the trial judge had not given examples of conduct that might, or might not, be classified as "legitimate" in the context of football nor had it been made clear to the jury that foul play, even serious foul play resulting in the offender being sent off, did not necessarily reach the threshold necessary to constitute criminal conduct. Further, where the trial judge had attempted to provide additional explanations, he had confused rather than clarified the position. The Court of Appeal held that the trial judge's misdirection was so serious that it rendered the conviction unsafe and on this ground

---

[35] See generally James 2010, Chaps. 4 and 5.

[36] *R v Barnes* [2005] 1 Cr App Rep 507, paras 21 and 24.

[37] *R v Barnes* [2005] 1 Cr App Rep 507, para 22.

[38] *R v Barnes* [2005] 1 Cr App Rep 507, paras 23 and 24.

Barnes' appeal was allowed and his conviction quashed. Although no retrial was ordered, despite the apparent strength of the prosecution case, a three-way clarification of the applicable law was provided by the judgment.

First, participation in contact sports is lawful therefore no criminal act of assault takes place when contact is made during the course of play. This part of the decision reiterates the long-established reasoning in *Bradshaw*, that sport is a lawful activity provided that it does not try to make lawful conduct that is inherently unlawful. In other words, contact sports are lawful activities unless they have as their specific object or purpose the causing of death or serious injury.

Secondly, it is not desirable and therefore not usually in the public interest to bring criminal actions based on sporting activities. As most organised sports have their own internal disciplinary procedures for dealing with breaches of their rules, these alternative dispute mechanisms should be resorted to in the first instance in the vast majority of cases. This partial acceptance of sport's ability to self-regulate through its networks of internal disciplinary procedures reduces the burden on the courts having to deal with cases that would be best heard by specialist tribunals.[39] It legitimises the use of alternative dispute resolution mechanisms to regulate low-level disorder and impose punishments, such as playing bans, that are perhaps more directly relevant to athlete-defendants and with the additional benefit that the violent player is removed from the context in which he has been acting violently.

Further, where injury is caused, a claim in negligence may be appropriate but a prosecution should only be pursued where the athlete's conduct is "sufficiently grave".[40] The court actively encourages injured athletes to use any additional dispute resolution forum, including the civil courts, to seek compensation for their injuries, thereby reducing further the impact of sporting cases on the criminal justice system. However, according to the Court of Appeal, the criminal courts should maintain their role as final arbiters of lawful conduct as per *Billinghurst* where the conduct is "sufficiently grave" to be properly categorised as criminal. Regrettably, the Court of Appeal offered little justification for the use of yet another new term to describe an athlete's criminality, which was the Court of Appeal's key criticism of the trial judge's original direction to the jury.

Thirdly, in order to determine whether or not an athlete's conduct should be categorised as criminal, Lord Woolf CJ eventually produced guidance of a similar level of detail to that which was available elsewhere. The type of sport; the level of play; the nature of the act; the degree of force used; the extent of the risk of injury; and the state of mind of the defendant must all be considered. The influence of the Canadian jurisprudence, in particular *Ciccarelli*, is clear and is almost directly replicated. Further, Lord Woolf CJ in the Court of Appeal in *Barnes* noted that in highly competitive sports conduct outside of the rules can be expected to occur in the "heat of the moment", and even if such conduct justifies being penalised by

---

[39] This is a long established principle in English law. See, for example, *Enderby Town FC v The Football Association* [1971] Ch 591.

[40] *R v Barnes* [2005] 1 Cr App Rep 507, para 5.

being either officially warned or "sent off", it may still not reach the threshold level of gravity required for it to be considered a criminal offence.[41] It follows that injury caused by conduct beyond the rules but in accordance with the practices of a sport, as per *Bradshaw*, or which is reasonably expected from participation in a particular sport, as per *Billinghurst*, or more explicitly, which is in breach of the rules but falls within the accepted standards by which a sport is played, as per *Cey*, is also lawful.

This approach is clearly contrary to an idealised notion that sport should be played only in accordance with its rules and that all acts of foul play are unacceptable to both the sport in question and to the law. It is, however, a pragmatic response to the acceptance that such play occurs and is generally accepted by the sub-cultural norms developed by each sport through the interpretation and application of its playing and disciplinary rules. This by no means gives sports participants an unlimited licence to use force against an opponent. It enables participants only to play the game in the manner in which it is expected to be played. Mistimed or misjudged challenges are lawful as is foul play where the risk of injury is low and/or there is an absence of intent to harm, such as one player tripping another in a game of football; however, deliberately violent or dangerous foul play can result in a prosecution being brought.

In a recent Canadian case, *R v CC*,[42] the defendant was convicted of unlawful act manslaughter following an incident in a game of rugby union in Ontario. The defendant performed an intentional "spear tackle" on the victim by driving his shoulder into the victim's stomach, lifting him up and propelling him backwards and head first into the ground. The victim died later as a result of catastrophic injuries to his spinal cord. The trial judge held that spear tackles are not within the rules of the game and further that this particular challenge was unconnected with the actual playing of this game as it occurred behind the play and was not a mistimed attempt to make a lawful challenge. As spear tackles are outside the accepted norms of rugby playing, the tackle was not within the implied consent of those who play rugby union and the offence of manslaughter was made out. Following *Barnes*, if an analogous situation were to occur in England, a similar approach and result could now be expected to be followed.

20.5 The Impact of *R v Barnes*

The Court of Appeal's judgment in *Barnes* provides a clear statement of the law that is easily applicable to a range of sporting situations. Perhaps the only controversial aspect of the decision was that the Court of Appeal quashed the conviction on the basis of the trial judge's misdirection of the jury rather than applying

[41] *R v Barnes* [2005] 1 Cr App Rep 507, para 15.

[42] *R v CC* (2009) ONCJ 249; 67 CR (6th) 183.

its own newly developed test to the facts as found by the jury. That aside, *Barnes* provides a workable, flexible and pragmatic means of determining the legality of sports participants' behaviour and, importantly, moves the criminal law away from proposals, such as those of Grayson, that all infringements of the rules of a game should be criminalised as a point of principle,[43] but without allowing sport an unqualified exemption from the operation of the law of offences against the person. Consequently, *Barnes* marks an important shift in emphasis by removing the vast majority of sports assaults from the jurisdiction of the criminal courts. In future, punishments will usually be imposed solely by the international, national, regional or local governing bodies of sport, providing them with the (long sought after) ability to self-regulate without "interference" from the courts.

Further, compensation will be awarded, where appropriate, by the civil courts rather than by compensation orders following conviction. This approach has been endorsed by Court of Appeal (Civil Division) in *Gravil v Carroll and Redruth RFC*,[44] where the law of torts has developed further and this shift away from regulation by the criminal law has been reinforced. *Gravil* centred on an altercation following a scrum in a semi-professional rugby union game. The defendant punched the claimant in the face after play had been stopped by the referee, causing the claimant serious facial injuries. The defendant was initially sent from the field of play for 10 min, i.e. "sin-binned". At his disciplinary hearing, it was found that the injuring player should have been sent off for the remainder of the game and was banned from playing rugby for eight weeks. In delivering the judgment of the Court of Appeal, Clarke MR held that the defendant-club was vicariously liable for the conduct of its player who threw the punch on the basis that his tortious conduct was so closely connected to his employment as a professional rugby player that his actions had to be considered to be within the course of his employment. Alternatively, the Court of Appeal ruled that it could be considered fair, just and reasonable to hold the club liable for the punch in circumstances where the defendant-player's conduct was an incidental risk of playing rugby pursuant—to his contract of employment.[45]

By allowing a claim for a deliberate punch, *Gravil* extends the scope of the law of torts significantly whilst at the same time reducing the potential scope for recourse to the criminal law for anything other than "off-the-ball" violence. Further, it highlights how an expanded law of torts, coupled with an effective internal disciplinary regime, can begin to claim jurisdiction over cases of a similar nature that would previously have been heard before the criminal courts.

---

[43] See Grayson 2000, 567–569 and in particular his "Draft Safety of Sportspersons Act".

[44] *Gravil v Carroll and Redruth RFC* [2008] EWCA Civ 689.

[45] *Gravil v Carroll and Redruth RFC* [2008] EWCA Civ 689, para 40. See further James and McArdle 2004.

20.6 Conclusion

The interpretation and analysis of the decisions of the two most senior members of the English judiciary—the Lord Chief Justice in *Barnes* and the Master of the Rolls in *Gravil*—means that the current approach of the law (both criminal and civil) to sports assaults can now be stated with a degree of certainty and confidence. First, contact sports are lawful activities provided that they do not have as their aim or purpose the deliberate infliction of death or serious injury. Secondly, all inter-personal contacts that are within the rules, or are in breach of the rules but within the accepted standards by which a sport is played, are lawful, regardless of the degree of injury sustained by the victim. "Tolerated risk-taking" is considered to be an integral part of the playing of contact sports. Actions in breach of the playing rules of the sport should be punished by the match officials or appropriate governing body. Thirdly, conduct that is beyond the accepted standards by which a sport is played is unlawful, however, following *Gravil*, such conduct is likely to be only tortious, not criminal. Again, any appropriate punishment should be imposed by the match officials or relevant governing body. Finally, following *Barnes*, any contacts that are unconnected with the playing of the game and/or are deliberately injury-causing will be criminal, regardless of any punitive action taken by the match officials or the relevant governing body. This clarity and certainty notwithstanding, the challenge for trial judges will remain in how *they* apply the *Barnes* and *Gravil* rulings in a manner that is both properly reflective of the regulated reality of the sports field and, more importantly, understandable to juries.

References

Anderson J (2005) Policing the sports field: the role of the criminal law. Int Sports Law Rev 5(2):25–32

Anderson J (2008) No licence for thuggery: violence, sport and the criminal law. Crim Law Rev 10:751–763

Cooper S and James M (2012) Entertainment—the painful process of rethinking consent. Crim Law Rev 2012(3):188–199

Gasser C, Schweizer E (2008) Switzerland: ice hockey/criminal law. Int Sports Law Rev 8(1):11–12

Grayson E (2000) Sport and the law, 3rd edn. Butterworths, London

Grayson E, Bond C (1993) Making foul play a crime. Solicit J 137(27):693

James M (2010) Sports law. Palgrave Macmillan, Basingstoke

James M, McArdle D (2004) Player violence or violent players? Vicarious liability for sports participants. Tort Law Rev 12:131–146

Law Commission (1994) Consultation paper no.134: Consent and offences against the person. HMSO, London

Law Commission (1995) Consultation paper no.139: Consent in the criminal law. HMSO, London

McArdle D (2005) The enduring legacy of reckless disregard. Common Law World Rev 34:316–335

Parrish R, Miettinen S (2008) The sporting exception in European Union law. TMC Asser Press, The Hague

Simester AP et al (2010) Simester and Sullivan's criminal law: theory and doctrine, 4th edn. Hart, Oxford

Williams G (1962) Consent and public policy. Crim Law Rev 1:74–83

Chapter 21
Animal Welfare and Blood Sports: *R (Countryside Alliance) v Attorney General* [2008] 1 AC 719

Laura Donnellan

Abstract The appellants appealed to the then House of Lords (now the UK Supreme Court) against a decision of the Court of Appeal that the Hunting Act 2004 was neither incompatible with the European Convention on Human Rights nor inconsistent with EU law. The 2004 Act prohibits the hunting with dogs of certain wild mammals, including foxes and hares. The appellants argued that the hunting ban infringed their rights under Article 8ECHR through the adverse impact the ban had on their private life, cultural lifestyle, the use of their home and loss of livelihood. They also submitted that the Hunting Act 2004 both infringed their "assembly" rights under Article 11ECHR and interfered with their "property rights" under Article 1 of protocol 1 to the European Convention on Human Rights. They further argued that the Hunting Act subjected them to adverse treatment, on the grounds of their "other" status under Article 14ECHR in so far as they compared to those who did not wish to hunt. In addition, some of the appellants, who supplied hunting-related goods and services, contented that the Hunting Act 2004 was inconsistent with Articles 28 and 49 of the EC Treaty (now Articles 34TFEU and 56TFEU) and sought references to the European Court of Justice (now the Court of Justice of the European Union, CJEU). The House of Lords dismissed the appeal holding inter alia that the instant case was far removed from the values that Articles 8ECHR, 11ECHR and 14ECHR sought to uphold and that "no good purpose" would be served by seeking a preliminary ruling from the CJEU if the hunting restrictions could, as they thought they might, be justified on the grounds of public policy under Article 30 of the EC Treaty (now Article 36TFEU) and Article 46 of the EC Treaty (now Article 52TFEU).

L. Donnellan (✉)
Lecturer in Law, School of Law, University of Limerick, Limerick, Ireland
e-mail: laura.donnellan@ul.ie

J. Anderson (ed.), *Leading Cases in Sports Law*,
ASSER International Sports Law Series, DOI: 10.1007/978-90-6704-909-2_21,

Contents

21.1 Introduction

The Hunting 2004 Act prohibits the hunting with dogs of certain wild mammals, including foxes and hares in England and Wales. Taking a long view, the origins of the legislation can be traced to 1800 and the beginning of UK parliamentary efforts to protect the welfare of animals by way of a measure seeking to prohibit bull-baiting.[1] These attempts were unsuccessful but as Lord Bingham reflected two centuries later, "the tide of opinion gradually changed" beginning with Martin's Act, "to prevent the cruel and improper treatment of cattle" in 1822.[2] Two years later, the Society for the Prevention of Cruelty to Animals was founded to secure "the mitigation of animal suffering, and the promotion and expansion of the practice of humanity towards the inferior classes of animated beings".[3] Thereafter a steady stream of measures to protect the welfare of animals and prevent the causing of suffering to them were enacted in 1833, 1835, 1837, 1844, 1849, 1850, 1854, 1876 and 1894. In 1900, the Wild Animals in Captivity Protection Act was passed and applied to any confined bird, beast, fish or reptile not included in the 1849 and 1854 Acts, and made it an offence wantonly or unreasonably to cause or permit any unnecessary suffering or cruelty to any of these creatures or to abuse, infuriate, tease or terrify it.[4] Section 4 of that 1900 Act specifically stated that the Act was not to apply to the hunting or coursing of any animal which had not been liberated in a mutilated or injured state in order to facilitate its capture or destruction, a provision, which Radford states, was inserted on the insistence of the House of Lords.[5] During the twentieth century, the stream of legislation continued,

[1] See generally Radford 2001, Chap 3.

[2] *R (Countryside Alliance) v Attorney General* [2008] 1 AC 719, para 37, Lord Bingham.

[3] Radford 2001, 41. It added "Royal" to its name, by permission of Queen Victoria, in 1840.

[4] *R (Countryside Alliance) v Attorney General* [2008] 1 AC 719, para 37, Lord Bingham.

[5] Radford 2001, 85.

with statutes directed to the welfare, protection and preservation of animals passed in (among other years) 1909, 1911, 1912, 1921, 1925, 1927, 1928, 1933, 1949, 1951, 1952, 1954, 1962, 1973, 1981, 1986, 1987, 1988, 1991, 1992, 1993 and 1996. As Lord Bingham noted, this long and deep legislative history on preventing the causes of unnecessary suffering to animals meant that "whatever one's view of the 2004 Act, it must be seen as the latest link in a long chain of statutes devoted to what was seen as social reform".[6] The Hunting Act as a socially reforming provision, as opposed to one which might have economic repercussions, is an important underlying element to this case analysis.

A slightly shorter view of the origins of the Hunting Act 2004 would begin with the Labour Party's victory in the UK Parliamentary elections of 1997. During that election campaign, Labour promised MPs a free vote on any provision seeking to prohibit and/or strictly regulate the hunting with dogs of certain wild mammals, including foxes and hares in England and Wales.[7] Michael Foster, a newly elected MP for Worchester, and a known anti-hunting campaigner, was the first MP to present a private member's bill on the matter. The bill won the support of more than 173 MPs in the House of Commons and progressed to a second reading. On second reading the bill was carried by 411 votes to 151. Following mass demonstrations by pro-hunting groups, including the newly created Countryside Alliance, the government backed down and Foster's bill collapsed. In December 1999, the then Secretary of State for the Home Department appointed a committee of inquiry ("the Burns Report") into hunting with dogs, with the following terms of reference:

> To inquire into: the practical aspects of different types of hunting with dogs and its impact on the rural economy, agriculture and pest control, the social and cultural life of the countryside, the management and conservation of wildlife and animal welfare in particular areas of England and Wales; the consequences for these issues of any ban on hunting with dogs; and how any ban might be implemented.[8]

The Burns Report reported back to the Home Secretary in June 2000 but did not determine definitively on whether hunting should be banned or restricted but simply outlined the "pros and cons" of the consequences and implementation of a ban on hunting with dogs. Eventually, the British government decided to give MPs three options: self-supervision on hunting; government regulation or an

---

[6] *R (Countryside Alliance) v Attorney General* [2008] 1 AC 719, para 37, Lord Bingham.

[7] In Scotland, the Protection of Wild Mammals (Scotland) Act 2002 prohibits the hunting of all wild mammals with dogs, with the exception of rabbits and rodents. The validity of this legislation was unsuccessfully challenged on human rights grounds in the Scottish courts. See *Adams* v *Scottish Ministers* [2002] UKHRR 1189 (Outer House) and [2004] SC 665 (Inner House). The Scottish statute is broadly similar to, but not identical with, the Hunting Act 2004. Moreover, the challenge in the Scottish courts was on broadly the same human rights grounds as were relied on in the present proceedings.

[8] The final report of the Burns committee of inquiry into hunting with dogs in England and Wales can be found online at www.defra.gov.uk/rural/countryside/hunting. Accessed 31 July 2012.

outright ban.[9] In broad terms, the House of Commons favoured a ban on hunting; however, the House of Lords favoured self-supervision. In 2001 and again in 2002, Hunting Bills seeking first to ban the hunting with dogs of certain mammals or second, in the alternative, to implement a strict licensing system, passed through the House of Commons but were defeated in the House of Lords. In September 2004, a bill banning hunting with dogs was accepted by nearly two-thirds of the House of Commons but was again rejected by the House of Lords until eventually, and by way of the Parliament Acts,[10] the Hunting Act received Royal Assent on 18 November 2004 and entered into force on 18 February 2005.

21.2 *Countryside Alliance* in the High Court

In 2005, the Countryside Alliance[11] and various individual claimants initiated High Court applications for judicial review of the lawfulness and integrity of the Hunting Act 2004 by way of challenges on various human rights and EU law grounds.[12] The "human rights" claimants included tenant farmers, Masters of the Hunt, a farrier, a Master and owner of a beagle pack, a landowner, trainer of coursing greyhounds, a livery yard owner, a professional huntsman and a professional terrier man. The challenges here were made variously under Article 8 (right to a private life); Article 11 (freedom of assembly); Article 14 (freedom from discrimination) and the Article 1 of the First Protocol (right to peaceful enjoyment of possessions) of the European Convention of Human Rights and Fundamental Freedoms ("ECHR" or "the Convention").[13] The "EU law" claimants included, among others, horse dealers based in Ireland with clients in the UK, a proprietor of a business who offered hunting holidays to foreign visitors, a horse breeder based in Ireland, a Belgian national, a German national and a Portuguese national who travelled to the UK specifically for hunting.[14]

[9] See the background in Griffin 2007, 228.

[10] In British constitutional law, the Parliament Acts 1911 and 1949 assert the supremacy of the House of Commons by limiting the legislation-blocking powers of the House of Lords i.e., provided the provisions of the Parliament Acts are met; legislation can be passed without the approval of the House of Lords. On the coming into force of the Hunting Act, the constitutionality of this process was challenged, That challenge was ultimately rejected by the House of Lords in *Jackson and others v Her Majesty's Attorney General* [2006] 1 AC 262.

[11] The Countryside Alliance was created in 1997 as a response to the newly elected Labour Government's pledge to ban hunting with dogs. An amalgamation of three organisations: the Countryside Business Group, the British Field Sports Society and the Countryside Movement, the Countryside Alliance is major British campaigning organisation or lobby group on rural issues and claims to have over 100,000 members. See www.countryside-alliance.org/ca.

[12] *Countryside Alliance & Ors v HM Attorney General & Ors* [2005] EWHC 1677 (Admin).

[13] Reproduced in full in the reference list to this chapter.

[14] See generally *Countryside Alliance & Ors v HM Attorney General & Ors* [2005] EWHC 1677 (Admin) at paras 27–55. There was some debate as to the standing of the Countryside Alliance to

The contention here was that the Hunting Act 2004 was inconsistent with the fundamental freedoms pursuant to Articles 34TFEU and 56TFEU. Both groups contended that the Hunting Act 2004 was a disproportionate, unnecessary and illegitimate interference with "their rights to conduct their lives in the manner they choose" and that the legislation would, so far from achieving its avowed aim of preventing cruelty to animals, "in fact promote such cruelty" and that reasonable alternatives to a prohibitionary approach existed.[15]

The High Court dismissed the applications for judicial review. It upheld the validity of the Hunting Act, holding that it was proportionate and legitimate and that Parliament had access to sufficient information (including the Burns Report) to make an informed and rational decision to enact the Act.[16] The legislative aim of the Act, the High Court concluded, was a "composite one of preventing or reducing unnecessary suffering to wild mammals, overlaid by a moral viewpoint that causing suffering to animals for sport is unethical and should, as far as practicable and proportionate, be stopped".[17] Without repeating now that which was raised subsequently on appeal and particularly with regard to the EU law arguments, two general points can be taken from the High Court. First, the High Court was of the view that with regard to the Convention-related allegations that much of the alleged interference was essentially economic and proprietary in nature, and was thus most appropriate for consideration under Article 1 of the first protocol.[18] In this, the High Court was prepared to hold that there was interference under Article 1 of the first protocol and that the Hunting Act did, to an extent that was significant, interfere with the peaceful enjoyment of possessions in so much as it prevented individuals from using land, animals and goods which they owned for the purposes of hunting and that the Hunting Act indirectly diminished the value of land or other property or had damaged the established goodwill of a business. Nevertheless, the High Court held that but that such interference mainly, if not entirely, constituted control of use, and not deprivation property.[19]

(Footnote 14 continued)
bring the proceedings on their own account. The issue concerned whether it was "a victim" for the purpose of section 7(3) of the Human Rights Act 1998 and, if it were not, whether this disentitled it from bringing the proceedings. In the end it was agreed, at para 30, that "the court should determine the challenges to the Hunting Act in the round and not by blinkered reference to individual claimants".

[15] *Countryside Alliance & Ors v HM Attorney General & Ors* [2005] EWHC 1677 (Admin), para 2.

[16] *Countryside Alliance & Ors v HM Attorney General & Ors* [2005] EWHC 1677 (Admin), para 337.

[17] *Countryside Alliance & Ors v HM Attorney General & Ors* [2005] EWHC 1677 (Admin), para 339.

[18] See, for example, the comments in the context of the Article 8ECHR claim in *Countryside Alliance & Ors v HM Attorney General & Ors* [2005] EWHC 1677 (Admin), para 137.

[19] See generally *Countryside Alliance & Ors v HM Attorney General & Ors* [2005] EWHC 1677 (Admin), paras 160–182.

Second, the High Court held that, in part, some of the "Human Rights" claimants and the "European Law" claimants had succeeded in demonstrating that the various provisions of the EU law and certain elements of the ECHR were engaged by the Hunting Act and that this then required the defendants to justify the Hunting Act as proportionate. Ultimately, the High Court held that the legislation passed the proportionality test because:

> It was within the proportionate rational competence of the legislature to conclude that the balance between the legitimate legislative aim and the interference with rights and freedoms which it would engender fell on the side of enacting the Hunting Act. It was intrinsically a political judgment and a matter of domestic social policy, incapable of measurement in any scientifically calibrated scale, upon which the domestic legislature had a wide margin of discretion.[20]

21.3 *Countryside Alliance* at the Court of Appeal

The applicants subsequently appealed the decision to the Court of Appeal.[21] In dismissing the appeals, the Court of Appeal upheld the decision of the High Court though it reached different conclusions on some of the issues. Most interestingly, it found that the argued provisions of EU law were not engaged,[22] and even if they were, then, judged against the relevant case law, principles and legal norms of EU law, the Hunting Act's interference with the values protected by Articles 34TFEU and 56TFEU was justified and proportionate. This was particularly the case here, the Court of Appeal held, because of the "extensive nature of the consideration given to the issue, and the unprecedented time allowed for the Parliamentary debates, that the democratic legislators considered the issue, and the values inherent in the legislation, to be of high importance. That in our view is more than sufficient to establish the legitimacy of the Hunting Act within the requirements of Community law".[23] In sum, the Parliamentary process undergone in the particular case of this legislation demonstrated, according to the Court of Appeal, that the hunting ban satisfied the requirement of "fundamental importance in the affairs of the member state" that is imposed by the principle of proportionality in EU law.[24]

---

[20] *Countryside Alliance & Ors v HM Attorney General & Ors* [2005] EWHC 1677 (Admin), paras 347–348.

[21] *R (Countryside Alliance)* v *Attorney General* [2006] EWCA Civ 817.

[22] On Article 34TFEU, see *R (Countryside Alliance)* v *Attorney General* [2006] EWCA Civ 817, paras 130–146 and concluding that the Hunting Act did not engage Article 34TFEU and thus largely but not entirely mirroring the analysis of the High Court at paras 204–228 of its judgment. On Article 56TFEU, see *R (Countryside Alliance)* v *Attorney General* [2006] EWCA Civ 817, paras 147–157 and concluding, differing from the High Court, that the Hunting Act did not engage Article 49.

[23] *R (Countryside Alliance)* v *Attorney General* [2006] EWCA Civ 817, para 165.

[24] *R (Countryside Alliance)* v *Attorney General* [2006] EWCA Civ 817, para 171.

Arguably, of greater overall interest is the Court of Appeal's identification of a difficulty in analysing the appellants' EU law-related arguments and one that might have wider connotations for national legislation which, although having an economic effect, is, at heart, social and ethical in nature. At first, the Court of Appeal reiterated that the importance EU law places on the fundamental freedoms of movement, services etc. and the "importance of the subordination of national to [Union] values, is underlined by the absence of a *de minimis* rule: any interference with interstate trade, however minor, engages this area of the Community's jurisprudence".[25] Therefore, the Court of Appeal noted, once the EU jurisprudence is "engaged by domestic legislation, the member state is required to justify that legislation in all of its aspects, and not merely in respect of any aspect of it that directly interferes with interstate trade".[26] Generally, the Court of Appeal observed, the application of EU law principles implementing the fundamental values of the Union to national legislation that interferes with cross border trade can be done in a "rational and coherent" way. However, the Court of Appeal stated, "the principles are a good deal less easy to rationalise when they are sought to be applied to social legislation [as is the case with the Hunting Act] peculiar to a particular member state, that is not in terms directed at all at, and only incidentally impinges on, the supply or acquisition of goods or services".[27]

In saying this, the Court of Appeal fully accepted that the Hunting Act had to be tested against EU jurisprudence and that if shown to engage the free trade provisions of the EU law, to however modest an extent, then none of the provisions of the Hunting Act could be enforced unless they could be justified in Community terms. Accordingly, the Court of Appeal said if, for instance:

> ...the only provable effect of the hunting ban on interstate trade was that someone currently exporting 25 horses [bred for hunting] per annum from the Republic of Ireland to England could no longer find a market for some of them, then on a rigorous view of the requirements of [article 34 TFEU] would be engaged. The justification that would have to be advanced would not simply be a justification of the interference with trade, but would have to be in terms of justification of the whole hunting ban. That is why in this case much time has been spent in debating....the permissibility of legislators bringing ethical principles to bear on the regulation of conduct within the state: [not a consideration] considerations with any obvious relevance to trade.[28]

Continuing on this line on the difficulties of examining the economic effect of "social" legislation, the Court of Appeal pointed to "more extreme" cases:

> Take the recent legislation in Scotland, and proposed in England & Wales, to ban smoking in public bars. It would seem that it would only require one current regular tourist from France to this country to prove that his pleasure in coming here was contributed to so greatly by the current freedom to drink and smoke at the same time that in future he will go elsewhere or stay at home (just some, will no longer come to England to hunt) for it to

---

[25] *R (Countryside Alliance)* v *Attorney General* [2006] EWCA Civ 817, para 126.

[26] *R (Countryside Alliance)* v *Attorney General* [2006] EWCA Civ 817, para 126.

[27] *R (Countryside Alliance)* v *Attorney General* [2006] EWCA Civ 817, para 127.

[28] *R (Countryside Alliance)* v *Attorney General* [2006] EWCA Civ 817, para 127.

> be necessary to justify in Community terms the whole of national policy as to smoking in public...The Community organs are well aware of these difficulties: difficulties that in their more extreme forms might be thought at least potentially to undermine the effective application of core Community values to the cases for which those values are necessary and appropriate. *As we will see as we address the current jurisprudence, much of it is concerned with exploring the limits to which the important principles as to free movement of goods and services can sensibly be taken*...in relation to the Hunting Act.[29]

"Sensibly", the Court of Appeal was of the opinion that EU free movement principles could not be taken to be engaged by the Hunting Act. Would the House of Lords hold similarly?

21.4 *Countryside Alliance* at the House of Lords: Human Rights

Although the rationale used individually by their Lordships differed, sometimes markedly so, the House of Lords ultimately and unanimously rejected the subsequent appeals on both the human rights and EU law grounds.[30]

21.4.1 Article 8ECHR

Lord Bingham began his review of the appellants' appeal under this heading by stating that the purpose of Article 8ECHR was clear: "It is to protect the individual against intrusion by agents of the state, unless for good reason, into the private sphere within which individuals expect to be left alone to conduct their personal affairs and live their personal lives as they choose".[31] Lord Bingham then reviewed the Article 8ECHR claim, and specifically the Article 8(1)ECHR claim, under four headings. The first point (concerning the phrase "private life and autonomy") relied principally on an interpretation of *Pretty v United Kingdom*,[32] where the claimants contended that "private life" is a broad term and covered the physical and psychological integrity of a person, sometimes embracing aspects of an individual's physical and social identity, protecting a right to personal development and the right to establish relations with others in the outside world, and extending to matters within the personal and private sphere, and all underpinned by a respect for personal autonomy.[33] Further and relying on *Peck v United*

---

[29] *R (Countryside Alliance)* v *Attorney General* [2006] EWCA Civ 817, para 127.

[30] *R (Countryside Alliance) v Attorney General* [2008] 1 AC 719.

[31] *R (Countryside Alliance) v Attorney General* [2008] 1 AC 719, para 10. See also Baroness Hale's view at para 116.

[32] *Pretty v United Kingdom* (2002) 35 EHRR 1, paras 61–62.

[33] *R (Countryside Alliance) v Attorney General* [2008] 1 AC 719, para 11, Lord Bingham.

Kingdom,[34] the appellants highlighted that the European Court of Human Rights in Strasbourg ("the Strasbourg court") had taken the view that Article 8ECHR protects a right to identity and personal development, and the right to establish and develop relationships with other human beings and the outside world, potentially including activities of a professional or business nature.[35]

Lord Bingham was not, however, convinced that the appellants' claim could be brought within Article 8ECHR:

> Fox-hunting is a very public activity, carried out in daylight with considerable colour and noise, often attracting the attention of on-lookers attracted by the spectacle. No analogy can be drawn with the very personal and private concerns at issue in *Pretty* [a case concerning the "right to die" by way of assisted suicide]...nor with the disclosure in *Peck* [concerning closed circuit television pictures of the complainant preparing to commit suicide]. It is not of course to be expected that there will be a decided case based on facts indistinguishable from those of the case in issue, but none of the decided cases is at all close. With their references to notions of privacy, personal autonomy and choice and the private sphere reserved to the individual, they are in my opinion so remote from the present case as to give no guidance helpful to the claimants.[36]

Lord Bingham's colleagues largely agreed with this approach,[37] and in doing so cited with approval the view north of the border of Lord Justice Clerk in *Adams v Scottish Ministers* who in that challenge to the Scottish hunting legislation had listed a number of aspects which, in that Scottish court's view, prevented fox-hunting from being part of the private life of the participants and including "when followers are taken into account, the hunt takes on the character of a spectator sport. It is also a public spectacle".[38]

The second heading advanced by the human rights appellants under Article 8ECHR pertained to "cultural lifestyle". They relied here on *G and E v Norway*,[39] which concerned Lapps working as reindeer shepherds, fishermen and hunters living and working in the far north of Norway, and *Buckley v United Kingdom*[40] and *Chapman v United Kingdom*,[41] which concerned gipsies seeking to live in their caravans. Lord Bingham held, however, that the Lapps in *G and E* and the gipsies in *Buckley* and *Chapman* belonged to "distinctive groups, each with a

---

34 *Peck v United Kingdom* (2003) 36 EHRR 719, para 57.

35 *R (Countryside Alliance) v Attorney General* [2008] 1 AC 719, para 11, Lord Bingham.

36 *R (Countryside Alliance) v Attorney General* [2008] 1 AC 719, para 15, Lord Bingham.

37 *R (Countryside Alliance) v Attorney General* [2008] 1 AC 719, paras 90–108, Lord Rodger who took a slightly broader view of privacy under Article 8ECHR as based on an interpretation of *von Hannover v Germany* [2005] 40 EHRR 1 and the claim by Princess Caroline of Monaco to a privacy right of being free from press intrusion. Nevertheless, Lord Rodger noted at para 109 that whether on a narrower or broader view of the scope of Article 8ECHR, the appellants' Convention right was not engaged.

38 *Adams v Scottish Ministries* (2004) SC 665, 680, para 66.

39 *G and E v Norway* (1983) 35 DR 30.

40 *Buckley v United Kingdom* (1996) 23 EHRR 101.

41 *Chapman v United Kingdom* (2001) 33 EHRR 399.

traditional culture and lifestyle so fundamental as to form part of its identity".[42] In contrast, the hunting fraternity could "not plausibly be portrayed in such a way" and adding, rather sharply, "the social and occupational diversity of this fraternity, often relied on as one of its strengths, leaves no room for such an analogy".[43] Again, there was general agreement on this point with Lord Hope, for example, noting: "The customs and beliefs which are shared by those who participate in [hunting] are different from those shared by others in the population generally. But they are a minority in numerical terms only".[44]

The third heading related to use of the "home" and specifically that "home" in Article 8ECHR is an autonomous concept and, on the Strasbourg court's ruling in *Niemietz v Germany*,[45] that the concept may extend to business premises and a professional person's office. Lord Bingham again quickly dismissed this argument by ruling "…it is one thing to recognise that the meaning of 'home' should not be too strictly defined or circumscribed, and quite another to suggest that the expression can cover land over which the owner permits or causes a sport to be conducted and which would never, in any ordinary usage, be described as 'home'".[46]

Finally, there was a "loss of livelihood" claim under Article 8ECHR wherein reliance was placed on *Sidabras and Dziautas v Lithuania.*[47] In that case, two men who had, some years before, been employed as KGB officers were, as a result of a statutory provision dismissed from their jobs and debarred from a very wide range of public and private sector employments. Further, they complained that they suffered constant embarrassment as a result of being publicly branded as former KGB officers. The European Court of Human Rights found that a far-reaching ban on taking up private sector employment did affect private life. It did not rule on whether Article 8ECHR had been infringed, but found a breach of Article 14ECHR of the Convention in conjunction with Article 8.[48] Lord Bingham found that *Sidabras* was "a very extreme case on its facts" wherein the claimant had been so effectively deprived of the ability to work that their ability to function as social beings was also blighted but that was "not the lot" of the appellants here "to whom every employment is open save that of hunting wild mammals with dogs".[49]

---

[42] *R (Countryside Alliance) v Attorney General* [2008] 1 AC 719, para 15, Lord Bingham.

[43] *R (Countryside Alliance) v Attorney General* [2008] 1 AC 719, para 15, Lord Bingham.

[44] *R (Countryside Alliance) v Attorney General* [2008] 1 AC 719, para 55, Lord Hope.

[45] *Niemietz v Germany* (1992) 16 EHRR 97, paras 29 and 30. Reference was also made to UK jurisprudence such as *Kay v Lambeth London Borough Council* [2006] 2 AC 465.

[46] *R (Countryside Alliance) v Attorney General* [2008] 1 AC 719, para 15, Lord Bingham and citing *Giacomelli v Italy* (2006) 45 EHRR 871, para 76.

[47] *Sidabras and Dziautas v Lithuania* (2004) 42 EHRR 104.

[48] *Sidabras and Dziautas v Lithuania* (2004) 42 EHRR 104, para 47 and paras 62–63.

[49] *R (Countryside Alliance) v Attorney General* [2008] 1 AC 719, para 15, Lord Bingham. But even on the extreme facts of *Sidabras* the court did not, as already noted, find a breach of Article 8 but contented itself with finding a breach of Article 14 in the ambit of Article 8.

21.4.2 Article 11ECHR

The essence of appellants' case here was that, since the only purpose of their assembling or associating was to hunt foxes, the prohibition of such hunting effectively restricted their right to assemble and associate. In advancing this argument the appellant's relied on the observation in *Anderson v United Kingdom* that "the right to freedom of assembly is one of the foundations of a democratic society and should not be interpreted restrictively".[50] Lord Bingham noted that the Court of Appeal,[51] in agreement with the High Court[52] had rejected the appellants' complaint under this head, holding that the effect of the hunting bans in England and Scotland respectively was not to prohibit the assembly of the hunt but to prohibit a particular activity once the claimants had assembled.[53] Lord Bingham questioned whether this was "a sufficient answer" and went on to observe that, "a right to assemble and protest is of little value if one is free to assemble but not, having done so, to protest. If people only assemble to act in a certain way and that activity is prohibited, the effect in reality is to restrict their right to assemble. I would not be content to treat Article 11 as inapplicable on the present facts".[54]

In this, Lord Bingham was supported by Lord Hope.[55] Nevertheless, both their Lordships agreed that there are limits to the application of Article 11ECHR, with Lord Hope stating:

> There is a threshold that must be crossed before the article [11ECHR] becomes applicable. The essence of the freedom of assembly that article 11 guarantees is that it is a fundamental right in a democracy and, like the right to freedom of expression, is one of the foundations of such a society...The situations to which it applies must relate to activities that are of that character, of which the right to form and join a trade union which article 11 refers to is an example. The purpose of the activity provides the key to its application. It covers meetings in private as well as in public, but it does not guarantee a right to assemble for purely social purposes. The right of assembly that the claimants seek to assert is really no more than a right to gather together for pleasure and recreation...I agree with Lord Bingham that, where the activity which brings people together is prohibited, the effect is in reality to restrict their right to assemble. But the claimants' position is no different from that of any other people who wish to assemble with others in a public place for sporting or recreational purposes. It falls well short of the kind of assembly whose protection is fundamental to the proper functioning of a modern democracy and is, for that reason, guaranteed by article 11.[56]

---

[50] *Anderson v United Kingdom* (1997) 25 EHRR CD 172, 174. See also *Chassagnou v France* (1999) 29 EHRR 615, para 100.

[51] *R (Countryside Alliance)* v *Attorney General* [2006] EWCA Civ 817, para 107.

[52] *Countryside Alliance & Ors v HM Attorney General & Ors* [2005] EWHC 1677 (Admin), para 82.

[53] *R (Countryside Alliance) v Attorney General* [2008] 1 AC 719, para 18, Lord Bingham.

[54] *R (Countryside Alliance) v Attorney General* [2008] 1 AC 719, para 18, Lord Bingham.

[55] *R (Countryside Alliance) v Attorney General* [2008] 1 AC 719, paras 56–57, Lord Hope.

[56] *R (Countryside Alliance) v Attorney General* [2008] 1 AC 719, para 58, Lord Hope.

21.4.3 Article 1 of the First Protocol to the ECHR

Lord Bingham was blunt on this issue: "I do not think that the effect of the 2004 Act is to deprive any of the HR claimants of his or her possessions. This is not a confiscatory measure".[57] That being said he held it "indisputable" that certain of the claimants have suffered "a loss of control over their possessions" in the sense that some of the appellant-landowners could not now hunt over their own land or permit others to do so and others (e.g., the farrier who used his equipment to shoe horses to be ridden for hunting), had lost their "marketable goodwill", suffering a reduction in trade. Lord Bingham observed that both Strasbourg[58] and domestic[59] jurisprudence draws a distinction between goodwill which may be a "possession" for purposes of Article 1 of the first protocol and future income, not yet earned and to which no enforceable claim exists.[60] Since the provision was applicable—and on this Lord Bingham was widely supported by his colleagues[61]—it was necessary to consider whether the interference imposed by the Hunting Act 2004 was justifiable and proportionate.[62] Baroness Hale's analysis on the Hunting Act's justification *vis a vis* the engagement of Article 1 of the first protocol to the Convention is worth citing at length as it has wider constitutional relevance:

> Even in the context of deprivation of property the Strasbourg court has said that 'finding it natural that the margin of appreciation available to the legislature in implementing social and economic policies should be a wide one [the Court] will respect the legislature's judgment as to what is in the public interest unless that judgment is manifestly without reasonable foundation': *Jahn v Germany* (2006) 42 EHRR 49…In determining whether a fair balance has been struck between the demands of the general interest and the interest of the individuals concerned, in control of use cases, 'the Court recognises that the State enjoys a wide margin of appreciation with regard both to choosing the means of

---

[57] *R (Countryside Alliance) v Attorney General* [2008] 1 AC 719, para 20, Lord Bingham.

[58] See, for instance, *Tre Traktörer AB v Sweden* (1989) 13 EHRR 309 (revocation of a restaurant's licence to sell alcohol had adverse effects on the value and goodwill of the restaurant and so was held to be a possession because an economic interest connected with running the restaurant).

[59] See Mr Kenneth Parker QC in *R (Nicholds) v Security Industry Authority* [2006] EWHC 1792 (Admin), paras 70–76.

[60] *R (Countryside Alliance) v Attorney General* [2008] 1 AC 719, para 21, Lord Bingham.

[61] See, for example, *R (Countryside Alliance) v Attorney General* [2008] 1 AC 719, para 65, Lord Hope; para 128, Baroness Hale; and para 146, Lord Brown.

[62] Lord Bingham answered in the affirmative at *R (Countryside Alliance) v Attorney General* [2008] 1 AC 719, para 47: "article 1 of the first protocol…is not to impair in any way the right of a state to enforce such laws as it deems necessary to control the use of property in accordance with the general interest…It is, in the first instance, for Parliament to decide what laws are necessary in accordance with what it judges to be the general interest. It has decided that the 2004 Act is necessary in accordance with the general interest. As already pointed out, Parliament's judgment is not immune from challenge. The national courts in the first instance, and ultimately the Strasbourg court, have a power and a duty to measure national legislation against Convention standards. But…respect should be paid to the recent and closely-considered judgment of a democratic assembly, and no ground is shown for disturbing that judgment in this instance".

> enforcement and to ascertaining whether the consequences of enforcement are justified in the general interest for the purpose of achieving the object of the law in question': *AGOSI v United Kingdom* (1987) 9 EHRR 1...On that basis, protecting wild animals from avoidable compromise to their welfare seems to me to fall well within the general interest and the means chosen to strike a fair balance.[63]

21.4.4 Article 14ECHR

The appellants also relied on Article 14ECHR. In order to engage Article 14ECHR it suffices to show that there has been discrimination on a proscribed ground within the ambit of another article of the European Convention on Human Rights.[64] The appellants contented that they were are subject to adverse treatment on the ground of their "other status" that is to say, as compared with those who do not wish to hunt and are in no way involved in hunting. Lord Bingham observed that the phrase "other status" in Article 14ECHR is "plainly incapable of precise definition" but that one of the better constructions of the expression was given by the Strasbourg court in *Kjeldsen, Busk Madsen and Pedersen v Denmark*—"discriminatory treatment having as its basis or reason a personal characteristic ('status') by which persons or groups of persons are distinguishable from each other".[65] Applying that construction to the present case, Lord Bingham, with which his colleagues were largely in agreement,[66] held that

> ...assuming in the HR claimants' favour that they are the subject of adverse treatment as compared with those who do not hunt and are in no way involved in hunting, and assuming further that their complaints fall within the ambit of one or more articles of the Convention, I cannot link this treatment to any personal characteristic of any of the claimants or anything which could meaningfully be described as 'status'.[67]

21.5 *Countryside Alliance* at the House of Lords: EU Law

On the EU law claims; there was general agreement that it could not be said with any reasonable certainty that either Articles 34TFEU or 56TFEU were engaged.

[63] *R (Countryside Alliance) v Attorney General* [2008] 1 AC 719, para 129, Baroness Hale.

[64] See *R (Countryside Alliance) v Attorney General* [2008] 1 AC 719, para 130, Baroness Hale.

[65] *Kjeldsen, Busk Madsen and Pedersen v Denmark* (1976) 1 EHRR 711, para 56. The House of Lords adopted this test in *R (S) v Chief Constable of the South Yorkshire Police* [2004] UKHL 39; [2004] 1WLR 2196, para 48, and again in *R (Clift) v Secretary of State for the Home Department* [2006] UKHL 54; [2007] 1 AC 484, paras 27–28.

[66] See similarly the analysis by Lord Hope at *R (Countryside Alliance) v Attorney General* [2008] 1 AC 719, paras 59–64.

[67] *R (Countryside Alliance) v Attorney General* [2008] 1 AC 719, para 24, Lord Bingham.

When pushed, the House of Lords[68] seemed to favour the position of both the High Court[69] and the Court of Appeal[70] that the Hunting Act 2004 did not engage Article 34TFEU, as based on an interpretation of that article by the CJEU in *Keck*.[71] Similarly, when pushed, the House of Lords[72] tended to agree with the High Court[73] that the hunting ban did engage Article 56TFEU but, as the Court of Appeal had concluded,[74] the EU jurisprudence leading to this determination was not entirely clear, and thus a reference to the CJEU might have to be considered if it were not a clear opinion that the ban on hunting could be justified under EU law.

In this, the House of Lords was generally agreed that "no good purpose"[75] would be served if, applying the relevant test under EU jurisprudence, that any such restrictions as result from the ban imposed by the Hunting Act were proportionate and justified on grounds of public policy under Article 30 of the EC Treaty (now Article 36TFEU justifying exceptions to the prohibition in Article 34TFEU on grounds of public morality, public policy and including the protection of the health or life of animals etc.) and Article 46 of the EC Treaty (now Article 52TFEU justifying exceptions to the prohibition in Article 56TEFU on grounds of public morality, public policy etc.). The House of Lords was in agreement that the Hunting Act 2004 was proportionate and could be justified under EU law. In reaching this conclusion, two central points were relied upon. First, that the Hunting Act 2004 as a measure to be justified under EU law must, principally, be seen as a measure of social reform, not directed to the regulation of commercial activity and of which any impediment to the intra-Union provision of goods or services is "a minor and unintended consequence and which bears more hardly on those within this country than outside it".[76] Second and relying by analogy on CJEU jurisprudence on restrictions justified for reasons of public policy such as in *Omega*,[77] (where the German authorities considered, and the ECJ accepted that the exploitation of games involving the *simulated* killing of human beings infringed a fundamental value enshrined in the national constitution, namely human dignity); the House of Lords noted equally that Parliament considered (through long and

---

[68] See, for example, *R (Countryside Alliance) v Attorney General* [2008] 1 AC 719, para 31, Lord Bingham. *Cf* Lord Hope at para 68.

[69] *Countryside Alliance & Ors v HM Attorney General & Ors* [2005] EWHC 1677 (Admin), para 228.

[70] *R (Countryside Alliance)* v *Attorney General* [2006] EWCA Civ 817, para 146.

[71] Cases C-267/91 and C-268/91 *Keck and Mithouard* [1993] ECR I-6097, 6131, paras 14–17.

[72] See, for example, *R (Countryside Alliance) v Attorney General* [2008] 1 AC 719, paras 34–35, Lord Bingham. Cf Lord Hope at para 71.

[73] *Countryside Alliance & Ors v HM Attorney General & Ors* [2005] EWHC 1677 (Admin), paras 231–43.

[74] *R (Countryside Alliance)* v *Attorney General* [2006] EWCA Civ 817, para 157.

[75] *R (Countryside Alliance) v Attorney General* [2008] 1 AC 719, para 73, Lord Hope.

[76] *R (Countryside Alliance) v Attorney General* [2008] 1 AC 719, para 50, Lord Bingham and para 131, Baroness Hale.

[77] Case C-36/02 *Omega* [2004] ECR I-9609, paras 28–31.

rigorous debate), the *real* killing of foxes, deer, hares and mink by way of recreation infringed a fundamental value expressed historically in numerous animal cruelty statutes and culminating in the 2004 Act.[78]

21.6 Commentary and Conclusion

In effect, the House of Lords, as the High Court and Court of Appeal had previously, held that the objective and intention of the Hunting Act was a composite one: to prevent or reduce unnecessary suffering to wild animals, overlaid by a moral viewpoint that causing suffering to animals for sport was unethical and should, so far as was practical and proportionate, be stopped.[79] The appellants, and particularly the EU claimants, although acknowledging that preventing unnecessary animal suffering was a legitimate objective, questioned the uncertain and unsatisfactory evidential basis for the claims of animal suffering. Moreover, they particularly questioned the "moral overlay" of the Hunting Act 2004 and the associated right of a member state of the EU to rely on public morality as a justification for a measure that quite likely engaged provisions fundamental to the Union's legal and economic values. The appellants were, however, to be disappointed, as they were subsequently at the European Court of Human Rights, which held that a state has a wide margin of appreciation in prohibiting an activity that, as validated by its parliamentary and democratic processes, it viewed as morally and ethically objectionable.[80]

In sum, the overall stated proceedings are noteworthy from a sports law perspective because the intention of the legislature was, outwardly, to decrease animal suffering caused by and for the purposes of what was purportedly "sport and recreation". The decision also provides an interesting revisionist perspective on Elias's application of the civilising process to sport,[81] revealing that in twenty-first century Britain hunting with dogs for foxes is no longer considered "an activity deeply embedded in the tradition, life and culture of the countryside, richly portrayed in art and literature, a highly cherished, skilful, health and useful form of communal outdoor exercise".[82] In sum, for a moral majority of the public and at Parliament, and to the legal satisfaction of the now UK Supreme Court, the pursuit of a small animal across the countryside until it is caught and destroyed by hounds is now considered "abhorrent".[83]

78 *R (Countryside Alliance) v Attorney General* [2008] 1 AC 719, para 50, Lord Bingham.

79 High Court, para 339; Court of Appeal, para 56; and House of Lords, para 80.

80 Friend and Countryside Alliance v United Kingdom [2009] ECHR 2068 (17 December 2009).

81 See generally Elias 1986, 150–174.

82 *R (Countryside Alliance) v Attorney General* [2008] 1 AC 719, para 1, Lord Bingham.

83 *R (Countryside Alliance) v Attorney General* [2008] 1 AC 719, para 1, Lord Bingham.

Appendix

Article 8 of the European Convention on Human Rights Convention:

8(1): Everyone has the right to respect for his private and family life, his home and his correspondence.

8(2): There shall be no interference by a public authority with the exercise of this right except such as is in accordance with the law and is necessary in a democratic society in the interests of national security, public safety or the economic well-being of the country, for the prevention of disorder or crime, for the protection of health or morals, or for the protection of the rights and freedoms of others."

Article 11 of the European Convention on Human Rights Convention:

11(1): Everyone has the right to freedom of peaceful assembly and to freedom of association with others, including the right to form and join trade unions for the protection of his interests.

11(2): No restrictions shall be placed on the exercise of these rights other than such as are prescribed by law and are necessary in a democratic society in the interests of national security or public safety, for the prevention of disorder or crime, for the protection of health or morals or for the protection of the rights and freedoms of others. This Article shall not prevent the imposition of lawful restrictions on the exercise of these rights by members of the armed forces, of the police or of the administration of the State.

Article 14 of the European Convention on Human Rights:

The enjoyment of the rights and freedoms set forth in this Convention shall be secured without discrimination on any ground such as sex, race, colour, language, political or other opinion, national or social origin, association with a national minority, property, birth or other status

Article 1 of the first protocol to the European Convention on Human Rights:

Every natural or legal person is entitled to the peaceful enjoyment of his possessions. No one shall be deprived of his possessions except in the public interest and subject to the conditions provided for by law and by the general principles of international law.

The preceding provisions shall not, however, in any way impair the right of a State to enforce such laws as it deems necessary to control the use of property in accordance with the general interest or to secure the payment of taxes or other contributions or penalties.

References

Elias N (1986) An essay on sport and violence. In: Elias N, Dunning E (eds) Quest for excitement: sport and leisure in the civilizing process. Blackwell Publishers, Oxford, pp 150–174

Griffin E (2007) Blood sport hunting in Britain since 1066. Yale University Press, New Haven

Radford M (2001) Animal welfare in Britain: regulation and responsibility. Oxford University Press, Oxford

Chapter 22
Gender and Equality: *Sagen v VANOC* [2009] BCCA 522

Hilary A. Findlay

Abstract Six months or so before the staging of the Winter Olympic and Paralympic Games of 2010 in Vancouver, Canada, the appellants, internationally ranked women ski jumpers, brought an application against the Vancouver Organizing Committee for the 2010 Olympic and Paralympic Winter Games ("VANOC") seeking a declaration that if VANOC planned for the staging of ski jumping events for men at the 2010 Winter Olympic Games, then a failure to plan a ski jumping event for women would violate their equality rights, as guaranteed under the Canadian Charter of Rights and Freedoms ("the Charter"). The two central issues in the proceedings were did the Charter apply generally to the claim of gender discrimination advanced by the appellants against VANOC and, if so, then, specifically, was VANOC breaching section 15(1) of the Charter by staging men's, but not women's, ski jumping events at the 2010 Olympic Games? Section 15(1) of the Charter holds that, "Every individual is equal before and under the law and has the right to the equal protection and equal benefit of the law without discrimination and, in particular, without discrimination based on race, national or ethnic origin, colour, religion, sex, age or mental or physical disability". The trial judge, in the Supreme Court of British Columbia, found that (a) hosting and staging the 2010 Olympic and Paralympic Winter Games was a "governmental activity" being performed by VANOC and that VANOC was, therefore, subject to the Charter; (b) that VANOC planned to host ski jumping events for men but not for women; and (c) that this differential treatment discriminated against the female skiers in a substantive sense. The trial judge nevertheless concluded that no violation of section 15(1) of the Charter had occurred. The Court of Appeal dismissed the skiers' subsequent appeal holding that the Charter did not apply to the selection of events for the 2010 Olympic Games and that, even if it did apply, the failure to include the women's ski jumping event would not constitute a breach of section 15(1).

H. A. Findlay (✉)
Department of Sport Management, Brock University, 500 Glenridge Ave, St Catharines, ON L2S 3A1, Canada
e-mail: hfindlay@brocku.ca

J. Anderson (ed.), *Leading Cases in Sports Law*,
ASSER International Sports Law Series, DOI: 10.1007/978-90-6704-909-2_22,

Contents

22.1 Introduction

Sagen v VANOC,[1] captured headlines leading up to the 2010 Winter Olympic and Paralympic Games, putting into question the inclusion of any ski jumping events—male or female. In this case, a group of fifteen female ski jumpers challenged the International Olympic Committee's ("IOC") decision not to include women's ski jumping in the 2010 Olympic programme. The trial judge, in the Supreme Court of British Columbia, found that the IOC's decision to include only ski jumping events for men, and not for women, was discriminatory. Notwithstanding this finding of discrimination under Canadian law, both the trial and appellate levels of court (the latter at the Court of Appeal of British Columbia), concluded that control over the decision of what sports to include in the Olympic programme rested solely with the IOC and was beyond the jurisdictional reach of a Canadian court to intervene in this instance. The decision was perplexing to many. How could something that was discriminatory under Canadian law, and which violated Canadian values, be allowed to be part of an event taking place on Canadian soil, organised by a Canadian organisation and which received significant public funding from all three levels of government—municipal, provincial and federal?

The case highlights a number of issues with respect to the governance of international sport and the oversight of such governance, particularly within the domestic forum. Three specific themes can be identified: the complex and diminishing role of national legal systems in regulating international sport (particularly when it occurs on national turf); the dominance of private institutions, such as the IOC and VANOC in international sport and a concern over the seemingly unfettered regulatory discretion of these private bodies, which is particularly evident when the decisions of international sport bodies conflict with legal principles of equality and respect for human rights, typically enshrined in and protected by national law.

[1] *Sagen v VANOC* [2009] BCSC 942 and *Sagen v VANOC* [2009] BCCA 522.

Ski jumping, at the time, had the dubious distinction of being the only sport in the Winter Olympics that was not open to both men and women. Nonetheless, support for the inclusion of women's ski jumping in the 2010 Winter Olympic programme had come from the International Ski Federation ("FIS"), the world governing body overseeing ski jump competition, which voted 114-1 in May 2006 to approve a recommendation that it be added. Six months later VANOC, at the request of the Canadian women's ski jump team, sent a letter to the IOC in support of the inclusion of women's ski jumping in the 2010 Olympic programme. Days later, however, the IOC Executive Board voted not to include women's ski jumping in the Games. The IOC claimed the ruling was based on "technical merit" and had nothing to do with gender discrimination. The women ski jumpers were not prepared to simply accept the verdict of the IOC. A discrimination suit was filed with the Canadian Human Rights Commission, which resulted in a mediated settlement requiring the federal government to lobby the IOC to include women's ski jumping at the 2010 Olympics. When efforts by the Federal Secretary of State for Sport were unsuccessful, fifteen elite women ski jumpers from six countries, including Canada, Norway, Austria, Germany, Slovenia and the United States, filed a lawsuit claiming that their non-inclusion in the Olympic Games constituted discrimination on the basis of their sex contrary to the Canadian Charter of Rights and Freedoms ("the *Charter*").[2]

The case was heard at two levels of court: on trail before the British Columbia Supreme Court; and on appeal to the British Columbia Court of Appeal.[3] This chapter will discuss the major elements of the trial and appellate courts' decisions and the repercussions for the regulation of international sport, such as the Olympic Games, particularly when such activities take place on national soil. The chapter is divided into four parts, each examining a different aspect of the case. The first part focuses on what became the pivotal issue of the case—jurisdiction. In order to bring themselves within the jurisdiction of the courts, the skiers needed to show that VANOC was either controlled by the government or carrying out a government function. Without this, the claimants would find themselves without a remedy. This section will focus on the analysis used by the court in distinguishing between private action and public, or governmental, action. The second part looks at the issue of discrimination. The trial court[4] had little difficulty finding discrimination; however, the actual source of the discrimination became a key concern here. Third, there is a

[2] Full citation: Canadian Charter of Rights and Freedoms, Part I of the Constitution Act 1982 being Schedule B to the Canada Act 1982 (UK).

[3] The appellants sought leave to appeal the decision of the British Columbia Court of Appeal to the Supreme Court of Canada. Their application was denied. See the filing docket to the Supreme Court of Canada at www.scc-csc.gc.ca/case-dossier/cms-sgd/dock-regi-eng.aspx?cas=33439.

[4] Only the trial court found discrimination. The BC Court of Appeal looked only at the threshold issue of whether the inclusion of an event in the Olympic programme was a "benefit of the law" to which section 15(1) of the *Charter* (i.e., the equality section) applied. Since the Court of Appeal concluded that the availability of ski jumping events at the 2010 Games was simply not a "benefit of the law" for the purposes of section 15(1), it did not have to consider in any great detail whether discrimination existed. As it happened, the Court of Appeal held *obiter* that even if the *Charter* applied to VANOC in respect of the impugned conduct in this case; the appellants'

review of the remedies potentially available to the claimants and their usefulness in actually assisting the claimants in their quest for parity in the Games. The chapter ends with a concluding comment on the outcome of the case and a reflection on the eroding impact domestic law has on the governance of international sport.

22.2 Critical Jurisdictional Question: Did the *Charter* Apply?

Sagen v VANOC is a unique case. The fact of the discrimination was easily discerned and widely accepted by the trial court and yet the unique aspect of this case is that the ski jumpers were unable to bring themselves within the ambit of the *Charter* and show, pursuant to section 32 of the *Charter*, some form of "government action"[5] in association with their claim and activities of VANOC. In short, it was the skier's proposition that VANOC was so heavily engaged with government involvement that it could be described as a form of "government action" but the application of the *Charter* in this regard is complex. It relies upon a fundamental but somewhat amorphous distinction between government and non-government. Margot Young, an expert in Canadian constitutional law, explains:

> The *Charter*, like any other rights-protecting document, has a central (but impossible) necessity: it must articulate a coherent boundary between the public and the private, between government and non-government. And it must use this boundary to determine whether the *Charter* applies.[6]

The "boundary" further distinguishes between state power and individual liberty. Again, Young explains:

> The application of rights to non-state actors is thus contradictory within classical liberalism's prism. Liberal rights documents must preserve a sphere of untouchable private action clear of obligatory constitutional norms and 'state' virtues. And, this separation of the public sphere from the realm of private activity sets limits on the types of claims the courts recognize.[7]

(Footnote 4 continued)
claims under section 15(1) could not succeed. For the Court of Appeal's *obiter* reasoning, see *Sagen v VANOC* [2009] BCCA 522, paras 50–67.

[5] Section 32 of the *Charter* states: "This Charter applies (a) to the Parliament and government of Canada in respect of all matters within the authority of Parliament including all matters relating to the Yukon Territory and Northwest Territories; and (b) to the legislatures and governments of each province in respect of all matters within the authority of the legislature of each province". Essentially, therefore, the Charter applies only to government, and government action; not to private individuals, businesses or other organisations.

[6] Young 2010, 97.

[7] Young 2010, 97.

This distinction was recognised by the trial judge in *Sagen v VANOC* when Madame Justice Fenlon commented that "not every discrimination is a breach of the *Charter*".[8] This statement bespeaks the distinction between state action and private action with which both levels of court had to grapple. In other words, the trial court could find, and did find, discrimination in the treatment of the women ski jumpers but found it arose from an historical decision of the IOC, a private entity that is outside the purview of the *Charter*, and thus could not be remedied using the *Charter*.

The claimants argued that government, indeed all three levels of government, were so inextricably part of VANOC and its operations as to fall within the scope of "government action" and thus, via section 32 of the *Charter*, within the ambit of the *Charter* as a whole. Over the years, two lines of argument have emerged within *Charter*-related jurisprudence for holding an entity accountable as "government action". The claimants argued that VANOC was subject to the *Charter* along both lines. The first line of argument required the claimants to establish that VANOC was, by virtue of its very nature, governmental or substantially controlled by government. This test, known as the "control test", is one of form rather than function. The second line of argument examines the nature of the activity being performed by VANOC. This test is known as the "government activity test". If the activity is such that it can be ascribed to government (e.g., carrying out a government programme, policy or responsibility), then VANOC, although a private entity (i.e., not a government-controlled entity under the first test), will nonetheless be subject to the *Charter* when performing that activity. This second test looks at the activity and not the nature of the entity itself.[9]

22.2.1 The Control Test

The control test was relevant in *Sagen v VANOC* only at the trial level. The fundamental premise of this aspect of Canadian public and constitutional law is that an entity that is not part of government is nonetheless subject to the *Charter* if it is subject to "routine or regular control" by government (in this instance, the Governments of Canada (federal), British Columbia (provincial) and two

---

[8] *Sagen v VANOC* [2009] BCSC 942, para 7.

[9] Note the cited case law relating to, and the analysis of, section 32 of the *Charter* by the Canadian Supreme Court in *Greater Vancouver Transportation Authority v Canadian Federation of Students* [2009] SCC 31, [2009] 2 SCR 295, paras 13–16. In that case, the appellant public transit authorities refused to post the respondents' political advertisements on the sides of their buses on the basis that their advertising policies permitted commercial but not political advertising on public transit vehicles. The respondents commenced an action alleging that the transit authorities' policies had violated their right to freedom of expression guaranteed by section 2(b) of the *Charter*. The Canadian Supreme Court held that both transit authorities were "government" within the meaning of section 32 of the *Charter* and that the *Charter* applied to all matters within the authority of those entities, including the operation of the buses they owned.

municipal governments were all involved with VANOC).[10] Previous case law had identified a number of factors indicative of a level of government control and including government funding; control over budget allocation; power of appointment (e.g., appointment of board members); control over terms of appointment (i.e., serving at the "pleasure" of the appointee or for a specified term); approval, or other control, over by-laws or other guiding documents of the entity; whether the entity is a creature of statute; and statutory provisions declaring government control.[11]

In this instance, the claimants argued that VANOC was controlled by government in three broad areas: governance, funding and operations. With respect to governance, the claimants pointed to the fact that 10 of the 12 directors of VANOC were appointed by the various levels of government. VANOC acknowledged that the four contributing governments had representatives on VANOC's Board and have some other limited supervisory roles, but argued that this still fell far short of the degree of control required to bring it within the ambit of section 32 of the *Charter*. Similarly, VANOC argued that the four governments did not, either individually or collectively, exercise routine or regular control over VANOC's day-to-day activities. Rather, it said, that the IOC exerted this kind of control over it. The trial court rejected the defendant's argument, finding that it would be inconsistent with what is referred to in Canadian public law as the "anti-avoidance principle"; that is, an otherwise "governmental" entity ought not, simply by creating bodies distinct from themselves and vesting those bodies with the power to perform governmental functions, thereby avoiding the constraints imposed upon their activities through the operation of the *Charter*.[12]

On the issue of funding, the trial court noted that, although three levels of government provided a large amount of financing to VANOC, this funding paled in comparison to that provided by the private sector (including the IOC) and thus the court rejected the claimants' second argument under the control test.[13]

[10] *Sagen v VANOC* [2009] BCSC 942, para 12.

[11] *Sagen v VANOC* [2009] BCSC 942, paras 12–48 and including reference to *McKinney v. University of Guelph* [1990] 3 SCR 229 (university); *Harrison v University of British Columbia* [1990] 3 SCR 451 (university); *Stoffman v Vancouver General Hospital* [1990] 3 SCR 483 (hospital); *Douglas/Kwantlen Faculty Assn v Douglas College* [1990] 3 SCR 570 (college); *Lavigne v. Ontario Public Service Employees Union* [1991] 2 SCR 211 (college); and *Eldridge v. British Columbia (Attorney General)* [1997] 3 SCR 624 (medicare programme).

[12] The anti-avoidance principle was applied implicitly in *Sagen v VANOC* [2009] BCSC 942, paras 17–24. The rationale for the broad "anti-avoidance" reach of section 32 of the *Charter* is explained in *Godbout v. Longueuil (City)* [1997] 3 SCR 844, para 48, La Forest J.

[13] *Sagen v VANOC* [2009] BCSC 942, paras 25–29. The various levels of government provided almost all of the $592 million development budget for the construction of new venues and the renovation of existing facilities. However, that amount pales in comparison to the 2010 Games' operating budget of $1.75 billion, which came from corporate domestic sponsorship ($760 million) and IOC broadcast rights ($450 million), and the remainder from ticket sales and international sponsorship. See *Sagen v VANOC* [2009] BCSC 942, para 27.

Finally, on the issue of government control over VANOC's operations, although the business plan of VANOC was approved by both the Canadian and British Columbian governments, VANOC argued that government oversight did not extend to its day-to-day operations. Indeed, VANOC contrasted the governments' high level oversight with the IOC's routine control over VANOC's operations. The focus of this argument was the VANOC "Master Plan". The Master Plan was a detailed planning tool that co-ordinated the activities that VANOC had to carry out as part of the planning, organisation, financing and staging of the Games.

> The Master Schedule lists each of VANOC's core activities; for each activity, it sets out the division within VANOC that is responsible for it, its expected completion date, its level of importance (whether it is a milestone, a deliverable or a key action in order of importance), whether it is an obligation owed to the IOC or the International Paralympic Committee, and if it involves interfacing with government, then which government. The Master Schedule records further comments and the date the activity is actually completed.[14]

The fact that the Master Schedule had to be approved by the IOC, but not the collective governments, was accepted by the trial court as compelling evidence that the IOC was, in fact, the ultimate controlling influence over VANOC.[15]

Overall, the fundamental question to address for the trial court was what was the nature of the purported control by government over VANOC's operations? In this, the trial court utilised the legal distinction in the jurisprudence surrounding the interpretation of section 32 of the *Charter* between "day-to-day" control and "ultimate or extraordinary" control; with only "day to day control" attracting the remit and obligations of the *Charter*.[16] In summary, the trial court ultimately found there was not sufficient "day to day" control by the government over the areas of governance, funding and operations to bring VANOC within the scope of the *Charter* under the "control test". The trial court concluded that, in contrast, the IOC's control over the minute details of VANOC's operations in planning and staging the 2010 Games was cogent evidence of the IOC's "day-to-day" control of VANOC's operations. Indeed, the sort of "day to day" control exercised by the IOC was seen as antithetical to government control of a similar kind.[17]

Finally, and to reiterate, at the Court of Appeal, this "control" point was not argued, as the appellants did not contest the trial judge's finding that the governments did not exercise "substantial control" over VANOC.[18]

---

[14] *Sagen v VANOC* [2009] BCSC 942, para 33.

[15] *Sagen v VANOC* [2009] BCSC 942, paras 30–48.

[16] See the phraseology of the Supreme Court of Canada in *Stoffman v. Vancouver General Hospital* [1990] 3 SCR 483, 513–514, La Forest, J.

[17] *Sagen v VANOC* [2009] BCSC 942, para 39.

[18] *Sagen v VANOC* [2009] BCCA 522, para 34.

22.2.2 The Government Activity Test

The key question on this test is whether there is a sufficient connection between the government "activity" and the action that is alleged to have infringed a right under the *Charter*. The question centres therefore on how narrowly the impugned action can be defined. This ultimately became a pivotal issue within *Sagen*.[19] The claimants argued that the planning, organising, financing and staging of the Winter Olympic Games, in other words, the "hosting" of the Games, was a government activity. While the trial judge noted that the IOC owned the Olympic Games and had control over its delivery; the IOC did not actually "stage" the Games. In that regard she concluded, consistent with the assertion of the claimants, that hosting the Games "is uniquely governmental in nature"[20] and that, as a result, VANOC was subject to the *Charter* when it carried out the activity of planning, organising, financing and staging the Games.[21]

In reaching her conclusion, Madame Justice Fenlon took particular note of the bidding process for the Games, which "could not have been undertaken by any other entity [than government]"[22] and the contracts entered into by all three levels of government and under which the Games were being staged, i.e., the "Host City Contract". Clause 1 of the Host City Contract stated clearly that the 2010 Games were awarded to Vancouver: "The IOC hereby entrusts the organization of the Games to the City and the NOC which undertake to fulfill their obligation in full compliance with the provisions of the Olympic Charter and of this Contract…".[23] Moreover, Fenlon J quoted Rule 34(3) of the *Olympic Charter,* which requires that the "National Government of the country of any applicant city must submit to the IOC a legally binding instrument by which the said government undertakes and guarantees that the country and its public authorities will comply with and respect the Olympic Charter".[24]

On this point, the Court of Appeal came to a different conclusion regarding the application of section 32 of the *Charter* and the appellate court concluded that the *Charter* did not apply to VANOC in this case.[25] To reiterate, the court found that when deciding whether the *Charter* applies to an entity using the ascribed "activity test", it is necessary to examine the specific action that is alleged to have caused the *Charter* infringement, i.e., in determining the scope of the application of the *Charter* to an entity such as VANOC, it would be necessary "to look not only to the activities or function of the entity itself but also to the nature or function of the

---

19 See generally *Sagen v VANOC* [2009] BCSC 942, paras 49–65.

20 *Sagen v VANOC* [2009] BCSC 942, para 56.

21 *Sagen v VANOC* [2009] BCSC 942, para 63.

22 *Sagen v VANOC* [2009] BCSC 942, para 63.

23 Cited at *Sagen v VANOC* [2009] BCSC 942, para 60.

24 Cited at *Sagen v VANOC* [2009] BCSC 942, para 61.

25 *Sagen v VANOC* [2009] BCCA 522, paras 44–50.

specific act or decision of the entity that is said to infringe a Charter right".[26] In this, the Court of Appeal was at one with the Supreme Court is opining that if the impugned action could be characterised as a "government activity" then the *Charter* applied; if it did not, then the *Charter* had no application. Put simply, the activities of a private entity (such as VANOC) would not generally be subject to the *Charter* but some specific activities of a identifiably "governmental" nature, delegated or assigned to that private entity, could be subject to the *Charter*.

Crucially, the Court of Appeal found that the alleged *Charter* infringement arose specifically from the IOC's decision not to include women's ski jumping in the 2010 Olympic programme. The court concluded that VANOC had no authority to make or alter the IOC's decision. The court reached this conclusion after considering the contractual terms of the Host City Contract. This contract was an agreement between the IOC, VANOC and the Canadian Olympic Committee, mandated under IOC Rules once Vancouver was selected to host the 2010 Olympic Games.[27] Under the standard Host City Contract, the IOC is always recognised as having the exclusive authority to determine what events are to be staged at that Games. Further, the agreement also provides that the national government in question is to have no legal authority to manage or direct the activities of VANOC as they relate to the planning or staging of the Olympic Games. Accordingly, the appellate court concluded that, although VANOC could be said to be carrying out a government activity when *hosting* the Olympic Games, the decision not to include women's ski jumping in the Olympic programme could not be linked to any government activity: the decision was neither made nor endorsed by the Canadian government. As a result, the *Charter* did not apply to the complaint. The Court of Appeal summarised its position as follows[28]:

> The case authorities support the view that, in determining the scope of the application of the *Charter* to an entity such as VANOC, *it is necessary to look not only to the activities or function of the entity itself but also to the nature or function of the specific act or decision of the entity that is said to infringe a Charter right.* Regardless of whether VANOC's hosting of the Games can properly be considered to be a governmental activity because of the substantial commitments made by the several levels of government to secure and hold the Games in Vancouver, *it is clear on the facts that neither government nor VANOC had any authority either to make or to alter the decision of the IOC not to include a women's ski jumping event in the 2010 Games.* The decision of the IOC not to add women's ski jumping as an event in the 2010 Games is not a "policy" choice that could be or was made by any Canadian government and the staging by VANOC of only those events authorized by the IOC cannot reasonably be viewed as furthering any Canadian government policy or program.

---

[26] *Sagen v VANOC* [2009] BCCA 522, para 49.

[27] Rule 34(3) of the IOC's *Olympic Charter*: "The National Government of the country of any applicant city must submit to the IOC a legally binding instrument by which the said government undertakes and guarantees that the country and its public authorities will comply with and respect the Olympic Charter".

[28] *Sagen v VANOC* [2009] BCCA 522, para 49. [emphasis added].

In sum, while the two levels of court may have disagreed with regard to the scope and basis of the application of the *Charter*, they agreed that the actual act forming the basis of the claimants' claim (i.e., the impugned action) was not one within the control of VANOC. Fundamental to this finding was the (uncontested) fact that the IOC had sole and exclusive responsibility for the decision not to add women's ski jumping to the Winter Olympic program.[29]

On this aspect of the case, *Sagen* makes clear two points. First, a private entity (such as VANOC) is subject to the *Charter* only when it is carrying out a specific activity that can be ascribed to government. Failing that, the *Charter* cannot provide a remedy against the entity for the impugned activity. The result is odd indeed. VANOC can effectively "stage" a government programme, or activity, with a discriminatory element, and remain immune from the equity provisions of Canadian law, so long as control over the discriminatory element is contractually left with a third party (in this case, the IOC[30]). Second, it illustrates the extent to which countries defer to the authority of the IOC and the *Olympic Charter* when agreeing to host the Olympic Games; and, by so doing, may find themselves in a position of diminished control over matters involving national interests and values.

22.3 Was There Discrimination?

In defence of the claimants' claim of discrimination, VANOC also argued that it was simply implementing a decision of the IOC and one over which it had no control but had, nonetheless, a contractual obligation to implement. In addition, the IOC for its part always maintained that its decision not to include women's ski jumping in the 2010 Olympic programme was based on "technical merit" and had nothing to do with gender discrimination. In its view, women's ski jumping had not yet reached the "level of maturity and universality" required of a sport or discipline to be included as part of the Olympic programme. The women ski jumpers, on the other hand, identified this aspect of IOC policy as the primary source of discrimination, and as claimants they specifically targeted the IOC's criteria for adding new events to the Olympic programme and the application of these criteria by the IOC (and subsequently, VANOC's role in implementing the IOC's decision).

The starting point here is Rule 47 of the *Olympic Charter* which states, in part:

> 3.2: To be included in the programme of the Olympic Games, events must have recognised international standing both numerically and geographically, and have been included at least twice in world or continental championships.

---

[29] *Sagen v VANOC* [2009] BCCA 522, paras 17–23.

[30] The IOC, as noted by the trial court, was neither a party to the suit nor within the jurisdiction of the Canadian court. *Sagen v VANOC* [2009] BCSC 942, para 132.

> 3.3: Only events practised by men in at least fifty countries and on three continents, and by women in at least thirty-five countries and on three continents, may be included in the programme of the Olympic Games.[31]

There are thus numerical, geographic and competitive requirements to be met to be included in the Olympic programme. On its face, the rule appears neutral, applying to both men and women and, if anything; the regulation favours women by applying a lower participatory threshold.[32] Rule 47 had its genesis in 1949 when in order to stem the proliferation of new sports, the IOC introduced selection criteria for determining whether sports, disciplines and events were to be included in the Olympic programme. At the time, men's ski jumping was part of the Olympic programme (as it had been since 1924) but women's ski jumping was not. At the same time as these selection criteria for inclusion of sports to the Olympic programme were introduced, an exception to the criteria was also created for sports that had traditionally been part of the Olympic Games (for e.g., men's ski jumping). The current Rule 47(4.4) reflects this "Olympic tradition" exception:

> 47(4.4): Sports, disciplines or events included in the programme of the Olympic Games which no longer satisfy the criteria of this rule [Rule 47(3.2 & 3.3] may nevertheless, in certain exceptional cases, be maintained therein by decision of the IOC for the sake of the Olympic tradition.[33]

Men's ski jumping was thus "grandfathered" into the Olympic programme.[34] Indeed, this "Olympic tradition" exception disproportionately applied to and benefited men's sports since, prior to 1949, the number of men's sports vastly outnumbered those for women, whose participation in the Olympic Games was limited to events considered "particularly appropriate to the female sex"[35] (which was a significant factor barring women's ski jumping from the Olympics at the time).[36] In short, men's ski jumping was never subjected to the selection criteria of Rule 47, and if it had, it would not satisfy the regulation's criteria. Even in 2010,

---

31 When the IOC adopted a new version of the *Olympic Charter* in 2006, these criteria were removed; however, as noted by the trial court, they continue to be applied "in practice" today. *Sagen v VANOC* [2009] BCSC 942, para 81.

32 This was the conclusion of the federal court in *Martin v IOC*, 704 F 2d 670 (9th Cir 1984) where women from 21 nations alleged discrimination in the exclusion of both 5,000 and 10,000 metre track events for women at the 1984 Summer Olympic Games in Los Angeles. The *Martin* court did not go beyond this formal analysis of the rule in coming to its decision. In *Sagen*, consideration was given to the "adverse effect" of the application of the rule.

33 Emphasis included by the trial court at *Sagen v VANOC* [2009] BCSC 942, para 84.

34 A North Americanism, typically used for a clause exempting certain pre-existing classes of people from the requirements of a legislative provision.

35 *Sagen v VANOC* [2009] BCSC 942, para 89.

36 Concerns about women's health, particularly reproductive health, the physical risk of certain activities and gender stereotyping typified a prevailing paternalistic attitude towards the inclusion of women in the Olympic Games and, to the extent the discriminatory decisions of the past persist today, reinforce and perpetuate those attitudes and ideas. See Vetinsky et al. 2009, 30 and Laurendeau and Adams 2010, 436.

men's ski jumping represented only 58 % of the required number of jumpers under the Rule 47 criteria and women, 52 % of the required number of jumpers.[37]

The trial court in *Sagen* recognised the significant disadvantage suffered over the years by women ski jumpers over men ski jumpers by virtue of the historical inclusion of the latter in the Olympic Games.[38] The court noted that without Olympic recognition it is difficult for women to get the training and support, both financial and competitive, necessary to reach world class levels. At the international level for example, without recognition at the Olympic Games, there was no urgency for FIS to establish a competitive circuit for women ski jumping. Indeed, such a circuit was not established until 2004,[39] and the first world championships for women were not established until the 2008–2009 season. At the national level, funding from national Olympic committees, and other sources including sponsorship, is tied to the sport's Olympic status, as are competitive opportunities. Consequently, without high level competitive and training opportunities women ski jumpers collectively were unable to meet the Olympic selection criteria under Rule 47(3.2 & 3.3). The argument was therefore that the resulting exclusion of women's ski jumping from the Olympic Games simply perpetuated the disadvantage.

In concluding on the decision not to include women's ski jumping in the 2010 Olympic programme, the trial judge was "satisfied that the differential treatment of the plaintiffs resulting from the application of the Olympic Charter Rules that grandfathered men's ski jumping, while requiring women's ski jumping events to meet the criteria for inclusion of new events, discriminates against the plaintiffs in a substantive sense".[40]

Unfortunately for the claimants, however, and as previously described, both the trial court and the appellate court determined that the *Charter* did not apply to the IOC or the Rules of the *Olympic Charter*, and thus did not apply to the IOC's decision not to include women's ski jumping in the Olympic programme. Nor did the *Charter* apply to VANOC when it implemented the IOC's discriminatory decision. The women were without recourse.

---

[37] *Sagen v VANOC* [2009] BCSC 942, paras 89–90. The claimants pointed out that the IOC has made a number of exceptions to the selection criteria. For example, even as the IOC voted to exclude women's ski jumping (which, at the time, had 135 elite female ski jumpers registered in 16 countries), it voted to include women's ski cross (30 skiers from 11 countries). See Vetinsky et al. 2009, 41. When asked about the admission of women's ski cross, which did not meet the selection criteria, leading members of the IOC Executive pointed to its popularity with the public and its appeal to "youth" (Pound 2008, 3: "There has been some pressure on the IOC to expand the program of the Games to include sports that have an appeal to today's 'youth', which has led to inclusion of such sports and disciplines as triathlon, snowboard, snow cross, freestyle skiing, synchronized diving and the like".).

[38] See generally *Sagen v VANOC* [2009] BCSC 942, paras 80–96.

[39] Vertinsky et al. 2009, 37, notes that, as recently as 2005, the head of FIS commented he was not sure ski jumping was either safe or appropriate for women.

[40] *Sagen v VANOC* [2009] BCSC 942, para 103.

22.4 Remedy

It is interesting to note that at no point did the claimants ask that women's ski jumping be added as an Olympic sport. They acknowledged that VANOC did not have the authority to add events to the Olympic programme and that a domestic Canadian court did not have jurisdiction over the IOC in this case. It followed that their litigation strategy was to ask that VANOC be enjoined from staging the men's ski jumping events in the hope that the IOC, faced with the dilemma of cancelling the men's events or asking VANOC to host women's ski jumping events, would opt for the latter. Any other domestic legal remedy ordered by a court would likely have been of limited practical value. As the Supreme Court noted, if VANOC were ordered to stage an alternative event for the female ski jumpers, it would not have been officially recognised as being part of the Olympic Games, since "only the IOC may grant the imprimatur of 'Olympic'".[41] Moreover, the staging of Olympic events requires the cooperation and involvement of both the international federation and national Olympic committees, "all of whom are part of the Olympic Movement and under the authority of the IOC"[42] and would, therefore, be unlikely to act in a manner contrary to the wishes of the IOC for fear of retribution. Indeed, FIS, although initially recommending in favour of adding women's ski jumping to the Olympic programme, subsequently made it clear it would support the position of the IOC in the legal dispute.[43] In short, from a pragmatic perspective, the domestic judicial system would have had little, if any, influence in the circumstances.[44]

22.5 Conclusion

The decision in *Sagen* was not a popular one among the public. According to one public opinion poll at the time, nearly three quarters of Canadians supported the inclusion of women's ski jumping in the Games.[45] Even the trial court found "something distasteful about a Canadian governmental activity subject to the *Charter* being delivered in a way that puts into effect a discriminatory decision made by others..."[46] From a national perspective, the case highlights the fuzzy line between public and private, between governmental and non-governmental. The 2010 Vancouver Winter Olympic Games illustrates how the "public" and

[41] *Sagen v VANOC* [2009] BCSC 942, para 116.

[42] *Sagen v VANOC* [2009] BCSC 942, para 117.

[43] *Sagen v VANOC* [2009] BCSC 942, para 117.

[44] The same would have been true had the skiers persisted in their action under the *British Columbia Human Rights Code,* RSBC 1996, c 210.

[45] Noted in Young 2010, 97.

[46] *Sagen v VANOC* [2009] BCSC 942, para 124.

"private" both influence and reinforce each other. It is difficult, if not specious; to attempt to draw a clear and predictable line between what is the exercise of state power and what is not. Arguably, in *Sagen*, the distinction reflects a dangerous construct within Canadian public, human rights and constitutional law "behind which private power thrives relatively unchecked and substantive issues are arbitrarily and unjustly resolved".[47] In plainer terms, VANOC became contractually obliged to perpetuate an IOC decision on Canadian soil even though that decision was found contrary to Canadian law by the trial court, one the Canadian courts were arguably unwilling, if not unable, to affect. As noted by one commentator,[48] the fact the case involved sport and, more particularly, women in sport, is an important context we should consider in looking at the judicial analysis and outcome of the case:

> Imagine if the exclusion had been of some other group, say black or Jewish participants, and if the event had been some other form of international meeting hosted by our governments. Would the courts have been as hands-off in such a case? Would the governments and local organizers been as quick to defer to an extra-national decision maker?

The case also illustrates the extent to which countries defer to the authority of the IOC and the *Olympic Charter* when agreeing to host the Olympic Games. In doing so, national authorities may find themselves unable to intervene, even where, as was the case in *Sagen*, the decisions of the IOC violate fundamental legal principles of equity and fairness. Further, it would seem relying on national courts to regulate international sport bodies may have little effect. There is, however, another level of regulatory oversight of international sport bodies. The Court of Arbitration for Sport (CAS) is emerging as an important and effective authority over international sport bodies. The *Olympic Charter,* for example, requires all athletes to sign a declaration stating that all disputes arising during or in connection with the Olympic Games will be submitted exclusively to the CAS. In many ways, CAS was intended to usurp the role of domestic courts in the resolution of sport disputes at the global level. Although the full scope of CAS's ability to intervene is unknown—there has never, for example, been a test of the IOC's anti-discrimination rules[49]; perhaps the women ski jumpers would have been more successful taking their case there?

---

[47] See Hutchinson and Petter 1988, 297.

[48] Young 2010, 97.

[49] The fourth and fifth "Fundamental Principles of Olympism" of the *Olympic Charter* provides as follows: 4. The practice of sport is a human right. Every individual must have the possibility of practising sport, without discrimination of any kind and in the Olympic spirit which requires a mutual understanding with a spirit of friendship, solidarity and fair play. The organisation, administration and management of sport must be controlled by independent sport organisations. 5. Any form of discrimination with regard to a country or a person on grounds of race, religion, politics, gender or otherwise is incompatible with belonging to the Olympic Movement. [emphasis added].

References

Hutchinson A, Petter A (1988) Private rights/public wrongs: the liberal lie of the *Charter*. Univ Tor Law J 38:278–297

Laurendeau J, Adams C (2010) 'Jumping like a girl': discursive silences, exclusionary practices and the controversy over women's ski jumping. Sport Soc 13:431–447

Pound R (2008) The future of the olympic movement: promised land or train wreck? In: Barney R et al (eds) Pathways: critique and discourse in olympic research, 9th international symposium for Olympic research at the Capital University of Physical Education, Beijing. International Centre for Olympic Studies, London

Vertinsky P et al (2009) 'Skierina' in Olympics: gender justice and gender politics at the local, national and international level over the challenge of women's ski jumping. Olympika 28:25–56

Young M (2010) The IOC made me do it: women's ski jumping, VANOC, and the 2010 winter Olympics. Const Forum 18:95–108

Table of Cases*

***Featured cases are in bold**

Australia

Canada

Court of Arbitration for Sport

(continued)

ASSER International Sports Law Series, DOI: 10.1007/978-90-6704-909-2,

(continued)

CAS 98/214 *B v International Judo Federation*	[11.5]
CAS 98/222 *B v International Triathlon Union*	[11.7]
CAS OG 2000/011 *Raducan v IOC*	[18.7]
CAS 2000/A/281 *H v. International Motorcycling Federation*	[11.7]
CAS 2002/A/370 *L v IOC*	[4.3]
CAS 2002/A/397 *L v FIS*	[4.3]
CAS 2002/A/371 *D v IOC*	[4.3]
CAS 2002/A/386 *Kabaeva v FIG*	[11.7]
CAS 2002/A/397 *D v FIS*	[4.3]
CAS 2004/0/607 *B v IWF*	[12.2]
CAS 2004/O/645 *USADA v Montgomery*	[12.1]; [12.3]; [12.4]; [13.2]
CAS 2004/0/649 *USADA v Gaines*	[12.3]
CAS 2004/A/651 *French v Australian Sports Commission and Cycling Australia*	[12.2]
CAS 2005/A/951 *Canas v ATP*	[4.3]
CAS 2007/A/1298-1300 *Webster, Hearts & Wigan Athletic FC*	[5.4]; [6.6]
CAS 2008/A/1480 *Pistorius v IAAF*	[14.2]; [14.3]; [14.4]; [14.5]
CAS 2008/A/1519-1520 *Matuzalem, FC Shakhtar Donetsk (Ukraine) & Real Zaragoza SAD (Spain)*	[6.6]
CAS 2009/A/1912-1913 *Pechstein v International Skating*	[13.1]; [13.3]; [13.4]; [13.5]; [13.6]
CAS 2009/A/2012 *Doping Authority Netherlands v N*	[18.7]

Europe

AGOSI v United Kingdom (1987) 9 EHRR 1	[21.4]
Anderson v United Kingdom (1997) 25 EHRR CD 172	[21.4]
Buckley v United Kingdom (1996) 23 EHRR 101	[21.4]
Chapman v United Kingdom (2001) 33 EHRR 399	[21.4]
Chassagnou v France (1999) 29 EHRR 615	[21.4]
Engel v The Netherlands (No. 1) (1976) 1 EHRR 647	[19.3]
Friend and Countryside Alliance v United Kingdom [2009]ECHR 2068	[21.6]
G and E v Norway (1983) 35 DR 30	[21.4]
Garyfallou AEBE v Greece (1997) 28 EHRR 344	[19.3]
Giacomelli v Italy (2006) 45 EHRR 871	[21.4]
Handyside v the United Kingdom (1976) 1 EHRR 737	[16.3]
Jahn v Germany (2006) 42 EHRR 49	[21.4]
Kjeldsen, Busk Madsen and Pedersen v Denmark (1976) 1 EHRR 711	[21.4]
Peck v United Kingdom (2003) 36 EHRR 719	[21.4]
Pretty v United Kingdom (2002) 35 EHRR 1	[21.4]
Perna v Italy (2004) 39 EHRR 28	[16.3]
Lauko v Slovakia (1998) 33 EHRR 439	[19.3]
Niemietz v Germany (1992) 16 EHRR 97	[21.4]
Sidabras and Dziautas v Lithuania (2004) 42 EHRR 104	[21.4]
Tre Traktörer AB v Sweden (1989) 13 EHRR 309	[21.4]
von Hannover v Germany [2005]40 EHRR 1	[21.4]

(continued)

(continued)

European Union

Court of Justice

Bernard Case C-325/08; [2010]ECR I-2177	[3.5]; [6.6][9.7]; [16.4]; [17.5]
Bond van Adverteerders et al v Netherlands Case 352/85; [1988]ECR 2085	[17.3]
***Bosman* Case C-415/93; [1995]ECR I-4921**	[3.3]; [3.4]; [3.5]; [3.7]; [5.1];[5.5]; [6]; [9.2]; [9.7]
Coditel SA et al v Ciné-Vog Films SA et al (Coditel II) Case 262/81; [1982]ECR 3381	[17.4]
Commission v France Case C-334/94; [1996]ECR I-1307	[3.7]
Commission v Infront WM AG Case C-125/06 P; [2008]ECR I-1457	[16.2]
Defrenne Case 43/75; [1976]ECR 455	[3.5]
Deliège Cases C-51/96 and C-191/97; [2000]ECR I-2549	[3.3]; [3.7]; [6.5]; [9.4]
Deutscher Handballbund eV v Kolpak Case C-438/00; [2003]ECR I-4135	[6.7]
Donà v Mantero Case 13/76; [1976]ECR 1333	[3.3]; [3.4]; [3.7]; [6.2]; [6.7]
***FA Premier League and others v QC Leisure and others; and Karen Murphy v Media Protection Services Ltd* Cases C-403/08 and C-429/08; 4 October 2011**	[9.7]; [17]
GlaxoSmithKline Services et al v Commission et al Cases C-501/06 P, C-513/06 P, C-515/06 P and C-519/06 P; [2009]ECR I-29	[17.4]
Grzelczyk Case C-184/99; [2001]ECR I-6193	[3.7]
Hoeckx Case C-249/83; [1985]ECR 973	[3.7]
Keck and Mithouard Cases C-267/91 and C-268/91; [1993]ECR I-6097	[21.5]
Konsumentombudsmannen v De Agostini et al Cases C-34–36/95; [1997]ECR I-3843	[17.3]
Laval un Partneri Ltd v Svenska Byggnadsarbetareförbundet et al Case C-341/05 [2007]ECR I-11767	[17.4]
Lehtonen et al v FRSB Case C-176/96; [2000]ECR I-2681	[6.5]; [9.4]
***Meca-Medina* Case C-519/04 P;** [2006]ECR I-6991	[3.7]; [3.8]; [6.5]; [9.1]; [9.2]; [9.3]; [9.4]; [9.8]; [12.1]; [17.4]
Roman Angonese Case 281/98; [2000]ECR I-4139	[3.5]
Simutenkov v Ministerio de Educación y cultura and RFEFI Case C-265/03; [2005]ECR I-2579	[6.7]
Sky Österreich GmbH v Österreichischer Rundfunk Case C-283/11; [2011]OJ C269/25	[16.3]
Sot Lélos kai Sia et al v GlaxoSmithKline AEVE Farmakeftikon Proionton Cases C-468/06 to C-478/06; [2008]ECR I-7139	[17.4]
Sotgiu Case 152/73; [1974]ECR 153	[3.4]
Stichting Collectieve Antennevoorziening Gouda et al v Commissariaat voor de Media Case C-288/89; [1991]ECR I-4007	[17.3]

(continued)

(continued)

(continued)

England and Wales

(continued)

(continued)

Bath and North East Somerset Council v HM Attorney General and Anor [2002]EWHC 1623 (Ch)	[1.3]
Blundell v Catterall (1821) 106 ER 286; 5 B & Ad 553	[1.5]
Bradley v Jockey Club [2004]EWHC 2164; [2005]EWCA Civ 1056	[5.4]; [8.4]; [18.7]
Breen v. AEU [1971]2 QB 175	[8.3]
Caldwell v Maguire and Fitzgerald [2001]EWCA Civ 1054	[20.1]; [20.3]
Chambers v British Olympic Association [2008]EWHC 2028 (QB)	[5.4]
Clark v University of Lincolnshire & Humberside [2001]1 WLR 1988	[8.2]
Condon v Basi [1985]1 WLR 866	[20.1]; [20.3]
Countryside Alliance & Ors v HM Attorney General & Ors [2005]EWHC 1677 (Admin)	[21.2]; [21.4]; [21.5]; [21.6]
Davis v Carew-Pole [1956]1 WLR 833	[5.4]; [10.6]
Doughty v. Rolls-Royce Plc [1992]ICR 538	[8.3]
Doyle and Others v R [2012]EWCA Crim 995	[19.3]
Dyce v Hay (1852) 1 Macq 305	[1.5]
***Eastham v Newcastle United Football Club* [1964]1 Ch 413**	**[5]**
Enderby Town FC v The Football Association [1971]Ch 591	[20.4]
FA Premier League and others v QC Leisure and others [2012]EWHC 108 (Ch)	[17.2]; [17.3]
Fitch v Rawling and others (1795) 126 ER 614; 2 Hy BL 393	[1.5]
Gasser v Stinson, Unreported, Queen's Bench Division, 15 June 1988, Scott J	[5.4]; [10.6];
Gough and Smith v Chief Constable of Derbyshire [2002]QB 459	[19.3]
***Gough and Smith v Chief Constable of Derbyshire* [2002]QB 1213**	[19.1]; [19.3]
Gravil v Carroll and Redruth RFC [2008]EWCA Civ 689	[20.1]; [20.5]; [20.6]
Greig v Insole [1978]1 WLR 302	[5.4]
Griffin v Slough West Water Services Ltd [1995]IRLR 15	[8.3]
Kingaby v Aston Villa (1912) *The Times* 28 March	[5.2]
Korda v International Tennis Federation Unreported, Court of Appeal, Morritt LJ, Auld, LJ and Clarke, LJ, 25 March 1999	[10.6]
Law v National Greyhound Racing Club Ltd [1983]1 WLR 1302	[5.4]; [8.2]
Mercury Communications Ltd v Director General of Telecommunications [1996]1 WLR 48	[8.2]
McInnes v Onslow-Fane [1978]1 WLR 1520	[5.4]
Miller v Minister of Pensions [1947]2 All ER 372	[18.4]
***Modahl v British Athletic Federation Limited (No 1)* Unreported, Queen's Bench Division, 28 June 1996, Popplewell J**	[10.5]
***Modahl v British Athletic Federation Limited (No 1)* [1997]EWCA Civ 2209**	[10.5]
***Modahl v British Athletic Federation Limited (No 2)* Unreported, Queen's Bench Division, 14 December 2000, Douglas Brown J**	[10.5]; [10.6]

(continued)

(continued)

(continued)

Table of Legislation

Australia	
Competition and Consumer Act 2010 (Cth)	
Section 45	[7.4]
Protection of Aborigines Act and the Restriction of the Sale of Opium Act 1897 (Qld)	[7.2]
Trade Practices Act 1974 (Cth)	
Section 45	[7.4]
Austria	
Ordinance on events of substantial social interest 2001	[16.2]
Belgium	
Order of the Flemish Government establishing the list of events of major importance to society, 2004	[16.2]
Canada	
Canadian Charter of Rights and Freedoms, Part I of the Constitution Act 1982	
Section 15(1)	[22.2]
Section 32	[22.2]
Europe	
European Convention for the Protection of Human Rights and Fundamental Freedoms of 4 November 1950	
Article 6	[19.3]; [19.4]
Article 8	[21.2]; [21.4]
Article 10	[16.3]
Article 11	[21.2]; [21.4]
Article 14	[21.2]; [21.4]
First Protocol, Article 1	[16.3]; [21.2]; [21.4]
European Convention on the Recognition of the Legal Personality of International Non-Governmental Organizations of 24 April 1986	[4.3]

(continued)

J. Anderson (ed.), *Leading Cases in Sports Law*,
ASSER International Sports Law Series, DOI: 10.1007/978-90-6704-909-2,

(continued)

European Union

Charter of Fundamental Rights of the European Union	
Article 11	[16.3]
Article 16	[16.3]
Article 17	[16.3]
Directive 89/552/EEC,	
Television without Frontiers Directive [1989]OJ L 298/23	[16.2]; [17.5]
Directive 93/83/EEC,	
Satellite Broadcasting Directive [1993]OJ L 248/15	[17.3]; [17.4]
Directive 97/36/EC,	
Amendment of Television without Frontiers Directive [1997]OJ L 202/60	[16.2]
Directive 98/84/EC,	
Conditional Access Directive [1998]OJ L 320/54	[17.3]
Directive 2004/38/EC	
Citizenship Directive [2004]OJ L 158/77	[3.7]
Directive 2010/13EU	
Audiovisual Media Services Directive [2010]OJ L 95/1	[16.2]; [16.3]
Treaty of Rome 1957	
Article 2	[3.3]
Article 48	[3.5]
Article 59	[3.5]
Article 85	[8.3]
Article 86	[8.3]
Article 177	[3.2]
Treaty of Amsterdam 1997	
Declaration 29	[3.7]
Treaty on European Union 1992	
Article 9	[3.7]
Treaty on the Functioning of the European Union	
Article 2	[3.3]
Article 3	[3.3]
Article 4	[3.3]
Article 5	[3.3]
Article 6	[3.3]; [9.6]
Article 18	[3.7]; [6.7]
Article 20	[3.7]
Article 21	[3.7]
Article 34	[21.2]; [21.3]; [21.4]; [21.5]
Article 36	[21.5]
Article 45	[3.5]; [3.7]; [6.7]
Article 52	[21.5]
Article 56	[3.5]; [6.7]; [17.2]; [17.3]; [17.4]; [17.7]; [21.2]; [21.3]; [21.4]; [21.5]

(continued)

(continued)	
Article 101	[3.7]; [8.3]; [9.3]; [17.2]; [17.4]; [17.5]; [17.6]
Article 102	[8.3]
Article 165	[3.7]; [6.5]; [9.6]; [9.7]; [16.4]; [17.5]
Article 267	[3.2]

Germany

Interstate Treaty on Broadcasting of 31 August 1991	[16.2]

International

International Convention on the Elimination of all Forms of Racial Discrimination of 21 December 1965.	[7.2]
International Covenant on Civil and Political Rights of 16 December 1966	
Article 19	[16.3]
International Declaration against Apartheid in Sports of 14 December 1977.	[7.2]
New York Convention on the Recognition and Enforcement of Foreign Arbitral Awards of 10 June 1958.	[4.3]
UNESCO International Convention Against Doping in Sport of 19 October 2005.	[12.5]
Universal Declaration of Human Rights of 10 December 1948	
Article 19	[16.3]

Ireland

Broadcasting (Major Events Television Coverage) Act 1999 (Designation of Major Events) Order 2003, S.I. 99/2003	[16.2]

Italy

Decision No 8/1999 of 9 March 1999	[16.2]
Decision No 172/1999 of 28 July 1999	[16.2]

New Zealand

Race Relations Act 1971	[7.2]
Immigration Act 1964	
Section 14(1)	[7.2]

United Kingdom

Pre-1800 by regenal year, chronological order

39 Edw 3 c23, Unlawful Games (1365)	[1.2]

(continued)

(continued)

(continued)

Human Rights Act 1998	
Section 6	[8.3]; [8.4]
Hunting Act 2004	[21]
Law of Property Act 1925	
Section 193	[1.6]
Section 194	[1.6]
Licensing Act 1872	
Section 17	[1.4]
Metropolitan Commons Acts 1866–1878	[1.6]
Metropolitan Police Act 1839	
Section 54(17)	[1.2]
Offences Against the Person Act 1861	
Section 20	[20.4]
Open Spaces Act 1890	[1.6]
Parliament Acts 1911–1949	[21.1]
Prevention of Corruption Act 1906	
Section 1	[18.5]
Public Order Act 1986	
Section 4	[19.4]
Section 5	[19.4]
Public Health Acts 1875–1890	[1.6]
Public Order Act 1936	
Section 5	[7.4]
Race Relations Act 1976	
Section 71	[7.4]
Restrictive Trade Practices Act 1976	[8.3]
Settled Estate Acts 1856–1877	[1.3]
Settled Land Acts 1882, 1890 and 1925	[1.3]
Sporting Events (Control of Alcohol etc.) Act 1985	
Section 2(2)	[19.4]
Southampton Marsh Improvement Act 1844	[1.4]
Supreme Court Act 1981	
Section 31(6)	[8.3]
Violent Crime Reduction Act 2006	[19.2]
Section 27	[19.4]
Wild Animals in Captivity Protection Act 1900	
Section 4	[21.1]
Windsor Forest Enclosure Act of 1813	[1.3]
Scotland	
Protection of Wild Mammals (Scotland) Act 2002	[21.1]

United States

Federal

Clayton Act 1914	[2.2]; [2.3]
Curt Flood Act 1998	[2.8]

(continued)

Switzerland

Contributors

Roger I. Abrams is the Richardson Professor of Law at the School of Law, Northeastern University, Boston, Massachusetts. Professor Abrams is a prolific author and leading authority on sports and labour law and legal education. He has served as a salary arbitrator for major league baseball and as a permanent arbitrator for the television, communications, electronics and coal industries; for the US Customs Service; the Internal Revenue Service; Walt Disney World; and Lockheed-Martin Company.
Professor Abrams has published five books on the business and history of sports: *Legal Bases: Baseball and the Law* (1998); *The Money Pitch: Baseball Free Agency and Salary Arbitration* (2000); *The First World Series and the Baseball Fanatics of 1903* (2003); and *The Dark Side of the Diamond: Gambling, Violence, Drugs and Alcoholism in the National Pastime* (2008). His most recent book, *Sports Justice*, was published in 2010.
Professor Abrams was appointed to lead the law school at Northeastern University in July 1999 and stepped down in 2002. He previously served as dean of both Rutgers University's law school in Newark, New Jersey, and Nova University Shepard Broad Law Centre in Fort Lauderdale, Florida. He began his academic career on the Faculty of Case Western Reserve University School of Law in Cleveland, Ohio, where he became the youngest tenured full professor in the history of that university. After graduating from Harvard Law School *cum laude* in 1970, he clerked for Judge Frank M. Coffin of the US Court of Appeals for the First Circuit in Boston, and then practiced with the Boston firm of Foley, Hoag & Eliot in the areas of labour law and civil rights litigation. Professor Abrams is an elected member of the American Law Institute, the American Bar Foundation, the National Academy of Arbitrators and the Massachusetts Historical Society.

Jack Anderson is a Professor at the School of Law, Queen's University, Belfast. His primary research interest is the relationship between sport and the law and he has published widely in the area including, most recently, *Modern Sports Law*, Hart, Oxford, 2010. His current research interest is in the legal issues surrounding the possible links between gambling, financial crime and corruption in sport.

J. Anderson (ed.), *Leading Cases in Sports Law*,
ASSER International Sports Law Series, DOI: 10.1007/978-90-6704-909-2,

In 2011, aspects of this research interest were carried out by way of a fellowship to the Australian Research Council's Centre of Excellence for Policing and Security in Brisbane and with the support of a Leverhulme Trust Study Abroad Fellowship. Jack contributes regularly to the media in Britain and Ireland on sports law matters and blogs at http://blogs.qub.ac.uk/sportslaw. He is a qualified arbitrator, being a Fellow of the Chartered Institute of Arbitrators (FCIArb) and is a member of a number of sports dispute resolution tribunals including the UK Sports Dispute Resolution Panel, Just Sport Ireland and the Gaelic Athletic Association's Disputes Resolution Authority.

Michael J. Beloff The Honourable Michael J. Beloff QC was educated at the Dragon School, Eton and Magdalen College, Oxford. He has degrees in history (first class) and law from the University of Oxford, where he was President of the Oxford Union and later President of Trinity College, Oxford 1996–2006. He is an FRSA, FICPD, an Academician of the Academy of Learned Societies for the Social Sciences and a member of ASPE. He is an Honorary Fellow of the Institute of Advanced Legal Studies, an Honorary Fellow of Trinity College, Oxford, an Honorary Vice-President of the Oxford University Law Society and has an honorary doctorate from Farleigh Dickinson University (USA) and from De Montfort University. Called to the Bar by Gray's Inn in 1967, he became a Queen's Counsel in 1981, a Recorder of the Crown Court from 1984 to 1995, a Master of the Bench of Gray's Inn in 1988, a Deputy High Court Judge from 1989 to 1996 (designated to sit in the Crown Office list), Senior Ordinary Judge of the Courts of Appeal of Jersey and Guernsey from 2005 (Judge of the Courts of Appeal of Jersey and Guernsey from 1995) and a Member of the Court of Arbitration for Sport ("CAS") from 1996. He has been Chairman of the International Cricket Council's Code of Conduct Commission from 2002, and was on the main dispute resolution panel for the World Cup (cricket) 2007 and World Cup 20/20 (2009). In November 2010, Michael was elected as one of the judges of the FIA's International Court of Appeal. In February 2011 he was appointed to the International Cricket Council's World Cup 2011 dispute resolution panel and is Chairman of the ICC's Code of Conduct Commission. A Steward of the Royal Automobile Club, Michael Beloff QC was also the Ethics Commissioner for the London Olympics in 2012.

Michael had lectured on law worldwide and his extensive publication portfolio includes *The Sex Discrimination Act* (Butterworths, 1976) and *Sports Law* (Hart Publishing) 1999 (2nd edn., 2012); and contributions in *Public Law*, *Current Legal Problems*, *Modern Law Review*, *Commercial Law Review*, *European Human Rights Law Review*, *Statute Law Review*, *Political Quarterly*; *European Current Law*, *Irish Jurist*; *The Journal of Environmental and Planning Law*; *New Zealand Law Journal*, *Denning Law Journal*, *Justice of the Peace*, *Jersey Law Review*, *Judicial Law Review* (Consultant Editor) and The Sweet and Maxwell *International Sports Law Review* (General Editor).

Ian Blackshaw is an International Sports Lawyer and Visiting Professor and Fellow at the TMC Asser Institute's International Sports Law Centre, The Hague. A prolific author of sports law literature—for example, *Mediating Sports Disputes* (2002); *Sport, Mediation and Arbitration* (2009); and *Sports Marketing Agreements* (2011)—Professor Blackshaw is also a contributing editor to the *International Sports Law Journal* and a consulting editor of *Global Sports Law and Taxation Reports*. Professor Blackshaw is a member of both the WIPO Arbitration and Mediation Centre in Geneva and the Court of Arbitration for Sport in Lausanne, Switzerland.

Simon Boyes is a Senior Lecturer at Nottingham Law School, Nottingham Trent University where he devised and designed the School's LLM Sports Law programme and the Sports Law module for students studying its undergraduate law programmes. His primary research interests are in the self-regulatory aspects of sport; the relationship between sports bodies and the law; and the influence of EU law on sport. His work, which has been cited as authority in the Court of Arbitration for Sport, includes contributions to the *International Sports Law Journal*, the *Entertainment and Sports Law Journal*, the *Sport and the Law Journal* and as a co-author in Gardiner et al. (2012) *Sports Law*, 4th edn., Routledge. In 2011, Simon was awarded a João Havelange Scholarship. Simon's scholarship supported a year-long project examining the legitimacy of legal intervention in football.

Steve Cornelius is a Professor in the Department of Private Law at the University of Pretoria in South Africa. Professor Cornelius and holds the degrees BIuris LLB (Unisa) LLD (Pret). The title of his LLD thesis was "The Interpretation of Contracts In South African Law". He is admitted as Advocate of the High Court of South Africa. Steve joined the Department of Private Law as Professor in 2010 after serving for 11 years in the Department of Private Law at the University of Johannesburg, where he was appointed as Senior Lecturer in 1999, promoted to Associate Professor in 2003 and to Professor in 2007. He was also Head of the Department of Private Law at UJ. Before that, he served for 11 years in the Department of Justice, briefly as a Public Prosecutor and mostly as a Legal Officer in the Branch: Legislation Research, where he played an important part in the drafting of regulations required for the functioning of the Human Rights Commission, the Truth and Reconciliation Commission and the Special Investigating Unit. He has published widely in his areas of research expertise (contract law and sports law) and notably *Principles of the Interpretation of Contracts in South Africa* (2002 and 2007); as co-author with Cloete et al. on *Introduction to Sports Law in South Africa* (2005); and as a co-editor with Blackshaw and Siekmann on *TV Rights and Sport—Legal Issues* (2009). Professor Cornelius had been a Visiting Fellow at Anglia Ruskin University, Chelmsford, England and is a member of the Editorial Advisory Board of the *International Sports Law Journal* which is published by the TMC Asser Institute in The Hague, The Netherlands. Steve is also a national rapporteur for the *International Sports Law Review Pandektis*, which is the official journal of the International Association of Sports Law.

Neville Cox LLB, Ph.D. is Associate Professor of Law and a Fellow of Trinity College Dublin and a practising barrister in which capacity he has been involved in a number of sports doping cases. He is the author of *Blasphemy and the Law* (2000) and *Defamation Law* (2007) and co-author of *Sport and the Law* (2004) and co-author of *Employment Law in Ireland* (2009). He has also published on a wide variety of topics in law journals and books and is co-editor of the *Employment Law Review*. He teaches and researches predominantly in the areas of Islamic law, employment law, defamation law, medical law and sports law. He has been a Visiting Professor at the University of San Francisco and Indiana University (Bloomington) and a scholar-in-residence in Washington & Lee University in Virginia. Professor Cox is Director of Teaching and Learning (Postgraduate) and Director of the Law School's LLM Programmes.

Dr. Chris Davies has an extensive association with James Cook University in Queensland, having completed three undergraduate degrees at the university, including his LLB, and tutoring and lecturing in law since 2000. After graduating in 2000, Chris commenced his Ph.D. at the Faculty of Law, University of Sydney on the subject of restrictive practices in sporting organisations. Dr. Davies was also a National Technical Official at the 2000 Sydney Olympic Games and in that capacity was responsible for the operations of the running component of the modern pentathlon. A contributor to both the "sport" section of Halsbury's Laws of Australia and the leading sports law text in Australia (Thorpe et al. (2009) *Sports Law*, Oxford University Press, Melbourne), Chris continues to publish frequently and widely in leading periodicals such as the *Bond Law Review*; *European Competition Law Journal*; *Malaysian Journal of Sport Science and Recreation*; *International Sports Law Review*; and the *Victoria University of Wellington Law Review*.

Laura Donnellan has an LLB (Law and European Studies) and an LLM in European and Comparative Law from the University of Limerick, Ireland and now lectures there in European law, sports law and the law surrounding animal welfare. Laura is currently an external examiner for employment law at Galway/Mayo Institute of Technology. Laura Donnellan has published extensively in her areas of expertise and notably a text entitled *Sport and the Law: A Concise Guide*, published by Blackhall Publishing, Dublin in 2010. Her work has also appeared in periodicals such as the *Commercial Law Practitioner*; *Hibernian Law Journal*; *Journal of Sport and the Law*; *Animal Law*; and *Sports Law Administration and Practice*. Laura is a contributing editor to the *Journal of Animal Ethics* and an Associate Fellow at the Oxford Centre for Animal Ethics.

Hilary Findlay is an LLB and Ph.D. from Canada. She is a founding partner in what was originally the *Centre for Sport & Law* and is now known as the *Sport Law & Strategy Group*, and she continues to consult with the Group. In 2000, Hilary joined the Department of Sport Management at Brock University in St. Catharines Ontario, Canada, as an Associate Professor. Hilary's research and publishing interests focus on three areas: Canadian and international sport

arbitration; the regulation of international and global sport bodies and issues of accountability; and, issues of procedural justice as they relate to sport disputes. Hilary currently sits on the Anti-Doping Review Board and Ethics Review Board of the Canadian Centre for Ethics in Sport (CCES) and is Chair of the Ontario Universities Association's (OUA) Appeal Committee hearing appeals of the organisation's decisions.
The chapter in this book was written in conjunction with Marcus F. Mazzucco, legal counsel with the Ministry of Tourism, Culture and Sport of Ontario. The authors have previously combined to write several articles around principles of international governance in sport. including, "Degrees of Intervention in Sport-Specific Arbitration: Are We Moving Towards a Universal Model of Decision-Making?" published in the Penn State Dickinson School of Law's *Arbitration and Mediation Yearbook* of 2010 and, "The Supervisory Role of the Court of Arbitration for Sport in Regulating the International Sport System", which appears in the *International Journal of Sport and Society.*

Simon Gardiner is a Reader in Sports Law at Leeds Metropolitan University and has published widely in a number of areas of sports law. He is lead author of Gardiner et al. (2012) *Sports Law*. 4th ed, Routledge and author of "UK Sports Law" in Blanpain R. and Hendrickx F., eds (2008) *International Encyclopaedia of Sports Law*. Kluwer. Simon has also co-edited on *EU, Sport, Law and Policy: Regulation, Re-regulation and Representation*, 2nd edn., TMC Asser Press, The Hague and he is the chief editor of the *Sport and the Law Journal* and is on the editorial board of the *International Sports Law Journal*. He has researched and published widely on the issue of sports player mobility inter and intra Europe; sports governance; racism; and the construction of national identity in sport.

Hazel Hartley studied at Leeds Polytechnic and Leeds University at undergraduate and Master's level and worked in teaching and coach education before working at Leeds Metropolitan University. Hazel works in the area of socio-legal studies and ethics applied to a range of sport, recreation, business and coaching contexts. She is currently the course leader for the MA Sport, Law and Society at Leeds Met. Hazel is also a member of the advisory board of the International Sports Law Centre at the Asser Institute in The Netherlands.
Hazel's doctoral thesis at the University of Lancaster was in Critical Criminology, focusing on a socio-legal study of the 1989 Hillsborough and Marchioness disasters. It embraced the political economy of disasters and risk, contemporary legal problems in nervous shock mass actions, reckless manslaughter, statutory regulation of health and safety, public inquiries and inquests, before moving on to the main case studies in sport and leisure contexts. The research made sixty recommendations for further research and legal reform. In applying her research to policy and practice, Hazel previously contributed to the Centre for Studies in Crime and Social Justice at Lancaster University on the topic "Disasters and the Law". Her research has contributed to processes of legal reform and consultation in the areas of corporate manslaughter, health and safety duties of managing directors, arguments for a public inquiry into the 1989 Marchioness Disaster, the

role of the Health and Safety Commission and HSE in the regulation of workplace health and safety. She has submitted evidence to various House of Commons Select Committees and government proposals in the areas of legal reform.
Hazel has published widely in the field of sports law—e.g., *Sport and the Law Journal*; *Journal of Legal Aspects of Sport*; *International Sport Law Journal*—and in 2009 published the well-received *Sport, Physical Recreation and the Law* with Routledge.

Anastasios Kaburakis holds Ph.D. and MS degrees from Indiana University and a law degree from Aristotle University of Thessaloniki, Greece. He has previously had faculty appointments at Southern Illinois University and Washington University Law School. He is currently an Assistant Professor of Management and Sports Business in the John Cook School of Business, Saint Louis University. Prior to academia, he practiced law and is licensed through the Thessaloniki Bar Association. While in Greece, he coached basketball at the junior and professional club levels, the national teams of Greece, and served the Greek Basketball Federation, FIBA, and several European educational institutions on legal and policy matters. He has published widely on international comparative sport law, NCAA compliance, particularly pertaining to international student-athletes, recruiting, amateurism, gambling, coaches' contracts, institutional liability, and intellectual property applications in sport. He regularly consults international sport governing bodies, NCAA Division I governance committees, policy-drafting actors in member conferences and coaches' associations, member institutions' compliance and coaching staff members on international recruiting, amateurism policy, and legal issues in intercollegiate athletics settings. He serves as an advisor for various international sport consulting firms. His main research interests and publications can be found at www.kaburakis.com.

Dr. Mark James is a Reader in Law at the University of Salford, Manchester. He has published widely in the area of sports law, currently serving as the Editor for the *Entertainment and Sports Law Journal*. He is the author of *Sports Law* and co-author of *Core Statutes on Criminal Law*, both published by Palgrave Macmillan in the UK. Previous research on the topic of the criminality of violence in sport and football banning orders has been published in leading periodicals such as the *Criminal Law Review* and the *Journal of Criminal Law*. Mark's current research is on how the UK Parliament has overseen and regulated the London Olympic and Paralympics Games of 2012, including issues such as planning and transport, ticket sales and trade, and the use of the Olympic symbol, as well as the diverse sports law literature which informs the holding of sports mega events. In 2011, an article by Mark (with G. Osborn) relating to London 2012 and the impact of the UK's Olympic and Paralympic legislation appeared in the prestigious *Modern Law Review*.

Katrien Lefever obtained her law degree at the KU Leuven, Belgium in 2005. After these studies, she went to Antwerp to undertake an Advanced Academic Study of Journalism at the Lessius Hogeschool, in association with the KU Leuven. During the FIFA World Cup of 2006, she did an internship with a Flemish

TV production company and later that summer with ROB TV, a broadcaster in the Flemish Community. Katrien joined the Communications Law Department of the Interdisciplinary Centre of Law and ICT (ICRI) at the KU Leuven in October 2006. Her research has focused on the regulatory consequences of liberalisation and convergence of the telecommunications and broadcasting sectors. Through a number of projects, she has contributed to policymaking and the drafting of legislation at Belgian and Flemish level. In October 2011, she successfully defended her Ph.D. thesis entitled "Access to Live and Full Sports Coverage on Digital Media: An Intradisciplinary Study of Media and Competition Law". In this Ph.D. thesis, which will be published in monograph form by TMC Asser Press, she provides a critical analysis and evaluation of the EU's attempts to ensure public access to sports coverage. Currently, she is working as an affiliated researcher at ICRI and as a company lawyer at a media company, VMMa, the parent company of the first Flemish commercial television station: vtm.

Johan Lindholm graduated from law school at Umeå University in Sweden during which time he also studied law at the University of Mississippi. He began working at the Department of Law, Umeå University in 2002 and has been a guest lecturer and visiting scholar at a number of international institutions such as the University of Virginia, the National University of Laos and Anglia Ruskin University in England. Currently a senior lecturer in law, Johan now teaches different aspects of constitutional and substantive EU law, comparative law and private international law. Johan's current and previous research mainly centers on the topics of EU law and sports law. The former concerns the constitutional aspects of EU law and especially the impact of EU law on national courts and national court proceedings. This topic was the basis of Dr. Lindholm's doctoral thesis entitled "State Enforcement of Union Rights", which was completed in 2007. Johan's sports law-related research concerns legal aspects of sports in general but especially the impact of EU law on sports. This has resulted in numerous individual publications concerning the relationship between EU law and sports. Since 2009, Johan has been conducting a large research project in sports law entitled "Doping: an Issue for the Legislator?". The project is financed by Centrum för Idrottsforskning and is expected to continue until 2012.

David McArdle is a Senior Lecturer in Law at the University of Stirling in Scotland. Having read Law at the University of Wales, Aberystwyth and worked in legal publishing, he commenced his Ph.D. studies in 1993 under the supervision of Professor Steve Redhead at Manchester Metropolitan University. Prior to moving to Scotland in 2002, he held research posts at Manchester Metropolitan, De Montfort and Middlesex Universities. David's research on various legal aspects of sport has been quoted in debates in both the House of Lords (by Lord Moynihan in a debate on the gender recognition bill, 14 January 2004) and the Scottish Parliament (in a debate on the Offensive Behaviour at Football etc. Bill, 23 June 2011). From September 2012 and for a three year period, he will be seconded as a Senior Research Fellow in International and Comparative Sports Law to the TMC Asser Institute's International Sports Law Centre in The Hague. An editor of the

Entertainment and Sports Law Journal since 2001, David has published extensively in sports law in numerous internationally excellent periodicals. He has also written *From Boot Money to Bosman*: *Football, Society and the Law*, published by Cavendish, London in 2000 and in 2006 was the co-editor (with Giulianotti R.) of *Sport, Civil Liberties and Human Rights* published by Routledge, London. David's monograph *Athletes: Law and Arbitration* will be published by Taylor Francis in 2013 and in the following year David will author the sports law volume of LexisNexis's *Laws of Scotland*: *Stair Encyclopaedia*.

Matt Mitten Professor Mitten is the Director of the National Sports Law Institute and the LLM in Sports Law programme for foreign lawyers at Marquette University Law School in Milwaukee, Wisconsin. He served as the Law School's Associate Dean for Academic Affairs from July 2002 to June 2004. He currently teaches courses in Amateur Sports Law, Professional Sports Law, Sports Sponsorship Legal and Business Issues, and Torts, and has also taught Antitrust Law, Comparative Sports Law, International Sports Law, Legal Ethics and Professional Responsibility and a Sports Law seminar.
Professor Mitten earned a BA in Economics from the Ohio State University and his JD, *magna cum laude*, from the University of Toledo College of Law. He practiced antitrust and intellectual property law as well as commercial litigation with Kilpatrick, Townsend & Stockton in Atlanta, Georgia from 1984 to 1989. He taught at South Texas College of Law in Houston from 1990 to 1999 and has served as a Visiting Professor at the University of Toledo College of Law as well as a Visiting Lecturer at the University of Tennessee Graduate School of Medicine. Matt has been appointed a Senior Fellow at the University of Melbourne Law School in Australia (2006, 2008, and 2010) and is a member of the International Advisory Board for its Graduate Diploma in Sports Law programme. He has also taught sports law courses at the University of Barcelona in Spain and the University of Queensland in Australia and discussed a wide variety of sports law topics at numerous conferences and seminars throughout the United States as well as in Australia, China, England, the Republic of Korea and Turkey.

Professor Mitten has co-authored a textbook entitled *Sports Law and Regulation*: *Cases, Materials, and Problems* (Aspen Publishers, Inc. 2009), which is currently in its second edition. A leading sports law scholar, he has published articles in several of the US's leading law reviews and is a member of the Court of Arbitration for Sport (Lausanne, Switzerland), the American Arbitration Association's Commercial Arbitration, Olympic sports, and United States Anti-doping Agency panels, and the Ladies Professional Golfers Association's Drug Testing Arbitration panel. He currently serves on the Sports Lawyers Association's Board of Directors and is an Executive Member of the International Academy of Sportslaw Practitioners & Executives. He formerly chaired the American Association of Law Schools' Section on Law and Sports and the National Collegiate Athletic Association's Committee on Competitive Safeguards and Medical Aspects of Sports, and has served on the Board of Directors of the Forum for the Scholarly Study of Intercollegiate Athletics.

John O'Leary is a Senior Lecturer in Law and member of the International Law Unit at the Anglia Law School, Anglia Ruskin University. He is co-author in Gardiner et al. (2012) *Sports Law*, 4th edn., Routledge and the sole editor of *Drugs and Doping in Sport* published by Cavendish in 2000. His particular research interests focus on the rights of athletes in doping disputes, employment right in team sports and the law relating to the regulation of sports stadiums. His recent publications have focused on developments in the World Anti-Doping Code and their conflict with the rights of athletes to compete in sport. He is a member of the editorial board of the *International Sports Law Journal.* He is a sports law consultant and has published extensively on contractual, employment and doping issues in professional sport. He was joint author of a report undertaken on behalf of the European Commission on Doping in Sport, which was used as a reference work by the World Anti-doping Agency and has advised UK Sport on legal aspects of their anti-doping policy.

Richard Parrish is Professor of Sports Law and the Director of the Centre for Sports Law Research at the Department of Law and Criminology at Edge Hill University, Ormskirk, Lancashire. His research explores the interface between sport and European Union law. He is the author of two monographs and two edited collections and he has co-authored sports law reports for the European Commission and the European Parliament. Professor Parrish is a member of the European Commission's Group of Independent Sports Experts (2010) and acts as an expert adviser for the European Commission's TAIEX programme with work having been undertaken in the Ukraine, Albania, Belarus and Turkey on the approximation of European laws relevant to sport. He is also a Specialist Adviser to the House of Lords Inquiry into Grassroots Sport and the European Union (2010/11). He is the Honorary Chair of the Association for the Study of Sport & the European Union, a group now numbering over 400 members. Professor Parrish is an editorial board member on the *International Sports Law Journal*, the *International Journal of Sports Policy and Politics*, *Sport and the Law Journal* and the *European Sports Law and Policy Bulletin.*

Dr. Geoff Pearson is a Lecturer in Law at the University of Liverpool Management School and Director of Studies for the University of Liverpool's MBA (Football Industries) programme. Geoff graduated from the University of Lancaster in 1995 with an LLB (with honours) in law before completing a Ph.D. thesis in 1999 entitled "Legal Responses to Football Crowd Disorder", at the same institution. Geoff joined the Football Industry Group (then known as The Football Research Unit) at Liverpool in 1999. His research interests include Law and Civil Liberties; the Policing of Football Crowds; Football Hooliganism; Intellectual Property Theft; and Professional Football in the EU. Geoff has worked with various football governing bodies and governmental/intra-national bodies during the course of his research and has acted as an expert witness on football crowd behaviour. He is the convenor for the University of Liverpool Ethnography Knowledge Platform and is also on the organising committee for the annual

Ethnography Symposium organised by the Ethnography at Liverpool and Keele Group and he was co-chair of the 7th Symposium, held in August 2012 at the University of Liverpool. Geoff has published widely in leading journals such as the *International Review for the Sociology of Sport*; *Policing and Society*; the *International Journal of Social Research Methodology*; *Ethnography; Journal of Criminal Law, the Howard Journal of Criminal Justice, Entertainment and Sports Law Journal*; *European Sports Management Quarterly*; *Journal of Social and Legal Studies*; *Journal of Civil Liberties*; and the *Liverpool Law Review*. In 2007, he wrote (with Dr. Clifford Stott) *Football Hooliganism: Policing and the War on the English Disease* published in London by Pennant Books. 2012 saw the publication by Manchester University Press of Geoff's monograph *An Ethnography of Football Fans: Cans, Cops and Carnivals*.

Stefaan Van den Bogaert is Professor of European Law and Director of the Europa Institute at Leiden Law School, Leiden University, The Netherlands. Van den Bogaert is also Visiting Professor of European Sports Law at the University of Brussels (VUB), Belgium and is a member of the editorial committee of the *Common Market Law Review*. Before joining Leiden Law School, Stefaan worked at Maastricht University, initially as lecturer, and later as senior lecturer in European law. His main research interests are EU internal market law, EU competition law, EU institutional law, EMU, and sport. Stefaan graduated from the Faculty of Law at the Catholic University of Leuven. He holds an LLM from the University of Cambridge (in European and Commercial Law) and obtained a Ph.D. from the European University Institute in Florence with a thesis on the regulation of the mobility of sportsmen in the European Union in the post-*Bosman* era. The thesis was subsequently published in monograph form in 2005 by Kluwer Law International. He is the main author of the *Study on the equal treatment of non-nationals in individual sports competitions* for the European Commission. Recent publications include, in particular, a supplement ("The Netherlands and EU Law") to Craig and de Burca (2012) *EU Law: Text, Cases and Materials*, 5th edn., Oxford University Press and an article (with A Cuyvers) on the regulation of gambling in the case law of the CJEU in the *Common Market Law Review* (2011).

An Vermeersch obtained her Ph.D. from the University of Ghent, Belgium in 2008 for a doctoral thesis entitled "Sport as a New Competence for the EU". An continues to be a Visiting Professor at the Department of Penal Law and Criminology at the University of Ghent offering classes in sports law and, since 2011, she also teaches EU law at Ghent University College. From 2009 to 2011 An Vermeersch was the Project Manager for Sports Policy for the Belgian EU Presidency (Flemish administration). An is currently a Legal Advisor at the cabinet of the Flemish Minister for Sport with particular responsibility for doping and European and International affairs. An has written extensively on EU sports law matters and her work has been published in leading periodicals such as the *European Law Review*, the *Common Market Law Review* and the *International Sports Law Journal*. An was one of the founding members of Sport & EU, the association for the study of sport and the European Union.

Stephen Weatherill is the Jacques Delors Professor of European Law at the University of Oxford. He also serves as Deputy Director for European Law in the Institute of European and Comparative Law at the Faculty of Law, Oxford and is a Fellow of Somerville College, Oxford. His research interests embrace the field of European Law in its widest sense. He is the author of numerous books—most recently *Cases and Materials on EU Law* (9th edn., Oxford University Press, 2010)—and the areas in which he has published papers in journals and edited collections in recent years include the impact of subsidiarity in EU law; the involvement of the EU in private law; aspects of "flexible" integration in Europe; the elaboration of strategies for the management of the internal market; the law and practice of product safety; and sport and the law. The leading writer in the area of European sports law; a number of Stephen's writings in the area were published in book form in 2007 as collected papers by TMC Asser Press. Before joining the Oxford Faculty, Professor Weatherill held the Jean Monnet Chair of European Law at Nottingham, and he has also previously held positions at the Universities of Manchester and Reading since beginning his academic career at Brunel University.

MIX
Papier aus verantwortungsvollen Quellen
Paper from responsible sources
FSC® C105338

If you have any concerns about our products,
you can contact us on
ProductSafety@springernature.com

In case Publisher is established outside the EU,
the EU authorized representative is:
Springer Nature Customer Service Center GmbH
Europaplatz 3, 69115 Heidelberg, Germany

Printed by Libri Plureos GmbH
in Hamburg, Germany